2004.6.1

OLIVER POLLOCK

MUSEUM of AMERICAN FINANCE

OLIVER POLLOCK

The Life and Times of an Unknown Patriot

BY

JAMES ALTON JAMES

BOOKS FOR LIBRARIES PRESS
FREEPORT, NEW YORK

First Published 1937
Reprinted 1970

INTERNATIONAL STANDARD BOOK NUMBER:
0-8369-5527-7

LIBRARY OF CONGRESS CATALOG CARD NUMBER:
70-130554

PRINTED IN THE UNITED STATES OF AMERICA

TO
MY SONS
MAURICE ALTON JAMES
AND
HUBERT E. JAMES

PREFACE

THE NAME Oliver Pollock has not heretofore been given a place in American historical literature.[1] My interest in him was begun through the years spent in collecting documentary evidence preparatory to writing *The Life of George Rogers Clark*. This interest was quickened through Clark's own statement that without the financial assistance of Pollock, his conquest of the Northwest during the American Revolution would have been impossible, and that without such aid this territory could not have been held for the United States.

During the nine years since the volume on Clark was published, while engaged in the collection of evidence relating to Pollock, I have been enabled to bring to light much new material which necessitates changes of emphasis and revision of judgment on the significance of the Revolution west of the Allegheny Mountains. It is planned to bring out these documents as separate volumes as was done in the study of Clark.

Conditions, civic, economic, and social, in New Orleans during the last half of the eighteenth century are naturally stressed, for it was in that center that Pollock was gaining a reputation as a leader among the traders and planters of the period. At the same time, he was profiting through carrying on commerce with the Illinois country, with the upper Louisiana ports, with the West Indies, and with the Atlantic ports, especially Philadelphia and New York.

Not only was he entitled to the praise bestowed upon him by Clark for his contributions and sacrifices in behalf of the Revolution in the West, but his assistance to George Washington and to Robert Morris was likewise noteworthy. It seems certain, also, that Governor Bernardo de Galvez of Louisiana

---

[1] For a biographical sketch see *Dictionary of American Biography*, Vol. XV, pp. 50, 51.

would have chosen to remain neutral if it had not been for the influence of Pollock.

The free navigation of the Mississippi River was one of the most difficult problems to be considered by the leaders of the new government. The interpretation of the views of the "men of the Western waters" by Pollock contributed to the only solution of this question that could at that time have preserved national unity.

While it has been my desire to present a sympathetic interpretation of the personality and influence of Oliver Pollock, I have not approached the subject in an attitude of eulogy or defense. I have sought to interpret him through his own words and through the testimony of those who knew him personally. After these years of study I have come to the conviction that no man in our whole history more nearly represents the highest type of patriotism.

Among the manuscript collections that have been drawn upon in the preparation of this volume were the Pollock Letters and Papers in the Library of Congress, the Draper Collection, the Bancroft Collection, the British Museum and Public Record Office Collections, the Ayer Collection, containing transcripts from Spanish Archives, the New York Public Library and the New York Historical Society, the Wyoming County, Pennsylvania, Historical Society, the American Antiquarian Society, the Pennsylvania Historical Society, and the Virginia State Archives. The courtesies extended to me by those in charge of these documents are recalled with lasting gratitude. Much assistance has been given also by Librarian Theodore W. Koch and members of the staff of the Deering Library, Northwestern University.

Among those persons from whom I have received advice on special points have been Dr. Louise Phelps Kellogg, in charge of the Draper Collection; Dr. Nelson Vance Russell of the National Archives; Dr. Lawrence Kinnaird of the California State Teachers College, San Francisco; Dr. Max Savelle, Leland Stanford University; Librarian R. W. G. Vail, American Antiquarian Society; Mr. T. E. Cassidy, New Rochelle, New

PREFACE

York; Rev. W. F. Mullaney, Washington, D. C.; Mrs. Guiles Flower, Carlisle, Pennsylvania; and Dr. I. J. Cox, Northwestern University.

For a critical reading of portions of the manuscript I am indebted to the following persons: Dr. Clyde L. Grose, Northwestern University; Librarian Robert J. Usher, Howard Memorial Library, New Orleans; Dr. E. M. Violette, Louisiana State University; Miss Estelle Ward and Mr. George Ward, Evanston, Illinois. The interest and suggestions of Mrs. James, at all times, cannot be adequately evaluated.

J. A. J.

Northwestern University
Evanston, Illinois

CONTENTS

		PAGE
PREFACE		vii

CHAPTER		
I.	A SUCCESSFUL TRADER IN NEW ORLEANS	1
II.	NEW ORLEANS AND THE ILLINOIS COUNTRY	21
III.	RIVALRY FOR CONTROL OF THE MISSISSIPPI VALLEY	34
IV.	AMERICAN APPEAL AND SPANISH RESPONSE	61
V.	SPANISH ASSISTANCE BECOMES MORE GENEROUS	74
VI.	EARLY STAGE OF THE REVOLUTION IN THE WEST	85
VII.	PENSACOLA AND MOBILE: AMERICAN OBJECTIVES	105
VIII.	AN AMERICAN RAIDER ON THE MISSISSIPPI RIVER	117
IX.	POLLOCK SUPPORTS CLARK: KASKASKIA	131
X.	POLLOCK AND THE FATE OF THE WEST: VINCENNES	153
XI.	DETROIT LOST FOR WANT OF A FEW MEN	172
XII.	CONTROL OF THE LOWER MISSISSIPPI	191
XIII.	WERE AMERICANS TO RETAIN THE WEST?	205
XIV.	THE NORTHWEST: CONQUEST OR GIFT?	222
XV.	"THE NAVIGATION OF THE MISSISSIPPI RIVER MUST BE FREE."—OLIVER POLLOCK	250
XVI.	POLLOCK'S FORTUNE ANNIHILATED; HIS FAMILY DEPENDENT ON FRIENDS	269
XVII.	OUR FLAG INSULTED; POLLOCK IMPRISONED	285
XVIII.	POLLOCK CHARGED WITH MISCONDUCT IN OFFICE	297
XIX.	FATE OF THE WEST IN THE BALANCE	308
XX.	"POLLOCK MEETS ALL DEMANDS OF HIS CREDITORS"	327
XXI.	"IN THE JUSTICE OF CONGRESS, I REPOSE THE FULLEST CONFIDENCE."—POLLOCK	338

APPENDICES:

I.	EVENTS IN THE PUBLIC CAREER OF OLIVER POLLOCK, 1776–1782, AS RELATED BY HIMSELF	347
II.	OLIVER POLLOCK AND THE DEVELOPMENT OF THE $ MARK	356

BIBLIOGRAPHY	360
INDEX	369

ILLUSTRATIONS

	PAGE
MAP OF THE REVOLUTION IN THE WEST	84
THE CLARK MEMORIAL AT VINCENNES	*facing* 248
POLLOCK'S RESIDENCE AT SILVER SPRING . . .	*facing* 306
DEVELOPMENT OF THE $ MARK	358

OLIVER POLLOCK

CHAPTER I

A SUCCESSFUL TRADER IN NEW ORLEANS

"FROM the opening of the Revolution, my soul panted for the success of the American arms, nor could I omit any opportunity of manifesting the sincerity and ardor of those feelings, when it was in my power to be useful either to the public interest or to any individuals who had embarked their fortunes and their lives in an enterprise so hazardous and so glorious." [1] This expression of patriotic fervor is more remarkable when we learn that it is the language of one who at the outbreak of the American Revolution had resided in one of the colonies for only two years.

In 1760, when he was twenty-three years of age, Oliver Pollock came with his father Jaret, two brothers and a young nephew, from Coleraine, Northern Ireland, to Philadelphia. Little is known regarding the members of the Pollock family in their former home. No record has been found which might serve to interpret Oliver's life in boyhood and young manhood. We find no account of his personal appearance. What education he obtained we do not know, but his many letters give ample evidence that he acquired a good use of the English language.

While little mention is made of Jaret Pollock after his arrival in America, it appears that he and three of his sons had been small landholders in Ireland. One of the brothers who remained in Ireland, evidently contrasting his hard lot with an imaginary life of ease enjoyed by Oliver in the New World, wrote: "Received yours which gives me pleasure to hear of your wellfare. I am to let you know that my misfortunes hurt me so much, that I will be obliged to go to you, if you do not

[1] Memorial of Oliver Pollock to the Legislature of Virginia, "Clark MSS.," *Virginia State Archives*, Pamphlet, October 26, 1811.

come home. Having one cow, was obliged to sell her from my poor helpless family; As for Brother Thomas he is very cruel to me. Notwithstanding he sits free, your father's land paying the whole rent." [2]

From Northern Ireland during the preceding years of the eighteenth century had come to America large numbers of Protestants of Scotch ancestry and also some Roman Catholics. The destruction of the linen and woolen manufactures in which they were chiefly engaged was threatened by British commercial restrictions. Neither the Presbyterians nor the Catholics were willing to lend their support to the Anglican Church. Some of these immigrants found homes in Massachusetts and New Hampshire but larger numbers were attracted to the Susquehanna and the Shenandoah valleys of Pennsylvania. By 1735, their settlements were to be found also in western Virginia and as far south as Georgia. They were possessed of little personal property and were engaged in tilling the small farms.[3]

From the "Sign of the Indian Queen," a Philadelphia hotel, the Pollocks, of Scotch-Irish descent, migrated to Carlisle, Pennsylvania, known as the capital of the Scotch-Irish settlements. Here one of the Pollock brothers erected and operated a grist-mill near Silver Spring, while another acquired a tavern and became a large land-owner in Cumberland County.[4]

[2] Charles Pollock to Oliver Pollock, January 10, 1767. *Letters and Papers of Oliver Pollock*, Library of Congress. The letter was written from Donagheady, Ireland. This village is a few miles from Londonderry.

[3] The Irish famine of 1740 and 1741 accelerated the migrations and it is said that for a number of years the Protestant immigrants from Ulster, alone, numbered 12,000 annually. It has been estimated that 200,000 immigrants came from Ireland to the British colonies and the West Indies during the last fifty years of the eighteenth century. Charles A. Hanna, *The Scotch-Irish or the Scot in North Britain, North Ireland and North America*, II, 194.

[4] The Spring, originally known as Silvers's Spring, was named after James Silvers who came into the valley in 1730 and took out a land-warrant for a tract of 500 acres. In later years, by common usage, the name of the Spring and the township became "Silver Spring." The Spring is one of the most beautiful in the Cumberland Valley.

That such a career made no appeal to the adventurous spirit of young Oliver is evident for after two years he returned to Philadelphia where he secured a vessel and crew and persuaded a group of merchants to entrust a cargo to him. Sailing to the West Indies, as many American traders were then wont to do, he began trading from port to port with headquarters at Havana. One of his earliest commissions reads: "You have herewith Inclosed Invoice and Bill of lading for Sundreys amounting to One Hundred and twenty-four Pounds two shill[ings] and sixpence which we desire you may dispose of at whatever Port you meet the best Market and as soon as an opportunity serves. We desire you may send us a Remittance in Dollars or Johanna's. If molasses can be had at 12 pence per gallon would recommend to you to ship us eight hogsheads and some for yourself." [5] The following commission was of the same date: "Enclosed you have Invoice and bill of lading for 38 barrels light flour and 16 barrels shipbread which desire you may sell to the best advantage in your Power, at any island you may choose to sell at and remit the proceeds in good molasses if to be had at from 12 d to 14 d pr. same bottom or first oppertunity of which shall expect to be advised in Due Time as to make Proper Insurance on. If none of the above Artikles to be had Remit in Dollars or Gold as may be most for Advantage of our Markitt advise as per above." In addition to molasses, he brought to the Philadelphia and New York markets, tea, coffee, spices, and sugar. Flour, rum, lumber and indigo were among the articles listed as suitable for Cuba and Santo Domingo.

His success in disposing of such consignments soon enabled him to secure other vessels and to become an independent trader and merchant attached to an "eminent house" in Havana. In this manner, for five years, he continued to expand his resources. He became proficient, also, in the use of Spanish. As he wrote: "In about eighteen months of assiduous study, with the constant practice of mercantile transactions I became master of it so as to do all my business

---

[5] Philadelphia, October 27, 1767. *Pollock Letters.*

without an interpreter." This acquisition was to constitute an important factor in his career, for within a decade he was to become the unofficial and then the official agent of the United States in dealing with the most influential representatives of Spain residing at New Orleans.[6]

While still at Havana, he succeeded in gaining the confidence, among others, of Alejandro O'Reilly, Irish soldier of fortune, who having saved the life of King Charles III during a Madrid insurrection, had been rewarded with the title of count.[7] Because of distinguished service in the Spanish Army, he had been promoted to the rank of major general and second in command at Havana.[8] He was regarded as Spain's leading general and as a man of excellent ability, possessed of great knowledge of men as well as of things.[9]

After removing to New Orleans in 1768, center of his later trading ventures, Pollock married Margaret O'Brien. Her ancestors were of the well-known Irish families of Clare and Kennedy of Ormond.

New Orleans then offered unusual opportunities for trade with Havana and other ports on the Atlantic seaboard. It was the chief market, also, for products from the Illinois country. Pollock was prepared to profit to the full from these conditions and his vessels were to be seen, at times, in English, French, and Spanish Continental ports. Moreover, his good fortune was advanced beyond that of any other trader because of the following incident.

On August 17, 1769, General O'Reilly with twenty-four vessels, carrying 2,600 picked and well-armed troops, arrived at New Orleans. He demanded the surrender of the town in con-

---

[6] James Wilkinson, *Memoirs of my Own Time*, II, Appendix 1. It may be assumed that he became familiar with French also, since this was the language of most of the inhabitants of Louisiana.

[7] Pollock was introduced to Count O'Reilly by his good friend Father Butler, President of the Jesuit College. *Ibid.*

[8] For an excellent account of O'Reilly and his influence, consult John Walton Caughey, *Bernardo De Galvez in Louisiana, 1776-1783*.

[9] The language of John Jay who met him later in Spain. Justin Winsor, *Westward Movement*, p. 37.

formity with the treaty of cession made with France whereby Louisiana was to become a Spanish possession.[10]

Spain, seemingly indifferent, had made no effort, until 1766, to take formal possession of this colony.[11] Opposition to the first Spanish governor, Don Juan Antonio de Ulloa, a well-known scientist, traveler, and naval officer, but ruler in name only, was continuous on the part of French leaders. He took little interest in the performance of his official duties. Moreover, French colonists could not believe that the cession of Louisiana to Spain had really been consummated. They were humiliated by the thought that without their consent they had been bartered to the Spanish king. "As colonists, as property owners, as members of a civilized society, they were agitated by all the apprehensions consequent upon a change of laws, manners, customs, habits, and government." [12] With a guard of only ninety men, Ulloa was helpless in quelling an

[10] November 3, 1762, the preliminaries of a treaty between France and Great Britain were agreed upon. Early the following year, ratifications of the definitive treaty were exchanged. France ceded to Great Britain all of her possessions east of the Mississippi River with the exception of the town of New Orleans and the island upon which it stood. She retained, also, certain small islands on the Canadian coast. Spain ceded Florida to Great Britain. By separate agreement, Spain received Louisiana from France. The generally accepted view of this transaction has been that Spain was given Louisiana as compensation for the loss of Florida. Interpretation of new evidence has shown that the cession was, in fact, a bribe proffered by France in order to win the consent of Spain to "an immediate signing of preliminaries of a peace that promised all that France could hope for under the circumstances." Arthur S. Aiton, "The Diplomacy of the Louisiana Cession," *American Historical Review* (1931), XXXVI 701–720. *Consult also* William R. Shepherd, "The Cession of Louisiana to Spain," *Political Science Quarterly* (1904), XIX, 439–458.

[11] Throughout the years of French rule, Louisiana had been a burden on her treasury. In the last years, the subsidy amounted annually to between 800,000 and 900,000 livres. Charles Gayarré, *History of Louisiana* (New Orleans, 1903), II, 73, 78, 82. Reluctance, on the part of Spain, to take possession of the French gift, was largely due to a knowledge of the great burden which would be imposed on the Spanish treasury. On the other hand, it was recognized by Spanish officials that Louisiana would constitute a barrier against the advance of the English.

[12] *Ibid.*, 113.

insurrection which became general among the rank and file of the French. So desperate was the situation that hundreds of persons under well-known leaders from the town and country, assembled in the public square at a time appointed, shouting, *"Vive le Roi de France."* Within three days, following the demand of the Superior Council, Ulloa with his family was forced to seek refuge on board a Spanish frigate which sailed for Havana, November 1, 1768.[13]

But insurgent opposition vanished overnight with the coming of O'Reilly as Governor and Captain General of Louisiana. Great display marked the formal surrender. The scene has been described as follows: "He was received with all the honors due to a captain-general, drums beating, banners waving, and all sorts of musical instruments straining their brazen throats and by their wild and soul-stirring sounds causing the heart to leap and the blood to run electrically through the hot veins. He was preceded by splendidly accoutered men, who bore heavy silver maces; and the whole of his retinue, which was of the most imposing character was well calculated to strike the imagination of the people. The French flag being lowered and the Spanish flying on top of the mast, O'Reilly, attended by Aubry, former French governor, and followed by the officers of both nations perambulated the square, in token of his being in possession of the colony. His suite then followed him to the cathedral where a solemn Te Deum was chanted." [14] But accepting the account of a careful observer who visited New Orleans in 1767, the gorgeous colors of the scene are somewhat dimmed. "The Church," he states, "dedicated to St. Louis had, because of its ruinous condition, not been used as a place of worship since 1766. One of the King's store-houses was used for that purpose." [15]

General O'Reilly quickly realized that to capture, with an overwhelming military force, a town of two thousand white

---

[13] For an account of the uprising, *see Ibid.*
[14] *Ibid.*, 297.
[15] Captain Philip Pittman, *The Present State of the European Settlements on the Mississippi,* ed. F. H. Hodder (Cleveland, 1906), p. 42.

inhabitants and half as many slaves was a far simpler task than it was to supply his troops with necessary provisions.[16] The colony was threatened with famine. Flour quickly rose to $30 a barrel and was obtained with difficulty at that price. Here was Pollock's opportunity. He had recently arrived on board his ship, the *Royal Charlotte*, with a cargo of flour from Baltimore. The market was under his control but he tendered the flour to the general on the latter's own terms. Fifteen dollars a barrel were finally paid for the flour but for this mark of generosity Pollock was granted freedom of trade in Louisiana. "And I did," he wrote, "enjoy that privilege so long as I staid in the country." [17]

At this time, other British traders in New Orleans were complaining bitterly of the restrictive system inaugurated by Spain which prohibited the mooring of their ships on shore and forbade British officers and sailors from setting foot on Spanish soil. How was such a trade handicap to be overcome? For years, British officers gave attention to the problem of a secure communication between West Florida and the Mississippi. "From authentick accounts of the Lands upon the Mississippi," one of them writes, "it can't be doubted that they are rich and fertile, and would yield Rice and Indigo; and this is such a temptation, that People are anxious at all hazards to make settlements upon them; But unless some better communication is discovered with British Territorys, there is little appearance that Establishments there would be of much advantage to Great Britain. A strange Situation for British Settlers to be obliged to pass Foreign Garrisons with the Produce of their Plantations or else dispose of it to Foreigners." [18]

---

[16] According to a census made by O'Reilly, 1769, New Orleans contained a population of 3,190. Alcée Fortier, *History of Louisiana* (New York, 1904), II, 9.

[17] James Wilkinson, *op. cit.*, II, Appendix 1.

[18] Lieutenant General Gage to the Earl of Hillsborough, July 1, 1772. From *The Correspondence of General Thomas Gage*, ed. Clarence E. Carter, I, 330.

To open communication between West Florida and the Mississippi,

The formalities, including the taking of the oath of allegiance to the King of Spain by selected leaders, ended, O'Reilly issued a proclamation demanding the arrest and trial of the conspirators, who were denounced as, "a few ambitious and fanatic men of evil intent who had rashly abused the ignorance of the public." The execution of five of these leaders who were from the best French families, followed the finding of the tribunal. Six others were imprisoned, one of them for life, and the property of all was confiscated to the king's treasury. To strike at insurrection, without mercy, was thought by O'Reilly to be his first duty and he was commended by the king. But as interpreted by one of Louisiana's well-known historians: "Posterity, the judge of men in power, will doom this act to public execration. No necessity demanded, no policy justified it. Ulloa's conduct had provoked the measures to which the inhabitants had resorted." [19]

Nevertheless, his critics who bewail the fate of the "Martyrs of Louisiana" acknowledge the good results of his rule, for it was under O'Reilly's direction that a reorganization of governmental administration was effected which in large measure endured throughout the Spanish period and continued in some phases even to modern times. For the Superior Council which had existed as a court for over a half-century, he substituted the *Cabildo*, which became the municipal government of New Orleans.[20] Every Friday this council composed of

it was proposed to send boats from Pensacola and Mobile by way of Lakes Ponchartrain, Maurepas and the Iberville River to the head of navigation. But a portage of ten miles was necessary before the Mississippi at Fort Bute could be reached. Therefore, it was recommended that a canal twelve feet wide and twelve feet deep should be dug, making possible direct communication by water. *Ibid.*, pp. 111, 138.

[19] F. X. Martin, *History of Louisiana* (New Orleans, 1882), p. 208. "The prisoners argued that they had committed no act of insubordination against Spain, as Ulloa had not exhibited his credentials and had not taken possession in the name of the King of Spain." Fortier, *op. cit.*, I, 224.

[20] For the records of the Superior Council *see Louisiana Historical Quarterly*, Vols. XIV and XXI. For the *Cabildo*, see *Ibid.*, XI, No. 4, 607.

A SUCCESSFUL TRADER IN NEW ORLEANS

six Regidors assembled, with the governor as chairman, to deliberate on matters which concerned the public welfare.[21] Spanish laws were introduced. The Spanish language, only, was recognized by the courts but French continued to be in common usage.

New Orleans, which was enclosed on three sides by a stockade, contained seven hundred dwellings. An insubstantial levée kept the River within its channel. The streets, described as too narrow even for that day, crossed one another at right angles, thus dividing the town into thirty-six squares, each one hundred yards in length. The street names, such as Duc de Chartres, Condé, Dauphine, Royale, Bourbon are seen to-day.

At the rear of a large square, Place d'Armes, now Jackson Square, stood the dilapidated cathedral, St. Louis. Near this structure, on the left, was the residence of the priests. The house and gardens of the governor were on the right side of the square and on the left were the king's storehouse and an artillery yard. A square beyond was the convent of the Ursuline Sisters, built of brick and tile and set back within a walled garden. Completed in 1734, this structure, still standing, would not be out of place in Rouen or any other French city where architectural types of that century are carefully preserved. In the language of an American architect: "With its center pedimented pavilion and its shuttered windows with their sunken panels, its high roof, its rusticated quoins, its picturesque conciergerie, it is perhaps our best example of Bourbon architecture." [22]

In general, the houses were one story with an attic and the

---

[21] In the absence of the governor, one of the ordinary alcaldes presided. The results of the meeting were immediately reported to Governor O'Reilly. For a more minute study of his administration, *consult* Fortier, II, pp. 4, 5.

[22] From T. E. Tallmadge, *The Story of Architecture in America* p. 133. This is probably the oldest structure in the Mississippi Valley. After the building was given up by the Ursuline nuns, it became the home of the archbishop and later on a school.

two-story "shop-homes" of the merchants. They were built on high foundations, were constructed of timber frames filled in with brick and had wide verandas on one or more sides. Within the patios were to be seen flowers, shrubs and fountains. At the sides and rear of the town were the vegetable gardens and the orchards where were grown oranges, figs, peaches, melons, currants, plums, cherries and apples. Wild grapes were to be found in abundance and wine, both domestic and imported, was a common beverage.

The approach to the *parade* on the water-front was guarded by twenty-one cannon mounted on platforms. Police protection was furnished by the soldiers. Ringing of bells in the guard-house constituted the fire alarm and at this signal all the "carpenters, joiners and slaves" were required to hasten promptly "with axes, gaffs, pick-axes, and clubs to the place where fire has broken out, to cut and throw down entirely or in part, the building in danger of burning." The penalty for failing to render "so important a service to their country," was imprisonment and a small fine.[23]

From an inventory of a public sale of house furnishings may be gained a picture of the interior of the home of a man whose family had been distinguished in the army and navy and in diplomacy.[24] With his yearly salary of 3,985 livres, as engineer-in-chief supervising all the public work done in Louisiana over a period of forty-six years, M. de Verge is said to have died comparatively poor. The house which was forty-six feet by twenty feet, containing a parlor, a dressing-room, a study and four other rooms, stood on a lot one hundred and twenty feet square. There were three fireplaces with brick chimneys and an attic. On the lot was an outbuilding, the kitchen, containing a large room with fireplace and attic and a small room used as a cellar. In the yard enclosed by a picket

[23] *La. Hist. Quar.*, IV, No. 2, p. 202.
[24] *Ibid.*, VII, No. 1, pp. 80–86. The sale was advertised in appointed public places and announced by sound of trumpet in all the streets and cross-roads. In the event of failure of the sale, the announcement was again made by trumpet as the people emerged from church after high mass.

fence there was also a brick well and a brick-and-frame structure for the slaves.

Among the articles offered for sale were tables and card-tables of cypress; chairs with cane seats, rocking-chairs covered with scarlet and velvet and easy arm-chairs of leather with cushions, and bolsters; eight framed pictures, one mirror, and ninety-one assorted books. Evidently napkins both plain and embroidered, and china plates, cups and saucers were used. Silver knives, spoons, cups and salt-cellars were mentioned, but for ordinary occasions there were earthenware dishes, knives with horn handles, and salt-cellars and oil-cruets of glass.

Included in the inventory were five cotton-caps, one small bathtub, four lanterns, three copper candlesticks, 120 drinking glasses, 291 empty bottles, a china water-cooler and cooking utensils. Excluding the silverware, the value placed upon the furnishings was 2,073 livres, but the two slaves in the household were appraised at 3,800 livres.

Three miles above New Orleans was "Trianon de Verge," the country home of the engineer. Here the articles inventoried for sale were 8 slaves, 4 oxen, 6 cows, 2 heifers, 11 sheep, and 8 lambs.

The inventory of the estate of a man well known for his social and financial prestige, an agent of the Company of the Indies, includes additional objects which assist in gaining a picture of domestic life during this period.[25] The New Orleans residence of M. Prevost located on the levée contained fourteen rooms and there were the usual outbuildings.

In the parlor were found an inlaid India table on a gilt pedestal, a walnut table, a mantel with its large mirror in gilt frame, and a second mirror, thirty by forty inches in size, eight arm-chairs, six other chairs and a settee all made of cane, and a clock with brass ornaments. On the hearth were a

[25] *La. Hist. Quar.*, IX, No. 3, 411–457. This remarkable document was discovered among the Spanish records in New Orleans by Laura L. Porteous and was translated by Edith Dart Price. Henry P. Dart, editor, supplied the marginal notes and references.

pair of andirons, shovel and tongs. There were three red-plush portières and a tapestry hanging of printed calico or linen.

Especially notable was the library which, with its gallery, contained over three hundred volumes. Among the titles were: *History of France,* 5 volumes; *History of America,* 4 volumes; *Historical Dictionary,* 4 volumes; Cæsar's *Commentaries;* Writings of Lucien, 3 volumes; Homer's *Odyssey; International Law,* 3 volumes; John Locke, *Essay on the Human Understanding;* Writings of Molière, Voltaire, Racine, Montaigne, Rousseau, Montesquieu; one volume on the *Education of Children,* and a pamphlet, *Children's Magazine.* There were also a four-volume treatise on *Police;* a three-volume *Dictionary of Commerce;* a German Grammar and Dictionary and a *Dictionary of the Bible* and a *New Testament.*

The following articles belonging to the household were listed: walnut bedsteads with horse hair spring mattresses, and feather beds, lamp with three pewter branches, silver and brass branched candlesticks, a small telescope, a magnifying-glass, opera-glass, snuff-boxes, razors, backgammon-board, cribbage-board, dice-boxes, waffle-irons, chafing-dish and a "small" brass bathtub.

There were five Negro house-servants. On his two plantations a short distance down the River were fifty slaves. Evidently M. Prevost rode in an ornamented coach, or in a chaise, or on horseback. His saddle was trimmed with crimson velvet and the harness, bridle and stirrups were ornamented with silver or copper and gilt buckles.

From these statements may be gathered something of the home surroundings of Oliver Pollock, who for sixteen years was one of the leading traders and land-owners of New Orleans. Writing of the effects of a hurricane which destroyed the greater part of New Orleans in 1779, he said: "The scene was too distressing for me to describe on paper. I and my family as well as many others, had a narrow escape for our lives." His books and papers, he saved, "the only articles in

A SUCCESSFUL TRADER IN NEW ORLEANS 13

my house I could keep dry."[26] To Mrs. Pollock, he never failed to ascribe credit for making what was evidently an ideal home for themselves and their family consisting of four sons and three daughters.

Social usages bore a striking likeness to those current in France during the reign of Louis XV. We read of the yellow, white, pink, blue, and cherry embroidered jackets with gold and silver trimmings.[27] At social gatherings and on holidays there were to be seen also, black velvet suits, silk and gold flowered coats, scarlet and white silk vests, trousers of blue sateen lined with red serge, red-heeled shoes, silk hose, and silver shoe- and knee-buckles. Conspicuous on such occasions were the women with their velvet, silk, and brocaded gowns trimmed with lace. Head-dresses topped off with aigrets, and gold and silver earrings were also worn. The ordinary dress of the men was a jacket and long breeches, "to protect them from the mosquitoes that abound here in the summer."

In the letters to her parents of a young postulant who accompanied the Ursuline Sisters to Louisiana is to be caught a glimpse of one phase of society during a somewhat earlier period. She writes that the women are expert in the art of displaying their beauty and that there is little distinction in dress among the classes. "Most of them reduce themselves and their family to the hard lot of living at home on nothing but sagamity, and flaunt abroad in robes of velvet and damask ornamented with the most costly ribbons. They paint and rouge to hide the ravages of time, and wear on their faces as embellishment small black patches."[28] Some years later, a French traveler writes: "As to the fair sex whose only art is that of pleasing, they are already born with that advantage here and have no need to acquire it in Europe."[29]

The Ursuline Sisters were in charge of the orphans and of

[26] *Pollock Letters*, August 25, 1779.
[27] *La. Hist. Quar.*, I, No. 3, p. 103.
[28] Grace King, *New Orleans, The Place and the People*, p. 67.
[29] N. Bossu, *Travels*, I, 23. Bossu visited Louisiana in 1752 and again in 1764.

the military hospital and devoted themselves also to the education of girls. Some of the well-to-do parents, like Oliver Pollock, sent their sons to France or to Spain for their education, and private teachers were at times employed who resided in the homes. By order of the king, teachers were to be sent over at public expense, who were to offer instruction to the youth of Louisiana in reading, writing, arithmetic and in Christian doctrine. Evidently General O'Reilly favored a requirement that all the sons of colonists who might come to Louisiana should serve two or three years in the battalion—"This is essential, as in case of war all these young men come as soldiers under the flag, and will be firm defenders of the State and of their common country." [30]

In the court records are to be found instances of cruelty on the part of husbands and of the legal separation of wife and husband with the granting of alimony to the wife. In one case the record shows that a husband had met with financial reverses and in his petition to the governor he asserted he was unable to satisfy his numerous creditors because of the obligation to pay his wife an allowance of 125 livres in cash; thirty-five livres for board and lodging and to supply two and one-half barrels of maize and one cord of wood each month. He asked for a reduction of the alimony or that Mrs. Populus be ordered to return to him. Two arbitrators were named to hear all the evidence and upon their decision "the Court will order that justice shall be done." [31]

There were suits for libel, cases against debtors, and arrests for the selling of stolen property. A court decision enjoins a woman "to cease vexing, ill-treating, and insulting the plaintiff under penalty of corporal punishment."

During the French period, the Capuchins, the first missionaries to arrive, and the Jesuits contended over the administration of the spiritual needs of Louisiana. In 1767 the

[30] Fortier, *op. cit.*, II, 50. From a *Memoir* submitted to the Spanish Government by Francisco Bouligny, who was a captain of infantry and *aide* to Governor O'Reilly.
[31] Index to the Spanish Judicial Records, *La. Hist. Quar.*, VII, No. 3, p. 525.

Jesuits were banished and upon the coming of General O'Reilly, the Superior of the French Capuchins, Father Dagobert, a name well known in Louisiana history, was in charge. His policy met the approval of O'Reilly and of his successor, Don Luis de y Ameraga Unzaga, both of whom were desirous of gaining the loyalty of their French subjects. "An enlightened prudence and a good deal of toleration are necessary here," Unzaga declared in a communication to a minister of Charles III, "for although this is a Spanish province and although Count O'Reilly endeavored to make its inhabitants forget the former domination under which they had lived so long, still I cannot flatter His Majesty so much as to say that the people have ceased to be French at heart, and that in them is not to be found that spirit of independence which causes resistance to oppressive laws. . . . After the blow that the colonists drew upon themselves by their late revolution, the infliction of another would be tantamount to utter destruction." [32]

Meantime, Father Cyril of Barcelona with four other Spanish Capuchins had come to New Orleans with a commission from the Bishop of Cuba to look into the spiritual affairs of Louisiana. Thus a controversy between the two leaders was begun and continued until 1793 when Father Cyril was constituted the first Bishop of Louisiana. He established his See in New Orleans.

Evidently the "liquor shop" as a social center was not lacking. Provision was made, about the year 1745, for licensing six taverns. Keepers were permitted to dispense wine or spirits to "travelers, sick people, the inhabitants and seafaring men; and this they must do with the requisite moderation," but taffia, or "kill devil," made from the scum of sugar, was obtainable.[33] No liquor might be furnished a soldier under the severest penalty, nor to Indians and Negroes. The license received for the privilege of keeping a tavern was paid into the ecclesiastical treasury of the parish, "which

[32] Fortier *op. cit.*, II, 15, 16.
[33] Regulations of Police, *Gayarré, op. cit.*, II, 362.

needs very much such relief and for the maintenance of the poor of this town, who are in a great state of destitution."

Under the O'Reilly code, revenue for carrying on the government of New Orleans was procured through a tax placed upon buildings, especially those used for taverns, coffee-houses, billiard-rooms, boarding-houses and slaughter-houses.[34] A dollar a barrel was the tax imposed on all brandy brought into New Orleans.

The law applicable to Negro slaves, *le code noir,* had been in force since the time of Bienville. Under no circumstances were husbands and wives, nor mothers and young children to be sold to separate owners. Baptized into the Catholic Faith, they were to be exempt from field work on Sundays and other holidays and their marriages were to be recognized. While the assemblies of slaves were forbidden, permission was granted them to attend the first morning mass. "In the country, they shall be led to church by the overseer of each gang, who shall take them back immediately after divine worship is over." A slave was usually granted a piece of land upon which he might grow a crop of corn or rice and raise chicken and hogs. There were instances in which certificates of freedom were gained by slaves through service in the army. Slaves were permitted to purchase their own freedom and a free Negro might purchase the freedom of his slave wife. To freed Negroes were granted the same privileges and rights as to those born free.

In dealing with the Indians, O'Reilly continued the French policy of councils with accompanying speechmaking, ceremony, and presents. Indians were at times held as slaves but their number seems never to have been large and the service they rendered was unsatisfactory. It was proclaimed by O'Reilly that holding Indians as slaves was contrary to the wise and pious laws of Spain.[35]

---

[34] For the rules of civil procedure under this code, *see La. Hist. Quar.,* XII, No. 1, pp. 33–120.

[35] At a sale, 1739, Engelique, a Negress, was purchased for 1,500 livres and 311 livres were paid for "Marie a savagess."

A SUCCESSFUL TRADER IN NEW ORLEANS 17

A good road "for carriages" extended along the levée, some forty miles north to the German Coast. Here were settlements of peasants, descendants of the colony of Germans who had been brought over to promote the ingenious scheme of John Law. They were referred to as "very laborious providers and victuallers of the town," the markets of New Orleans being supplied by them with chickens, ducks and turkeys. An official writing the Spanish Government declared that a contract for 1,000 German families would be cheap at any price.[36]

Beyond the German Coast were the villages of the French Acadians, made famous through the story of Evangeline. Here were some eight hundred families of these refugees, industrious, law-abiding and useful subjects who "had acquired good stocks of cattle and Begin to purchase negroes." [37]

Included within the Province of Louisiana farther north were settlements at Point Coupée, Natchitoches and Arkansas, about half-way to the Illinois Country, and Ste. Genevieve and St. Louis. There were a few plantations south of New Orleans for a distance of thirty miles but because of the low swampy ground within thirty miles or so of the mouth of the River, settlement was not thought possible.

After thoroughly informing himself regarding the different districts, O'Reilly appointed officials and issued instructions which they were required to observe strictly. Upon his tours of inspection, he is said to have traveled one hundred and fifty miles up the Mississippi River. Particular attention was paid by him to promoting the settlement of unoccupied lands. To every family desiring to settle within the province, he granted a homestead of six or eight acres on the River with the ordinary depth of forty acres. Settlers were required to construct, at their own expense, the levées, dikes and roads.

Plantations of indigo, tobacco, beans, and peas were to be seen on both banks of the river for a distance of forty miles

---

[36] *La. Hist. Quar.*, VII, No. 2, 203.
[37] From "The Two Putnams," ed. Albert C. Bates, p. 219.

north of New Orleans. Small quantities of cotton were produced. Rice, easily grown, was one of the prime necessities for food, a traveler remarking: "There is hardly a house where they do not place on the table a dish of rice—in the morning, at noon and in the evening. The children especially are accustomed to it." [38] Corn was cultivated and "it is so necessary to this country that were it to fail, the greater part of the negroes would perish, as they are accustomed to this food and prefer it to the best bread." [39]

Because of excellent pasturage, cattle, sheep, horses, noted for their strength and endurance, and mules and hogs were raised. Distemper was a common disease among animals, "for which there was no remedy." So prevalent was it that "not one in five of the cattle arrives at the age of four years." An ordinance of 1737 made the slaughter of domestic animals, not inspected by an official, illegal. Private persons were forbidden to slaughter even their own live stock without permission from the Council. Game might be sold upon the streets only after inspection.

Indigo, valued at 100,000 pistoles, was shipped from Louisiana in 1763. Ten years later, a plantation with seventy slaves, across the River from New Orleans, produced in one year, 6,000 pounds of indigo which sold at one dollar a pound. Other exports included rice, deer-skins and naval stores. On some of the plantations sugar of inferior quality was grown. Numbers of planters operated saw-mills, boards and shingles finding a ready market in the West Indies. Cypress wood was most in favor for building purposes and there was said to be one hundred square miles of cypress on the Island of Orleans alone, the trees standing "as thick as the hair on the head." Live-oaks, superior for the interior construction of ships, were abundant. Plentiful supplies of turpentine and resin were to be gotten from the pine forests.

Various herbs suitable for all kinds of sickness were to be

[38] Francis Bouligny, *Memoir on Louisiana* in 1776, quoted in Fortier, *History of Louisiana*, II, 30.
[39] *Ibid.*

A SUCCESSFUL TRADER IN NEW ORLEANS 19

found in quantities, their virtues being known especially to the Indians. Mention is made of some of the common medicines and drugs to be found in an apothecary shop such as powdered rhubarb, sassafras, camphor, opium, tartar emetic, brandy, and taffia, the last two "sold only for medicinal purposes." Surgeon Alexandre was referred to as a "Correspondent of the Spanish Royal Academy of Sciences." Frequent reference is made to the recurrence of malaria, small pox and yellow fever.

When Pollock began trading on the Mississippi, the total population of Louisiana was probably 10,000. From the founding of New Orleans, trade with the Illinois country had been one of the chief supports of its inhabitants. As stated by a representative of the British Government: "New Orleans is but a small town, not many good houses in it, but in general, the inhabitants healthy and well looked. Its principal staple is the trade for furs and skins from the Illinois." [40]

Outfitted by Pollock and other merchants, traders, numbering from 400 to 500, ascended the river during the spring or fall in little fleets of seven to twelve bateaux. These boats, usually covered, manned by eighteen to twenty-six hands, were some forty feet long and nine feet wide. Ordinarily, three months were consumed in reaching the Illinois villages, for the labor was arduous consisting of rowing, poling, and warping, although sails were used in propelling the craft as far as practicable. The return trip took from fourteen to sixteen days. At an earlier period, piroques, made by hollowing the trunks of trees, were used. But they were unfit for sails and were easy prey for bands of Indians. Canoes driven with four oars were, at times, used as dispatch boats between the capital and the Spanish Illinois. With the founding of St. Louis in 1764, that post became the leading center for trade on the upper Mississippi River.

Not only were the traders forced to combine for protection

---

[40] From "Journal of Captain Harry Gordon, 1766," *Travels in the American Colonies*, ed. Newton D. Mereness, p. 483.

from attacks by Indians and robber bands, but snags and the caving-in of the banks made navigation dangerous. A traveler writes:

> On one side is a Bank from 25 to 30 feet high, where very often you see and hear great pieces of mud or clay, on which are growing trees, tumbling into the torrent. Round you is the stream running from three to five knots an hour in which are huge trees in the current fast to the bottom but bent by the impetuous stream and some of them only bobbing up their Heads when their own elasticity gets the better of the strength with which the water bends them down. On the other Hand, there is a large beach of mud spread over sometimes with sand, in which one or more spots are seen covered with trees. Before you is a quick descent of Country appearing much under you. This you see divided sometimes with sandy Beaches and at others with streams of Water interspersed with a thousand Logs and through which to direct your course is a great incertainty.[41]

Upon arrival at the Illinois country, the packmen scattered out along the various trails for trade with the Indians. They ascended as far as the source of the Mississippi River and to the upper waters of the Missouri. The portages to Lakes Superior and Michigan were familiar to them. European goods valued at 8,000 pounds sterling were consumed annually, in the Missouri trade alone.

In the Illinois villages, Kaskaskia, Cahokia and Vincennes, George Rogers Clark, well-known Virginia leader, was, as we shall see, to initiate those movements which led ultimately to the conquest of the old Northwest and its acquisition by the United States. With these events the name of Oliver Pollock was to be indissolubly connected. Lacking the financial support and advice of this trader, planter, and diplomat, the cause of the American Revolution west of the Alleghanies would have run a different course. An effort to picture something of the life in these French villages, so intimately associated with Louisiana, as they passed in succession from French to British and then to American control is, therefore, of interest and significance.

[41] Pittman, *Mississippi Settlements*, p. 36.

CHAPTER II

NEW ORLEANS AND THE ILLINOIS COUNTRY

IN THE Illinois District of the Province of Louisiana was officially included the territory on the whole course of the Ohio River and on both banks of the Mississippi from the line of the Ohio to that of the Missouri and the Illinois rivers. Repeatedly, the question of the inclusion of this territory as a part of New France was agitated during the French régime. But economic interests seemed to connect it more intimately with Louisiana.

French life, in the Illinois district, centered in the little villages of the "American Bottom," Kaskaskia, Prairie du Rocher, Nouvelle Chartres, St. Philippe and Cahokia, and in Vincennes on the east bank of the Wabash River, one hundred and fifty miles from its mouth. Ouiatanon was an important trading-post one hundred miles above Vincennes where a dozen French families resided under the protection of a palisaded fort. While St. Louis was the leading center for trade, Ste. Genevieve (Misera) was a well-known settlement across the Mississippi from Kaskaskia, having a population of some four hundred whites and three hundred slaves.[1]

The American Bottom, from three to seven miles in breadth, extending north one hundred miles from the confluence of the Kaskaskia River with the Mississippi, contained 300,000 acres. It was noted for the fertility of the soil,

---

[1] Detroit was a thriving center for trade with the Illinois country and with Montreal. There were French hamlets, also, at Green Bay and Prairie du Chien. Other French posts were Presque Isle, on the site of Erie; Du Quesne (Pittsburgh); Le Boeuf; Niagara; St. Joseph; Michilimackinac (Mackinac). Fort Massac was on the Ohio and there was a fort on the Maumee. Juchereau's Post was begun in 1702 at the mouth of the Ohio but was soon abandoned.

the gift of the Mississippi River. Kaskaskia, the largest settlement, was located six miles above the mouth of the river having the same name.[2] At this spot, the River was eighty yards wide and of depth sufficient to permit the loading of large bateaux from its banks. The population of Kaskaskia, together with that of the four other villages within the American Bottom was probably never greater than 1,600. After the exodus of numbers of the French to St. Louis and Ste. Genevieve, in order to escape English rule, a census of 1767 showed that there were 600 white persons living in Kaskaskia; 125 at Prairie du Rocher; 15 at St. Philippe; 15 at Nouvelle Chartres; and 300 at Cahokia.[3] While Negro slavery existed in all of these villages, the total number of slaves was not large, possibly five hundred all told. The use of slaves was not regarded as an economic success by the royal government.

One who visits the village of Prairie du Rocher to-day, may readily reconstruct many phases of French life which were to be seen in these hamlets of the eighteenth century. Three-fourths of a mile away was the site of the original village of that name, nestling picturesquely at the base of the limestone crags which rise one hundred feet above the river plain. The visitor may even now hear stray bits of French patois; may find evidence of land-holding resembling that of the French period; and may see the *habitans* types as they gather in their little "cathedral."[4]

Traveling over the "King's Highway," three miles to the west one comes to the ruins of Fort de Chartres, so named in honor of a regent of France, the Duc de Chartres. Here resided the commandant, for it was the center of French civil

[2] During the year 1881, the Mississippi at a time of flood cut through to the channel of the Kaskaskia and left the larger part of the village on an island. A flood during 1899 swept most of the village into the river.

[3] Cahokia ultimately became a part of East St. Louis. St. Philippe and Nouvelle Chartres disappeared. The population of St. Louis in 1772 numbered 400 whites and 200 slaves.

[4] For the description of an earlier church building at Kaskaskia, *see* James, *Life of George Rogers Clark* (Chicago, 1928), pp. 75, 76.

THE ILLINOIS COUNTRY

government in the Illinois. In 1720 a wooden fort had been completed on this site, one of the links in a chain of posts which was to reach from Quebec to the Gulf of Mexico—a dream of La Salle. This stronghold, rebuilt in 1753 at a cost of some 250,000 livres, was an example of the engineering skill of the school of Vauban and was regarded as the strongest fortification in America. It was intended to be the chief seat on the Upper Mississippi, of the Royal Company of the Indies, center for trade and for the operation of the lead mines. The lead ore, after it was mined and smelted and shaped into flat bars, was taken to the New Orleans market.[5]

The enveloping walls of the fort, 490 feet in length, two feet thick and fifteen feet high were built of stone and plastered over with mortar.[6] They were pierced with loop-holes at regular intervals and the four bastions had two port-holes for cannon on each of their faces and flanks.

Here were stationed from two to three hundred soldiers, although the fort was capable of housing four hundred. The officers came from good French families, while the soldiers in general were recruited from the poorest class in French cities or from the prisons. In this miniature Versailles on the banks of the Mississippi, the gay colors of the dress of the officers, consisting of long coats, embroidered vests and knee-breeches, formed a striking contrast to the poorly clothed, underfed private soldiers, frequently seeking their freedom by desertion. From this post a company had descended the Mississippi and then proceeded up the Ohio in time to assist in avenging the death of Lieutenant Jumonville de Villiers, who lost his

[5] One of the lead mines was located across the Mississippi River fourteen miles from Kaskaskia. This "La Mothe Mine" during 1741 yielded 25,000 bars of lead each weighing from sixty to eighty pounds. *La. Hist. Quar.*, I, 114.

[6] Pittman, *European Settlements*, p. 88. The Illinois State Park Commission, of which the author of this volume was chairman, purchased this site for the State in 1913. The walls, at present from two to four feet in height, enclose an area of some four acres of ground. The powder magazine was restored; the officers' quarters and well have been located. This fort is the remnant of the oldest structure in the Upper Mississippi Valley. *See Life of Clark,* p. 70.

life at Fort Necessity in 1754. At the opening of the French and Indian War, Fort du Quesne, cut off from Canada by the British, was provisioned by boatloads of flour and pork from Fort Chartres. Reinforcements sent from this fort under Charles Philippe Aubry, the last acting governor, aided in holding Fort du Quesne for France until 1758, when he was forced to retire before a superior force of British led by General John Forbes. In November of that year, Governor Aubry retreated to Fort Chartres, the French having determined to abandon the upper Ohio region. The Illinois country still remained loyal to France after Wolf's victory on the Heights of Abraham (1759). By the fall of 1761 the French flag ceased to float north of the Ohio River save in this district.

Notwithstanding the surrender of New France to the British, the Illinois country was not at once abandoned by the French. A force of 132 soldiers was led through the wilderness from Michillimackinac by the Sieur de Beaujeu-Villemonde to strengthen the garrison at Fort Chartres. It was to this stronghold that Pontiac, able chief of the Ottawa, after his unsuccessful attempt to capture Detroit, retired, still hoping to secure French aid in carrying out his plan for confederating the tribes of the Northwest and thus prevent possession of that territory by the British. His advances were rejected by Louis St. Ange, the commandant, who had been left at the fort with a detachment of forty men. This disappointment, together with the knowledge of the successful advance of Colonel Henry Bouquet with a force of 1,500 from Fort Pitt to the Upper Muskingum, where he made advantageous treaties with the Indians, led Pontiac to see the hopelessness of his cause. In July, 1765, therefore, he set out to meet Colonel George Croghan, a deputy Indian agent, wise in Indian diplomacy, who represented Sir William Johnson. A council was held at Ouiatanon where the humbled chieftain promised to offer no further resistance to the British. Croghan then advanced to Detroit, where another important

THE ILLINOIS COUNTRY

conference was held with the Indians during the summer of 1765. This resulted in the general pacification of all the Western tribes. The flag of the Bourbons continued to float over Fort Chartres until October 10 of that year, when the veteran St. Ange, who for half a century had been a leader in the Northwest, surrendered the post to Captain Sir Thomas Sterling, commanding a hundred men of the forty-second Highlanders belonging to the celebrated Black Watch regiment. Thus passed the last vestige of French authority in the upper Mississippi Valley.

The natural fertility of the soil in the American Bottom, "one of the finest countries in the world," the so-called terrestrial paradise, constituted a common theme for travelers at the close of the eighteenth century. It is not surprising that this area was to become the most historic within the limits of the present State of Illinois rather than Starved Rock and the valley of the Illinois River as foretold by La Salle.

Before the opening of the recorded history of the region, it was the scene of a highly developed Indian culture, made known to us through the excavation of the mounds which rise above the level of the American Bottom. One of these, Cahokia, known as Monk's Mound, is the most imposing monument of the mound-building age within the United States.[7]

Near the French settlements in the American Bottom were the huts of the remnants of the four Illinois tribes of Indians —the Kaskaskia, Cahokia, Tamaroa, and Michigamea—numbering four hundred warriors. In spite of governmental prohibitions and the protestations of missionaries, brandy was furnished them by French soldiers and traders and they are described as a poor, debauched and dastardly people. Under

[7] This mound is located eight miles east of East St. Louis. Its shape is that of a truncated pyramid with a base extending 1,080 feet from east to west. From the top, 100 feet high, may be seen, within a radius of two miles, some sixty other mounds which vary in height from 10 to 50 feet. Cahokia Mound is now a part of the Illinois State Park System. For a more complete statement, see James, *Clark, op. cit.*, Appendix II.

the tutelage of Jesuit priests, the habits of the Indians were much improved. Not only did they attend mass but certain barbarities, such as the torture of prisoners, were in part abandoned. They learned to use the plow. Indian women adopted the use of dresses and petticoats which were woven out of the hair of the buffalo. Friction between Indians and whites was of frequent occurrence. Stock belonging to the villagers at times destroyed the crops of the Indians, and animals of the Indians strayed over the fields of the white man. An Indian's lands were ceded without his consent, demands for payment being denied.

In the early years of French occupation marriages between *coureurs de bois* and Indian women were common. The best solution of the Indian problem, it was advocated, was to be found in this absorption of the natives by the whites. But half-breed children were often found to be more depraved than Indians and by order of the government (1735) priests were prohibited from solemnizing these marriages without approval by the commandant. This restriction did not end the practice. There were a few Indian slaves, but their labor was unprofitable and the number decreased.

So lavish was nature in her gifts that the French acquired habits of indolence. Buffalo, beaver, elk, and deer were plentiful, as were ducks, geese, turkeys, and pheasants. The streams and small lakes teemed with fish. In the forests, along the rivers, there grew hickory, black-walnut, mulberry, persimmon, sycamore, oak, cottonwood and maple trees. Pecans and cherries were also plentiful, and the thickets of wild plums, crabapples, and blackberries were matted together with the wild grape-vines. These vines were to be found climbing to the tops of the tallest trees. To secure the grapes it was necessary to cut down the trees. As a traveler relates—"they make the vintage with the hatchet." From the grapes, the French manufactured a wine which was high in alcoholic content.

Travelers, English and French, agree with regard to the

main features of society in these villages. Some of the inhabitants were well educated. There were those who came from the better classes of France and Canada and a few were of noble birth. Among them were many well-to-do men, some of whom had risen to prominence in the Illinois, chiefly as traders. Others, possessing some patrimony before migrating, had increased their property through trade. The democracy of the frontier was lacking, for social lines were drawn between the "gentry," men of ability and influence, and the poorer and more ignorant. Fully two-thirds of the villagers could neither read nor write. The wives of the lower class, indolent and shiftless as their husbands, neglected their homes and spent their time in that more pleasurable pursuit, gossiping with neighbors. Honesty and punctuality in their dealings, courtesy, politeness, and hospitality in their social relations were general among all classes. While drinking and gambling were common, these communities were not conspicuously different in such respects from the society of other frontier settlements.

The usual dress of the laborer consisted of pantaloons made of a coarse blue cloth or of buckskin, held in place with a sash; a colored cotton shirt and a blanket-coat with a cape which might be drawn over the head. Short overskirts, reaching to the knee, over a longer petticoat, were worn by the women of this class. Moccasins and rude leather boots and shoes were worn by both men and women. In place of hats, they commonly tied handkerchiefs, blue or red, over their heads, although home-made straw and fur hats were used. The fringed leather shirt and brightly colored cap, with a tassel, made the dress of the *voyageurs* conspicuous.

Men and women of the well-to-do class, as far as possible, took on the fashions in dress of New Orleans and Paris, and luxuries such as richly trimmed coats, embroidered waistcoats, silk hose and silver buckles were to be seen. A French traveler, at the close of the eighteenth century, describing the life at Vincennes, wrote: "All their time, too, is wasted in prating endless stories, insignificant adventures and journeys to town to see friends. That is to New Orleans nearly five hundred leagues down the river." [8]

French life, as in Canada, centered in the village communities and the isolated farm-house was rare. The houses, placed close to the front of the lots along the narrow streets, were usually a story and a half high with wide verandas on the sides.[9] While a few houses were built of stone, most of them were of wood set on stone foundations, one or two feet in height. Less pretentious houses were built of upright beams set in horizontals at the top and bottom. The interstices between the uprights were filled in with "cat and clay," a mortar which was made of a mixture of common clay and finely cut straw. Glass was used in some of the windows, but in the older houses scraped skins or oiled paper was used as a substitute for glass. Thatched roofs were common but shingles attached by wooden pegs were used. The puncheon floor and spacious fireplace and chimney completed the structure, whose interior and exterior were whitewashed. Houses of the more wealthy were comparatively well furnished, with "plate" on the sideboards and French mirrors on the walls. A few men owned billiard-tables. Each dwelling was set in a yard surrounded by a picket fence. Within the enclosure were peach, apple, pear, and other fruit-trees and the flower and vegetable garden wherein were raised potatoes, melons and squash.

The nightly dances in the puncheon-floored cabins furnished amusement for all ages and all classes, for there was no distinction of wealth on these occasions. The village priest was frequently in attendance. The first of the year was ushered in by formal New Year's Day calls. On January 6 the carnival season began and continued during a number of days. Balls, with cotillions, reels, and minuets were a part of

[8] C. F. C. Volney, *A View of the Soil and Climate of the United States of America* (Phila., 1804), p. 374.
[9] John M. Reynolds, *The Pioneer History of Illinois* (Belleville, 1852), p. 50.

the festivities on this occasion. The *charivari* was likewise a time for good-natured fun for it had not degenerated into the characteristic debauch of the later frontier society.

Rarely did a festival of the calendar go unobserved, for the ceremony and discipline of the church laid a firm hold upon all. Processions and festivals were important events in their lives. The church building was a conspicuous structure in each village. While one twenty-sixth of the produce of the farms was collected for the support of the church, it was necessary to supplement this contribution by donations from parishioners, gifts from the king and from other persons in France. The income from lands held by the religious orders constituted the chief source of support for the churches.

"Criminal offenses were almost unknown among the French. They readily acquiesced in the interpretation of laws by judge or notary and submitted to the regulations of the district commandant or of the village priest. For some years, the decrees of the British government for the Illinois district were administered by military officers from Fort Chartres. Each village maintained its own militia company which was organized primarily for defense against the Indians. The captain was the chief officer of the community. He represented the major commandant, put into execution the decrees of the judge, and performed functions similar to those of an English justice of peace." [10]

Adjoining the village were the narrow strips of land, the "common fields" from one-half to a mile long and varying in width from ten to forty rods. The *habitans* cultivated these fields, which were plowed, sowed, and reaped according to rules agreed upon in the public assembly which was made up of all males of military age. Upkeep of roads and the repair of churches were likewise under control of the assembly. It was at the door of the church, after mass, that the assembly met. Here the royal notary offered property for sale, in a "high and audible voice," payments being made in

---

[10] *Life of Clark*, University of Chicago Press, p. 76.

silver, peltry, or slaves. "The *syndic* was the official elected to carry out the will of the assembly, and so long as the individual complied with the restrictions he was entitled to hold his land in fee simple. The 'commons' was a tract set aside for pasturage and woodland." [11] Each cultivator was required to build and keep in repair the fence along his farm separating it from the commons. After the crops were harvested, horses, cattle and hogs were permitted to run in the common fields. The assembly agreeing, portions of the commons might be assigned as common fields to young married persons and to new-comers in the community.

While encouragement had been given by the French Government to settlers to develop the land, the ordinary villagers were at best but indifferent farmers. Labor on the larger holdings was poorly performed by slaves. Although the soil was capable of yielding large returns of wheat, corn, tobacco, hemp, flax, hops, fruits, and vegetables, the cultivation was so primitive that wheat, for example, produced only from five to eight fold.[12] Tilling the soil was burdensome when hunting, fishing and trading yielded an easier livelihood. Corn was raised only in small quantities as food for stock. Cultivation of wheat was begun by the French in the Illinois country, as early as 1687. Although it was grown later, under orders from the Company of the West, well down the Mississippi, the Illinois and Wabash settlements alone produced a surplus for the New Orleans market. Lower Louisiana always counted on securing flour from this region. In the year 1746, 800,000 pounds, produced north of the Ohio, were sold in New Orleans.[13] During the last ten years of French control the growing of wheat increased rapidly, at least three-fourths of the crop finding ready markets at New Orleans and Detroit. After the transfer of Kaskaskia to Great

[11] *Ibid.*, p. 79.
[12] *Jesuit Relations*, ed. R. G. Thwaites (Cleveland, 1904), LXIX, 219.
[13] Henry M. Brackenridge, *Views of Louisiana* (Pittsburgh, 1814), p. 272. During the year 1738, 300,000 pounds of Illinois flour were shipped to New Orleans. Rowland and Sanders, *Mississippi Provincial Archives, 1729–1740* (Jackson, Miss., 1927), I, 401.

Britain, M. Beauvais, with an estate on which he kept eighty slaves, furnished the king's magazine with 86,000 pounds of flour, representing a portion only of his harvest for a single year. In each village were water-mills for grinding corn and sawing boards, and grist-mills which were operated with horse- or water-power.

Agricultural methods were those of a century earlier, the clumsy wooden plows being drawn by oxen. There was no effort to renew the fields with fertilizers. Farmers were well supplied with a hardy breed of cattle originally brought from Canada and there were sheep and poultry, but their stock had degenerated in size for want of proper care. Hogs in large numbers roamed the forests. The horses resembling mustangs were noted for their strength and endurance. A few horses of superior breed were brought from the Pawnee Indian country, some 600 miles to the southwest, or from New Mexico.[14] The inhabitants traveled on horseback or rode in the clumsy wooden carts, *charrettes*, with two horses driven tandem.

But the fur-trade, in one way or another, furnished the means of employment for the majority of the inhabitants. In the villages were the merchants who on their own account, or more frequently serving as agents or partners of New Orleans and Canadian merchants, furnished the supplies used in exchange for furs such as hatchets, knives, kettles, blankets, ribbons, and glittering trinkets. Dry goods amounting to 400,000 pounds sterling were said to have been imported to New Orleans (1763) for town, country and Indian trade. At times, the village merchants, accompanied by *voyageurs* who propelled the canoes and carried the packs of goods and furs, traded with the Indians in person. They outfitted, usually on credit, the *coureur de bois*, who through love of adventure spent most of their lives in the woods. By twos and threes these wood rangers sped along the waterways in their canoes and crossed the country to trade with distant

[14] Clark to Patrick Henry, March 9, 1779. James, *Clark Papers*, I, 303, 304.

tribes. They were to be found among the Indians on the head-waters of the Mississippi and the Missouri. Others, following the south fork of the Platte River, passed through Colorado to the southern spurs of the Rockies where there was considerable trade with the Spaniards of Santa Fé.

To most of the *coureur de bois* the restraints and privations of civilized life were unbearable. They were merry, patient, and industrious in the performance of tasks, usually faithful in keeping engagements and warm in their friendships, but revengeful and ready to take advantage of an enemy. Their lawlessness when among the Indians was proverbial. Disregarding regulations of government and protests of missionaries, they demoralized the Indians by trading them rum and whiskey. After months spent in a life of barbaric pleasure and hardship, toil and peril, with cargoes of furs and game, they returned to the villages where they dissipated their energies and squandered their earnings in drinking and gambling, and then with new packs returned to the wilderness to repeat the same round of life again.

A report to Governor O'Reilly on the Spanish Illinois gives the following description:

> Besides the *habitans* who are settled, there are other unattached persons who are wanderers from will, who serve but to increase the excess and to consume uselessly the products of the country. For although they are wont to employ themselves from four to six months in the hunt, they quickly waste whatever they gain in revelling. They do not apply themselves to agriculture, or to any other work, but are forever wandering; and although they have not at times the means for their sustenance and vices, as they find men to back them, who will supply them on account of the future trade, they come out on top and always live in idleness, although it is known that they corrupt the native youth by their evil example.[15]

In addition to flour, the Illinois posts sent to New Orleans peltry and furs, tobacco, salted buffalo-meat, buffalo-tongues,

---

[15] From *The Spanish Régime in Missouri*, ed. Louis Houck I, 71.

venison, cured hams "equal to those of Bayonne," tallow, bear's oil and lead, in exchange for liquors, groceries, dry goods and commodities used in the Indian trade. Selling prices were ordinarily 100 per cent higher than those for the same articles in the Paris markets. Droves of cattle were also driven from the Illinois country to New Orleans. The Spanish governor offered to contract (1767) for 8,000 barrels of flour and pork with which to supply the Havana market. During the next decade, as we shall see, competition between the Spanish and English authorities for control of trade on the Mississippi River and its tributaries became so intense that these nations were brought to the verge of war. This was the period when Oliver Pollock was building up his fortune.

CHAPTER III

RIVALRY FOR CONTROL OF THE MISSISSIPPI VALLEY

FURS were becoming of increasing importance to the British in their effort to establish a monopoly of manufactures. Influenced by this motive, certain clauses of the well-known Proclamation of 1763 found expression. "All the lands and territories," this mandate reads, "lying to the westward of the sources of the rivers which fall into the sea from the west and northwest are reserved under the sovereignty, protection, and dominance of the king." Settlement on these lands was forbidden, but trade with the Indians was to be free and open to all British subjects.

After the treaty of Paris, however, there developed a new impulse on the part of men of the coast for the establishment of colonies in the West.[1] Financial backing and political influence were sought in Great Britain by promoters of colonies. "Half of England," an American traveler reported, "was new land mad and everybody there has their eye fixt on this country."

Early in the summer of 1763, before the ministry had evolved a definite policy regarding the newly acquired territory, "the Mississippi Land Company" was formed. The purpose of the organizers, thirty-eight well-known residents of Virginia and Maryland, was to secure a grant of land in the Illinois country. Among the names are found George Wash-

---

[1] During the year 1749, the Ohio Company secured a grant of 500,000 acres located between the Monongahela and Kanawha rivers. There were a number of petitions for other projects. See George H. Alden, *New Governments West of the Alleghanies Before 1780*. Bulletin of the University of Wisconsin. Vol. II, no. 1. Consult also C. W. Alvord, *Mississippi Valley in British Politics*. Vol. I, II. These volumes are invaluable for a study of this phase of Western history.

RIVALRY FOR THE MISSISSIPPI VALLEY

ington, Richard Henry Lee and Arthur Lee. In their petition to the Crown, they plead for a grant of 2,500,000 acres which was to include the Southern Illinois District and the western portions of the present States of Kentucky and Tennessee. Some of the arguments advanced in favor of the petition were: That immigrants drawn to the colony, because of the fertility of the soil and mildness of the climate, would produce hemp, flax, indigo, silk and other commodities much in demand for British manufactures. Beyond the extension of trade and increase of revenues, such a colony, it was asserted, would serve as a buffer against Spanish encroachments.[2]

Among other colonial plans, equally ambitious, was one urging a grant of 1,200,000 acres between the Illinois and the Ohio rivers which was sponsored by Sir William Johnson, Superintendent of Indian Affairs, George Croghan, William Franklin, Governor of Pennsylvania, son of Benjamin Franklin, and a number of other prominent Pennsylvanians. Then in London, Benjamin Franklin was constituted a special advocate before the ministry for this memorial.[3] Rivalry for the exploitation of the same territory on the part of Pennsylvanians and Virginians was to continue a leading factor in Western history during the entire Revolution. By charter, the western boundary of Pennsylvania was defined, but her citizens sought to exploit the West through the creation of new colonies. Virginia advanced claims to the whole of the Northwest because of the terms of the sea-to-sea charter of 1609. Opportunity for speculation in land stirred her leaders to advocate westward expansion.

Franklin favored the idea of western settlements at the Albany Congress in 1754. Shortly afterward, he recommended the establishment of two colonies which were to be located between the Ohio River and Lake Erie, but suggested it might

---

[2] For material on the organization of this company, *consult* F. J. Turner, *The Frontier in American History* (New York, 1920), pp. 517, 518, 570–572.

[3] Alvord, *op. cit.*, I, pp. 86–101.

require "some centuries" for its realization. To George Whitefield he wrote in 1756: "I sometimes wish that you and I were jointly employed by the Crown to settle a colony on the Ohio, I imagine that we could do it effectually and without putting the nation to much expense; but I fear we shall never be called upon for such service. What a glorious thing it would be to settle in that fine country a large, strong body of religious and industrious people! What a security to other colonies, and advantage to Britain, by increasing her people, territory, strength, and commerce. Might it not facilitate the introduction of pure religion among the heathen, if we could, by such a colony, show them a better sample of Christians than they see in our Indian traders—the most vicious and abandoned wretches of our nation." [4] In a letter to his son he declared: "A settlement should be made in the Illinois Country by raising a strength there which on occasion of a future war might easily be poured down the Mississippi upon the lower country and into the Bay of Mexico to be used against Cuba, the French Islands or Mexico itself." [5]

The project was approved by the Earl of Shelburne, Secretary of State for the Southern Department, who had advocated a more liberal policy for the colonies. He favored the movement of settlers across the mountains and the establishment of colonies at Detroit, and at the mouth of the Ohio and of the Illinois rivers. With the reorganization of the ministry (1768), a new office, Secretary of State for the Colonies, was created with the Earl of Hillsborough in charge. Representing conservative opinion, which opposed colonial expansion, he urged that the management of Indian trade should be transferred to the colonies. Interior forts were to be abandoned and no western colonies were to be sanctioned.

During December, 1771, General Gage, military commander at New York, was directed to withdraw the troops from Fort Chartres and Fort Pitt and to demolish both forts.

[4] Benjamin Franklin, *Complete Works*, ed. John Bigelow, II, 467.
[5] *Writings of Benjamin Franklin*, ed. A. H. Smyth (New York, 1905), IV, p. 141.

Major Isaac Hamilton, the following year, in carrying out this order, declared that "he had destroyed Fort Chartres in such a manner that at present it cannot afford the least shelter to an enemy, and that he removed the stones which protected the banks of the river and opened drains to admit the waters, so that the floods in the Fall will entirely wash away the front of the fort." Leaving fifty soldiers at Kaskaskia, Major Hamilton returned to Fort Pitt with the remainder of his force and then went to Philadelphia.

At the same time, Hillsborough opposed the scheme of a group of Pennsylvania land speculators to establish the colony of Vandalia south of the upper course of the Ohio. Because of this opposition, he was driven from office and Lord Dartmouth, who favored a progressive policy of expansion to the West, was named as his successor. The proposal to abandon the Illinois country was defeated and General Gage was instructed to leave the troops at Kaskaskia as a guard for the country along the Mississippi River, over which the Spanish were gaining too great influence. The Vandalia grant was made, but the outbreak of the Revolution prevented the consummation of the plan.

Meantime, in spite of British efforts to prevent it, Virginia and Pennsylvania backwoodsmen, after the retaliatory expedition of Colonel Henry Bouquet in 1764, were soon pushing into the Monongahela Valley and the Ohio country. By blazing a tree and marking the date and number of acres they set up what were known as "tomahawk claims." After clearing and planting a certain portion of this land, they established what were designated "corn titles." These pioneers completely ignored the expression of "royal will and pleasure" as set forth in the Proclamation of 1763. Lord Dunmore, Governor of Virginia, characterized their disregard for measures of restraint in the following letter to the colonial secretary: "I have learnt from experience that the established authority of any Government in America, and the policy of government at home are both insufficient to restrain the Americans; and that they do and will remove as their avidity and restlessness incite them. They acquire no attachment to Place; but wandering about seems engrafted in their nature; they do not conceive that Government has any right to forbid their taking possession of a vast tract of country either uninhabited or which serves only as a shelter to a few scattered tribes of Indians. Nor can they be brought to entertain any belief of the permanent obligation of Treaties made with those People whom they consider as but little removed from the brute creation." [6] But Dunmore, himself, had come to America with the purpose of improving his fortune and was not unmindful of the opportunities for financial advancement through speculation in western lands. The Proclamation of 1763 declaring these lands reserved "for the present" for the use of the Indians checked for a brief time only the westward movement of population.

But British Crown officers in America were soon aware of the futility of efforts to enforce its provisions. Forcible removal of those occupying lands beyond the established line was of no effect. An officer writing of settlers driven from lands on the Monongahela, said: "I have Since received Advice that those intruders are not only returned upon their encroachments, but that they have been joined by some hundreds more. [I am] not without a suspicion of their being encouraged in those lawless Proceedings by some principal People." [7] Backwoodsmen could not be held in check awaiting the outcome of the deliberations of the British ministry. Some 30,000 settlers, it has been estimated, had settled beyond the mountains between 1765 and 1768.

Discontent increased among the Indians at encroachments upon their hunting grounds. Finally, in November, 1768, Sir William Johnson, famous as Superintendent of Indian affairs, in a treaty with the Iroquois chiefs at Fort Stanwix, was enabled in consideration of two hundred boatloads of presents valued at 10,000 pounds sterling, to secure the establishment

---

[6] *Dunmore's War*, ed. Reuben G. Thwaites and Louise P. Kellogg (Madison, 1905), p. 371.
[7] From *The Correspondence of General Thomas Gage*, ed. Clarence E. Carter I, 157.

of a boundary beyond which the English agreed to prohibit settlement. In general, starting at the east end of Lake Ontario, this line ran south to the Delaware River, west to the Allegheny and down the Ohio to the mouth of the Tennessee. A month earlier, the Cherokee, at the "Treaty of Hard Labor," South Carolina, met John Stuart, Superintendent of the Southern Indians, and agreed to a boundary line by which they surrendered their claim to territory east of the Kanawha.

The British purpose, as revealed in these treaties, was to control westward expansion. General Gage in 1770 voiced the sentiment which no doubt influenced the views of the government. He wrote:

As to encreasing the Settlements to respectable Provinces and Colonization in general terms in the remote Countrys, I conceive it altogether inconsistent with sound Policy. They can give no encouragement to the Fishery; tho' the Country might afford some kind of naval stores, the Distance would be too far to transport them; and for the same reason they could not Supply the Sugar-Islands with Lumber and Provision. As for the raising of wine, silk or other commodities, the same may be said of the present Colonies without planting others for the purpose, at so vast a distance. . . . The pretense of forming barriers will have no end; whereever we settle, however remote, there must be a Frontier, and there is room enough for the Colonists to spread within our Limits for a Century to come. If we reflect how the people of themselves, have gradually retired from the Coast, we shall be convinced, they want no encouragement to desert the sea Coasts, and go into the back-Countrys; where the lands are better and got upon easier terms. They are already, almost out of reach of Law and Government, neither the endeavors of Government, or Fear of Indians has kept them properly within bounds.[8]

But the colonists argued that settlement in the upper Ohio Valley was in keeping with treaty terms. Following the first pioneers, Virginians of Scotch-Irish and German parentage pressed on to the head-waters of the Monongahela, the Great Kanawha and the Tennessee. On and on they went, paying little heed to the terms of Indian treaties. Accounts are fre-

[8] *Ibid.*, I, 277.

quent of these hordes of surveyors, speculators, and homeseekers, searching for the choicest locations. Said George Washington, who, in 1770, had made a trip down the Ohio River to the Great Kanawha: "The people of Virginia and elsewhere are exploring and marking all the lands that are valuable, not only on the Redstone and other waters of the Monongahela but along down the Ohio as low as the Little Kenawha; and by the next summer I suppose will get to the Great Kenawha at least." [9]

Interest on the part of the general public grew as new prospects for gain were blazoned in vivid colors. It is almost a proverb in this neighborhood (Philadelphia), a letter of 1768 states, discussing the possibility of investment in western lands, that every great fortune made here within these fifty years has been by land.[10] "All this spring and summer," George Croghan wrote in 1770, "the roads have been lined with waggons moving to the Ohio." [11]

Investment in lands on the lower Mississippi likewise furnished thrills to speculators, big and little. The British Government had encouraged immigration to West Florida from the time of the organization of civil government in that district under the first governor, Captain William Johnstone. Arriving at Pensacola early in 1764, he established garrisons at Mobile (Fort Charlotte), at Manchac (Fort Bute), and at Natchez (Fort Panmure). A road was constructed from Mobile to Natchez for the purpose of deflecting to the English settlements trade which was then going to New Orleans.

Colonization was greatly stimulated after the arrival of Governor Peter Chester at Pensacola in 1770. Mobile was particularly favored as a place for settlement according to the reports of English official observers. With a fort suitable for

[9] Washington, *Writings*, ed. Ford, II, 310.
[10] C. W. Alvord, "Virginia and the West," *Miss. Valley Hist. Rev.*, III, 21.
[11] He estimated that between four and five thousand families settled west of the Alleghenies within two years after the Treaty of Fort Stanwix.

defense, settlers were free to engage in growing cotton and vegetables. Pasturage was abundant and one plantation-owner possessed one thousand head of black cattle. Timber was plentiful, turpentine being easily produced.[12]

With the arrival of four score persons and eighteen Negroes from the frontiers of Pennsylvania and Virginia, at Natchez in 1770, a new era of immigration was inaugurated. Their appeal to Governor Chester for grants of land, met with favor. He referred the petition to Hillsborough, pointing out the advantages of promoting settlement. The upper country, as far north as the Illinois, could be supplied with merchandise from the towns which would be established along the Mississippi. In this manner, the superiority of New Orleans could be overcome. Many of the French, dissatisfied with Spanish rule, would be led to settle on the British side of the River. "I flatter myself," he concluded, "that we have great tracts of very excellent land, that if protection and encouragement is given to us, and your Lordship would deign to adopt and patronize this infant child, measures might be pursued to place us in a more respectable situation." [13] While Hillsborough did not oppose migration to this region, he failed to make a definite reply and the immigrants were left to shift for themselves.

Interest of speculators and settlers in West Florida was stimulated by the publication, in 1770, of the volume to which reference has been previously made. It was the first account of the West in English. *The Present State of the European Settlements on the Mississippi* was dedicated to Hillsborough. Captain Philip Pittman, the author, was an engineer who had visited the Western settlements in person. His primary objective was to "impress the English people with the advantage of the possession of the Floridas and to wipe off the unfavora-

---

[12] *The New Régime,* eds. C. W. Alvord and Clarence E. Carter, Ill. Hist. Coll's. (Springfield, 1909), XI, 307.

[13] Cecil Johnson, "Expansion in West Florida, 1770–1779," *Mississippi Valley Hist. Rev.,* XX, No. 4, 486.

ble impressions that have taken place in the minds of many people from the unjust reports of the climate of West Florida and which still retards the settlement of the country." Typical of his descriptions is that of Natchez, "which from its situation and soil, is the finest and most fertile part of West Florida. . . . The country is well watered, hops grow wild, and all kinds of European fruits come to great perfection. The fences of many of the gardens made by the French still remain, and several fruit-trees, mostly figs, peaches and wild cherries. The French always esteemed the tobacco produced here as preferable to any cultivated in other parts of America." [14]

General Phineas Lyman of Connecticut, an officer in the French and Indian War and a well-known lawyer, representing the "Company of Military Adventurers," attempted to plant a colony near Natchez.[15] Among his associates were the two Putnams, Colonel Israel and Lieutenant Rufus. For seven years, Lyman had been in London coöperating with Franklin in a vain effort to secure a grant of land on the Mississippi. Twenty thousand acres in West Florida were finally granted to him.[16] A committee of the Company, upon visiting the region, found all desirable lands taken up as far north as Natchez. They referred in their report to the healthful climate, to the fertility of the soil and to the increasing number of settlers from Europe and America who were flocking to this

[14] Pittman, *op. cit.*, pp. 78–80.

[15] A regiment of 1,050 Connecticut men under General Lyman had together with volunteers from Massachusetts, New York, and New Jersey, taken part with the British Army and Navy in the seizure of Havana in 1762. Only about one-third of this regiment survived the expedition. Considerable booty was divided among the survivors. At the close of the War they were organized into the "Company of Military Adventurers" with the objective of procuring a grant of land within the territory acquired by Great Britain. "The Two Putnams, Israel and Rufus, in the Havana Expedition, 1762 and in the Mississippi River Exploration 1772–73 with some account of The Company of Military Adventurers," *Connecticut Hist. Soc'y*. Quoted with permission from Albert C. Bates, ed. (1931).

[16] General Lyman had no document as proof of this grant, but his statement seems to have been accepted without question by the members of the Company in a meeting held at Hartford, November 18, 1772.

RIVALRY FOR THE MISSISSIPPI VALLEY

part of the Mississippi Valley.[17] "The neighboring plantations, which are settled on the river not far below, abound with large herds of horses, meat cattle, swine etc. which may be purchased at low rates, and which are fattened by the spontaneous productions of the Country, without the fatigues and labour of their owners. Indian corn is produced in great abundance with little more labour than planting it; with many other matters of fact that render this country peculiarly inviting. And on the whole it is a very easy Country to live in, and independent fortunes may be made there equal to almost any country in the world." [18]

Authorized by Governor Chester, nineteen townships of 23,000 acres each were reserved for the Company. It was determined to settle four townships at the earliest possible date "for the adjacent country was settling in the most rapid manner settlers flocking to it from all quarters, and that they could not expect this tract of country would long be reserved and locked up from cultivation." [19]

Several companies of persons, one of them headed by General Lyman, set out by sea for West Florida early in 1774. Again, Lyman was disappointed. Upon arrival, he found that all governors and commanders had been forbidden to issue further warrants or to make additional grants except under authority of a royal order or according to the terms of the Proclamation of 1763. Lyman's disillusioned colonists were able to procure only squatter rights.[20] With the opening of

---

[17] Israel Putnam, Rufus Putnam, Captain Roger Enos and Thaddeus Lyman, son of General Lyman, constituted this committee of exploration. They returned to New York, August 6, 1773.
  An agent of the Company reported that seventy sailing vessels had been counted between New Orleans and Manchac.
  [18] *Ibid.*, Journal, p. 42. Report of the Board, based on the statement from the Committee.
  [19] *Ibid.*, Introduction, p. 40. Twenty-five thousand acres, near Natchez were reserved by Governor Chester and his Board for Samuel Sweeney of New Jersey. He had already, April 1773, brought a number of settlers to that region.
  [20] Upon the arrival of Mrs. Lyman with another company, she found that both her husband and their son, Thaddeus, who had accompanied his father, were dead. She survived only a few days.

the Revolution, the British Ministry, desirous of rewarding those who remained loyal, suspended the instruction which forbade the granting of land to settlers. All reservations and restrictions were relaxed. West Florida was proclaimed by Governor Chester as a refuge for the distressed friends of England. Loyalists in considerable numbers, from practically all of the colonies, took advantage of this opportunity to escape the turmoil of armed conflict. While Pensacola and Mobile attracted some of them, larger numbers procured grants near Natchez, Baton Rouge and Manchac. So rapid was this immigration that by 1774 it was officially estimated the English population in the lower Mississippi region numbered 2,500 and there were 600 slaves.[21]

Meantime, Pollock, while extending his trade relations, was profiting through land speculation and by the transportation of settlers and providing them with necessary equipment. In addition to operating his own plantation near Baton Rouge, he bought and sold lands at Manchac and up the River as far as Natchez. Some of his correspondents resided at Pensacola. In language not unlike that current in our *relator age,* one of his agents writes as follows:

> Soon after the receipt of yours, of the 18th. Ulto. I took every opportunity of talking with Mr. Marshall about lands on the Mississippi without giving in the least to understand that I had orders to purchase from him, and by this method see if I could get the Lands lower than your Limits. But after speaking to him on this subject for several days and finding he was determined not to sell on any other terms but on those he had made the conditional agreement with Mr. Henderson (which I heard was set aside by your advice before you went to Philadelphia) and some New Settlers arriving who were able to purchase, made me afraid they might make him some offers, and thereby he would rise in his demand. This together with your being so very anxious to get those Tracts, induced me to close the bargain. . . . The 200 acres joining Doctor Flowers lower line I would sell, but not for three dollars per acre. I expect also that tract of 500 acres which I got

---

[21] During the succeeding five years, it has been estimated that this number was doubled. Johnson, "Expansion in West Florida," *Miss. Valley Hist. Rev.,* XX, No. 4, 496.

RIVALRY FOR THE MISSISSIPPI VALLEY

from you, being one of the nearest back tracts to Manchac, the price is 2 dollars, 2000 acres at Point Coupée, it is 10 years free from quit rent, 1900 acres joining where Blanchard is settled, allowed to be as good a tract as is on the River, most of the front is cleared. Several tracts on Buffalo Creek and some fronting the River both below and above Natchez, 700 acres on the forks of the Iberville, the cart road to Manchac goes through it, all which I will sell if we can agree about the price. Some of them I would give a long Credit for the purchase money on the buyers paying Interest.[22]

The relation established through one of these land deals was to prove of inestimable value to the colonial cause during the Revolution. Fifteen hundred acres of land near Baton Rouge, adjoining a tract of 500 acres of which Pollock was owner, were purchased by him for Thomas Willing and Robert Morris of Philadelphia. Pollock visited this city occasionally on his trading ventures, receiving such commissions in person.

The control of Indian trade was intimately connected with the British attitude toward the establishment of colonies in the West. In the rivalry for this trade before the outbreak of the French and Indian War, the French had been victors over the British. Frenchmen won the friendship of the Indians by living among them, by affecting their manners and by supplying their supposed wants. French missionaries also aided materially in winning the good-will of the natives.

Causes for complaint against the English were due, in the main, to the activities of irresponsible traders, "abandoned wretches" as Franklin dubbed them, who furnished rum to the Indians and then defrauded them of their furs. Moreover, goods were at times sold by British firms to French traders, a practice which enabled the latter virtually to throttle competition. But could the avenue of trade be turned up the Ohio to Fort Pitt, to the coast and to London, thus breaking the commercial connection between the Illinois country, New Orleans, and French and Spanish old-world ports? To this

[22] *Pollock Letters*, March 25, 1775.

end, British authorities favored the promotion of trade with the Indians of the Northwest immediately after its military occupancy.

The problems connected with the tribes of the Southwest were not essentially different. While welcoming the trader, they also protested the coming of permanent settlers who transformed the character of their hunting grounds. Their demand was for definite boundary lines. In proposing certain limitations to white settlements, a Creek chief declared "that the Red men were formerly ignorant, but God-Almighty and the King of England had made them otherways." He urged that the villages of Pensacola and Mobile should extend only "as far as the ebbing and flowing of the tide." [23] Commercial opportunities in the trans-Mississippi region were likewise beckoning English traders. Governor Dobbs of North Carolina expressed this ambition (1763) as follows: "The English can now extend their trade beyond the Mississippi and reach the Spaniards of New and Old Mexico by pushing on our discoveries and traders by the Missairi (Missouri) and the rivers West of the Mississippi, and so secure an open trade to the westward American ocean." [24]

Best known among the firms coming to the French Illinois villages, following the possession of Fort Chartres, was the one operating under the name, Baynton, Wharton and Morgan, with Philadelphia as headquarters. On the advice of the junior member, George Morgan, a graduate of Princeton, branch stores were established for trade and land speculation at Kaskaskia, Cahokia and Vincennes. He visited these villages and became noted for his influence over the French. Information gained on these trips furnished the foundation for his plans for the conquest of the West during the Revolution.

During the fall of 1766, this company proposed to employ sixty-five flat boats, each with a crew of five, to transport their

---

[23] Helen Louise Shaw, *British Administration of the Southern Indians, 1756–1783* (Lancaster, Pa., 1931), p. 24.

[24] F. A. Ogg, *The Opening of the Mississippi*, p. 322.

merchandise down the Ohio. One of the four convoys, sent from Fort Pitt, within a year carried goods which had been brought from Philadelphia to Carlisle by wagons and thence across the mountains by a train of six hundred pack-horses. Without mishap, twenty days was the average time consumed in the trip down the River. Among the articles listed in the shipments, were clothing, ruffled shirts, silk handkerchiefs, shoes, blankets, looking-glasses, jews-harps, black and white wampum, guns and munitions, brooches, earrings, silver arm and wrist bands, bells, medals and vermilion.[25] There was also much demand for tea, chocolate, sugar, and spirits. In exchange, the Indians brought in the skins of fur-bearing animals, such as otters, bears, and buffalos. Little money was to be found in the villages and the inhabitants used wheat and other produce of the farms in trade. Traders, merchants and clerks representing Eastern firms came in such numbers that Morgan was able to write in 1768 that an English militia company had been formed at Kaskaskia containing sixty members.[26] The profits from trade were not as great as had been anticipated. The value of goods sent from Philadelphia by this firm in one year, was estimated at 400,000 pounds. The expense of sending a single convoy of forty-five boats from Fort Pitt to Fort Chartres was some 5,000 pounds. It was found to be too expensive to row the boats up stream to Fort Pitt. Moreover, prices higher by from 10 to 25 per cent were paid for peltries at New Orleans than in the Eastern markets. Appreciating these facts, General Gage wrote the Earl of Shelburne in 1767:

That the trade will go with the stream is a maxim found to be true, from all accounts that have been received of the Indian Trade carried on in the vast Tract of Country, which lies on the back of the British Colonies; and that the Peltry acquired there, is car-

[25] At times wagon-trains carried the goods to Fort Pitt. For a good account of the organization and carrying on of this trade with the Illinois country, see Max Savelle, *George Morgan, Colony Builder* (Columbia University Press, 1932), p., 18 *et seq*.
[26] C. W. Alvord and C. E. Carter, "The New Régime," *Ill. Hist. Coll's.* (Springfield, 1915), pp. 19–21.

ried to the Sea either by the River St. Lawrence, or the River Mississippi, as the Trade is situated on the Lakes, Inland Rivers and streams whose waters communicate respectively with these two immense Rivers. The part which goes down the St. Lawrence we may reckon will be transported to Great Britain, but I apprehend what goes down the Mississippi will never enter British ports; and I imagine that nothing but a Prospect of a superior Profit or Force, will turn the Channel of the Trade contrary to the above Maxim.[27]

French traders, remaining in the Illinois villages, carried their furs secretly across the River to trade with friends in St. Louis or transported them to New Orleans. Bribes to some of the British officers, it was said, caused them to wink at this practice. Even British traders from Fort Pitt and West Florida were smuggling furs and skins to New Orleans.[28] It was estimated (1771) that peltries worth between 75,000 and 100,000 pounds sterling were exported, annually, from that port to France.

The effect of illicit trade, spoken of as immense, found expression in a letter of Morgan:

The French in open Day and without the least Ceremony [he wrote], send their Peltries from hence [Ft. Chartres] to New Orleans or to the West side of the Mississippi. . . . This with the very large Quantity of Peltry taken from the Wabache to New Orleans, is certainly highly prejudicial to the English Interest, as we are thereby prevented from vending English Merchandise to

---

[27] *Ibid.*, p. 506.

[28] General Gage reported at the close of 1766 "that the traders in West Florida carry most of their Skins to New Orleans, where they sell them at as good a price as is given in London. As I had before some Intelligence of this, the Officer commanding at Fort Pitt had orders to watch the traders from Pennsylvania who went down the Ohio in the Spring to Fort Chartres; and to report the quantity of Peltry they should bring up the Ohio in the Autumn. He has just acquainted me, that the Traders do not return to his Post, that they are gone down the Mississippi with all their furs and Skins, under Pretence of embarking them at New Orleans, for England." Carter, *Gage Correspondence*, p. 117. *See also* pp. 122, 168, 350.

the very numerous Tribes and the British Nation is deprived of the Opportunity of manufacturing vast Quantities of Skins and Furs which are now all sent to France, as also from receiving a great Annual Revenue which would Necessarily result therefrom. . . . In short, unless very diff't Measures to what are at present pursued, are taken, the Country had much better be abandoned, as it is very evident that not a single Advantage can arise from it as yet, otherways than by a proper Regulation and Encouragement of the Peltry Trade, which from many calculations would be more than 3000 Packs per Annum. . . . The great Number of French Hunters that are procuring Meat up the Ohio for New Orleans as well as for the Settlements on the West Side of the Mississippi, have so thinn'd the Buffalo and other Game there, that you will not see the one-twentieth part of the Quantity as formerly. . . . Our present Com'd'r looks no further than to-day, and if he could get Fees from a Thousand he would permit them all to hunt there.[29]

With the coming of Lieutenant John Wilkins, as commandant, to the Illinois country, August 4, 1768, Morgan foresaw great improvement in business. According to his instructions, Wilkins was directed to aid English traders, especially the firm of Baynton, Wharton and Morgan, in all possible ways, and attempt to remedy the evil conditions resulting from the absence of civil government. Shortly after his arrival at Fort Chartres, Wilkins began to show favors to William Murray, an agent of the David Franks Company, also of Philadelphia. Because of his antagonism to Wilkins, growing out of the loss of monopoly in trade, Morgan returned to Philadelphia. Goods belonging to his company were sold to the rival company. Unpaid accounts were entrusted to an agent who was to take in payment bills of exchange or peltry which were to be sent to New Orleans, consigned to Oliver Pollock. He,

[29] Fort Chartres, December 10, 1767. *Trade and Politics*, 1767–1769, ed. C. W. Alvord and C. E. Carter (Springfield, 1921), pp. 128–132. "It is known to everyone that whoever desires to carry a point with Col. Reed [Commander at Ft. Chartres] must not be empty handed. He has not yet nor never shall recieve a — from me. He has therefore repeatedly declared that he would do our dam'd Company all the Injury he could, as he had never reaped a Farthings Benefit from Us."

as agent for the company, was to send the peltry in ships bound for Philadelphia.[30]

St. Louis rapidly became the center for the Missouri River trade which had earlier gone to the Illinois villages. To this post and Ste. Genevieve migrated large numbers of the French who were dissatisfied with British rule and who had hopes that in Louisiana they might enjoy privileges formerly accorded them. An English traveler described this condition as follows:

> There is no settled administration of justice but the whole depends upon the meare will or fancy of the Offr. commanding the Troops; and whose disposition is displeasing to all Ranks under his command, as well as an ensociable desire to get money by any means ever so low. Its displeasing to me to give such a character for a Man of his Rank, but I am afraid it will be found to be too just and from the treatment the French inhabitants there received most of them has left us. . . . At the village of Kaskaskia there is indeed several, who support themselves chiefly by Hunting and in performing Voyages to and from New Orleans, but none of those would I believe, remain, if their property interest were not so materially concerned.[31]

Notwithstanding the protests of Spanish officials, traders from St. Louis, with goods obtained at New Orleans, pushed their way up the Ohio, the Wabash, and the Illinois and trafficked also with the Indians of the Wisconsin and the Fox rivers. In the journal of a British officer whose mission was to

---

[30] Morgan, while in the favor of Commandant Wilkins, had been permitted to purchase some 24,000 acres of land from the French. This was a violation of the Proclamation of 1763. On a portion of the land, Morgan proceeded to make a farm. The experiment was a success and during the first year he is said to have raised from eighty to one hundred bushels of corn an acre. Tobacco and wheat were also grown. From the East, Morgan brought fruit-trees and the best seed available. He built a grist-mill, operated a distillery and imported sheep. The experiment is of interest for it marks a transitional step from fur-trading to the agricultural stage.

For a good summary, consult Savelle, *George Morgan, Colony Builder*, pp. 52–75.

[31] April 15, 1768. *Trade and Politics*, p. 248.

determine methods by which the Indian trade of the Northwest might be secured to the English, is found this statement:

> The Village of Pain Court (St. Louis is pleasantly situated on a high ground which forms the West Bank of the Mississippi, it is 3 Miles higher up than Kyahokia, has already 50 Familys Supported Chiefly from thence, and seems to flourish very quick. At this place Mr. Le Clef [Laclede], the principal Indian Trader resides, who takes so good measures, that the whole Trade of the Missouri, that of the Mississippi Northwards, and that of the Nations near La Baye [Green Bay] and St. Joseph's by the Ilinois River is entirely brought to him. He appears to be sensible, Clever and has been very well Educated; is very Active, and will give us some trouble before we get the parts of this Trade that belong to us, out of his Hands.[32]

To prevent illicit trade, it was recommended by British authorities that the Indians should be required to trade with licensed traders only; that forts should be erected near the junction of the Ohio and the Illinois rivers with the Mississippi; and that armed boats should "scour" the rivers. A fort was erected, also, by Spanish officials, at the mouth of the Missouri, which was to constitute a check upon British traders who were pushing up the Missouri Valley. Rivalry between the traders of the two nations for the trade of the Sauk Indians of Iowa was likewise keen. We find Don Pedro Piernas, Lieutenant-Governor of the Spanish Illinois, petitioning for flags which might be used as evidence to the Indians of Spanish domination and to neutralize the effect of boats passing down the Mississippi flying British colors.

It was clear to British leaders that Louisiana, as a Spanish possession, would increasingly menace their commercial and political supremacy in the West. An officer declared, in 1768:

> The acquisition of the Country of the Illinois I am afraid will turn out to be but of small advantage to us. But really at present it is not very material, for as long as New Orleans is in the hands of another Power, the whole produce of that Country must center

---

[32] *Journal of Captain Harry Gordon*, 1766, ed. Newton D. Mereness, *Travels in the American Colonies*, p. 475.

there. For our merchants will always dispose of their Peltry or whatever the Country produces at New Orleans. So little attention had been paid to render the Country in any means serviceable to us, for the expence it costs in keeping it; that you would imagine pains had been taken to induce the Inhabitants to remove from our side. . . . But had we the Island of New Orleans, that Country [Illinois], in a very short time would I believe be equal to any of our Colonies. At present we are allowed the free navigation of the Mississippi but the Spaniards may prevent us from landing and we cannot anchor a Vessel in the River but is obliged to make them fast alongside the Bank of Trees.[33]

During the following year, 1769, British traders were denied the right of mooring their ships on the Spanish shore. In this way, Article VII of the Treaty of 1763, whereby the free navigation of the Mississippi River had been guaranteed to the subjects of Great Britain, was virtually nullified.[34] As a further step toward preventing foreign commodities entering New Orleans, O'Reilly forbade Englishmen and other foreigners to reside in or sell merchandise in New Orleans.[35]

Open warfare for the trade monopoly of the Mississippi and its tributaries seemed inevitable. Plans for the capture of the Spanish possessions were discussed by British authorities. From the British Government came orders to their officers to procure intelligence regarding the defense of New Orleans and other Spanish posts, "whether they have any or what fortifications, and if so, in what state and condition, what number of regular troops they have and what number of Colony Troops or Militia they could assemble on any emergency." [36]

[33] *Trade and Politics,* 1767-1769, pp. 242-244.
[34] To the protest that "warping and tacking" were essential in navigating the river, O'Reilly paid no heed. Vera Lee Brown, "Anglo-Spanish Relations in the Closing Years of the Colonial Era," *Hispanic American Historical Review,* V (1922), p. 370.
[35] John Fitzpatrick, MSS., *Letter Book,* 1768-1790. New York Public Library. Fitzpatrick was a trader at Manchac and carried on a correspondence with Pollock.
[36] Quoted with permission from *The Correspondence of General Thomas Gage,* ed. Clarence E. Carter, I, 77.

RIVALRY FOR THE MISSISSIPPI VALLEY

The two nations were on the verge of war in 1770, because of a dispute over the Falkland Islands. General Gage was ordered to take steps preparatory to an attack on New Orleans. With the ultimate capture of the entire province of Louisiana in mind, the mobilization of troops at New York was begun early in 1771. "From all accounts," Gage wrote, "that have been received hitherto, of the state and condition of Louisiana, an Attack upon that Province is very practicable, and of the different means of approaching New Orleans the River Mississippi is judged the most advantageous; tho' feigned attacks might at the same time be of service, on the side of the Ohio, and West Florida. . . . Orders have been transmitted for the 64th and 65th Regiments to embark at Halifax for Boston, from whence they will march into some of the Colonys the most contiguous to this, till further orders." [37] But the King of Spain, before hostilities were actually begun, agreed to the terms submitted by Great Britain.

The contest for commercial supremacy grew more intense during the years immediately preceding the American Revolution, with the odds in favor of British traders. The administration of affairs in Louisiana was now in the hands of Unzaga, who had been appointed governor by O'Reilly before his departure for Spain, early in March, 1770.[38] Commercial regulations under the new governor were enforced with greater leniency. Certain privileges were accorded British traders in New Orleans. Spanish planters were even permitted to buy certain products from the "floating stores" and other British boats continuously on the Mississippi. Some idea of the volume of trade may be gained from the statement of a captain on the lower Mississippi who reported, May, 1774, that "seventy sail of vessels" were to be seen between New Orleans and Man-

---

[37] John Caughey, "Bernardo de Galvez and the English Smugglers on the Mississippi, 1777," *The Hispanic American Historical Review*, XII, No. 1, pp. 50, 51.

[38] Count O'Reilly lived until 1794, receiving numerous honors from the King of Spain. Unzaga continued to serve as governor for seven years.

chac.[39] According to the report of a Spanish officer, 1776, the commerce of Louisiana amounted to $600,000 annually.[40] Only $15,000 of this amount represented the trade of the six or eight Spanish vessels and of the two ships which were permitted to take cargoes to France. The remainder of this commerce was carried on mainly by English traders.

To offset this advantage, it was advised that Spanish merchants should be granted freedom of trade as at an earlier period; that an army should be maintained which would be adequate, not only to defend Louisiana, but, in case of necessity, furnish reinforcements for Mexico and Havana; and that forts should be built opposite the mouths of the rivers flowing into the Mississippi. The positive advantages accruing to Spain through the completion of these projects would be the control of the navigation of the Mississippi, possession of Mobile and Pensacola which were dependent on returns from illicit commerce, and the consequent increase of income to the Royal treasury.

With the concession of complete freedom of trade accorded him by O'Reilly, this period of bitter commercial rivalry proved to be Pollock's golden opportunity. His activities as trader and planter showed marked expansion. Describing the years immediately preceding the outbreak of the Revolution, he writes: "I was supplied with drygoods from London, Negroes from Africa, and flour from Philadelphia to the River Mississippi (for all which I had no bills protested); and by the correspondence I had with the principal commercial houses in Philadelphia, I became known to the United States." [41]

Commissions sent him, such as the following, were common:

Being inform'd on Coming hear last night of your arrival in the River with a cargo of Negroes I have to request in case you should

[39] Captain Michael Martyn to Rufus Putnam (MS. letter, Northwestern University).
[40] Don Francisco Bouligny, *Memoir Concerning the Province of Louisiana*, Alcée Fortier, *History of Louisiana* (New York, 1904), II 38.
[41] This letter of January 22, 1791, was addressed to Governor Beverly Randolph of Virginia. *Calendar of Virginia State Papers*, IV, 251.

RIVALRY FOR THE MISSISSIPPI VALLEY 55

send any to your own plantation, you will by the same opportunity send the two you were to supply me with last year for the land according to agreement.[42]

Another order was as follows:

I understand you have a large cargo of Negroes to dispose of: I should be very glad you would let Mr. James Rumsey have on my account four hundred dollars in negroes and I will pay you next Fall in cash or peltries. Last September I sold Mr. James Rumsey a negro man for four hundred dollars, who ran away and came here about Christmas last and Mr. Rumsey hath wrote to me that if I will give him four hundred dollars by letting him have two negroes below, he will pay the difference between the value of the negroes and the four hundred dollars in Cash. If, Sir, you will do me the favor to settle this matter with Mr. James Rumsey you will greatly oblige me. Also, Sir; Mr. Donnellan told me you sould out your negroes ten in a lot, payable next Fall. If so and you have confidence enough to trust me with a lot I can pay you for 'em at that time.[43]

From a journal kept by one of Pollock's neighbors, we glean something of the routine of plantation life of that period:

Four Negroes a sawing, 2 cutting logs, 12 hoeing rice and cutting canes, 5 sick. Four men rowing in the boat with me in quest of bottles and cross cut saws—got cross cut saws and 25 bottles at Pollock's and 9 bottles at Watt's. . . . Two negroes ran away but were catched and brought back. Condemned them to receive 500 lashes each at 5 dif't times and to carry a chain and log fixt to the ancle. Poor Ignorant Devils; for what do they run away? They are well cloathed, work easy, and have all kinds of Plantation produce at no allowance. . . . Yesterday being New Year's day, the Gentlemen of the Settlement dined with me, celebrated the day with mirth and good humor, Our Spirits being elivated by the moderate use of good Madirra, wine and Claret.[44]

In Pollock's bills of sale, in addition to Negroes and flour, evidently his most important sources of profit, there were

---

[42] January 25, 1775. *Pollock Letters.*

[43] February 16, 1775, *Pollock Letters.* Two young women were sold at $250 each. Letter of October 10, 1775.

[44] *Life, Letters, and Papers of William Dunbar* (Jackson, Miss., 1930), pp. 25, 26, 56.

items such as: refined sugar, indigo, saltpeter, coffee, tea, butter, claret, taffia, plates, knives and forks, tumblers, wine-glasses, frying-pans, candlesticks, blue and red ginghams, buckram, Irish linen, muslin both flowered and striped, flannel, silk and cotton stockings for men and women, silk and cotton gloves, parasols, boots and shoes for children, women and men, Russia boots, slippers, shoe-brushes and hair-trunks; also white and blue handkerchiefs, hats, plain and ruffled shirts, napkining, sheeting, black crepe, black satin, satinet, and blue, gray, green and scarlet bombasine.[45] There was a ready market for these articles in the villages of the upper Mississippi River and the Wabash.

Evidence is abundant that Pollock, at the opening of the year 1776, was well on his way toward financial success as promising as that of any American of the eighteenth century. He was known throughout the colonies as a most successful trader, merchant, and planter. The greater number of his correspondents were individuals and firms in Philadelphia. There were many transactions carried on by him, also, for men residing in Richmond, Natchez, Pensacola and Manchac. Representing the firm of Willing and Morris, he purchased cargoes of rice which they disposed of in the Philadelphia market and of Illinois corn and wheat which they sold in the West Indies. By the close of the year 1776, he held a balance in favor of this company amounting to $42,000.

Moreover, he was, as he says, "particularly favored and countenanced" by Spanish officials. Not only was he accorded freedom of trade on the Mississippi, but he was awarded the contract for furnishing flour for the New Orleans garrison (1772). So intimate were his relations with the Spanish governors, that through their loans to him, he was enabled to expand his commercial ventures. Their private funds, also, were entrusted to him for investment, a portion of any profits being left "to my own decision."

While he was possessed of capital and property conservatively estimated as amounting to $100,000, a sum surpassed

[45] Letter of April 23, 1776. The total amount of this bill was $7,560.

by only a few of his American contemporaries, his credit, as will be seen, was easily double that amount.

His place of leadership among the numerous traders resident in New Orleans, could not be challenged. Such an achievement is noteworthy, when it is recalled that nine years only had elapsed since as a young immigrant he was entrusted with a commission, evidently his first, which reads: "Inclosed you have Invoice and Bill of Lading for 10 Baralls of Flouar amounting to 20–9–10 which you'l please to Dispose of to the Best Advantag. Remit the Proceeds in what you think will answer this Market and you'l oblidg your Frand [friend] and Homb. servt." [46]

To account for his rapid advancement is impossible, unless it is conceded that he was possessed of outstanding business acumen and other qualities which were summarized by one of his associates as, "personal respectability which gave him an elevation and opened prospects, as flattering as his most sanguine hopes could have desired."

To what extent his trade had been extended through the establishment of friendly relations with representative leaders in the Illinois villages cannot be accurately estimated. Among others, James Rumsey, previously mentioned, and William Murray, both well-known traders and land-speculators, migrated from Illinois and took up their residence in New Orleans. As early as December, 1767, we find that Rumsey took a cargo of Negroes from New Orleans to the Illinois villages where there was a ready market for this sort of labor. From these men, Pollock gained an intimate view of the attitude of the Illinois inhabitants toward the colonial cause. For a year Rumsey had served, at Kaskaskia, as one of the six members of a court of judicature for the settlement of all disputes. George Morgan was president of this court during the period of its existence, some eighteen months. Dissolution followed a dispute with the English commandant.

William Murray came from Philadelphia in 1767 to Fort Chartres and served, for a time, as agent and later as a mem-

[46] Philadelphia, July 3, 1767. *Pollock Letters.*

ber of the David Franks Company, rivals in trade with Morgan's company. Like other traders, he became interested also in acquiring land. Writing in 1769, he said: "I have lately made a small purchase in the land way; and had I hands with a genius for husbandry all would turn out to good account. I wish we had a number of industrious Germans, which wou'd make this one of the finest Countrys in the World."

Because of small profits in trade, this company, together with a number of other men from Philadelphia, organized under the name of the Illinois Land Company, turned to land speculation, with Murray as their agent. Of two large tracts secured by him, one was located on the Illinois River and the other south of Kaskaskia on the Ohio. The Wabash Land Company, made up largely of men from Maryland, through their agent Louis Viviat, an associate of Murray procured two tracts of land on the Wabash River near Vincennes.[47] These transactions were carried on without the sanction of British officials and their validity was denied by Captain Hugh Lord, officer in command at Kaskaskia. Any settlement of these lands, he declared, would be expressly contrary to His Majesty's orders.

A year earlier, the British Ministry, aroused by the unfavorable reports on Illinois conditions due to the lack of civil government, the incoming of new settlers, and such lawless enterprises as that of Murray, decided upon a new Western policy. In their judgment, these problems would be solved through placing the Old Northwest under the government of Quebec.

Moreover, Scotch merchants of Montreal, with political influence in Parliament, had been gradually gaining control of the fur-trade of the Northwest and hoped to preserve it for that purpose by the exclusion of settlements. Arguments in favor of the Quebec Act, 1774, whereby French law would be extended over this region, were: that it would serve as a deterrent to settlement by English colonists; that it would

---

[47] *American State Papers*, Public Lands (Washington, 1833–1861), II, 108 *ff*.

RIVALRY FOR THE MISSISSIPPI VALLEY 59

prevent the repetition of illegal purchases of land companies and would serve to regulate the fur-trade. In this way, the charter claims of Virginia, Massachusetts and Connecticut to portions of the Northwest were virtually disregarded. The Roman Catholic Church was to be reëstablished in the villages of the Northwest. This, likewise, as interpreted by Protestant leaders of the movement for Revolution in the East, was a step toward interference in religious beliefs elsewhere.

Thus foiled in carrying out their schemes, the promoters of these companies bitterly opposed the Quebec Act. Some of their agents remaining in the Illinois country became active opponents to British authority. Among others, Murray sought refuge at New Orleans and, as will be seen, became a confidant of Pollock.

No positive statement can be made, however, on the decisive factors which determined Pollock to use his influence and his wealth in behalf of the colonial cause. No reference is made, in his correspondence, to the results of the Stamp Act, of the Coercive Acts, or to the events connected with the meeting of the First Continental Congress. In describing the sentiment of the colonists, then prevalent, General Gage wrote: "The Fury into which People were thrown and which spread like an Infection from Town to Town and from Province to Province is hardly to be paralleled where no Oppression was actually felt, but they were stirred up by every Means that Art could invent; they were made to believe that their Religion was in danger, their Lands to be taxed, and that the Troops were sent to enforce the Measures, and wantonly to massacre the Inhabitants. People well disposed caught the popular Fever, and when it raged at the highest the delegates were chosen for the Continental Congress, so that we are told, the greatest Incendiarys in most Provinces were elected." [48]

By early April, 1776, Pollock's decision had been made through obeying, as he states, "the dictates of my own Zeal. . . . And from the beginning to the end I was deaf to every

---

[48] *Gage Correspondence*, I, 392.

motive except an ardent affection for our righteous cause." Alone and without credentials from any authority, could he win from Spanish officials and from their government, support for the American cause? Such was the difficult task which he elected to undertake.

CHAPTER IV

AMERICAN APPEAL AND SPANISH RESPONSE

DURING early August of 1776, George Gibson, a Pennsylvanian in the disguise of a trader, through the mediation of Pollock, was granted an audience at New Orleans by Governor Unzaga. The "humbly clad citizen," as he was called in a dispatch of the governor, was captain of a militia company, "Gibson's Lambs," which had been enlisted in the region of Fort Pitt.[1] He was accompanied by Lieutenant William Linn and fifteen other "traders." The mission upon which they came was one of the most interesting and significant undertakings in our annals. It was to prove of vital importance throughout the Revolution, not alone to Virginia but to the cause of America. The plan, originating with Gibson, looked toward securing from New Orleans a supply of gunpowder then greatly needed for frontier protection and for securing the friendship of Indian tribes.[2] Powder and arms had heretofore been purchased in England and the West Indies, but with the opening of hostilities these sources of supply had been cut off.[3] Instances are to be found early in 1775, of the

[1] Captain Gibson's company was used to reinforce the Virginia Line commanded by General Charles Lee.

[2] Captain Gibson, in 1768, secured and took possession of a patent for land in that part of Cumberland County where the relatives of Oliver Pollock lived. It seems evident, therefore, that he probably knew of the success of Pollock in New Orleans. The friendly relations between the two men were to continue throughout their lives.

[3] October 19, 1774. Earl of Dartmouth to the Governors in America: "It is His Majesty's Command that you do take the most effectual measures for arresting, detaining and securing any Gunpowder or any sort of arms or ammunition, which may be attempted to be imported into the Province under your Government, unless the Master of the Ship having such Military Stores on Board shall produce a License from His Majesty, or the Privy Council, for the exportation of the same from some of the Ports of this Kingdom," *N. Y. Col. Doc's.*, VIII, 509.

disposal of arms to Americans by British private soldiers, notwithstanding the punishment for those found guilty was five hundred lashes.[4]

Captain Gibson was bearer of a letter from General Charles Lee, who spoke for the Virginia Committee of Safety. General Lee was the Commander-in-Chief of the Southern District and second to Washington in command of the American Army.[5] The content of the message was well calculated to win the favor of Governor Unzaga and, more important, of Charles III, ablest king of the Spanish throne since the reign of Philip II. "It must be known, Sir," Lee wrote, "that these provinces wearied with being oppressed and having flattered themselves for a long time, but in vain, for a redress from their ills by means of prayers and remonstrances, have at length determined to break all intercourse with a country which they had always regarded as their mother but which they can now no longer regard else than as a scourge of injustice and cruelty. They lack neither force nor courage to maintain their rights, but do lack the means necessary to maintain war. It is difficult not to say impossible, for them to obtain those means by sea, since all the ports are blockaded by the English fleet." In return for the known "generosity of the Spaniards," which he plead should be further extended, he set forth the advantages which would accrue to Spain from the establishment of a systematic trade with the thirteen United Provinces. Should Great Britain succeed in subjugating the colonies, her great army and fleet would then be in position to conquer Cuba and Mexico. But with America independent, Spanish possessions need not fear attack. Great Britain, single handed, would be incapable of raising an army adequate to even at-

---

[4] *Diary of Frederick Mackenzie* (Harvard University Press, 1930), I, 6–12. Lieutenant Mackenzie was an officer in the regiment of Royal Welsh Fusiliers, 1775–1781, serving in Massachusetts, Rhode Island, and New York.

[5] The Southern District comprised Virginia, the Carolinas, Georgia and the country extending to the Mississippi River. Lee had seen service as lieutenant colonel in England, colonel in Portugal, and major general in Poland.

AMERICAN APPEAL

tempt such a conquest. The superiority of her maritime force, supreme at the moment, would be greatly reduced through the loss of America, "Nor need there be any apprehension," he continues, "that the colonies having once established their independence would molest any other power; for the genius of the people, their situation, and their circumstances engage them rather in agriculture and a free commerce which are more important to their interests and to their inclination." Not only the spirit of humanity and generosity but also the interest and the security of Spanish sovereignty in America should convince the governor of the desirability of procuring for the American Army such necessities as guns, blankets, and medicines, especially quinine.[6]

For upwards of two years the Revolution had been gaining momentum in Virginia, as in the other colonies. After the hasty exit of Governor Dunmore from his "Palace" and later from Williamsburg, June, 1775, the House of Burgesses organized as the "Convention" and proceeded to put the colony on a war-footing. Into the hands of the Committee of Safety, consisting of eleven members, was placed the executive authority. Enlistment of two regiments of troops was ordered and provision was made for an efficient militia.

Lord Dunmore had taken refuge at Norfolk, with a handful of British regulars, under the protection of a small fleet of men-of-war. Because of numerous depredations, the Committee decided to send against him an armed force consisting of eight hundred men. After a brief engagement, in which he lost a number of his followers, Dunmore abandoned the town and with his remaining regulars and a number of Tories and runaway slaves took refuge on board his ships.

On the afternoon of January 1, 1776, he began the bombardment of Norfolk. Under cover of the guns, sailors landed and set fire to the wharves and some of the houses. Provincial soldiers, after breaking open warehouses and rum-shops, began

---

[6] This letter, May, 1776, accompanied one sent by Governor Unzaga to Spain, dated September 7, 1776. *Archivo General de Indias*, Seville, Estante 87, Cajon I, legajo 6.

looting the houses before they applied the torch— "The destruction caused by the ships was confined to the water-front but the Virginia soldiers involved the whole place in the catastrophe."[7] By the third day, two-thirds of Norfolk lay in ashes. A month later, the remainder was destroyed, thus depriving Dunmore of a place of shelter.

General Lee, arriving at Williamsburg March 29, took command of all the forces in Virginia. Advancing to Norfolk, he attacked the British ships and shortly afterward the fleet sailed away with Dunmore and his followers on board. Under these circumstances Lee prepared the communication to Unzaga.

That the Virginia captain was granted a hearing by Governor Unzaga was due to the influence of Oliver Pollock. His success as mediator he explained as follows: "The same intimacy subsisted with him that I before enjoyed with O'Reilly and during the whole of his government I supplied the country frequently with provisions, dry-goods, and negroes."[8]

Pollock translated into Spanish the message from Lee, provided accommodation for the entire party, and took the necessary measures to conceal them and their business from the many British spies then in New Orleans.[9]

But was Pollock, influential as he had become in Spanish mercantile and official circles, to win favorable consideration for the request of General Lee? Four months earlier, his efforts with Unzaga to secure Spanish protection for some American vessels against their seizure by a British sloop-of-war, on the representation that they were in a neutral port, proved unavailing. To what extent the governor was influenced through Pollock's interpretation of the contents of the letter, can only be conjectured. Back of the appeal—and it is to be recalled that Pollock was adept in the use of Spanish—was the

---

[7] Quoted from H. J. Eckenrode, *The Revolution in Virginia* (with permission from Houghton, Mifflin Company, Publishers, Boston, 1916), p. 87.

[8] Wilkinson, *Memoirs*, II, Appendix 1.

[9] Later, Pollock gave an account of his transactions to the President of Congress. *See* Appendix I.

conviction and enthusiasm of one who had determined at whatever cost to support the cause of America. How wholehearted was his allegiance is manifest in his first message to a committee of Congress— "As I conceive myself too much interested in everything that concerns America (notwithstanding my present situation is remote from the scene of action) I eagerly embraced the opportunity of exerting my utmost endeavours for the glorious cause." [10]

To furnish assistance to colonists in rebellion, was an appeal which might find favor with an O'Reilly wrought up over the transgressions of British contraband traders but would, it might be conjectured, be denied as a breach of neutrality by the more pacific Unzaga. "I have kept the neutrality that I had proposed to myself, in order not to give reasons for complaint to either side," Unzaga wrote, in asking for instructions; "but since something may happen in the future that may make it necessary for me to tip the scales in favor of the side which I judge to be more advantageous to his Majesty's service, I beg you to inform me of the royal intentions in order that I may perform them to the letter in the delicate and troublesome matter." Although lacking specific authority, he finally permitted the sale of ten thousand pounds of powder to Pollock.

Pollock declared that the change of attitude manifested by Unzaga was, in part, a result of the adoption of the Declaration of Independence, news of which was brought by Captain Gibson. How influential the pleadings of Pollock were in winning the acquiescence of the governor may be understood from the following statement.

Replying briefly to the message of Lee, Governor Unzaga proffered his services "for employment by you in accordance with your good pleasure and desire as well as for the advantage and benefit of those provinces. Be assured of my good will to please you, as can be testified by the Ambassador [Pollock] of those provinces to whom I have lent my aid, and to whom I have granted the means that may expedite for him

[10] October 10, 1776. *Pollock Letters.*

his purpose of succoring those provinces." But he was not ready to assent to a systematic trade with the Americans, as proposed, until authority had been granted by his Sovereign.

Judged by his dispatch to the Spanish Secretary-of-State, three days later, Unzaga was manifestly disturbed over the imaginary picture vividly sketched by Captain Gibson. An army of 80,000 Continental troops together with 120,000 minute-men were already in action. Boston was evacuated by the British and their fleet was repulsed at Charleston. In the spring, it was planned, he said, to send a strong detachment down the Mississippi River in order to seize any English property between the mouth of the Ohio River and Manchac.[11] After passing through Lakes Maurepas and Pontchartrain, the objectives were to be Mobile and Pensacola. Deprived of the use of these ports, the British would be unable, it was believed, to launch an attack by sea.

This apparition was very real to Unzaga, for he writes: "I have always feared the ease with which they can enter this river and descend in six day's time as far as this town without our being able to know of it or to prevent it; and coincident with their arrival will come the news from our posts, for it is impossible to bring news earlier overland because of the inaccessibility of the country. Now I am making it possible by constructing batteries on the aforesaid river for the placing of the only 18 pound cannon belonging to his Majesty in this province, in order that the troops serving them may defend the province more safely from any insult to which their forces may be opposed." He recommended that an armed frigate should be used to patrol the river as protection to the works under construction.[12]

But the thought of a British invasion from Pensacola haunted Spanish officials at all times. They were fully aware that New Orleans was in an exposed position and open to attack by the Mississippi from both directions. They knew

---

[11] Manchac was located some forty miles above New Orleans.
[12] To José de Galvez, September 7, 1776. *Archivo General de Indias*, Seville, Estante 87, Cajon 1, legajo 6.

that their defenses were wholly inadequate. General Lee, in soliciting aid for Virginia, strengthened this fear by calling attention to "the innumerable armies" and "immense fleets" which the British would muster if the colonists were defeated, and the resultant peril to all Spanish possessions. The coming of an American force, in the spring of 1777, as foretold by Gibson, with the aim of capturing Mobile and Pensacola, would have been heartily welcomed by Unzaga. With the loss of these ports, Great Britain would cease to be a menace to the Spanish colonies.

Were the instructions of the Spanish ministry to be in keeping with these facts? Six months earlier Count Vergennes, French Secretary of Foreign Affairs, had sent a message to Ossun, Spanish minister in Paris, in which he pleaded for joint action in furnishing the Americans with clothing, arms, and munitions [13]— "This would indicate our opportunity is to furnish them, and where can there be better means of accomplishing it than through Louisiana. Spain has good motives to fortify and provision this colony. . . . The insurgents being without money and their produce being unsuited to this commerce, it would be necessary to deliver supplies to them on credit. . . . After all, a few barrels of powder would signify little to a power like Spain." [14]

Vergennes, master in diplomacy, was jealous of the British advance to maritime supremacy after the Seven Years' War. His one aim was to restore French prestige in Europe. He welcomed, therefore, the evidence of disruption of the British-American colonies which for years had been foretold by French leaders. "To watch the Colonies; to foment, as far as possible, their discontent; to aid them in insurrection against England, so far as this could be done without prematurely engaging in a war with England; was the policy of the ministry of Louis XV from the time of the humiliation of 1763." [15]

[13] March 17, 1776.
[14] Henri Doniol, *Histoire de la Participation de la France a l'Establissement les Etats-Unis D'Amerique*, I, 339, 340.
[15] Francis Wharton, *Diplomatic Correspondence of the American Revolution*, I, Introduction, 36 *ff*.

French assistance to America would serve, Vergennes thought, as a means to cripple their natural enemy. While winking at the aid secretly given the colonies through French ports, he secured, on June 10, 1776, a million livres from the national treasury for this purpose. Two months later, the Duke de Grimaldi, Spanish prime minister, influenced by Vergennes, induced Charles III to contribute a like sum. A continuation of the War would enable Spain, it was believed, to attack Portugal while Great Britain was unable to come to her rescue. She awaited, also, an opportunity to regain Gibraltar. Moreover, she desired to protect her own interests in the new world, now seriously threatened by British aggression.

The reply of Ossun to the suggestion of Vergennes indicates that Spain was not yet fully prepared to follow his suggestion— "Spain is not in the habit of sending ships to Louisiana often. All the arms manufactured in Spain bear the insignia of the King. It would be necessary, then, that supplies be sent by France, apparently to one of our colonies but really to Louisiana. . . . His Majesty would pay one-half of all expenses of the expedition." [16]

But the reply to the communication of Governor Unzaga is couched in language much more positive. His statement to General Lee was approved. The Americans were to be assured that Spain would be pleased to have them seize Pensacola and the other English settlements on the right bank of the Mississippi, and that "as soon as their independence is assured the transfer of territory that they promise will be discussed." "In order to facilitate both objectives, the governor of Louisiana is also advised that he will obtain through Havana and by as many other ways as possible, aid in arms, ammunition, clothing, and quinine asked for by the colonies. The most prudent and secret methods are to be preferred by him so that he may secretly supply them in such a way that these things shall appear to be sold to them by private traders. For this purpose, the proper secret instructions shall be sent, and some trader

[16] Doniol, *op. cit.*, I, 343.

AMERICAN APPEAL 69

who is to be used as a stool pigeon." [17] The Governor of Cuba was advised that he was to transmit without delay to Unzaga, arms, powder from the factory in Mexico, and goods—all with the greatest secrecy.[18]

Meantime, Lieutenant Linn, with forty-three men, on September 22, 1776, set out up the Mississippi River with nine thousand pounds of the powder which had been procured by Pollock after many interviews with the governor. He purchased and fitted out a vessel which was used to carry the powder up the River. That the purpose of the expedition was divulged to British officials may be gathered from the report of one of their traders at Manchac. "We have nothing new," he wrote, "which is worth mentioning excepting that the American Barge that went to New Orleans some time ago has repassed here on her way to Fort Pitt the other Day. It is said she has 15,000 some hundred pounds of gunpowder on Board. She never called here going up or down." [19]

Upon arrival at the Arkansas Post, the strength of the crew was spent through labor at the oars and lack of food.[20] They were given a most kindly reception by the Spanish commander. "It was hard," Linn wrote Pollock, "for men almost half dead to work, when the one-half was obliged to help the other half every night off the boats, some they had to carry out in Blankets to the fire and the rest had to be helped to walk out." [21] At this post they passed the winter.

With the coming of spring, meat having been procured by

---

[17] December 23, 1776. *Pollock Letters.*
[18] December 24, 1776. *Ibid.*
[19] Fitzpatrick, *Letter Book,* p. 223. This statement appears at the close of a letter to the English governor in which Fitzpatrick petitions for a grant of land. He based his claim upon service in the French and Indian War, in which he was taken prisoner by the Indians.
[20] This post was located ten miles up the Arkansas River from its mouth. It served as a means of protection for the commerce between the Illinois posts and New Orleans, and also for trade with the Arkansas Indians.
[21] Linn to Pollock, November 30, 1776. "Clark MSS.," *Virginia State Archives.*

hunting, and with rice and other provisions purchased from the Spanish stores with orders drawn on Pollock to the amount of $2,400, the voyage was resumed. Linn declared in a letter to Pollock that their supplies would suffice until they got to the Ohio River.[22] That he was to procure this assistance from someone with whom he had a secret understanding is evident. The connection of this incident with the course of the Revolution in the West will later appear. The expedition reached Wheeling on the second of May, at a time when that post and Fort Pitt greatly needed the powder for their protection and for assistance in dealing with the Indians.

In the meantime, Captain Gibson, who remained in New Orleans, had been imprisoned by decree of the governor, in order to quiet the suspicions of the British consul. During October, however, he was permitted to take passage for Philadelphia on a vessel purchased and dispatched by Pollock. Captain George Ord, whose vessel had been seized by a British sloop and who, with his men, had been protected and furnished with supplies by Pollock, accompanied Gibson. To each of them was given information regarding the situation at New Orleans, Gibson carrying a letter from Pollock addressed to the Virginia Council of Safety. To Captain Ord was intrusted another communication intended for a committee of Congress of which Robert Morris was a member.[23] Both messages closed with the significant words: "Permit me, therefore, to make tender of my hearty Services, and to assure you that my Conduct shall be ever such as to merit the Confidence and approbation of the Country to which I owe everything but my birth." This promise, together with the 1,000 pounds of powder brought by Gibson, must have renewed hope in the mind of Morris, who was then declaring that the calls upon him for money were "loud, large, and constant." [24]

[22] Linn to Pollock, November 30, 1776. "Clark MSS.," *Virginia State Archives*.
[23] October 10, 1776. Addressed to Andrew Allen and Robert Morris. *Pollock Letters*.
[24] Quoted from E. P. Oberholtzer, *Robert Morris, Patriot and Financier*.

Because of the lack of gunpowder, Washington at the siege of Boston had been in almost perpetual alarm. When he was preparing for the siege of Dorchester Heights he wrote Governor Trumbull of Connecticut: "My situation in respect to this Article is really distressing and while common prudence obliges me to keep my want of it concealed, to avoid a discovery thereof to the Enemy; I feel the bad effect of that concealment from our friends, For not believing our distress equal to what it really is they withhold such small supplies as are in their power to give; I am so restrained in all my military movements, for want of these necessary supplies, that it is impossible to undertake anything effectual; and while I am fretting, at my own disagreeable situation, the World I suppose is not behind hand in censuring my inactivity. . . . This my dear Sir, is Melancholy." [25]

To large numbers of Americans at the close of the year 1776, the promise for independence seemed well nigh hopeless. While the British had evacuated Boston, they were in possession of New York and Newport. Washington, with his little army of five thousand men, reduced at one time to only three thousand effectives, was being forced by General Howe to retreat across New Jersey. From a package of letters stolen from Washington's headquarters, the enemy was made aware of the critical situation in the American Army. In these letters, Washington was complaining to Congress of the lack of discipline in his army, of the deficiency of good officers and a scarcity of arms and powder. Although he was in great need of an Adjutant General, he had no one qualified for the office. The army was decimated by sickness, and was in dire need of clothing, blankets, and equipment. Large numbers of men

---

p. 30. As a reward, Captain Gibson was advanced in rank to that of colonel and joined Washington's army. At the close of the Revolution he returned to Cumberland county where he became a county lieutenant. He led a regiment to the support of General Arthur St. Clair and was killed in battle.

[25] February 19, 1776. David M. Matteson, "George Washington Every Day," *United States George Washington Bicentehnnial Commission* (Washington, 1934), p. 351.

were even without shoes and stockings. British assurance of the ultimate outcome was expressed as follows: "Under all the disadvantages of want of confidence, clothing, and good winter quarters, and constantly harassed by a victorious and incensed Army, it will be astonishing if they keep together 'till Christmas." [26]

Merchants in Philadelphia closed their shops and martial law was proclaimed. Congress fled to Baltimore (December 12) leaving a committee of three, of which Morris was a member, in charge of Continental affairs. "It is very mortifying for me," he wrote Congress, "when I am obliged to tell you disagreeable things; but I am compelled to inform Congress that the continental currency keeps losing its credit, many people refuse openly and avowedly to receive it. . . . Some effectual remedy should be speedily applied to this evil or the game will be up." [27]

Writing of the gloomy cowardice of the times, John Adams uttered this apostrophe: "Posterity! You will never know how much it cost the present generation to preserve your freedom! I hope you will make good use of it. If you do not, I shall repent it in heaven that I ever took half the pains to preserve it." [28]

Washington was given full power by Congress to conduct the War as he saw fit. That this confidence was not misplaced was demonstrated by his surprise attack and the defeat of two battalions of Hessians who were sleeping off their Christmas debauch at Trenton. One week later, by a masterly movement, on the night of January 2, 1777, he won an important engagement over two isolated British regiments at Princeton. These two victories, characterized by Frederick the Great as the most brilliant in military history, served for a time to re-

---

[26] Quoted from *Diary of Frederick Mackenzie*, I, 96.
[27] Quoted from Oberholtzer, *Robert Morris*, pp. 26, 27. Morris was virtually the Committee.
[28] John Adams, *Familiar Letters to his Wife*, p. 265.

vive the flagging spirits of the Americans. The outlook was brighter also through the coming to New Orleans of a new governor who soon manifested willingness to assist Pollock in carrying out his objectives.

CHAPTER V

SPANISH ASSISTANCE BECOMES MORE GENEROUS

THE promotion of Don Bernardo de Galvez, a magnetic and successful leader, to the post of Governor of Louisiana in February, 1777, was of greatest significance for the American cause. He was a member of one of the most influential Spanish families, descended from the ancient nobility. His father was Viceroy of Mexico. José de Galvez, his uncle, was the power behind the throne as Secretary of State and President of the Council of the Indies. Distinguished service in the Spanish Army in Portugal and while in charge of an expedition against the Apaches on the Spanish frontier in America, led to his appointment as colonel of the fixed regiment, and as Governor of the Province of Louisiana.[1] Although only thirty years of age, the new governor was known for his ability, energy, and ambition.

The accession of Galvez was welcomed by Pollock, who evidently had been baffled by the half-hearted support of Unzaga. As he wrote: "My eagerness to seize every opportunity of serving my country had led me into such frequent importunities to Governor Unzaga that I had just reason to fear his displeasure." Evidently he was mistaken, for in presenting Pollock to his successor, Unzaga characterized him as "a faithful and zealous American in whom he might repose implicit confidence."

Galvez tendered his services, at once, to Pollock and assured him he would go every possible length for the interests of Congress. He declared that the port of New Orleans would be open and free to American commerce and to the admission and sale of prizes made by American cruisers or privateers. This was in keeping with the royal order of October 23, 1776.

---

[1] Caughey, *op. cit.*, 62–65.

SPANISH ASSISTANCE

A month earlier, the British minister at Madrid had urged the Spanish court to take action similar to that of Portugal whereby American vessels were to be forbidden to enter her ports. Instead of treating Americans as rebel subjects of a friendly power, however, the King of Spain directed that American vessels should be granted any hospitality in Spanish ports which might be accorded those of France or Great Britain.

Moreover, Galvez declared to Pollock that he was prepared to suppress the commerce with Great Britain and engage in trade with the United States. By his order, a number of British vessels were seized because of contraband trade. A sloop, the property of Pollock, having been captured at the same time, was freed when its ownership was established. Seizure of an American schooner in the Lakes, provoked an order for the capture and confiscation of all British vessels between "the Balize and Manchac." [2] To the captain of a British frigate who protested against the protection accorded an American privateer, Galvez replied that his king had granted immunity on the Mississippi to all such ships. "Whoever fights on the River," he continued, "will incur the disapproval of My Sovereign and in consideration of my duty I would have to oppose to the extent of my power."

American trading vessels, upon arrival at the mouth of the Mississippi River, were taken over as Spanish property in order to protect them from a British sloop-of-war. This decree of the governor was entrusted to Pollock, who dispatched it to Robert Morris, on a vessel chartered for the purpose by Pollock and two of his friends at an outlay of $1,000. "The execution of this will make some noise," Pollock writes, "and will, no doubt, create a jealousy between this Government and Great Britain, but as the saying is, 'the more Mischief the better sport on the present occasion.' " [3]

---

[2] Pollock to the President of Congress, September 18, 1782. *Pollock Letters.*

[3] The letter is undated but it seems probable that it was written early in April, 1777.

Judged by these early communications from Pollock, do we not see portrayed a man who is already a striking illustration of devotion to a great cause? We are to recall that no official recognition had, as yet, been accorded him by the American Government. A group of traders, however, "a small faction of Americans" as Galvez styled them, agreed that Pollock was to serve as agent for the United States at New Orleans.

Although he was aware that the captain of a war-sloop was under orders from Governor Chester, at Pensacola, to seize his person and property, Pollock had no fear since he had been assured special protection by Galvez. "But in case of an accident which may happen of being taken prisoner," he writes the Committee, "I would be happy to have something to show from you either in the Character of Civil or Military as you may think proper, so that it would only entitle me to be treated as a Gentleman, for at present I am threatened with only Death, which in the Service and legally appointed I should not dread."

In addition to the bills already assumed by Pollock he declared: "I have often been obliged to advance money for the benefit of the Cause, which I have made no account of; but in future I shall furnish you with the particulars. At present, all the reward I want is to be in the Service in what Rank or Station of Life you may think I merit, so that I may have something to show if called upon." He asks that the Committee should manifest confidence in him through establishing some form of credit in Spain or elsewhere in Europe for the money which he might advance. Supplies of flour or Negroes would be equally satisfactory.

That he gained the complete confidence of Galvez and won his interest for the cause of America is clear from the statement: "I prevailed also on the Governor to write and express those friendly assurances which have been already mentioned." [4] In presenting Pollock to his successor, Unzaga had

---

[4] As viewed by Dr. Caughey, in his study of the life of Galvez, the governor would probably have maintained strict neutrality had it not been for the influence of Pollock.

SPANISH ASSISTANCE

declared: "that if the Court of Spain was going to take part with Great Britain, Oliver Pollock should not remain in the country twenty-four hours; but if the reverse, that they were going to take part with France, Pollock was the only man that he could confide in in the colony, meaning an English merchant." [5]

In addition to possessing a good personality, Pollock's approach in private interviews was more direct because of his ability to use, as we have noted, the Spanish language, then an exceptional accomplishment among Americans. To Pollock, Morris wrote regarding the generous proposals made by Galvez: "Herein you will find inclosed a letter for the Governor which please to deliver and procure it to be well translated into Spanish for him." How difficult diplomatic rapprochement was may be inferred from a letter from Morris to Galvez—"We were happy to receive your letter of June second but it was our misfortune that in this place [Philadelphia] there was no one familiar with the Spanish language who could make a translation of it."

To Galvez, it was clear, as it had been to his predecessor, that British plans contemplated an attack upon Louisiana. One of his earliest communications urged, as a means of defense, that the Southern Indians should be gained as allies. This could, he thought, be easily accomplished because of their former subjection to France. By means of gifts, friendly visits, and promises, some progress was made toward the accomplishment of this objective.

During May (1777), a conference was held at Mobile between John Stuart, British Superintendent of the Southern Indians and a man of excellent administrative ability, and the chiefs of the Chickasaw and Choctaw tribes. While the military strength of the Southern tribes has been variously estimated, it seems probable that the Chickasaw and Choctaw numbered between four thousand and five thousand braves. There were about the same number in the Creek, Cherokee and other tribes. The British policy aimed at overcoming the

[5] Wilkinson, *Memoirs*, II, Appendix I.

influence of American emissaries, who in the guise of traders visited the tribes urging them to preserve strict neutrality. "It is the declared intention," Stuart exhorted them, "to possess themselves of your Lands, it also becomes your duty and interest to unite yourselves firmly to the King's cause, to whose goodness and protection you have been and are so much indebted. I therefore warn you not to pay any attention to the stories and insinuations of bad designing men. . . . Listen only to my Deputies and Commissioners who live among you for your advantage and happiness."[6] We find Pollock urging that a force should be sent to capture Pensacola. This would lead, he thought, to the control of all the Southern Indians.

Early in 1777, Galvez requested that two frigates should be sent, at once, to defend the Spanish possessions against British aggression which had reached "a point of intolerable insolence difficult to be borne by a man of honor." Among the infinity of insults which could not be recounted he specified the following: that the English had plundered Spanish dwellings along the River and fired on the inhabitants; that a Spanish and a French vessel had been fired on, and after capture were delayed for periods of twenty-four and thirty hours, the communications under the seal of the governor having been read; and that boats loaded with pitch at New Orleans had been seized as contraband. Such evidence of presumption on the part of the British and the contempt in which they regarded the Spaniards determined Galvez to avenge what he referred to as "an infinity of insults each separate one of which appears deserving of punishment."

His quick response to the appeals of Pollock, may here find a satisfactory interpretation. "I wrote you fully yesterday," Pollock states in a letter to the Committee of May 5, 1777, "since which I had the Honor of conversing more particularly with his Excellency, the Governor, and upon stating some questions in regard to your sending an expedition against this River and Pensacola he desires me to assure you that he will

---

[6] Quoted with permission from, Helen Louise Shaw, *British Administration of the Southern Indians, 1756–1783*, pp. 109, 110.

assist your troops with stores, cash and in fine everything in his Power for the benefit of the Cause; therefore I hope your Honors will lose no time in sending down an express immediately by the way of the Ohio acquainting me with your intentions so that I may be prepared here with his Excellency." [7] He also urged that blank commissions should be sent in order that he might enlist troops at New Orleans and elsewhere for he was assured there were many persons, mainly traders, on the lower Mississippi who would welcome the opportunity of declaring openly for the United States.

Galvez became steadily more aggressive. During one night, eleven British boats, engaged in carrying on illicit commerce, were seized by his order. This was an act of reprisal for the seizure of three Spanish boats by the *West Florida,* a British frigate. In explaining his action, Galvez wrote: "Within twenty-four hours after the three mentioned boats of ours had been taken, I confiscated eleven which were employed in the contraband trade in this jurisdiction, and although most of these are entirely useless for navigation and only serve to store goods which have not a quick sale, nevertheless I have dealt them a blow which not only has thrown them into a panic but which I believe is such that for some time they will not think of returning to carry on their clandestine commerce." [8]

British armed vessels appeared before New Orleans with the demand that the captured vessels and crews should be released. Pollock, agent of the American rebels, was likewise to be given into their keeping. Hostilities seemed about to open but the British withdrew when Galvez showed no disposition to yield. "I received them," he wrote, "with match-rope in hand in order to prevent any violence."

Two of the vessels interned were the property of Americans. They were released secretly upon the request of Pollock. The nine others were confiscated and their cargoes were sold. At that time, owing to a shortage in food, there was much sick-

[7] *Pollock Letters.*
[8] Caughey, *The Hispanic American Historical Review,* XII, No. 1, pp. 52, 53.

ness at Pensacola. Galvez sent one hundred and fifty barrels of flour to relieve the distress and this spirit of generosity settled the controversy for a time. Although the immediate cause for dispute was adjusted, we find the governor calling for reinforcements, and both naval and military equipment with which to strengthen the fortifications at New Orleans.

Causes for strained relations continued to arise. The governor at Pensacola protested against the sending of arms and ammunition up the Mississippi under the protection of the Spanish flag. A mail-boat was attacked while ascending the River, presumably by a British armed sloop. British subjects were forbidden to transact any business within the Spanish boundaries, while French commercial concessions were extended. Two French commissioners at New Orleans declared that "the whole trade of the Mississippi is now in our hands." Compared with a statement of Galvez, uttered as late as October, 1778, this generalization does not square with the facts. Reasserting his inability to put an end to British contraband trade, he writes: "In these circumstances, it is impossible to attain the object of excluding foreigners, for as the consul says; 'English ships stocked with the necessary articles idle along the river and according to the treaties of peace, they cannot be prevented from anchoring and mooring wherever they see fit.' And what inhabitant having what he needs at the door of his house will fail to take advantage of the opportunity to obtain it, since there are no witnesses to accuse him of fraud? What vigilance, what force, or what body of customs officers would be able to keep watch to prevent this abuse over a distance of one hundred leagues of river whose banks are fringed with habitations?" [9]

Meantime, Galvez was becoming more war-minded, due, in part, to communications which he received during the early days of July, 1777, to the effect that hostilities were inevitable on account of the preparations which France and Spain were

---

[9] *Documents Relating to the Commercial Policy of Spain in the Floridas*, ed. Arthur P. Whitaker, p. 17.

SPANISH ASSISTANCE

making and because of the "bare-faced aid which they give to the Americans in their ports." He was cognizant, also, of a communication from Lord George Germaine to Governor Chester at Pensacola directing that he should use all of his resources to fortify that post and put it in a state of defense.

By the end of the year 1777, Pollock, aided by loans from Galvez, amounting to some $74,087 had been enabled to send arms, ammunition, and provisions to the upper Mississippi posts and to the frontiers of Virginia and Pennsylvania. For such advances he became personally responsible. Under Spanish colors, large bateaux, "deeply loaded," and propelled with twenty-four oars, managed to slip past Natchez with these goods. In eighty-five or ninety days, they arrived at the mouth of the Ohio and usually continued to Pittsburgh. Blankets, shoes, stockings, shirtings and medicines, especially quinine in quantities, procured from the Spanish storehouses at a cost of 25,000 pistoles, constituted a single shipment.

Early in 1778, merchandise purchased by Pollock on his own account, amounting to 10,900 pistoles, was sent up the River, then the safest route to Philadelphia. To the commander of the boats, orders were issued that officers of American troops descending the River, might, in case of need, be permitted to draw upon these supplies. In this consignment to the Committee of Congress, besides powder, gun-locks, musket-balls, and gun-worms, were horn and ivory combs, horn tumblers, scissors, razors, butcher's knives, hinges, nails, brass rings, blue and white handkerchiefs, needles, thread, flannel, cambric, mosquito gauze, table clothing, napkining, Irish linen, red, yellow and black calicos, men's hats, shoes, and stockings. Specific needs of the "gentry" were not omitted, for there was included in the shipment; fine ruffled shirts, metal buttons, red garters, silk breeches, silver breast-plates, wine, brandy, and taffia. In a supplementary note to another bill of goods sent Morris and his colleagues on the Committee, Pollock writes: "I have taken the liberty of forwarding a box of Havanna Segars which I wish safe."

In spite of his efforts to prevent extraordinary charges,

rowers could not be secured except through the payment of very high wages. "Hurry down those batteaux again" was Pollock's command, "In order that I may dispatch them back with more goods." Shortly afterward he wrote the Committee: "I found it highly necessary and indeed the only method of saving the goods or getting them forwarded was by sending them all under Spanish Colors, which I have conducted in the most secret manner possible. . . . All sorts of Goods are very scarce and dear here just now as there has been no Arrivals for a long time past and for fear this should be the case next Fall I have purchased about p^{s}20,000 [pistoles] worth of Peltries and Indigo and shipped to the Amount of p^{s}11,000 from here for France and the remaining p^{s}9000 I have shipped via the Cape all addressed to Mons. Geronimo La Chappelle. . . . The Brig they are shipped in from here is a very good vessel under French Colors and regularly cleared. . . . This speculation is made entirely with the View of having it in my Power to supply you with such Goods as you may require this Fall. . . ." Again he wrote the Committee: "I have more goods on hand which if I can get Hands enough to fit out another Batteaux, I will send one up, but I am afraid that will not be practicable as the number of Batteaux gone up this year has thinned the men so that Monsr. Connand has the greatest difficulty in procuring them at very high price as the common wages for the run is from 40 p^s [pistoles] to 45 p^s and now he has been obliged to pay 70 p^s. This runs away with a great deal of ready cash and no such thing as doing anything without it. I thought to make out an estimate or sketch of my advances and engagements for goods to be paid for by the month of December for the States, but as my time is now precious must only observe I shall want about 50,000 p^s to clear off what I have undertaken and paying off the goods purchased and the expenses of the men here. This [is] exclusive of the goods received from the Governor here and which sum I shall depend on your supplying me with by that time." [10]

The balance in trade which he held as agent for Willing

[10] May 7, 1778. *Pollock Letters.*

and Morris, $42,000, had been much reduced through his remittances to France. "But this shall not prevent your being supplied with what you call for," he wrote; "as the G[governor] has promised to assist me with some cash tho' he has not as yet received any orders for so doing. The rest I shall make up out of the prizes and my own Stock and Credit shall be immediately employed. I do not know yet whether I can get the boats dispatched under Spanish Passports or not. If I cannot get this done, I will have them manned and armed as you order, as in all probability they will be attacked by a party of White men and Indians they may send from Pensacola, but we shall be prepared to receive them as I am now engaging a parcel of resolute batteaux men well attached to the Cause and shall make all the expedition possible."

Instructions sent by Pollock to commanding officers descending the River to New Orleans were very definite. In this, also, there was manifested complete coöperation with Galvez. To escape possible attack from Indians or from British armed vessels near Manchac, they were directed to call at the Spanish posts, Arkansas or Point Coupée, for instructions, where they "may get every intelligence necessary of the enemy." Of this service, one captain writes: "I had the good fortune to meet with Mr. L. Sweet who delivered me a Letter from You dated Orleans April 22 [1778] which (although not very satisfactory) was great service, by your great care in being so particular in advising how to act in so critical a situation." After drawing on Pollock, as advised by the commanding officer at Pittsburgh, for $2,500 which was invested in merchandise, he returned to that post.

In the meantime, through timely loans by Galvez, Pollock holding himself responsible for their payment, and by his own personal advances for the purchase of goods, American agents had been enabled to cope with the British in the contest for ascendancy over the Indian tribes of the Northwest. We now turn to an account of this phase of the Revolution.

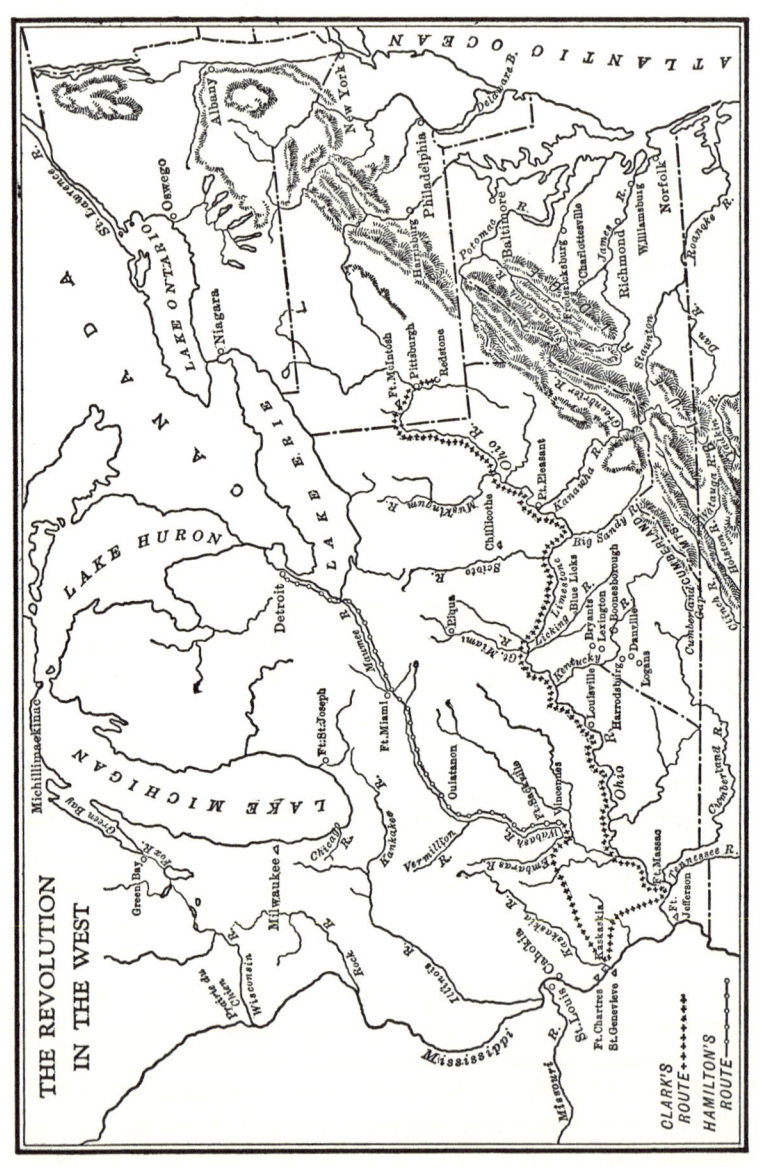

CHAPTER VI

EARLY STAGE OF THE REVOLUTION IN THE WEST

FROM the outbreak of the Revolution, American leaders were urging the capture of Detroit, which was the most important British post in the West—the key to the fur-trade and to the control of the Indian tribes northwest of the Ohio River. Throughout the War this post continued, as Washington wrote, "to be a constant source of trouble to the whole Western country."

The fort at Detroit was a small wooden structure surrounded by a "Stocade of Picquets about nine feet out of the earth, without Frize or ditch"—furnishing defense only against Indian attack. At the opening of the year 1776, the garrison consisted of two companies of the King's Regiment numbering 120 men, commanded by Captain Richard B. Lernoult. Out of a population of some 1,800 in the town and near-by country, 350 militia, French and English, were capable of bearing arms.[1]

On the south side of the strait connecting Lakes Michigan and Huron was a poorly constructed wooden fort, Michillimackinac, in which was housed a garrison consisting of about 120 men, commanded by Captain Arent Schuyler de Peyster.

As we have seen, the Illinois villages were likewise under the control of the British. After the abandonment of Fort Chartres in 1772, because of the encroachment of the Mississippi River on its walls, the garrison was removed to Kaskaskia, where the house of the Jesuit missionaries, recently vacated, was fortified and named Fort Gage. Two companies of soldiers, under Captain Hugh Lord who had made himself popular with the French inhabitants, constituted the garrison.

---

[1] For the further defense of Detroit, *see* James, *Life of Clark*, p. 30.

In order to save unnecessary expense, the troops were recalled to Detroit during the spring of 1776, Captain Lord entrusting the administration of affairs to Philippe François de Rastel, Chevalier de Rocheblave. After distinguished service during the French and Indian War, like many other Frenchmen, the new commander sought refuge under the Spanish flag. For a time he was entrusted with the command at Ste. Genevieve, but because of difficulties with Spanish officials, he returned to the British Illinois. Here, as the successor to Captain Lord, he was employed, as Sir Guy Carleton wrote: "to have an eye on the proceedings of the Spaniards, and the management of the Indians on that side."

By what means Spanish influence was to be overcome demanded his immediate attention and continued his most pressing problem during the two years he was in command. Experience with the Spaniards had developed in him a personal hatred for them and his ambition was quickened by the hope of becoming Governor of New Orleans in the event of its capture by the British. Therefore, he requested that all Spanish trade on the Ohio River should be cut off; called attention to the aid which the Americans were receiving from New Orleans; declared that Spanish agents were stirring up the tribes on the Illinois River to attack British posts and, during the summer of 1777, demanded: "Shall we make the first move or shall we permit it to be made?" [2]

The chief American post (1775) guarding the frontier stretching from the Greenbrier River to Kitanning on the Upper Allegheny was Fort Pitt. Restored in 1774, by order of Governor Dunmore, it was the point of departure for an expedition of some three thousand Virginia militia, led by Dunmore against the Shawnee strongholds, "nests of hornets," in

[2] The post at Cahokia in 1775 was without a commanding officer. At Vincennes Edward Abbott, serving as lieutenant-governor, built a stockade post, which he named Fort Sackville. Early in 1778, he was recalled to Detroit. There were little French settlements, also, at Ouiatanon, near La Fayette, Indiana, Fort Miami (now Fort Wayne), Fort St. Joseph (Michigan), Peoria (Illinois), and at Green Bay and Prairie du Chien (Wisconsin).

THE REVOLUTION IN THE WEST 87

the Scioto Valley. During the summer of 1774, the atrocities of bands of these Indians had stirred the frontiersmen to a frenzy of rage. Associated with Dunmore on the expedition were Colonel Andrew Lewis, Colonel William Fleming, Colonel William Preston, Colonel William Christian, Captain Evan Shelby, Lieutenant James Robertson, George Rogers Clark, recently made a captain of militia, and other leaders whose names were to become famous in frontier annals.

In the decisive battle at Point Pleasant, at the mouth of the Kanawha, October 10 of that year, one of the bloodiest combats in the history of Indian warfare, the Indians under Chief Cornstalk were worsted. At the Treaty of Camp Charlotte they agreed to accept the Ohio as the boundary between them and the whites. They were to restore all prisoners and agreed to permit the navigation of the Ohio without further molestation.[3]

After the treaty, Dunmore returned to Williamsburg, leaving Major John Connolly as his agent in charge of the garrison of seventy-five men at Fort Dunmore, formerly Fort Pitt. In conference at the Capital, February, 1775, Dunmore, then in trouble with the rebellious colonists, instructed Connolly to use every effort to induce the Indians across the Ohio to espouse the cause of the British.

Responding to the message from Connolly, chiefs of the Delawares and some of the Mingo gathered at Fort Dunmore in June, 1775. They were assured that a general treaty with all the Ohio tribes would follow.[4] On the last day of the treaty, a committee of patriots from West Augusta County was present, and, notwithstanding the opposition of Connolly, through

[3] It was claimed in British official dispatches that Governor Dunmore, associated with Virginia land speculators, had undertaken the expedition in order to nullify the ministerial prohibition on Western purchases and grants. See Alvord, *Miss. Valley in British Politics*, p. 193. The victory was really that of the left wing of Dunmore's army under Colonel Andrew Lewis, composed of 1,100 militia. For a more complete account of Dunmore's war, consult James, *Life of Clark*, pp. 15-20.

[4] *The Revolution on the Upper Ohio, 1775-1777*, eds. R. G. Thwaites and Louise P. Kellogg (Madison, 1908), p. 35.

friendly messages to the chiefs and the distribution of goods, prepared them for later negotiations. Disbanding the garrison in July, Connolly returned to the East where he found that Dunmore was a fugitive on board a British man-of-war off the Virginia Coast.

Fearful of a rupture with the Western Indians, the Virginia House of Burgesses, in their last session, appointed six commissioners to carry on negotiations. Captain James Wood, one of the number, who was well versed in frontier affairs, was delegated to visit the Ohio tribes in order to extend an invitation to them to attend a conference at Pittsburgh; to explain the dispute and "assure them of our peaceable Intentions towards them and that we do not stand in need of or desire any Assistance from them."

Captain Wood, with Simon Girty, an interpreter, as his sole companion, set out on his hazardous journey.[5] His reception by the Shawnee was friendly as the fear excited by the Battle of Point Pleasant was still upon them. He carried his messages as far as the Wyandot villages near Detroit. Two British emissaries, he learned, had already presented belts and strings of wampum to seventeen nations, inviting them to unite with the French and English against the Virginians.[6]

Despite this opposition, chiefs and tribesmen from the Delaware, Wyandot, Mingo and Shawnee tribes gathered for the conference at Pittsburgh in September. Each tribe, upon arrival, was received with "Drum and Colours and a Salute of small arms from the Garrison."

The Virginia commissioners, assisted by two commissioners sent by the Continental Congress, strove through speeches and by presents of clothing and strings of wampum, to convince the Indians that they should keep the hatchet buried and endeavor to induce the Six Nations and other tribes to remain absolutely neutral.

---

[5] As a boy, Girty was captured by the Seneca and lived with them for three years. He became a Tory, hated by the borderers because of the atrocities committed by Indian bands under his leadership.

[6] *American Archives*, 4th series, III, 76 *ff.*

THE REVOLUTION IN THE WEST 89

They were assured that the cause of Virginia was the cause of all America. "In this dispute," Lewis Morris, Continental Commissioner, said, "your Interest is involved with ours so far as this, that in Case those People with whom we are Contending should subdue us, your *Lands,* your *Trade,* your Liberty and all that is dear to you must fall with us, for if they would Distroy our flesh and spill our Blood which is the same as theirs; what can you who are no way related to or connected with them Expect? . . . We only ask you to stay at home, to take care of your women and children, and follow your usual occupations; we are not afraid these People will conquer us, they Can't fight in our Country and you know we Can; we fear not them, nor any Power on Earth."

The natives were invited to send their children to be educated among the white people. Finally, after three weeks given over to discussion, they accepted the offer of friendship which was "to endure forever." [7] In general, the terms of the treaty were kept for upwards of two years and in the meantime settlements in Kentucky were established. This made possible the advance into the territory north of the Ohio River. With these events the name of George Rogers Clark is indissolubly associated.[8]

Soldiers in the armies of Lewis and Dunmore had heard from their companions, the hunters and surveyors, such as Clark, wonderful tales of Kentucky. Western Kentucky had been frequented earlier by French boatmen, from New Orleans and the Illinois country, bringing trappers in pursuit of the fur-bearing animals. Later on, British trading companies sent their hunters up the Kentucky rivers for buffalo-meat with which to supply the garrison at Fort Chartres. Land companies, likewise, such as the Mississippi Company of Virginia and the company of Military Adventurers represented by General Lyman, desired to exploit this region.[9]

---

[7] *Revolution on the Upper Ohio,* 25 *et. seq.*
[8] For a plan originating with Major Connolly which threatened the American Union, *see* James, *Life of Clark,* pp. 35, 36.
[9] *The Miss. Valley in British Politics,* II, p. 172.

In June of 1772, Clark, leaving his home in Carolina County, Virginia, struck out with a few other adventurers from Pittsburgh to explore the lands on the upper Ohio and its tributaries. That the journey was well suited to inure these young men to lives of adventure and hardship may be gathered from statements of one of the party. They crept past Indian villages, fearing discovery, and the narrator exclaims: "Instead of feathers my bed was gravel stones by the river side." Clark's return to his home was an event of importance for he was the first from that section who had gone out to the *New World*, as the Ohio country was called. His glowing account of the fertile soil, of the exquisite beauty and stateliness of the trees of various kinds and his stories of the buffalo, deer and turkeys, so plentiful in that region, induced his father, among others, to journey with him on his return.

One hundred and thirty miles below Pittsburgh, at the mouth of Fish Creek, Clark had selected a body of fine land, where he left the company, and with a single companion descended the River 170 miles further. By the middle of November they returned to Fish Creek where they spent the winter, their friends going back to Virginia. Hunting, cutting rails, girdling trees, and burning brushwood were the winter tasks of the two in preparation for planting corn the next season. By that time, settlers had pressed on to the mouth of the Scioto River and Clark was given opportunity to practice his calling as a surveyor.

Early in 1774, a band of some ninety men, of which Clark was a member, gathered at the mouth of the Little Kanawha for undertaking a settlement in Kentucky. The alarm was then general in the frontier communities over the report that the Shawnee were determined to kill all Virginians and rob all Pennsylvanians who should be found on the Ohio. With other frontiersmen they mustered for Dunmore's War which, as we have seen, broke out in the late summer.

The spring following, Clark set out for the Kentucky River where he surveyed lands for the Ohio Company and located lands in his own name in what he declared was one of the richest and most beautiful countries to be found in America.[10] He found Captain James Harrod and fifty companions engaged in reoccupying the site they had abandoned the year before which was, as Harrodsburg, the first permanent settlement in Kentucky.

Fifty miles east of Harrodsburg, he found Daniel Boone and a company of thirty backwoodsmen beginning a settlement, Boonesborough, which was planned as the capital of the independent government of Transylvania, the design of Judge Richard Henderson. Delegates from Harrodsburg and two other settlements, within the bounds of the colony, were called by Henderson to meet with those from Boonesborough for the purpose of drawing up a plan of government. The eighteen delegates thus assembled May 23, 1775, constituted the first representative body of American freemen west of the mountains. Their foresight is manifest in the compact agreed upon and in the laws which were formulated. From the Continental Congress, Transylvania sought recognition as the fourteenth member of the United Colonies.

Aware of the discontent among Kentuckians because of the claims of the Transylvania Company, Clark decided to contest these claims. The revolt which he led found expression in a general meeting at Harrodsburg in June, 1776. In the petition which was to be presented to the Virginia Assembly, it was urged that relief and protection should be furnished them and that they should receive recognition as a separate county. The journey over the Wilderness road by Clark and his companion, John Gabriel Jones, who were selected to carry the memorial to Williamsburg, was one of hardship because of their suffering through cold and hunger and constant fear of ambush by Indians. With a letter of introduction from Governor Patrick Henry, who was himself the owner of Kentucky land, Clark appeared before the Executive Council. Replying to his request for five hundred pounds of powder needed for defense, since Kentucky was not legally united to Virginia, they suggested that a loan of the ammunition should be made.

[10] James, *Clark Papers*, p. 10.

"If a Cuntrey was not worth protecting, it was not worth Claiming" was his challenge, which brought favorable action and the order for the delivery of the powder at Pittsburgh subject to his order.

In the meeting of the Assembly he defended the petition for the recognition of Kentucky as an independent county of Virginia. His victory over Judge Henderson, who was assisted by the best of legal talent, was complete.[11] Out of the ill-defined territory constituting Fincastle County, Virginia, were created the three counties, Kentucky, Montgomery, and Washington. As compensation for his claim, Henderson received a grant of 200,000 acres of land from Virginia. Later on, North Carolina made a like grant of land located between the Powell and the Clinch rivers.

With great difficulty and the loss of two lives from Indian raids, the powder was brought to Harrodsburg. It came at the right moment, for the Kentuckians, cooped up within their stockaded forts at Harrodsburg, Boonesborough, and Logan's Station, were forced to defend themselves against a succession of Indian attacks, organized by British officials at Detroit, by which they hoped to gain control of the whole region west of the Alleghenies.

Affairs at Detroit were under the direction of Lieutenant-Governor Henry Hamilton, who had knowledge of the treaty made at Pittsburgh through reports of an Indian who was present and a Frenchman who was stationed nearby. Hamilton was convinced that any treaty which might be made would endure for a brief period only, on account of the "haughty, violent dispositions" of the Virginians. Indian jealousy was easily aroused by accounts of encroachments upon their lands. In spite of the declaration of American commissioners, that it was their intention to retain only the areas

[11] For this attempt to set up a proprietary colony, *see* James, *Life of Clark*, pp. 21–27. Archibald Henderson, *The Significance of the Transylvania Company in American History*, gives an authoritative interpretation of Daniel Boone's influence in our history. Address delivered October 12, 1935.

THE REVOLUTION IN THE WEST

acquired by treaty, frontiersmen continued to push the line of settlement forward regardless of boundaries. Some of them even hoped for a general Indian war in order that the seizure of lands might be promoted.

The attention of the natives was called to the fact that the "Big Knives" had been pushing them back for many years and would not rest until they were possessed of all this country. The origin of the following message from the Six Nations and the Chippewa, early in 1777, to the Virginians and the Pennsylvanians, may be readily discerned: "You have feloniously taken possession of part of our Country on the branches of the Ohio, as well as the Susquehanna, to the latter we have some time since sent you word to quit our Lands as we now do to you, as we don't know we ever give you liberty, nor can we be easy in our minds while there is an arm'd Force at our very doors, nor do we think you, or anybody else would. Therefore to use you with more lenity than you have a right to expect, we now tell you in a peaceful manner to quit our Lands wherever you have possessed yourselves of them immediately, or blame yourselves for whatever may happen."

Early in April, 1776, George Morgan, as Indian agent for the Middle Department, was selected to conduct affairs at Fort Pitt.[12] So far as possible he was to adjust all differences by arbitration and "inspire them with sentiments of justice and humanity and dispose them to introduce the arts of civil and social life, and encourage the residence of handicraftsmen among them." Assurance had already been given the Delawares by Congress that in addition to the establishment of satisfactory trade relations and the protection of their rights to the lands, there should be sent to them a schoolmaster, a Christian minister, and a competent instructor in farming.[13] The preceding November, two blacksmiths had been employed to reside among the Iroquois. The Western Indians

---

[12] Two other Departments, Northern and Southern, had also been constituted.
[13] *Jour. of Cont. Cong.* (new ed.), IV, 366.

were to be drawn to Pittsburgh for a second treaty at the earliest time convenient.[14]

Was Morgan or Hamilton to win in the matching of wits to gain support from the Northwestern tribes? Success, in the large, might conceivably mean gaining control over some eight thousand warriors.[15] Morgan proceeded at once to the Shawnee towns where he extended the invitation to come to Pittsburgh, September 10, for the purpose of making a treaty. To other tribes, as far west as the Wyandot villages opposite Detroit, were delivered the speech and belt sent by Morgan. The bearer of this message, William Wilson, crossed to Detroit with his three companions in response to the request from Governor Hamilton who assured him a friendly reception. Hamilton's purpose was not long a mystery. Two hundred Indians had been assembled, deputies, as Hamilton wrote, of the "Ottawas, Chippewas, Wyandotts, Shawanese, Senecas, Delawares, Cherakees and Potteowattamies." Explaining the message of the Americans to them, he declared that the people who sent it were enemies and traitors to his king. Tearing their message and speeches asunder and cutting the belt to pieces he spoke to them on the tomahawk belt. Chief White Eyes of the Delawares, who accompanied Wilson, was ordered to leave Detroit before sunset, "as he regarded his head." Wilson was likewise directed to leave at once, receiving a parting word which was intended to excite fear among frontier folk and enthusiasm for the British cause on the part of the Indians. As stated by Wilson: "He would be glad, he said, if I would inform the people on my return of what I had seen; and that all the Indians I saw there at the treaty were of the same way of thinking; and that he would be glad if the people would consider the dreadful consequences of going to war with so terrible an enemy, and accept the King's pardon while

[14] *Jour. of Cont. Cong.* (new ed.), IV, 268.
[15] At various times there were assembled for conferences, chiefs of the Delawares, of the Muskingum and the Ohio, the Shawnee and Mingo of the Scioto, the Wyandot, Ottawa and Potawatomie of Lake Michigan, the Chippewa of all the Lakes and the Miami, Sauk and other tribes. For number of warriors, *see Life of Clark*, p. 31, note 1.

THE REVOLUTION IN THE WEST 95

it could be obtained." In further council with the Indians, he declared that he would protect them from the Virginians and that if one tribe was attacked all would aid in repelling the assailant.[16]

In response to the invitation of Morgan, warriors and chiefs, representing the Six Nations, Delawares, Munsee and Shawnee, numbering 644, gathered at Pittsburgh. The conference served to dissipate the widespread gloom, for these envoys promised inviolable peace with the United States and neutrality during the War.[17] Twelve of the chiefs were induced to visit Philadelphia, where they were introduced to Congress.

The British policy of employing the Indians, as allies, has been generally condemned by Americans. To remain mere spectators in a conflict which so deeply involved their interests would have been, for the natives, an impossible rôle. In utilizing them as allies, British officials were prompted by the same motive that had dominated governments for all time, namely, that in waging war, the help of aliens is to be enlisted. In American colonial warfare, neither the French nor the English had hesitated to enlist Indians under their standards.

The principle of Indian neutrality was soon abandoned by both the British and the Americans. Asserting that the "Rebells" had excited the Indians to take part in the "Unnatural rebellion" and had enlisted a body of them "under arms," the Earl of Dartmouth, during July, 1775, issued the order that no time should be lost in inducing the Six Nations, their allies, to take up the hatchet against "his Majesty's rebellious subjects in America."[18] On the day the message was penned, five hundred Indians were brought to Montreal to join the English Army. Early in September, 1776, Hamilton proposed the employment of Indians against the frontiers of Virginia and Pennsylvania. In the orders which followed, General Carleton was directed to make use of every means "that Prov-

[16] Louise Phelps Kellogg, "Indian Diplomacy During the Revolution in the West," *Transactions of the Illinois State Historical Society.* Publication No. 36, p. 8.
[17] Morgan, *Letter Book*, I, November 8, 1776.
[18] July 24, 1885. *N. Y. Col. Doc's.* VIII, 596.

idence has put into his Majesty's Hands for crushing the rebellion and restoring the Constitution." Hamilton was commanded to assemble as many Indians as convenient to carry out this decree. By June of 1777, he felt assured from the friendly disposition manifested by the representatives of many leading tribes at Detroit, that one thousand warriors were ready to overrun the frontiers. Thereafter, the British were to enroll Indians for service with their regular army as well as to employ them with more terrible results in raiding the frontiers and cutting off outlying settlements.

While urging Indian neutrality, there is evidence that the colonists, likewise, early adopted a policy similar to that of the British. During April, 1775, the Massachusetts Provincial Congress appealed to the Iroquois "to whet their hatchets and be prepared, together with the colonists to defend their liberties and lives." [19] In May, 1776, the Continental Congress resolved "that it is highly expedient to engage the Indians in the service of the United Colonies," and fifty pounds were offered for every prisoner brought in. Notwithstanding the arraignment of the British Government in the Declaration of Independence for the enlistment of savages, Congress granted Washington power to use Indians as auxiliaries and to offer them bounties for all their prisoners.[20]

During the spring of 1776, also, John Stuart and other British agents were engaged in stirring up the Cherokee and other Southern Indians for attacks on the Tennessee settlements and the frontiers of the Carolinas and Georgia. The brunt of the first attack fell on Watauga, the first permanent settlement in what is now the State of Tennessee. For three weeks, the fort, crowded with women and children and defended by forty men, was besieged. So well organized was the defense under James Robertson and John Sevier that the attack was frustrated. Because of the depredations of the Cherokee, a combined force of militia from North Carolina, South Carolina and Virginia was sent against them. Defeated by

[19] *American Archives*, 4th series, I, 1349.
[20] *Jour. of the Cont. Cong.*, IV, 395, 452.

superior forces and with their cabins and crops in ashes, the Indians willingly submitted to the terms proposed.[21]

Arms, ammunition, rum and other presents in ever-increasing quantities were the ready means employed by British leaders for winning savage favor. "But the Indians must have presents," an official exclaimed. "Whenever we fall off from that article they are no more to be depended upon." [22] British officers at Detroit were generous not only with their presents but were lavish in hospitality, partaking with Indians in the feasts of roast ox and as the natives said, "covering their dead anew with rum." Even Hamilton himself, cultured Englishman that he was, painted and dressed as a red-man and joined the savage hordes in the wild yelps and dances incident to these councils. The colonists might make a show of presents at first but that they would be unable to furnish the different nations with their necessary wants was an argument shrewdly used, for the Indians were already aware of American poverty. Threats to send canoe-loads of goods back to Montreal were effective whips upon such tribes as might show any signs of wavering.

That complete control over the Indians of the Northwest was not won by the British during the critical months of 1777, was largely due to the opportune arrival of Lieutenant Linn at Wheeling early in May, and to the coming of other boats sent to Pittsburgh by Pollock, loaded, as we have seen, with powder, arms and supplies to be used, in part, in treating with the Indians. A conservative estimate of the value of the contributions of Governor Galvez, for which Pollock became responsible together with Pollock's own shipments, amounted by the close of 1777, to $100,000.

Early in this year, memorable to frontiersmen as "the year of blood," the British inaugurated more aggressive measures with a view of distressing the frontiers of Virginia and Pennsylvania as much as possible and with the hope that the American Army would be weakened through a withdrawal of forces

---

[21] For the establishment of the Tennessee Settlements and a more extended account of these attacks, see *Life of Clark*, pp. 8, 9, 46–49.
[22] *Mich. Pioneer and Hist. Coll's.*, IX, 375.

to meet these attacks. Although war-bands, fifteen in number as stated by Hamilton, were urged to act vigorously, they were ordered to act with humanity. Resolutions voiced by chiefs to heed the injunction that they should spare the blood of the aged and of women and children were idle. Presents for proofs of obedience signified little.

In isolated localities men were killed or captured while at work in the fields or out hunting. Women and children were burned in the homes and entire families were carried off as prisoners. Arriving at an Indian village, men prisoners were forced to satisfy the savage instincts of their captors by running the gauntlet or by being subjected to untold cruelties. Some were sold to British and French traders and later effected their escape or were ransomed. Women were forced into slavery and children were adopted into the tribe.

That Hamilton, known by frontiersmen as the "hair-buyer general," offered rewards for scalps cannot be positively proved. The testimony of prisoners and spies who visited Detroit, contains evidence that scalps were paid for. Among articles listed at that post—which included blankets, kettles, knives, razors, and rum, were one hundred and fifty dozen scalping-knives. Hamilton's own dispatches indicate that the securing of scalps was by no means exceptional. During January, 1778, he wrote General Carleton that the Indians had brought in seventy-three prisoners and 129 scalps. In a letter of September, he states: "Since last May, the Indians of this district have taken 34 prisoners, 17 of which they delivered up and 81 scalps." [23] At the same time, he declares that it was customary to present a gift on "every proof of obedience they shew in sparing the lives of such as are incapable of defending themselves." [24]

But charges of inhumanity cannot be brought against all British officers. Lieutenant-Governor Abbott, in command at Vincennes, asserted: "It is not people in arms that Indians will ever daringly attack, but the poor inoffensive families

[23] *Mich. Pioneer and Hist. Coll's.,* IX, 469.
[24] *Ibid.,* pp. 430, 465.

who fly to the deserts to be out of trouble, and who are inhumanly butchered, sparing neither women nor children. It may be said it is necessary to employ Indians to prevent their serving our enemies, I will be bold to say their keeping a neutrality will be equally (if not more) serviceable to us, . . . surely the presents they receive will prevent their acting against us." [25]

The policy of enlisting Indians was vigorously opposed in parliament by both Edmund Burke and William Pitt. "There were no means," a member asserted, "which God and Nature might have placed at the disposal of the governing powers, to which they would not be justified in having recourse." "But who is the man," Pitt replied, "who has dared to authorize and associate to our arms the tomahawk and scalping-knife of the savage? . . . What! to attribute the sanction of God and nature to the massacres of the Indian scalping-knife. . . . They shock every sentiment of honor. They shock me as a lover of honorable war and a detestor of murderous barbarity. These abominable principles, and this more abominable avowal of them, demand a most decisive indignation." But among Americans, there were individuals, also, who were not guiltless of this practice, one governor and his council sanctioning it by the offer of premiums for the scalps of enemy Indians and Tories.[26]

Among the defenders of Kentucky during the critical year 1777, was George Rogers Clark. His leadership had been more firmly established, after his victory over Judge Henderson, through setting in motion the machinery of government for Kentucky County. Some form of civil organization was demanded, for personal rights were about to yield to the assertion of individual might. "I'm afraid," John Todd, Jr., writes, "to lose sight of my house lest some invader should take possession. . . . But why do I preach politicks? Tis a country failing. . . . I'm worried to death almost by this learned

---

[25] *Clark Papers,* p. 47. For other illustrations, *see Life of Clark,* p. 53.
[26] *Frontier Retreat on the Upper Ohio,* ed. Louise P. Kellogg, *Wis. Hist. Coll's.* (Madison, 1917), XXIV, 183.

ignoramus set; and what is worse, there are two lawyers here and they can't agree." [27]

But the need for military protection was even more pressing than was that for civil organization. Heretofore, frontier military service had been voluntary. The pioneer, single-handed, defended his home, or combining with his neighbors under some leader chosen from their own number, carried on such retaliatory attacks against the Indians as were necessary for the protection of life and property. Armed with long rifles and hunting-knives and with their pockets full of parched corn, a substitute for bread, they pursued the foe and fought him in savage fashion. In this warfare, many Kentuckians won reputations for individual prowess. But attacks of Indian bands organized by the British called for more adequate means of defense.

Compulsory military service was inaugurated. The organization of the militia was entrusted to Clark, who was commissioned a major. Associated with him, as captains, were Daniel Boone, James Harrod, John Todd, Jr., and Benjamin Logan, all noted Indian fighters. The storm broke early in March when some two hundred warriors crossed the Ohio with the design of cutting off Harrodsburg, Boonesborough, and Logan's Station. Such a stroke, it was hoped by Hamilton, would put an end to American control in Kentucky. The fury of attack was met with a resistance born of desperation on the part of the one hundred and fifty men, defenders of the forts.

Having accomplished little at Harrodsburg and Boonesborough, the Indians appeared at Logan's Fort, which was besieged until the second of September. The timely arrival of one hundred Virginians, led by Colonel John Bowman, saved the defenders from starvation or surrender. From the Yadkin came forty-eight mounted men to the relief of Boonesborough, and one hundred expert riflemen arrived from Virginia in October. With these accessions, the outlook for the wearied Kentuckians seemed brighter, but their actual condi-

---

[27] Draper MSS., *Preston Papers*, June 22, 1776.

tion during the winter, because of this raid, was still desperate. Writing of this period, Clark said: "Our conduct was very uniform, the defense of our forts, the procuring of provisions or when possible supprising the Indians (which was frequently done) burying the dead and dressing the wounded seemed to be all our business." But in his diary he records: April 19, 1777: "Two burgesses were elected"; July 9: "Lieutenant Linn married, great merriment"; and September 2: "Court held." On the retaliatory expeditions, Clark led the militia. Many were advocating the abandonment of Kentucky but he quieted their fears by assurance of succor from Virginia.

The tendency toward American disaffection produced through the proclamations by Hamilton scattered along the trails, must, Clark knew, be overcome. To any who would join the British, generous rewards were offered in land and good quarters at Detroit. Through what means then would it be possible to capture this citadel of British power in the West? This objective was never absent from Clark's mind. It was clear to him, also, that the brunt of the attacks from both the north and the south would fall on Kentucky, and that Kentucky, if supported, might serve as a base for any offensive movement. The surest defense against savage forays, Clark concluded, would be, first, to capture the Illinois posts and win the friendship of the French inhabitants. As an initial step thereto, in April, 1777, he sent Benjamin Linn and Samuel Moore, hunters in disguise, as spies to Kaskaskia and Vincennes. What his designs were was a secret which he shared with no one.

After an absence of two months, his agents returned to Harrodsburg. There was no apprehension, they reported, of an attack from Kentucky on the part of Rocheblave or the inhabitants at Kaskaskia. The fort, containing large quantities of military supplies, was unguarded. Quantities of presents were being used by Governor Hamilton to induce the Indians to raid Kentucky.

That some of the English merchants were openly antagonistic to Rocheblave and favored the Americans must have been communicated to these messengers.[28] This treacherous element, Rocheblave claimed, were corresponding with Eastern leaders and carrying on trade with the rebels. An invasion of the Illinois villages was openly talked about by them and supplies were being collected for the American troops when they should come. One of these traders, Thomas Bentley, whose wife was a daughter of one of the most prominent Kaskaskian families, had expected the coming of spies and Daniel Murray, the brother of William Murray, had talked with them.[29]

It seems probable, also, that Clark knew something of these conditions before sending his spies to Kaskaskia.[30] Lieutenant William Linn, as we have seen, upon arriving at the mouth of the Ohio with his cargo of powder, secured, through the influence of Pollock, supplies which enabled him to continue his journey. That he was met, as prearranged, by Bentley's boat, is evident from an order for $60 which he drew on Pollock in favor of Bentley.[31]

[28] Accusations against Rocheblave were brought before Governor Carleton, March 31, 1777. Kaskaskia *Records*, 1778-1790, ed. C. W. Alvord, *Ill. Hist. Coll's.*, V, pp. 4-6. *Ibid.*, XVI *ff.* For the growth of an American party in the Illinois country and its significance, consult Alvord, "Virginia and the West," *Miss. Valley Hist. Rev.*, III, 31 *ff.*

[29] *Kaskaskia Records*, XXIII.

[30] Dr. Alvord suggested that Bentley, while on one of his trading expeditions, had met Clark.

[31] Finding this voucher establishes beyond question the fact that a Bentley boat met that of Linn. This was the original hypothesis of Dr. Alvord (1909). Eleven years later, he wrote: "At the time of writing this introduction [*Kaskaskia Records*], I stated that the evidence furnished was only a hypothesis, but later thought on the subject has led me to believe that the logic of events furnishes real proof." Alvord, "The Illinois Country" 1673-1818, *The Centennial History of Illinois* (Springfield, 1920), I, 322, note 31. The order on Pollock is proof, likewise, that the assertion of Bentley, that Linn had *seized* one of his boats and confiscated the corn, was false. In writing Daniel Murray, who doubtless was familiar with all conditions, Bentley says that he has been accused by Rocheblave of correspondence with the Americans —"You well know how much I abhorred the thought of interfering on either side. . . . I am not conscious that any part of my conduct will admit of an ambiguous interpretation and must imagine tis the corn

In his letter to Governor Henry, Clark writes that the principal inhabitants are "entirely against the American cause and look on us as notorious rebels that ought to be subdued." [32] But he continues, "I don't doubt but after being acquainted with the cause they would become good friends to it." The evidence shows, however, that there were some among the French leaders who were lukewarm in their attachment to the British flag. Glowing pictures of the joys of independence had been unfolded to them by Bentley, the Murrays, and other traders. That Clark preserved silence relative to these men may be accounted for because of his desire to protect them. The suggestion was made by a Virginia officer that Lieutenant Linn might be found at Kaskaskia by a company of militia sent to protect him in his ascent of the Ohio with the cargo of powder. Assurance of protection could alone have induced him to enter an enemy stronghold.[33]

Upon the charge of rendering assistance to the enemy, Bentley was imprisoned at Quebec. After his escape and return to the Illinois country, he resumed his policy of appearing friendly to both the British and the Americans and as Dr. Alvord states—"continued his double dealing up to the time of death." This judgment is confirmed in the following testimony

which was taken from Matthews that he wants to make handle of." The proceedings of the Court of Inquiry on the case are to be found in *Kaskaskia Records,* pp. 24–35.

[32] *Clark Papers,* p. 30.

[33] "If you should not fall in with Captain [Lieutenant] Linn . . . before you arrive at the mouth of the Ohio, I think it will be necessary that you pass up the Mississippi to the Kaskaskia Village, where you will make inquiry and probably meet with Captain Linn with his Cargo and if you don't meet him before you get there, when you meet him, you will conduct him with the utmost safety to the said Cargo up to the House of James Asturgass on the Monongahela River and immediately advise me thereof." Colonel Dorsey Pentecost to Capt. William Harrod—Thwaites and Kellogg, *Revolution On the Upper Ohio,* p. 228. That Linn secured, at the Arkansas Post, from Lewis Charleville, of Kaskaskia, goods amounting to $209 is evidence also that the French of Kaskaskia were probably aware of the friendly relations between the colonists and Spain. The bill was drawn on Pollock. Through Charleville, likewise, Linn must have gained information regarding affairs at Kaskaskia.

of Pollock: "Mr. Bentley is now desd [deceased] and it may be deemed improper to say what truth would support respecting his deposition or information, let it suffice that he and I did not speak from some of his manovres, which would not Redound much to his honor, full proof of which may be now had on the spott if necessary." [34]

In his communication to Governor Henry, Clark submitted a plan of action notable for its aggressiveness. Kaskaskia, he asserted, was of the utmost importance, for from this center the British were able to keep control of the Wabash tribes and send them against Kentucky; it furnished provisions for the garrison at Detroit and controlled the navigation of the Mississippi and the Ohio, thus preventing the Americans from securing goods from New Orleans with which to carry on trade with the Indians. "We must," he urged, "either take the town of Kuskuskies, or in less than a twelve month send an army against the Indians on Wabash, which will cost ten times as much and not be of half the service."

While Clark was urging the necessity for a military advance into the Northwest, conditions in the New Orleans sector were becoming of increasing importance.

[34] "Clark MSS.," *Va. State Archives.*

CHAPTER VII

PENSACOLA AND MOBILE: AMERICAN OBJECTIVES

FOR nearly a year, George Morgan had been advocating with all his fiery energy that an expedition against West Florida should be sent down the Mississippi. He made known his plan to the Board of War. Disappointed at the outcome, but not baffled, on July 6, 1777, he again brought the proposal to the attention of Congress. In the meantime, pursuing his own course, he opened correspondence with Galvez. He expressed his appreciation for the powder which had been procured by Pollock.

It was the purpose of the United States, he asserted, now free and independent, to maintain the closest relationship possible with Spanish subjects.[1] Very deftly, he outlined the military operations of the Americans: the evacuation of Boston by the British; the capture of New York by Lord Howe, and the successful retirement of Washington "disputing the ground by inches." Then followed Trenton and Princeton. In his optimistic manner, Morgan declared that Howe might, with his superior army of 15,000 troops, be able to capture "some of our deserted places which they themselves will be forced to abandon immediately." But Morgan does not explain the method by which this was to be accomplished since Washington's army was then reduced to 4,000 regulars and such militia as he was able to enlist.

It was effective propaganda, however, and as we shall see, produced good results. "But in that way," he continues, "America cannot be conquered not even with 50,000 men. By stratagem and delay we shall gain the upper hand and shall establish our empire. . . . Our army is composed of picked

---

[1] April 22, 1777. *Archivo General de Indias,* Seville, Estante 87, Cajon 1, legajo 6.

men; we have about 200 warships and privateers, carrying from 4 to 40 cannons with which we are infesting the coasts of England, Ireland and the Islands of America, and capturing their transports with their troops and provisions." He then submitted a plan for the conduct of the war in the West should Spain and France make common cause with America. This comprehended the capture of Niagara and Detroit, and also, if transports could be procured at New Orleans with the permission and concurrence of Galvez, a surprise attack on Mobile and Pensacola, the destruction of their fortifications and the capture of their stores.

"You may be assured that your desires are mine also," was the satisfying reply of Galvez. Back of this unequivocal answer may be seen the influence of Pollock. The governor goes on to say:

In regard to the hiring or purchase that you petition and the execution of your plan which is to be with my consent, permission, and aid, although I should be very glad, I may not take part therein, but you may, if you please come to an agreement with the same person resident in this city who was employed for the past commission. That person [Pollock] is one of the most interested, and you may be assured that I shall lend him my permission and all the aid that I can notwithstanding that I shall apparently feign not to understand anything about the matter. The trade desired by you with this district may be undertaken from whatever point you wish or is most convenient to you and you may be sure that those who take part in it, shall be welcomed and be well received by me and I shall be responsible for everything.[2]

By the close of the year 1776, Congress had declared a willingness to assist in reducing the town and harbor of Pensacola and to favor its cession to Spain providing that power should join the United States in the war against Great Britain, and in the event also that the United States should be granted the free navigation of the Mississippi River and the use of the harbor of Pensacola.[3] It is not surprising, therefore, that the

---

[2] August 9, 1777. Galvez to Morgan. *Archivo General de Indias*, Seville, Estante 87, Cajon 1, legajo 6.

[3] *Jour. of the Cont. Cong.*, VI, p. 1057.

PENSACOLA AND MOBILE

second proposal of Morgan, for an expedition against Pensacola, upon being presented to Congress, July 10, 1777, seemed scheduled for favorable action. A decided majority of the Board of War were keen on the project of preparing, immediately, a force of 1,200 men to be sent against Pensacola. Supplies, cannon and artillery were to be secured from Galvez. The attack by this force from the land side was to be aided by three or four frigates to be brought from Havana. The plan seemed promising for Pensacola was defended by a force of only 800 men and one or two sloops-of-war. Arguments in its favor, advanced on the floor of Congress, were: that the trade of the English, which was increasing, would be destroyed and their prestige with the Indians would be lost; that a vast store of merchandise would be captured; that it would be agreeable to the Spaniards and reflect luster on American arms.

Robert Morris, his judgment confirmed through favorable messages from Pollock, was among those who urged that the time was ripe for such a stroke. Provisions and military equipment, he declared, could easily be procured.[4] Opposition came from one member [Chase] who was demanding that West Florida should become the property of the United States. Such an expedition, another member added, would cause the British to concentrate their full force against the Southern States.

But Henry Laurens, who had recently taken his seat as a Representative from South Carolina, became the real spokesman for the opposition. As he wrote: "I was soon provoked to break through the proscribed bounds and to oppose a random scheme for a Western enterprize which had been proposed to the House as equally practicable and advantageous and which to my amazement the whole House appeared to have adopted; nothing remained to do on their part but to vote men and money."[5] Among his arguments were the following: the number of men proposed was too few and if there

---

[4] *Jour. of the Cont. Cong.*, II, 421.
[5] *Ibid.*, II, 443, 444.

were soldiers to spare they should be sent to the defense of Georgia; and that the Tories, the Choctaws, and fever and ague were enemies which had been left out of the reckoning in this proposed "mad expedition." "And where are the frigates," he ejaculated. "I can hardly forbear concluding that a great Assembly is in its dotage and that happily for us our Enemy is at the same time very infirm." [6] This scourging proved effective for the scheme received only a few affirmative votes.

Pollock seized every opportunity for imparting to Galvez full information on these possibilities. At all times he was an ardent advocate for such a stroke. That the imagination of the governor was having full exercise may be gathered from his report to his uncle that a force of from four to six thousand Americans was to come down the River during the summer for an attack on Pensacola. That Galvez was not without misgivings regarding the ultimate effect of such an expedition on the Spanish possessions may be sensed from the decision, on his part, to strengthen his own defenses.[7] No time was lost on the part of the Spanish Government in taking up this problem.

By July, 1777, the request embodied in the letter of General Charles Lee met with favor by the Spanish Government and there was deposited at New Orleans, subject to the order of Virginia, two thousand barrels of gunpowder, a quantity of lead, and a large amount of clothing.[8] This information was quickly forwarded to the Governor of Virginia by a special messenger sent on a boat chartered and paid for by Pollock. Intelligence of the exact strength of the enemy at Pensacola, secured with difficulty, was likewise dispatched. The efforts of Benjamin Franklin had now won the favor of Count d'Aranda, Spanish ambassador in Paris, but King Charles refused to declare openly for the American cause. On January 2, 1777,

---

[6] To John Rutledge, August 12, 1777. *Ibid.*, 447.
[7] Galvez to José de Galvez, June 2, 1777. *Ayer Collection.* Newberry Library.
[8] Stevens, *Facsimiles*, May, 1777, p. 151.

the Committee of Secret Correspondence notified Franklin of his appointment as commissioner to negotiate a treaty of friendship and commerce with Spain.[9] Some days earlier, Congress had instructed Franklin that the United States was prepared to assist Spain in an attack on Pensacola, providing that port and the Mississippi River should be open to American trade.[10] Before these messages were in hand, however, the American commissioners, in Paris, had authorized Arthur Lee to go to Madrid to solicit an alliance with Spain.[11]

Meanwhile, early in 1777, a Council of the Spanish Secretaries of Departments replied to a communication of Vergennes wherein he had proposed an open alliance with the Americans. Secret aid was to be continued but there was to be no alliance with the United States. France and Spain were to agree upon a plan for military action and to arm as rapidly as possible. It was also suggested that a combined fleet of twelve French and Spanish ships with some French troops should be sent to the Island of Santo Domingo. This plan did not meet with the favor of Vergennes for he feared lest the suspicions of the British should be aroused.

On February 18, 1777, Grimaldi was succeeded as prime minister of Count de Florida Blanca. With his ascendancy, the outlook for open assistance to the Americans was greatly lessened.

The new minister, forty-seven years of age, although not of the patrician class, had received a good education and become a lawyer of distinction. Turning to diplomacy, his first mission was that of ambassador to Pope Clement XIV. In this field, by sheer force of character, he achieved marked success. He was a liberal although his views were tempered with caution. He opposed England, was jealous of French ascendancy, and hated the spirit of revolution.

To the new minister, it was evident that should Spain assist

[9] *Secret Journals of Congress*, II, 42, January 2, 1777.
[10] *Ibid.*, II, 40. This confirmed an act of December 30, 1776, *Jour. of the Cont. Cong.*, VI, 1057.
[11] Franklin, because of his age, was unable to undertake the journey. *Writings of Benjamin Franklin*, ed. Smyth, VII, 32.

in securing independence for the British colonies, Spanish authority in America would likewise be endangered. Spanish domination of trade with her colonies would be jeopardized with a vigorous nation developing as their neighbor. Moreover, alliance with America meant war with Great Britain. The Spanish navy, army and treasury were in no condition to offer adequate defense against attack by the leading maritime power of the day. Assurances were given British authorities that no American representative would be received at Madrid.

In seeming keeping with this pledge, Arthur Lee, before his arrival at the Spanish border, received a message to the effect that he should not proceed to the capital city but that a conference would be granted him at Burgos.[12] Here, on March 4th, Lee was met by Grimaldi. He was informed that while an alliance could not be hoped for, the Americans would find deposited at New Orleans and at Havana stores of clothing and powder which their ships might procure and that supplies were likewise being collected at Bilbao for shipment to these ports.[13] In vain, Lee argued that the time was opportune for the immediate interposition of Spain and France. If Great Britain should again become united to America by conquest or conciliation, he declared, she "would reign the irresistible though hated arbiter of Europe." "You have considered your own situation, and not ours," Grimaldi replied. "The moment is not yet come for us. The war with Portugal—France being unprepared, and our treasure ships from South America not being arrived—makes it improper for us to declare immediately. These reasons will probably cease within a year, and then will be the moment." This argument seemed satisfactory to Lee for he returned to Paris convinced of the sincerity and well wishes of the Spanish Government.[14]

Aid continued, however, to be given surreptitiously to the Americans by the Spanish Government. The firm of Joseph

---

[12] Jared Sparks, *Diplomatic Correspondence of the American Revolution* (Boston, 1829–30), I, 400.
[13] Wharton, *Diplomatic Correspondence*, II, 279–80.
[14] *Ibid.*, II, 282, 283.

Gardoqui and Sons, operating at Bilbao, served as the leading agents for assisting America. Funds were collected by Diego Gardoqui, at Madrid, and forwarded to Arthur Lee. He, in turn, gave his orders for goods to the company at Bilbao. Transactions were on a cash basis, the Gardoquis drawing on Lee's bankers for payment.[15] During the year 1778, despite the watchful eyes of Lord Grantham and other British agents, Americans secured in this way 18,000 blankets, 11,000 pairs of shoes, 41,000 pairs of stockings, and shirtings, tent-cloth, and medicines in quantities.[16]

There can be little doubt Spanish officials were prompted to this seemingly generous conduct through the hope of ultimate gain for Spain. Patrick Henry, as Governor of Virginia, well understood what arguments would be most forceful in winning Spanish assistance. In acknowledging the aid already rendered by Galvez, he cited the rewards for its continuance as follows: The control by Spain of the trade of the Southern States and the deprivation of "their ancient and natural Enemy, the English, of all those vast supplies of naval stores and many other articles which have enabled them to become so powerful on the seas." Again in possession of Pensacola and St. Augustine, he thought the Spaniards would be in position not only to secure immense quantities of hemp, flax, furs, beef, pork, flour, shingles and other produce of the trans-Allegheny country, but would also "enjoy" a great part of the trade with the Northern States. To facilitate intercourse by way of the Mississippi, he proposed to establish a post at the mouth of the Ohio and urged the necessity for making New Orleans a free port.[17]

Governor Henry likewise pled with the Governor of Cuba for further assistance. "We are," he wrote, "well acquainted, Sir, with the Honour, Spirit, and Generosity of the Spanish nation and should therefore glory in an intimate connection

[15] *Ibid.*, II, 308.
[16] Edward Channing, *History of the United States* (New York, 1912), III, 284.
[17] October 18, 1777, Patrick Henry to Galvez. *Clark MSS.* (Virginia State Library).

with it. For I suppose, I need not inform your Excellency, that the States are now free and independent, capable of forming Alliances and of making Treaties." Of mutual benefit, he urged, would be the exchange of products shipped down the Mississippi for the woolens, linens, wines, and military stores to be gotten at Havana.

As he progressed, his imagination glimpsed the future but he caught no vision of that spirit of expansion which was to dominate American thinking even before another decade had elapsed— "And were you once restored to the possessions you held in the Floridas (which I sincerely wish to see, and which I make no Doubt these States would cheerfully contribute to accomplish) the advantage to us both in a Commercial View would be greatly increased. The English indeed insinuate that it would be impolitic in your Nation to assist us in our present situation, but you are too wise not to perceive how much it is their Interest that you should be imposed upon by this Doctrine and how much more formidable they must be to you with the assistance of America than without it and you must be too well acquainted with the nature of our States to entertain any jealousy of their becoming your Rivals in Trade, or overstocked as they are with vast tracts of land, that they should ever think of extending their territory." [18]

The effects of a conquest by the Americans of the British posts east of the Mississippi River had already been discussed by the Spanish Government. Secret royal orders were sent to Galvez defining their policy. In case the Americans seized the English settlements and desired to deliver them to Spain, Galvez was directed to receive them "in trust." But should British officials take umbrage at this act, they were to be assured that these possessions would be more secure under Spanish control than under the domination "of their enemies risen in rebellion." [19]

---

[18] Patrick Henry to the Governor of Cuba, October 18, 1777 (Va. State Library).

[19] José de Galvez to Bernardo de Galvez, August 15, 1777. A. G. I. *Papeles de Cuba*, Leg., 174.

Had he possessed only a slight sense of humor, the governor must have smiled as he read this message, well aware as he was that Spain had not forgotten the loss of the Floridas to England as a result of the Seven Years' War. It is evident that Florida Blanca was hoping to complete the plan which was clearly set forth by him in the following February.

In his offer to mediate, the United States was to be confined to the Atlantic Coast. Great Britain was to receive the valley of the St. Lawrence. Spain was to retain the Mississippi Valley east to the Allegheny Mountains.[20] In this wise, the future policy of Spain was forecast.

Three months later, however, in making application for a loan of 150,000 pistoles, which Pollock was to negotiate, Henry suggested that West Florida should be annexed to the United States. Such a cession, he argued, would be the means of cutting off the supplies of lumber and provisions procured from the Mississippi country by the British West India settlements and would prevent the progress of their rivalry to the Spanish colonies. "If the thanks of this free and independent country" for which Henry was speaking, was not an adequate equivalent for the loan, he proffered, as an added inducement, the "trade in one or in all its rich products and the friendship of its brave inhabitants. . . . Ignorant at the present time which of these products your Excellency prefers I offer them so that you may select those which are most pleasing to your Excellency and the Spanish Nation." Favorable consideration for the proposal by Galvez was gained through the mediation of Pollock.

Early in March, 1778, Pollock was gratified at receiving his appointment as commercial agent for the United States, resident at New Orleans. Although the commission had been agreed upon, June 12, 1777, it was withheld until the close of October when the Committee of Commerce, successor to the Secret Committee of Congress, reaffirmed the appointment. "The good disposition which you discover to our Cause

[20] Florida Blanca to Grantham, British Minister at Madrid, February, 1778. Wharton, *Diplomatic Correspondence* (Introduction), p. 87.

and the Character you bear," they wrote, "has determined us to employ you as our Commercial Agent in New Orleans, in full confidence that your conduct of our affairs would be such as to entitle you to our Approbation and future Favors; and should it at any time be your misfortune to fall into the hands of our Enemies as you have suggested, you have Liberty to claim the Protection of the United States of America as their Commercial Agent resident at New Orleans, and may depend that Congress will redeem you by Exchange or retaliate any Injuries or indignities that may be offered you." [21] In acknowledgment Pollock wrote: "I take this opportunity of returning you my sincere thanks for the Honor you have done me in placing your Confidence in me as your public Agent in this Part of the World, and you may depend there is nothing in my Power but shall be done to perform my duty in that Station." [22]

He was authorized to purchase and ship forty or fifty thousand dollars' worth of blankets and other supplies for the army. These goods were to be forwarded in fast-sailing vessels which he was directed to charter or buy. The drafts, amounting to $30,000, were sent in part payment. The balance was to be met by a shipment of flour. Just how this was to be accomplished, the Committee does not define. They declared: "We are desirous of sending you supplies of flour, as that would furnish Funds to answer the Demands this Business will occasion, but unluckily our Enemies Ships of war are so numerous as to block up effectually at present all those ports from wherever that article can be exported." [23] But they urged the necessity of getting goods "soon and safe to this part of America where they are very much wanted." Pollock was directed to forward the goods at once by sea, as transportation by the Mississippi was too slow and danger of capture by the Indians was constant. Within a month, however, he was advised to send part of the shipment up the River to Pittsburgh where

---

[21] *Papers of the Continental Congress*, No. 50, folios 29, 30.
[22] March 6, 1778. *Pollock Letters*.
[23] October 24, 1777. *Pollock Letters*.

a quantity of flour had been deposited to partially cover the cost. They intrusted him with three blank commissions for privateers which he might grant to persons whom he knew would comply strictly with the conditions imposed. "Rest assured," was his quick response, "everything you desire shall be put in execution immediately." Pollock, without delaying to translate the letters from Morris and his committee, communicated the contents to Galvez and secured the assurance that he was "still disposed to serve you."

An additional loan from the governor enabled Pollock to dispatch a small sloop loaded with taffia, sugar, and coffee secured at a cost of 4,000 pistoles. The government was in his debt for advances amounting to 50,000 pistoles and he was then "much distressed for want of cash." That there was no wavering in this crisis is clear from his statement made at a later time: "Sensible of the necessities of my Country, which at that period were extreme, the propriety of appropriating my Fortune to her Service would not admit of a moments deliberation. The Misfortunes of America rendered her Cause still dearer than before to every true American. And I was the more ready to repose confidence in the promises of remittances which those letters contained as I was determined to share the fate of my Countrymen if they should fail, and to rely on their justice if crowned with success." [24]

Early in 1778, Captain Jacinto Panis, representing Governor Galvez, appeared at Pensacola with the demand for prompt redress for the insults which the British were committing on the lower Mississippi. A "friendly" offering from Governor Galvez consisting of a box of white sugar and a cask of wine were gratefully received with a "thousand thanks" by Governor Chester. While pressing the request for greater "politeness" on the part of the British, Panis was to carry on negotiations, also, regarding the presence of English traders among the Indians west of the Mississippi, the return of fugitive slaves, and the "activities of an English corsair on Lake

---

[24] Pollock to the President of Congress, September 18, 1782. *Pollock Letters.*

Pontchartrain." [25] While little resulted from the negotiations, Galvez gained through this mission useful information on the defenses of Mobile and Pensacola.

Upon arriving at Mobile, Panis learned of the depredations committed by an American, Captain James Willing, who had descended the River to New Orleans with a crew of twenty-seven men on board an armed boat *The Rattletrap*. "The fear lest he should ascend with his followers to surprise this settlement and its inhabitants," Panis writes, "frightened everybody." At Pensacola, there was feverish haste in providing for adequate defense.

[25] For the results, *see* Caughey, "The Panis Mission to Pensacola," *Hispanic American Review*, X, No. 4, November, 1930.

CHAPTER VIII

AN AMERICAN RAIDER ON THE MISSISSIPPI RIVER

WILLING, who was a brother of the senior member of the firm, Willing and Morris, was commissioned by the Commerce Committee of Congress to procure the supplies deposited at New Orleans under the control of Pollock and bring them to Fort Pitt.[1] He was likewise directed to make prize of British property on the Mississippi River and win the neutrality of the inhabitants along its banks.

Through residence, for a time, at New Orleans, Willing was familiar with conditions on the lower Mississippi. During 1772, he served as a partner, in trade, with Pollock. Writing of this relationship, Pollock states:

> By the desire of my friend Mr James Willing, I take the liberty to trouble you with a few lines. By a letter from that Gentl[n.] to you of the 11th ult[o.] you'll see the desire he has of making a contract to supply the Troops at Pensacola with Flour etc. at same [time] acquainting you of my engagements here in that way which would make it suit us very well to enter into a contract at your place, in particular as the whole comes through the channel of Messrs. Willing and Morris, well known to your Honor for some time past. Should there be any hopes of making an advantageous contract, Mr. James Willing or self shall go over to Pensacola upon the first notice from your Honor and compleat it. In the meantime if theres any flour wanted for the troops I can spare some I have already ordered for this place.[2]

Shortly before, Pollock had been granted a contract to supply the Spanish garrison at New Orleans with flour. As

---

[1] As stated by Willing, he was expected to bring at least five boats loaded with dry goods. Thwaites and Kellogg, *Frontier Defense on the Upper Ohio*, p. 198.
[2] To General Haldimand, British Commanding officer. December 1, 1772. *Haldimand Papers*, British Museum, 1769–72, Vol. II, Add. MSS., 21,729, pp. 315, 316.

an argument for a similar concession at Pensacola, Willing writes:

> Upon my arrival I was much pleased to find Mr. O. Pollock about making a contract for supply of this colony. He has begun it and has delivered one cargo already and expects another Vessell here soon so that if Mr. Stephenson chuses he may in the meantime until we can hear from W & M [Willing and Morris] have 3, 4, or 500 Bblls. flour to begin with. I am certain that our House can supply upon better terms than any other in America and he will have a certainty of never being disapointed as in case a Vessel should not arrive there he can be supply'd from here, so that beg you'll push him to his word to give us preference.[3]

It was evidently a great disappointment to Pollock that he was unable to supply General Haldimand, commanding officer at Pensacola, to whom the letters were addressed, with claret and "sour kraut." As customary, a good-will offering was sent, consisting of a barrel of sweet oranges and a box of pecans, but the flour contract did not follow.

The town of Natchez where, for two years, Willing continued to carry on, without success, as a merchant, contained, in 1776, twenty log and frame houses. The Natchez district was, according to Pittman, the finest and most fertile portion of West Florida— "The country is well watered, hops grow wild and all kinds of European fruits come to great perfection. The fences of many of the gardens made by the French still remain, and several fruit-trees mostly figs, peaches and wild cherries. The French always esteemed the tobacco produced here as preferable to any cultivated in other parts of America."[4]

The number of inhabitants within the district was increased during the fall of 1776 through the coming of a numerous body of Scotch Irish from Pennsylvania, Virginia, and North Carolina, who sought to escape the turmoil of divided sentiment prevalent in the back counties. Other immigrants to the

---

[3] *Haldimand Papers, loc. cit.*, November 11, 1772, pp. 310, 311.
[4] Pittman, *op. cit.*, pp. 78–80.

A RAIDER ON THE MISSISSIPPI

region were Loyalists who had been driven from the frontier communities by their Whig neighbors.

With his force increased to nearly one hundred men, Willing surprised Natchez and secured an oath of neutrality from the magistrates. The persons, slaves, and any other property of the inhabitants were to be secure during the period of neutrality.[5]

Gaining other recruits, French and Spanish bateaumen, and a number of men from Natchez, Willing proceeded down the River, carrying on a ruthless warfare in which the crops of British planters were destroyed, their houses burned, their cattle and hogs killed and their slaves carried off. Many planters crossed the River, taking refuge under the Spanish flag. Others were held prisoners-of-war. The plundering was not carried on indiscriminately, for friends of the American cause were not molested.

One whose name headed the black-list wrote of the raid as follows:

The party was commanded by James Willing a young man who had left this Country the year before; perfectly and intimately acquainted with all the gentlemen upon the river at whose houses he had been often entertained in the most hospitable manner and frequently indulged his natural propensity of getting drunk. . . . This was the man who it seems had solicited a Commission by which he might have an opportunity of demonstrating his gratitude to his old Friends. . . . Profit and Nash are spared.—From hence they proceed to Baton Rouge, where they find no negroes on the English side, but those whom at that time they considered as Friends. Here the villains grow bold, finding small game on the English side, they pass over to the Spanish Territories & seize the negroes of Poupett and Marshall. The houses of the English Gentlemen on the British side were plundered & among the rest mine was robbed of everything that could be carried away—all my wearing apparel, bed and table linen; not a shirt was left in the house—blankets, pieces of cloth, sugar, silverware. In short all was fish that came in their nett. They destroyed a considerable quantity

[5] Caughey, "Willing's Expedition Down the Mississippi, 1778," *The Louisiana Historical Quarterly*, XV, No. 1, p. 10.

of bottled wine, tho' they carried away no liquor. The orders given by their head were to drive down my negroes & if opposed to shoot 'em down. In the whole I was plundered of £200 sterling value.[6]

With the aid of Pollock, who had sent a force of forty men up the River for his guidance, and with the sanction of Galvez, Willing arrived at New Orleans.[7]

Numbers of immigrants from West Florida, panic-stricken by the report, broadcast by Willing, that a still larger American force was to follow him, sought refuge under the Spanish flag with their Negroes, cattle and valuables. Galvez issued a proclamation confirming the hospitality extended and asserting perfect neutrality by Spain in the struggle between Great Britain and her colonies.

At New Orleans, Willing's outfit, due to the foresight of Pollock, was granted the freedom of the town. At a public auction, conducted by Pollock, the sum of $37,500 was realized from the sale of the plunder.[8]

A British sloop, the *Rebecca,* mounting sixteen guns, four pounders, and a number of swivels, had been captured by one of Willing's lieutenants. The seizure of this boat ended, for a time, British control of the lake and canal leading to New Orleans. Pollock was granted special permission by Galvez, whose conduct was characterized as "very extraordinary" by General William Howe, to fit her out as a cruiser, the *Morris.* She was to sail under American colors.

With the force increased at New Orleans, Willing's party, led by Captain Joseph Calvert, proceeded downstream. They captured the brig *Neptune,* and another English vessel, the *Dispatch,* which was seized near the mouth of the River.

Among the dispatches brought by Willing was the appointment of Pollock as agent of Congress. "This honorable mark

---

[6] Dunbar, *Life of William Dunbar,* pp. 60–62.
[7] Knowledge of Willing's approach was brought to Pollock by Lieutenant Thomas McIntyre.
[8] This was sold at public auction.

of their favor," as he wrote, "found in my bosom a new bond of duty and became an additional spring to actuate my conduct."

Shortly after, a British officer, on board a sloop-of-war, appeared at New Orleans with the demand that Galvez should offer an explanation for his unneutral conduct. It was held a breach of neutrality to allow the Americans to enter New Orleans, which thus became a base for operations against the British. All British persons and property illegally seized and held by Willing were to be released. Attacks upon British property, especially the *Rebecca,* which was captured "within gun-shot of a Spanish fort," should, they claimed, have been prevented. There was the demand, likewise, that all prizes made on the Mississippi River should be restored.

In seeking an adjustment of these questions, there was clearly manifest a dependence of Galvez on the judgment of Pollock. It is evident that Pollock possessed accurate knowledge of the principles of international usage then prevailing. British prizes taken on Spanish soil were to be restored. But Pollock insisted on his "undoubted right to seize and take the Persons, as Prisoners, and Property as legal prize, of or belonging to Subjects of Great Britain which I shall find in the River Mississippi or elsewhere not under your Excellency's immediate protection."

All persons engaged in carrying to the enemy at Vincennes, munitions of war and other merchandise were, he maintained, subject to capture:

> But even [he writes], supposing these Traders to be subjects of a neutral Power, the Property in question is still equally liable to confiscation to the said States, for it is notoriously known that during the present contest between Great Britain and the American States, the British Ships never fail to seize and their Admiralty Courts to condemn as legal Prizes all such Vessels as are found going to or coming from any Port belonging to the American States at war with Great Britain. It is equally the invariable practice of all nations with respect to the Vessels of neutral States found to be supplying the Enemys of either of the Belligerent Powers with warlike Stores, Arms, Provisions etc.

In his reply to British demands, Galvez declared that his protection of the Americans was in consonance with the position taken by the leading European Powers. Spain, he asserted, was under no obligation to protect British subjects on British soil or off the shore of British territory, and that the seizures made by Willing would not be released until the completion of an official investigation then being conducted. As finally determined, certain boats and cargoes which had been captured were to be restored to their owners. In the communication to Governor Chester, Galvez made it clear that he assumed no responsibility for any seizures made between Natchez and Manchac.

At the same time, he granted Pollock permission to dispose of all British property seized above Manchac, "either on the River or the English Territories and luckily the *Rebecca* is one of these prizes." Pollock wrote the Committee of Congress:

> I have also the pleasure to inform you that the number of Tories that were seated at Baton Rouge and who had formed a plan for cutting off our boats in going up we have totally routed. I have taken about 100 of their slaves, which I have sold at about 140 p^s round for ready cash. . . . This I can assure you is very hurtful to the Enemy as they have been supplying Jamaica constantly with lumber and Pensacola with provisions ever since the commencement of the war.

Two war-sloops were dispatched to the Mississippi by Governor Chester in order to enforce the demand for the restitution of British property, to prevent the return of Willing, and to intercept an expedition of two or three thousand men reported to be coming down the River for an attack on West Florida.

Galvez, with an inadequate force at his command, fully appreciated his critical situation. "He who commands these frigates," he writes, "is said to be a brutal man, capable of committing any atrocity without disturbing himself about the consequences. His intention apparently is to ask me to give up the prizes of the Americans and their persons, especially

A RAIDER ON THE MISSISSIPPI

the commander and officers of the party and if I do not comply, to open fire on the city and destroy it."

Judged by the communication from Chester, no adjustment could prove satisfactory so long as Pollock and Willing were at liberty under Spanish protection. A schooner, he maintained, had been seized by an agent of these two men and the passengers and crew had all disappeared.

There is the most violent presumption [he writes], that all the people have been inhumanly and barbarously murdered by the Rebels to prevent their crimes being brought to light. I therefore demand, not only that restitution be made of said Schooner, Dispatch, to her owners, with her cargo of negroes, and other property on board at the time of seizure but also that the master, passengers and crew may be produced by James Willing and Oliver Pollock, who fitted out the said Calvert and his party from New Orleans. And that the said Willing and Pollock, the principal instigators of this most horrid murder, and all the band of plunderers and robbers that have acted under their authority be delivered up to Capt. Ferguson in order to be brought here and punished agreeable to their deserts for the atrocious crimes they have committed, as they can be considered in no other light.[9]

He demanded, further, that all British property carried to Louisiana by the rebels should be restored. He protested the decree whereby all British as well as American subjects were to take an oath of allegiance to Spain or to quit Louisiana with the utmost precipitation. Concessions to Americans were objected to, such as the enlistment of Spanish subjects; patrolling the streets of New Orleans, under arms; the seizure and search of British subjects and holding others in irons. As further evidence of disregard for the spirit of neutrality, he accused Galvez of winking at the practice of fitting out armed boats by Americans and their destruction of British settlements on Lake Pontchartrain. This communication, bristling with protests, concluded with the following warning:

[9] Notwithstanding Pollock's protests, Galvez surrendered this prize, following his decision that no prizes should be taken between the mouth of the River and Manchac.

I cannot conclude this letter without once more Remonstrating against your Subjects transporting military Stores and Clothing up the River Mississippi destined for the Colonies in Rebellion, under Spanish Colours and Passports— Your Excellency cannot be ignorant of the General Principles which govern all States, and must know that by the Law of Nations "The Goods of an enemy on board the Ship of a Friend, may be taken, because supplying the Enemy with what enables him better to carry on the War, is a departure from neutrality. . . . I know you have it in your Power, and if you refuse to exert your authority for such unjustifiable proceedings, you alone must be answerable for all the Calamities and Consequences that may ensue.[10]

Yielding to these demands would, as will become apparent, have spelled disaster to the American cause in the West. How critical the situation was is set forth by Pollock in a letter written a few days earlier but which summarizes the situation:

Tho' I am now despatching the Batteau Speedwell under the care of Monsr. Connand and goes regularly cleared under Spanish Colours for the Illinois Country, yet so exasperated are they upon the River and at Pensacola that it is a doubt with me whether they will stop her above and perhaps take her tho Spanish Property as the Governor & the Captains of the Sloops from here a few days ago threaten vengeance against the Governor for not delivering up every American here with all the Prizes taken and say they will make Reprisals on this Town which in all probability will be the means of bringing on further Ceremonies betwixt the Court of Spain and Great Britain. . . . However I can not conclude this important subject without giving the greatest applause to Governor Galvez for his noble Spirit and Behavior on this Occasion for tho he had no batteries erected or even men to defend the Place against two sloops of war, the Hound and Sylph, and at the same Time a small sloop with 100 men in the Lakes all coming against him with Demands and Threats, yet in this situation he laughed at their Haughtiness and despised their attempts, and in short they returned as they came. But I have good Reason to suppose they are not yet satisfied and only wait for more Force.[11]

[10] *Letters and Papers Relating to American Affairs,* 1718–1796 (British Museum). Add. MSS., No. 24, 322, pp. 37–42.
[11] *Pollock Letters,* May 7, 1778.

Among other consequences resulting from the Willing raid may be mentioned its effect in weakening the morale of the British Indians on the lower Mississippi. As stated by Governor Chester: "The Indians that are come do not exceed one hundred. Thus the object formed by the rebels is attained, to make the Indians neutral as they failed in their attempts to persuade them to take a decisive part against his Majesty's loyal subjects." [12]

The initial success of the expedition, according to British officials, was due to the failure of John Stuart, Superintendent of the Southern Indians, to prevent the capture of Natchez. Referring to this negligence, Lord Germaine wrote:

It was surely a most unpardonable negligence in the officers you had appointed to watch their motions upon that River, not only to have been without intelligence of their coming but to have no parties of Indians at the Landing Places. . . . I cannot conceive it possible that after so large an expense incurred in the Indian Department, parties could not have been engaged to succeed each other in keeping a constant watch upon the banks of the River to give timely notice of the approach of the Enemy and of sufficient strength to defeat a much more formidable Detachment than that which has been suffered to do so much mischief.[13]

It now seems evident that, because of this raid, West Florida was, for the time, lost to the American cause. Pollock manifested keen disappointment that Congress had not sent a force sufficient to take Pensacola, "long wished for here. As the small Party you sent," he writes, "under the command of Capt. James Willing without order or subordination has only thrown the whole river into confusion and created a number of Enemies and a heavy expense which would not have happened had they been otherwise Governed and a proper number sent."

The British proceeded to strengthen their defenses in West

[12] "Historical Manuscripts Commission," *Report on American Manuscripts*, I, 213.
[13] Shaw, *British Administration of the Southern Indians, 1756–1783* (Lancaster, Pa., 1931), p. 121.

Florida. A new commander sent to Pensacola was directed to erect a fort near the former site of Fort Bute which should command the entrance to the Iberville River. Here was to be stationed a garrison of three hundred men. Two or more galleys were to protect the navigation of the River and prevent any rebel craft from descending to New Orleans.[14]

With Manchac once more in possession of a force sent against it from Pensacola, made up of seventy-five British regulars and a party of Carolina refugees and defended by an armed boat having a crew of 150; with Natchez recaptured and defended by a force of two hundred, communication by the River after the middle of June, 1778, was extremely hazardous. Spanish colors no longer afforded protection to shipments of goods and Pollock was forced to order the return of his boats. Boats descending the River, however, were saved from capture through timely warning by special agents of Pollock stationed at Arkansas Post. "A letter from you was of great service," a messenger from General Hand wrote, "by your great care in being so particular in advising how to act in so critical Situation. . . . I have this day drawn on you for two thousand nine hundred and fifty nine dollars in behalf of the United States on account of merchandise purchased by advise of Gen¹. [Hand] which I expect will be punctually paid, I have staid at this Post six days and intended to sett off for Fort Pitt this Evening."

In spite of the presence of British spies, Pollock proceeded to fit out his prize ship, the *Morris*. When fully armed, and with a crew of one hundred and fifty men, he hoped to use her to convoy boats loaded for Atlantic ports, to cope with any vessel under British colors, and thus protect his upriver shipments.

Even after the closing of the Mississippi, he continued to dispatch boats to Eastern ports loaded with sugar, coffee, and taffia. Securing these supplies was made possible through a further advance of $6,000 by Galvez, who again asserted that

---

[14] Historical Manuscripts Commission, *Report on American Manuscripts*, I, 323.

A RAIDER ON THE MISSISSIPPI

he lacked the authority from his government and that in case of a rupture with Great Britain, which he ardently desired, all of his resources would be needed for the defense of Louisiana.[15]

But Pollock succeeded in sending goods up the River, "in the most secret manner possible." Such communications as this were common:

> I thought it necessary to have another conference with the G. before I concluded this Letter, and am just now come from him and he agrees to supply me with some Indian goods such as strouds and Blankets and a number of other articles that will answer but in this expedition he expects a Concern for his Advances which will be advantageous to us as it will enable me to send more goods than I otherwise could.[16]

At the same time, he continued to urge upon Congress the necessity for an expedition against Natchez, defended by only two hundred men, and Manchac with only one-half that number. This accomplished, they could depend on a regular supply of goods. Great numbers of "true Americans," in New Orleans, were prepared to take part also in the capture of Pensacola which was protected by a force of not to exceed one thousand. Three thousand men, under experienced officers, would, he thought, suffice for the capture of that post and even with one-third that number the Mississippi could be held against any force then available to the British—

> But Pensacola is the chief objective and if you should determine on this, lose no time in acquainting me that I may have everything wanted ready for that purpose. I shall have letters lodged for the commanding officer at the Arkansas acquainting him with every particular for his government. The English are prompting savages to fall upon the Spanish inhabitants towards Manchac and to begin at my plantation as being the first and capital offender. This with what I mentioned to you in my former letters makes this Governor wish for a speedy arrival of your forces with a declaration of war betwixt Spain and Great Britain which will

[15] Pollock to the Commercial Committee, April 1 and May 7, 1778, Royal approval was granted, August 25th.
[16] To the Committee of Congress, April 1, 1778. *Pollock Letters.*

give us an opportunity to make up for past grievances and amply satisfy Governor Galvez who would write you on this subject but he is now dispatching a packet for Spain and I have acquainted him of a safe opportunity which I will dispatch in a few days by which he will write you fully.[17]

Further evidence is abundant that Pollock, as he expressed it, lost no opportunity of serving faithfully in the station to which he was called. Benjamin Franklin, then representing the United States in France, was given an account "of all which had happened." Like information was furnished General Hand at Pittsburgh. The special messenger by whom Pollock sent an appeal to Congress for an expedition, "to take possession of that immense country," was William Murray. "Murray," he wrote, "is a gentleman well known with you and whom we put the greatest confidence in, having experienced his zeal in the glorious cause in which he will be happy to serve in whatever Capacity you may chuse to honor him with, and particularly if there should be an Expedition towards this Part of the World he may be of infinite Service towards the Illinois country or down the River as he is well acquainted." [18]

For the capture of Pensacola, Galvez stood ready to contribute his services, although it was not approved by his Council, nor had Spain acknowledged American independence. In spite of threats and demands by British authorities, Galvez continued to grant protection to American vessels and citizens. The Courts of Spain and Great Britain were upon the best of terms, British officers declared, and satisfaction for the governor's unparalleled conduct would surely be demanded of the Court of Spain. His reply may be inferred from a dispatch by Pollock that, "in hopes of a speedy rupture with Great Britain and everlasting alliance with the States, he remains fully satisfied with what he has done."

To what extent this policy was a result of personal appeals by Pollock, may be conjectured only. Lacking this intimate

[17] July 6, 1778. *Pollock Letters.*
[18] To the Committee of Congress, May 7, 1779. *Pollock Letters.*

A RAIDER ON THE MISSISSIPPI

relationship, the reply of Galvez might well have been that of the Governor of Cuba. Pollock urged that American prizes might be brought into Havana and that freedom of trade between that port and the United States should be permitted. To open trade or commerce with any foreign power, without specific orders from his government was, according to the governor, not to be considered. American vessels in distress, entering the harbor, might hope only to secure necessary supplies.

Through spies at Pensacola, Natchez, and other posts, Galvez obtained full information on British plans. The situation was daily becoming more critical and an attack upon New Orleans seemed imminent. As reported, a campaign would be under way in July.

Early in the year 1778, the new commander-in-chief of the British forces at New York, Sir Henry Clinton, was secretly instructed to carry out a plan for the capture of New Orleans. One thousand troops, under General John Campbell, were to proceed to Pensacola. At the same time, a force of 3,000 was to be sent to St. Augustine. A new fort commanding the entrance to the Iberville River was to be erected and garrisoned by 300 men. Two or more galleys were to be stationed on the Mississippi in order to protect navigation and prevent any enemy craft descending to New Orleans. Because of a lack of convoys and uncertainty over the fleet under Count D'Estaing, November came before reinforcements were dispatched to the South.[19]

Meantime, troops were mobilized in New Orleans and supplies were collected. In response to the demand for aid, by Galvez, 212 men and twelve officers arrived from Havana. An elaborate system of fortifications was begun as protection for the outlying districts. All cannon were mounted in order that they might be moved from one section of New Orleans to the other. Surrounding posts were ordered to be in readiness against attack. In the open country, ditches were dug and trees felled to delay the advance of the enemy. An incident, trifling

[19] Stevens *Facsimiles*, 1207. Clinton to Germaine, November 8, 1778.

in itself, served, for a time, to offset the British menace and in turn to excite alarm at their posts. The Spanish commander at the Arkansas reported the arrival of twenty-five Americans on a boat which was bringing supplies for Willing. Informed by Pollock that there was no hope of their being able to run past the British posts, they returned to Fort Pitt. In the report which was spread throughout the lower Mississippi posts, sanctioned by Galvez, British and Spanish commanders were informed that "this force of 2,000 men" was about to descend the River for the purpose of taking all British settlements. Those who before had assumed a threatening attitude were now, Galvez wrote, seeking his friendship.

Once more, a joint communication from Pollock and Galvez besought Congress to send an expedition to capture the British posts on the Mississippi and in West Florida. After careful consideration by the Board of War, they replied: "From the variety of operations in which we are at this time engaged, it is impracticable for these States to undertake an enterprise the magnitude of that suggested." But Galvez was to be assured "that from the favorable aspect of our affairs, it is probable Congress will speedily be enabled to turn their attention to and operate effectually in that quarter." [20]

The hopes of Galvez and Pollock, again blasted, were revived in a manner unanticipated. By the middle of August, news of the success of the expedition under George Rogers Clark in the Illinois country had reached Pollock and was immediately transmitted to Galvez.

[20] *Jour. of the Cont. Cong.*, V, 1083.

CHAPTER IX

POLLOCK SUPPORTS CLARK: KASKASKIA

CLARK knew that taking Kaskaskia, the objective he had proposed in his letter to Governor Henry, could not be accomplished unless reinforcements should be sent from Virginia. On October 1, 1777, therefore, he set out for Williamsburg in order to lay his plans before the governor.[1] Arriving at the capital, he found the people greatly elated over the report of Burgoyne's surrender.

The favor of the governor was soon won through Clark's power of persuasion, but he hesitated to order an expedition into a region as far away as Illinois. To lay the plan before the Assembly, would deprive it of all secrecy and endanger any probability of success. Thomas Jefferson, George Mason and George Wythe, who were called upon for advice, recommended that the project should be carried out and promised to use their influence in securing three hundred acres of conquered land for each soldier going on the expedition. The consent of the Assembly was gained through the plea that it was designed as defense for Kentucky, Clark remarking naïvely, "but a few in the House knew the real intent of it."

Among the brief items which we find in Clark's diary during the sixty-one days of waiting are the following: "Bought a ticket in the state lottery, number 10,693 first Class; Sunday went to Church; Bought a piece of Cloth for a Jackote, Price £4,11,15; Started from my Fathers to Williamsburgh; Got to Williamsburgh, bought 2 shirts and a Book £5; Proposed an expedition against F. C. [French Country] to the Governor and Councill which they afterwards agreed to. I continue here until the 2."

---

[1] This journey of 700 miles from Harrodsburg is best described in Clark's "diary," *Clark Papers*, p. 26. See *Life of Clark*, pp. 113, 114.

Clark was appointed lieutenant-colonel and was authorized to raise, anywhere in Virginia, seven companies of militia, each to contain fifty men. He was advanced £1,200 in depreciated currency and was given an order on General Edward Hand at Pittsburgh for the necessary boats, ammunition and supplies. Final action was secured in the Council, January 2, 1778, and two days later he set out for Pittsburgh.

Strictly interpreted, his letter of instructions indicated that the expedition was intended to relieve Kentucky, but privately, Clark was directed to capture Kaskaskia. That his ultimate objective was Detroit, he kept a profound secret. "I should have mentioned my design to his Excellency," he wrote some years later, "but was convinced or afraid that it might lessen his esteem for me, as it was a general opinion that it would take several thousand to approach that Place." [2] So confident was he of the outcome that he entered into partnership with Governor Henry for securing possession of a tract of land.

Clark hastened to Redstone, the place of rendezvous. From the outset, his officers encountered difficulties in enlisting men. Virginians and Pennsylvanians were still contending for control of the Pittsburgh area and many leaders were opposed to making the sacrifice necessary "for the defence of a few detached Inhabitants that had better be removed." Indian marauders were causing havoc among settlers on the upper Ohio who had disregarded the warning of messengers to take shelter within the block-houses, flee to the fortresses, four being accessible at strategic points, Kitanning, Forts Pitt, Henry, and Randolph, or retire to the east of the mountains.

Since June 1, 1777, Edward General Hand, an experienced frontier officer, had been in command at Fort Pitt. Discretionary power was granted him by Congress to enlist one thousand or more men. But the militia failed to respond and five companies only were assembled at Point Pleasant where they awaited the arrival of General Hand with the object of invading the Indian Country. Thither the great Shawnee chief, Cornstalk, came, with a message of friendship, for he had kept

[2] *Clark Papers*, p. 116.

inviolate the terms of the Treaty of Pittsburgh. While being held prisoner, he was, together with his son, murdered by some mutinous soldiers. Thereafter, the Shawnee were inveterate foes of the Americans. Upon the arrival of General Hand, with but a handful of regulars and without provisions, the expedition was abandoned.

Congress, late that fall, once more ordered General Hand to prepare for an advance on Detroit and its dependencies. News of Burgoyne's surrender, interpreted as evidence of final colonial triumph, inspired frontiersmen to make renewed efforts.

During February, 1778, with a force of five hundred men, largely militia, General Hand set out for Sandusky, a British trading and recruiting center. Heavy rains and melting snow retarded his advance and flooded streams defeated his plans. After taking possession of some Indian villages, almost deserted, the expedition was abandoned. Thus the first organized advance by Americans into Indian territory was deemed a failure and the affair was dubbed "the Squaw Campaign." Disappointed at the outcome, "much pestered with the machinations of Tories," and believing that a new commander would be better supported, Hand requested his recall.[3] His petition was granted and General Lachlan McIntosh, whose military ability was highly esteemed by Washington, was named as his successor.

Under such adverse conditions, Clark's enlistments were greatly delayed. "I found my case desperate," he writes, upon learning that out of two companies enlisted by his captains, Joseph Bowman and Leonard Helm, two-thirds of the men had refused to serve. But assured that two hundred militia from the Holston settlements would join him in Kentucky, he determined to carry out his design. With one hundred and

[3] For a more extended statement, *consult* James, *Life of Clark*, pp. 58–64. A significant cause for Hand's resignation was the escape from Pittsburgh to Detroit of Alexander McKee, former Crown officer, Simon Girty, an interpreter, and Matthew Elliot. They were received with favor by Governor Hamilton and all became infamous as leaders of savage warriors. For Hand's account, *see Frontier Defense,* pp. 249–255.

fifty frontiersmen and a number of private adventurers and the families of twenty settlers, he "set sail" from Redstone on May 12, 1778.[4] Stores granted by General Hand, including powder and lead supplied through the influence of Pollock and brought from New Orleans by Lieutenant William Linn, were taken on at Pittsburgh. Linn, himself, joined the expedition and Clark must through him have learned of conditions at Kaskaskia and New Orleans and of the assurance of assistance from Pollock.[5] In fifteen days, the flotilla of flat boats arrived at the Falls of the Ohio, a point selected by Clark as the base for his future operations. It commanded the navigation of the River, since goods must be portaged around the Falls. It was on the route most practicable, also, between the Kentucky settlements and the Illinois country. Landing on an island in the midst of the rapids, in order to discourage desertions, Clark ordered the erection of a block-house. A small patch of ground of the seven acres not subject to overflow, upon which they were to cultivate a crop of corn, was apportioned to each of the families.

In place of four companies expected from the Holston region, Clark learned that part of a company only was available and that but few Kentuckians had arrived. For the first time, he disclosed to his followers the objective of the expedition. The proposal was enthusiastically received, except on the part of some of the Holston men who deserted during the night.

Clark was the more eager to advance upon receiving news of the French alliance, which was brought to him by a messenger from Pittsburgh. He counted on its effect with the Illinois French. On the morning of June 24, there was an almost total eclipse of the sun visible at the Falls of the Ohio.[6] Interpreted as a favorable omen by the majority, the boats containing the little army of one hundred and seventy-five men

[4] "Memoir," *Clark Papers,* p. 117.
[5] Captain James O'Hara also joined Clark. O'Hara was in charge of two boatloads of provisions which were being sent by General Hand for the use of Captain Willing's party. Captain O'Hara, likewise, knew of the influence of Pollock. *Clark Papers,* p. 221, note.
[6] *See Life of Clark,* p. 489, note 4.

shot the rapids and floated down the River to a spot near Fort Massac, an abandoned French post. They then struck off through the wilderness for Kaskaskia, 120 miles distant, marching single file in order not to excite the suspicions of any who might cross their trail.[7]

"Their dress, resembling that of the Indians, was common among the borderers of the time. The buckskin fringed hunting-shirt, covered the upper part of the body, reaching almost to the knees. This was girded about the waist with a broad leather belt, much decorated, from which hung the tomahawk. Leather breeches were worn by most of them, while others wore boots or leggings made of coarse woolen cloth wrapped loosely and tied with garters or laced on the outside. Moccasins were the usual covering for the feet. On the head was worn a broad-brimmed felt hat or a cap made of squirrel skin or fox skin with the tail dangling behind. Hanging over one shoulder was the shot-bag and powder-horn, and over the other a game bag which was used also for provisions. Clumsy flintlock rifles were carried by all."[8]

On the third day, upon coming to the stretches of prairie, their guide lost his way, and all were in greatest confusion. "I never in my life felt such a flow of Rage," Clark wrote, "to be wandering in a Country where every Nation of Indians could raise three or four times our Number, and a certain loss of our enterprise by the Enemies getting timely notice."[9] After two hours, the guide again got his bearings and the march was resumed.

On the evening of July 4, they stood on the bank of the Kaskaskia River across from the village of Kaskaskia, three-fourths of a mile distant. Six days had been taken for the

---

[7] The ordinary route would have been to the mouth of the Ohio and up the Mississippi. Clark wrote later: "As I knew that spies were kept on the River below the Towns of the Illinois, I had resolved to march part of the way by land." A party of American hunters, recently from Kaskaskia, gave him the desired information. *Clark Papers*, p. 225.
[8] *Life of Clark* (University of Chicago/Press), p. 118.
[9] *Ibid.*, 119.

march. For two days they had been without food, but these days of fatigue did not weaken the resolution, expressed by Captain Bowman, that they were all determined to take the town or die in the effort.[10]

Through his scouts, Rocheblave was informed that an expedition was on its way to attack the Illinois villages. His warnings were ineffective against the advice of American sympathizers who discouraged the militia officers.

In boats procured at one of the farm-houses, Clark and his men, about midnight, crossed the river.[11] No alarm was given, and while one division surrounded the town, the other, led by Clark, took possession of the fort and seized Rocheblave. Runners were sent throughout the town warning the inhabitants, on pain of death, to keep to their houses.

American traders in Kaskaskia, among them Daniel Murray and Richard Winston, received Clark with rejoicing and furnished his troops with "plenty of provisions" on the night of the capture. On numerous occasions thereafter, Murray delivered, for the use of Clark's followers, beef, pork, flour, Indian meal, wood and other supplies. So highly were the services of Winston regarded that within a month after the arrival of the Americans, he was given a captain's commission.

The villagers were disarmed and were in greatest confusion for they had been told of the savage nature of the Americans. They were shocked at the unkempt appearance of their conquerors whose clothes, because of the hard march, were dirty and ragged. "Giving all for lost," wrote Clark, "their lives were all they could beg for, which they did with the greatest fervancy, they were willing to be slaves to save their families." [12] Instead of employing extreme measures, Clark was de-

[10] July 30, 1778. *Ibid.,* pp. 614–617.

[11] The suggestion has been made, which I approve, that the boats had been placed at the farm-house by American sympathizers. C. W. Alvord, "The Illinois country 1673–1818," *Centennial History of Illinois,* I, 326. See evidence on Bentley, *ante.,* p. 102. The picturesque story which is told of the dance being given at the time of the capture is not supported by any contemporary evidence. See Theodore Roosevelt, *The Winning of the West,* II, 45, 46.

[12] *Clark Papers,* p. 120.

sirous of gaining their allegiance, for he was aware that with his small force it would be impossible to hold in subjection a town having a population of nearly one thousand.

Moreover, he hoped to gain their assistance in carrying out the rest of his plan. To the deputation of leading men, which he summoned, he explained the causes for the War and informed them that although, by the laws of war, they were completely at his mercy, yet it was an American principle to free, and not enslave, those whom they conquered. All who chose to become loyal citizens and took the oath of fidelity, he assured them should have all the privileges of Americans. Complete liberty was granted to any who chose to take their families out of the country. This promise of liberty, together with the news of the French alliance and the influence of the American traders, won the adherence of the French, who hailed the coming of Clark's men as the emissaries of their beloved and longed-for king.

Clark's assertion of the principle of religious liberty, not then recognized in Virginia, was serviceable in further exciting their enthusiasm. To Father Pierre Gibault, the village priest, who asked permission to conduct the usual services in his church, Clark replied that he had nothing to do with churches except to protect them from insult, and that the Catholic Church, under the laws of Virginia, would be granted as many privileges as any other. The effect of this conduct on the minds of the villagers was magical and was expressed by Clark as follows: "In a few minutes the scean of mourning and distress was turned to an excess of Joy, nothing else seen or heard— Addorning the Streets with flowers and Pavilians of different colors, compleating their happiness by singing etc." [13] In this spirit they took the oath of allegiance to the American cause. Rocheblave, because of his harsh language, was imprisoned, and was sent under guard to Virginia, where, by breaking his parole, he escaped. His slaves were sold and the proceeds were distributed among Clark's followers.

Clark immediately turned his attention to the capture of

[13] "Mason Letter," *Clark Papers*, p. 120. The "pavilians" were flags.

the other Illinois villages. With thirty mounted men, some of them French, Captain Joseph Bowman surprised and captured Prairie du Rocher and St. Philippe. Upon reaching Cahokia, they rode straight to the house of the commander and demanded the immediate surrender of the town. Without parley, the terms were accepted, and the next day the inhabitants, one hundred in number, took the oath of allegiance.

Friendly relations between Clark and Fernando de Leyba, Spanish lieutenant-governor at St. Louis, were established immediately after the capture of Kaskaskia and became continuously more intimate. "This gentlemen interests himself much in favor of the States," Clark wrote, "more so than I could have expected. He has offered me all the force that he could raise, in case of an attack by Indians from Detroit as there is now no danger from any other quarter." De Leyba had accompanied Governor Unzaga from Spain to New Orleans in 1769. He served also under Governor Galvez, by whom he was appointed nine years later to his post at St. Louis. Thus, the friendly relationship obtaining between Galvez and Pollock was reflected in the dealing of De Leyba with Clark. Four days after the capture of Kaskaskia, De Leyba wrote of a cargo of goods consigned to him by Pollock which were subject to Clark's order. "I should be glad to know by the first opportunity," Clark replied, "whether they were for the State of Virginia or for the Congress, otherways I should not know how to act as both have made Contracts." [14]

Colonel Francis Vigo, an Italian who actively favored the American cause from the time of the capture of Kaskaskia, was a partner of De Leyba in Indian trade. He had served in the Spanish Army but was discharged at New Orleans, where he became known to Pollock. Upon taking up his residence in St. Louis, he was spoken of as a trader of great influence and considerable property, and as a man of integrity and liberality. In the Illinois villages, he established branch stores and

---

[14] A. P. Nasatir, "The Anglo-Spanish Frontier in the Illinois Country During the American Revolution," *Journal of the Ill. State Historical Soc'y*, XXI, No. 3 (1928), p. 12.

from these furnished supplies to Clark, receiving in return orders drawn upon Pollock.

Gabriel Cerré was the real leader of the British faction in Kaskaskia. Like other Canadian youths, he had been drawn to the Illinois country by the opportunity for trade. By 1755, he was established at Kaskaskia, "that little Paris in the Wilderness." To Montreal he returned frequently with furs secured in trading ventures among the Peoria, the Kickapoo, the Mascoutin and other tribes. His success was such that he became known as the wealthiest, most enterprising and influential citizen of Kaskaskia. Clark referred to him as one of the most eminent men in the country and of great influence among the people. His assistance must be gained at any cost. When the village was captured, he was absent. His enemies, most of them his debtors, preferred charges against him of a sort which they hoped would win for themselves the favor of Clark. Clark demanded his immediate return in order to meet these criticisms. In his presence, his opponents failed to repeat the accusations. "I informed Mr. Cerré," Clark wrote, "that I was happy to find that he had so honorably acquitted himself of so black a charge, that he was now at liberty to dispose of himself and property as he pleased, If he chose to become a citizen of the Union that it would give us pleasure. He made many acknowledgements and concluded by saying that many doubts that he had were now cleared up to his satisfaction and that now [he] wished to take the oath immediately. In short, he became a most valuable man to us." So diplomatically did Clark conduct this critical affair that he won not alone the confidence of Cerré, but likewise the support of his associates, who were among the leading men of the village.

Following the advice of their leaders, the French were ready, at the outset, to accept Continental currency for supplies. That financial assistance had received but little consideration from Governor Henry or Clark is evident from the following statement by Clark: "The short notice I had of my destination not more than ten days, having to settle my business in so short a time, I never thought of asking anything about it. I remember that his Excelly the Governor told me I could get what I wanted from Mr. Pollock."

His money gone, Clark began drawing drafts upon the Treasurer of Virginia and upon Pollock. The second method proved acceptable to Vigo, Cerré, and all the other merchants and traders.

At the outset, such bills were received and paid at their face value, in silver, by Pollock. In his first communication, a letter of July 18th, Clark writes: "I have succeeded agreeable to my wishes and am necessitated to draw bills on the state and have reason to believe they will be accepted by you, the answering of which will be acknowledged by his Excelly, the Governor of Virginia." [15]

Pollock had been instructed by the Commercial Committee of Congress, also, to give all possible assistance to the expedition under Clark, to purchase goods on the best terms, to charter vessels, employ crews, or issue commissions to trustworthy persons for privateering.

Never does Clark fail to accord Pollock full credit for the aid furnished, whereby he was enabled to hold the Illinois country. From General Hand at Pittsburgh, as we have seen, he had received his first supply of ammunition which had been forwarded by Pollock.

Among Clark's first accounts, we find a draft for $285 drawn on Pollock to provide horses and to cover the other expenses of Father Gibault and Dr. Jean Laffont on their notable journey to Vincennes, where the priest had many friends. During the preceding ten years, he had been in charge of the church in that village in addition to serving parishes at Kaskaskia and Cahokia.

Learning that Clark was planning to capture Vincennes, the priest sought permission to win the support of the inhabitants in a peaceable way. While, as he expressed it, having nothing to do with temporal affairs, he assured Clark "that he

---

[15] *Clark Papers*, p. 55. The first bill was drawn on Pollock in favor of M. Prate for $208. It is endorsed, "accepted by O. Pollock, Agt., January 2, 1779. "Clark MSS.," *Va. State Archives*, Aud. 44.

POLLOCK SUPPORTS CLARK

would give them such hints in the spiritual way that would be very conducive to the business." Accompanied by Dr. Laffont, he set out upon this mission on July 14. They took with them an address prepared by Clark for the French at Vincennes, and numerous letters from their friends in Kaskaskia, which assisted materially in gaining their favor. Every effort was to be made to disabuse them of any fears they might have of the conquerors of the Illinois posts. Becoming citizens of the States meant, they were assured, protection for their persons and property and greatly extended commercial privileges. On the other hand, by refusing the offer, they would be forced to withstand the miseries of a war.[16]

The mission was completely successful. Early in August, they returned bringing the news that the American flag was floating over the Vincennes post. The additional expense of the expedition was met through further orders drawn on Pollock, amounting to $1,260.

Captain Leonard Helm was then sent to take command of the militia at Vincennes. Fort Sackville, which dominated the town, was a well-built wooden fort inclosing three acres of ground located on the bank of the Wabash River. The four bastions, each surmounted by three guns, were built of solid logs and stood twelve feet above the level of the fort walls which were eleven feet in height.[17]

Clark had succeeded in occupying Kaskaskia and Cahokia and was in control at Vincennes, but could he, removed as he was from any base of supplies, maintain control over this territory? His fund of Continental currency was quickly exhausted. During the summer of 1778, he continued to draw drafts in rapid succession on Pollock for "furnitures" supplied by traders and merchants. By the end of November, these orders amounted to $18,000.

We find among his earliest disbursements: $237 to ten men for bringing the boats from Wheeling to Redstone; $216 for linen to be used as boat covers; $1,351 for 12,189 pounds of

---
[16] *Ibid.*, p. 54.
[17] *Clark MSS.* (Indiana State Library, Indianapolis).

flour in barrels; $237 for ten beeves; $30 for a boat anchor; $6 for a treat to Capt. Helm's Company; $10 for four pair handcuffs; and $57 for hospital supplies.

Bread, flour, salt, meat, and drink were entered in his accounts as necessaries. Their meat supply came through hunting deer, buffalo, elk, and wild hogs. Salt was difficult to obtain and references are numerous of the loss of the winter's hunt because of the lack of salt. Liquors such as whiskey, rum, and taffia were required as a necessary part of the rations. Frequently they were used also in exchange for provisions. At best, the supply of liquors was limited. "I am under the necessity of putting a stop to the men's Rations of Liquor," an officer writes, "in order to purchase provisions. Please send us a little paper by the first opportunity as we can hardly carry on business for [lack of] that article."

Boats must be constructed and log houses built; suitable clothing was lacking and at times, like Washington's followers at Valley Forge, Clark's troops were barefoot and almost naked. "We shall use all our endeavors to furnish your men with necessary clothing," Clark was advised by Governor Henry, "but long experience renders it proper to warn you that our Supplies will be precarious. You cannot therefore be too attentive to the providing them in your own Quarter as far as Skins will enable you to do it. . . . The less you depend for supplies from this Quarter the less will you be disappointed by those impediments distance and a precarious foreign commerce throw in the way." Necessities for campaigning, in addition to food and clothing, included cannon, swivels, rifles, pistols, powder, lead and flints, knives and kettles. Numerous ledger entries show that small amounts of powder were obtained from the French villagers for $2.00 a pound and lead for $.50 a pound. The same account shows that bacon cost $.50 and flour $.11 a pound and that taffia was $6.00 a gallon. A day's wage for an armourer, and also for a carpenter, was $1.60.

That Clark provided for a well-organized commissary department becomes evident, as we read the many pages of his accounts with Virginia, including: the contracts drawn for supplies; the receipts for moneys disbursed; the orders on quarter-masters by officers, and the hundreds of vouchers, many of them for articles of even the smallest value.

Among such routine documents are found: "Let this man Have 4 lb. of pork for the people that are going down the River to Traverse the Horses"; "Issue to that Squaw that Furnished our men with Provisions, one Bushel of Corn and five Pounds of Pork"; "Please to issue for the use of the Kaskaskias Indians 40 weight of flour"; "The Commissary of Issues is amediately ordered to prepair one Thousand Rations to have them Ready to Imbark by 12 o'clock"; "Furnish Mr. Edward Murray with five gallons whiskey he having agreed to accept that Quantity in full for his pay as Express from this place"; "As there is a Party of militia going after a Party of Indians as have done mischief you will be pleased for to let me have one Pound of Powder and two Pound of Lead we haveing not a Sufficient quantity for to Persew them."

To meet such demands, orders on Pollock were drawn in favor of Cerré for $619, another for $2,000 and a third for $1,273; in favor of A. Chouteau for $2,100; of Laffont for $1,000 and in favor of a score of other well-known villagers, for various sums. From the first, the Charleville brothers, three in number, had coöperated to the full with Clark. The first draft on Pollock received by Charles Charleville was for $200. This was soon followed by a second for ten times that sum. Even before Clark's arrival, this family, together with the Lachances and the Janises, were of the group who favored the American cause.[18] All were traders whose boats plied between the Illinois country and New Orleans.

Men prominent at Vincennes, after the visit of Gibault, were ready, also, to furnish supplies for Clark's use, receiving, in exchange, orders on Pollock. Francis Bosseron had assisted his father in establishing the most successful trading company

---

[18] For an excellent summary of the supplies needed by Clark, see James G. Randall, "George Rogers Clark's Service of Supply," *Miss. Valley Hist. Rev.*, VIII, 256–263.

in this village. At twenty-six years of age, upon the death of his father, Francis came into full ownership of the business. So favorably known was the company that their drafts were honored from Montreal and Detroit to Virginia and New Orleans. It seems evident that no persuasion was necessary in winning the allegiance of Bosseron, who was the mayor of the town, to the American cause.

Returning to Kaskaskia, Gibault reported that Bosseron had been elected captain of the militia and commander of the fort, and to him was awarded the first commission issued by Clark in the West. Later, he was made a major. Very early, he was called on to furnish supplies for the Americans, receiving, in exchange, a draft on Pollock.[19] J. M. P. Legras, another well-known trader, followed the lead of Bosseron, and thus Vincennes was won. The following order, in the usual form, proved acceptable to Legras:

KASKASKIAS 2nd Feby. 1779

$1752
SIR

At Thirty Days sight of this my first of Exchange, second of same tenor and date not paid Pay to Mr. Legras or to his Order the Sum of One Thousand Seven Hundred and fifty two Dollars for sundry furnitures to the State of Virginia and Charge as pr. former advice from—

Sir
Your very obd^t. Se^{rvt},
G. R. CLARK

To OLLIVER POLLOCK
ESQ^r.
NEW ORLEANS

Early in August, 1778, the first of Clark's drafts, with an accompanying letter, had been received by Pollock. Forwarding the letter to the Commercial Committee, Pollock writes: "You'll see he is in possession of the Illinois and that he has drawn bills on me with the expectation of my honoring them for the State of Virginia. There is to the amount of 1,000 Dol-

[19] For an interesting account of the career of Major Bosseron and his assistance to Clark, see Janet P. Shaw, *Indiana Mag. of History*, XXV, pp. 204–241.

lars already come to hand which I have accepted payable in January next, and if any more are presented I shall accept them payable at the same time as I hope before that you'll have it in your power to furnish me with sufficient funds to wipe off the whole."

He was already obligated to pay $42,500 on the same date, because of indebtedness accrued on behalf of the géneral government. His responsibility, at that time, included, also, the $74,087 secured from Governor Galvez with which arms, ammunition, and supplies had been furnished the frontier posts of Pennsylvania and Virginia.

Without present resources with which to meet these obligations, he assures Clark that "the cause in which we are embarked urges me to strain every nerve, and luckily having a number of good Friends have hitherto enabled me to serve my Country. In consequence of this I have accepted your bills." [20] The serious situation with which he was then confronted was enhanced because of the fact that Willing and his men still remained at New Orleans and were dependent upon him for support.

The capture of the Illinois posts was interpreted by Pollock as a step toward opening communication by the Mississippi, securing control of the River posts and possibly Pensacola. In this manner, he hoped to be relieved from the burdens he had assumed on behalf of the American cause. Of the sums he had advanced, $14,445 had been invested in a cargo of peltries and indigo which he shipped under French colors to France. Goods suitable to the needs of the Commercial Committee were to be taken in exchange. The project proved a total loss for the cargo was seized by an agent of the United States who was stationed at Cape St. Francis. As justification it was claimed that the government was in his debt and that these goods had been shipped by an agent of the United States. "This," wrote Pollock, "was my first reward for serving America."

The British, fearing an expedition under Clark, began to strengthen their fortifications at Natchez and Manchac. In his

[20] August 18, 1778. *Draper MSS.*, 48J33.

first communication to Clark, a congratulatory message, Pollock urged the necessity for the capture of these posts before war should be declared between Great Britain and Spain. The task, he thought, could be readily accomplished by a force of three hundred men, for Natchez was defended by only eighty men and Manchac by one hundred—"Both posts are poorly entrenched and I believe keep themselves in readiness for starting on the first alarm or appearance of our troops. But if suddenly surprised in the night they may be made prisoners."

Clark's success was gratifying to Pollock in another respect, as he now found the opportunity to get rid of Willing and his troublesome followers. "I come now to my old grievance," he writes the Commercial Committee, "since he has excused himself by waiting the arrival of a packet which was on its way from the Arcansas supposed to contain letters from you. This packet however is now come to hand without any letters from you and now as little hope of his setting off as ever. What his next pretense for tarrying here will be God knows. But as there is a clear passage for him and his party to go up, part by land and part by water through the Spanish territories and join Colonel Clark, I am determined to stop all supplies in order to get him away."

Although he was "deeply indebted in this part of the world," Pollock had assumed orders drawn by Willing amounting to 11,967 pistoles—"for his men while here, which tho high and unprovided for I was under the necessity of supplying him with, for the Credit of the States in this Gov't." [21] The ultimatum to Willing states that the sixty men of this party, under the leadership of Lieutenant Robert George and Richard Harrison, were to march through Spanish territory to join Clark.[22] The mission upon which these officers had come was to procure the goods held for the general government at New Orleans. These had already been dispatched

[21] *Pollock Letters,* October 5, 1778.
[22] Judged by his letters to Clark, Willing was the sole promoter of this expedition. On September 1, he writes: "Annexed you have a Copy of a Letter I wrote by Lieut. Robert George who I sent off to you with

POLLOCK SUPPORTS CLARK 147

by Pollock under protection of the Spanish flag and were then at St. Louis awaiting orders from General Hand.

Willing, himself, was directed to leave for Philadelphia within ten days. His face was saved through a commission entrusted to him to appear before Congress and acquaint them with conditions in New Orleans. Before his leavetaking, Willing once more tested the generosity of Pollock by drawing on him for 919 pistoles. The sailing of the sloop under Spanish colors upon which Willing embarked was made possible through the assumption by Pollock of two months' pay for the quota of officers and sailors. A portion of the expense he hoped would be covered by a shipment of goods on account of Robert Morris and himself amounting to 5,500 pistoles.

Pollock's relief may be sensed in a communication which he forwarded to Clark: "This step was taken in order to get this party from here which has been living here for a long time at a heavy expense and doing no manner of service to the States. In consequence I have now dispatched them." He assumed the expense of equipping the party with horses and provisions to the amount of 1,000 pistoles.

Permission for the expedition having been secured from Galvez, minute instructions, showing Pollock's intimate knowledge of the route to be followed, were entrusted to the leaders. The sensitiveness of Spanish officials, with whom they would be brought into contact, was carefully protected. At Barataria they were to board an armed schooner which they would find awaiting them—"In consequence, I desire you'll immediately proceed over to that place and embark after which the Captain and pilot on board will directly make sail for the Appelansaas and land you there at the most Convenient place, as soon as wind and weather will permit, they having the necessary orders and directions for that purpose."

my Party consisting of about 60 men and they will either stay with you or proceed immediately according as they May receive Instructions from Genl. Hand or Congress with the State Goods."

Here they were to meet a Mr. Bacon, agent of Pollock, who was to have twenty-five to thirty horses or mules in readiness to carry their baggage and provisions. Two competent guides were also provided. Upon arrival at the Arkansas Post, they were to present to the commandant an order from Pollock for provisions or any other necessities. These drafts amounted to some $3,500.

Arriving at the Illinois, Lieutenant George was directed to inform Clark "of the necessity of opening the Communication on this River and taking possession of the Country immediately before war should be declared between Great Britain and Spain by which the latter will save us that Trouble and in consequence we will lose a valuable conquest which might now be easily obtained." [23]

Bills drawn on Pollock amounting to $8,500, for aid given Clark, had now reached New Orleans. "You'll find I am in great distress with respect to the payment of those bills," he writes Clark. "Notwithstanding this I have accepted all your bills in full expectation of the States supplying me with funds by the latter end of this year, a disappointment in which will effectually ruin me, and in consequence of which I hope you'll urge the State of Virginia, which seems to be the most convenient, to be speedy in forwarding down flour here to pay for those bills and lodge funds here for any future demands they may have for goods." But the wish was wholly vain.

Notwithstanding his uncertain future, 5,000 pounds of powder were at once dispatched to Clark and during September, 1778, supplies and 2,000 pounds of powder, valued at $7,200 were likewise sent by him for the use of the Illinois troops. As soon as men could be gotten to man the boats, an additional supply was to follow. Without "hard" dollars, importers refused to dispose of their goods, but Clark's necessities were to be met, in part, by supplies already purchased by Pollock. "Open the communication and commence your flour trade," he implores the Committee, "and then I will

---

[23] *Draper MSS.*, 48J34.

be able to supply you with all kinds of goods you may order for that use, as there are several vessels expected from France this Fall."

Conciliation of the Indian tribes was a gigantic task to which Clark early gave attention and his ability shown in handling this problem was a striking phase of the conquest of the Northwest. Tribes in the vicinity of Kaskaskia offered to treat for peace at once and those near Vincennes showed a like disposition. But how was the control by the British over the more distant tribesmen to be overcome?

To meet the needs of Indian councils demanded great administrative ability on the part of Clark. "An accomplished diplomat in Indian affairs," is a title to which he was justly entitled.[24] Impressed with the success of the French and the Spaniards in dealing with the Indian problem, he studied their methods and adopted them as his own.

His chief difficulty in winning Indian friendship was lack of supplies, for without powder, which in 1779 sold at $4 a pound, their hunters were unable to procure food for their families. Without whiskey and other commodities, little could be accomplished in councils. From Detroit and Montreal plentiful supplies were obtainable by British agents.

That no assistance was to come from Virginia, already burdened with war, may be gathered from a communication of Governor Henry:

> It would be well to communicate to them [the Indians] our present want of those articles necessary to them & our inability to get them, to encourage them to struggle with the difficulties as we do til peace when they may be confidently assured we will spare nothing to put their Trade on a comfortable and just footing. In the meantime, we must endeavor to furnish them with ammunition to provide skins to clothe themselves, with a disposition to do them every friendly office & gain their love.

Later, Jefferson issued instructions that "ammunition should be furnished gratis to those warriors who go actually on ex-

[24] Kellogg, *Indian Diplomacy During the Revolution in the West*, p. 11.

peditions against the hostile tribes." To this message John Todd, Jr., an associate of Clark wrote: "I wish you'd tell me how Mr. Machieval advises to keep up the Indian interest without goods, either to give or to sell." [25]

It was only through orders drawn on Pollock in favor of the French merchants, and the timely arrival of supplies forwarded by him, that Clark was able to cope with this problem. Early in August, 1778, Clark dispatched his second appeal to Pollock:

> The goods [he writes], that I have been necessitated to purchase have been at a most Extravagant Price and a great loss to the Soldiery. . . . I hope that you will send me an Assortment of Five Thousand Dollars worth of Goods most Suitable for Soldiers and Indians as my situation obliges me to give them small presents. I will make you immediate remittances in Bills. I am in great want of ammunition for this and other Garrisons in the Illinois Country. . . . I should be glad that you would send me four Thousand Pounds of Powder. Mr. Faggotts receipt and this letter shall be your security. No news worth relating but what you have heard by the Gentlemen already arrived except Post Vincent acceeding to us.[26]

Toward the close of August, 1778, a huge horde of savages gathered to hear what the chief of the Big Knives had to say. Some of them had come from villages five hundred miles distant. Among them were chiefs and warriors from the Chippewa, Ottawa, Potawatomi, Winnebago, Sac, Fox, Miami, and other tribes, a dozen or so in all, representing some four thousand warriors. Clark seemed to possess a full understanding of their natures. While treating them with justice, he adopted an attitude, as occasion demanded, either conciliatory or severe. While manifesting confidence, he was always on guard and prepared for an emergency. Assuming an air of bravado, he nevertheless confessed his apprehension "among such a number of Devils." His speeches were striking

---

[25] Kellogg, *op. cit.*, pp. 10, 11.
[26] August 6, 1778. *Clark Papers*, pp. 64, 65.

appeals to the prejudices and ideals of this primitive assembly. He said:

> I know that a mist is yet before your Eyes. . . . The Big Knife are very much like the Red people—they dont know well how to make Blanket powder and cloath. The English "would not let our women Spin nor the men make powder nor let us trade with anybody else but said that we should Buy all from them and since we had got saucy they would make us give them two Bucks for a Blanket that we used to get for one and that we should do as they pleased etc. killed some of us to make the rest fear. . . . Thus the war began and the English was drove from one place to another until they got mad and hired you the Red people to fight for them and help them. The great Spirit getting angry at this he caused your old Father the French King and other Great Nations to Joyn the Big knife and fight with them against all their Enemies so that the English is become like a Dear in the Woods. From this you may see that it is the great Spirit that caused your waters to be Troubled because you Faught for the people that he was mad with and if your women and children should Cry you must blame your selves for it and not the Big knife you can now Judge who is in the right.[27]

Protesting that they had been led astray by the British, they promised thenceforth to be friends of the Americans. In reply, Clark declared that he came not to ask peace from any nation; that he came as a warrior, not as a counselor, carrying in his right hand war and in his left hand peace; that they might go freely and fight for the English; his superiors had ordered him to ask peace of no people. Pointing to the war-belt, he challenged them to begin hostilities.[28] During five weeks, the council continued and at its close all united in a great feast.[29] So successful was Clark, that an English officer asserted that only the Sioux remained in the British in-

---

[27] *Clark Papers*, pp. 244, 245. On the second night of the Council, a party of warriors attempted to break into Clark's lodging in order to capture him. So skilfully did he handle this affair, that his general appeal was greatly strengthened. *Clark Papers*, pp. 249, 250; James, *Life of Clark*, pp. 128, 129.

[28] *Clark Papers*, p. 126.

[29] For a more extended discussion, *see Life of Clark*, pp. 127–130.

terest. "So great was our Interest among the Indians about this time," Clark writes at a later date, "that Governor Hamilton on his Expedition against St. Vincent with all his Influence could Raise not more than four or five Hundred Indians to accompany him."

CHAPTER X

POLLOCK AND THE FATE OF THE WEST: VINCENNES

LATE in September, 1778, Colonel David Rogers, accompanied by seven men, arrived at New Orleans and delivered a letter from Governor Henry to Galvez. Pollock serving as intermediary, Rogers's reception was satisfying. "O. Pollock presents his Compliments to Col. Rogers," a formal invitation reads; "and begs leave to acquaint him, His, Exly. Govr. Galvez will be glad to have the Honour of his Compy tomorrow at Dinner." [1] Once more, while serving as host to his Virginia guests, Pollock was forced to draw on his already depleted resources—to the amount of 3,459 pistoles.

"Were the amount not so large," Galvez stated, referring to the loan (150,000 pistoles) asked by Governor Henry, "and had I not given to Mr. Oliver Pollock the money that I was able to take from the surplus remaining from the sum assigned annually to this Province for its maintenance, I should immediately have resolved to send you a part of it in order to please you and to render that State a service, but this is impossible for me at the present as there is no money." Acting upon Pollock's advice, he recommended favorable consideration of the proposal by his government. Spain, he thought, would also look with favor upon joining West Florida to the United States in the event that British domination should be overcome.

In fact, he surmised it was "quite the thing for Spain to desire it." English communication with the gulf ports in which they were enabled to fit out expeditions would thus be

---

[1] Monday noon, 21st. Septr. 1778. "Haldimand Papers," British Museum, *Add. MSS.*, 21,844, p. 97.

prevented. Provisions and timber which they were procuring from the Mississippi would likewise be cut off.

Galvez consented, also, to advocate the construction of a fort at the mouth of the Ohio—"I consider the establishment of this fort very useful for facilitating the navigation of the Mississippi River. It will always be of use in restraining the Indian allies of the English who without that aid would more readily dare to molest those traveling from one part to the other." [2]

Pollock now appealed to Congress for an expedition against Pensacola, which had been devastated by a hurricane, "driving the vessels on shore which were lying at anchor in the harbor and oversetting their fortifications and houses." "In my opinion," he adds, "the free navigation of this river for many reasons is much wanted for the general good of the cause and may just now be very easily accomplished."

Demands on the part of creditors were insistent, but at no time does he acknowledge defeat. An additional financial burden of 4,349 pistoles was assumed in fitting out a vessel for the use of the general government. This action was due to information furnished him that the Committee was lacking vessels and West India products.[3] His plan included loading the ship with sugar cases which might be sold at a handsome profit in Havana and taking on taffia, sugar, and salt for Philadelphia. Additional cargo shipped from New Orleans included a supply of indigo valued at 1,378 pistoles. Instructions to the captain included drawing on Pollock for any sum necessary for the loading of the boat at Havana.

By the middle of December, 1778, he had advanced 8,500 pistoles, also, for fitting out the ship *Morris*. For the quota of officers and crew, numbering one hundred and fifty, he likewise became responsible, and, in meeting these obligations, he was forced to dispose of some of his plantation slaves at a discount.

[2] October 19, 1778. *Pollock Letters.*
[3] December 15, 1778. *Ibid.*

"Immediate relief," was his appeal to the Committee of Congress, in order to cover drafts amounting to $56,000, incurred on behalf of the general government. Failing in the request, the remainder of his slaves must go on the block within a month. "However," he writes with his never failing note of optimism, "I am still happy to have that resource upon this occasion to serve the Cause and make no doubt but you'll soon put it in my power to do honor to my engagements, as I am informed your coasts are now all clear of our enemies, you'll naturally forward me supplies of flour." Six thousand barrels of flour, he estimated, could be disposed of each year at New Orleans to good advantage and, providing Spain remained neutral, he believed two hundred thousand barrels might be consumed in the West Indies trade.

Not only had the authorities of the United States and of Virginia neglected to provide Pollock with funds necessary to meet their demands for goods, but they failed to advise him of the method by which such obligations would be covered.[4] This failure was due partly to the capture of Philadelphia by the British and the confusion incident to the removal of government papers, and in part to the deranged condition of affairs in Congress growing out of the frequent accession of new members. The conduct of affairs as viewed by Alexander Hamilton was due to the "degeneracy of representation in the great council of America." "What is the cause? And how is it to be remedied? are questions that the welfare of these States required should be well attended to. The great men, who composed our first council,—are they dead, have they deserted the cause, or what has become of them? Very few are dead, and still fewer have deserted the cause; they are all, except the few who still remain in Congress, either in the field or in the civil offices of their respective States; for the greater part are engaged in the latter. The only remedy then is to take them out of these employments,

[4] *Draper MSS.*, 48J37.

and return them to the place where their presence is infinitely more important." [5]

Owing to the short crop of wheat in 1778 and the necessity for furnishing supplies, not only for the American Army, but for the French troops accompanying Count D'Estaing, the government was forced to put an embargo on all provisions. Not one of the vessels dispatched by Pollock along the coast had reached its destination. The sloop upon which Captain Willing embarked was captured and he was sent as a prisoner to New York. The vessel was recaptured and run ashore and thus a portion of the cargo was saved. The attitude of the new Committee which was appointed the middle of December gave promise of greater regularity in the conduct of affairs at New Orleans. They were empowered by Congress to exert every possible effort in making remittances to Pollock and the unusual wheat harvest, "the finest crop that had been known for many years," gave assurance that the conditions would be fulfilled.

With no hope for immediate relief and with sacrifices most extreme, Pollock succeeded in forwarding to Clark during January, 1779, five hundred pounds of powder and four swivels. The Illinois French refused to accept Continental money, but were ready at all times to receive orders drawn on Pollock. By February, these drafts amounted to $30,000. Pollock met one-third of this amount through contracting for the use of his remaining slaves on the public works at New Orleans. This, he said, has only kept the constable from the door. But, in the language of his memorial to the Legislature of Virginia, he was compelled "either to honor that brave man [Clark], to dishonor the American government, to dishonor the great cause of human liberty, and to dishonor his own feelings, promises and character or to meet these demands as they occurred."

Clark's ability as a leader was now to be put to the test, for he was forced to meet a counter-attack by Governor

---

[5] Addressed to George Clinton. *Writings of George Washington*, ed. Jared Sparks, V, 508, 509.

Hamilton which involved the possession of Vincennes and probably the loss of the whole West. Such an outcome would have gone far, judged by British plans which were projected in the West during the following year, toward the ultimate defeat also of the American forces east of the mountains. By early August, Hamilton, at Detroit, knew of Clark's success in the Illinois country but supposed the attack had been made by a portion of the force under Willing. Preparations were immediately begun to regain these posts. Agents were sent among the Wabash, Miami, and Shawnee tribes, with liberal presents, to stir them up against the enemy. The Ottawa, Chippewa, and other tribes tributary to Detroit were called in council, were feasted in the usual fashion and told of plans which were about to be executed. Commandants at Michillimackinac and St. Joseph were urged to coöperate through sending forces down the Illinois River. Hamilton was more confident because of conditions described by him as follows: "The Spaniards are feeble, and hated by the French, the French are fickle and have no man of capacity to advise or lead them, the Rebels are enterprising and brave, but want resources, and the Indians can have their resources but from the English if we act without loss [of] time in the favorable conjuncture." [6]

Provisions, artillery stores, and presents for the Indians were collected, and on October 7, some 175 white troops, two-thirds of them volunteer French militia, and sixty Indians were ready for the expedition. Led by Hamilton, they set out on their six-hundred-mile journey which was to consume seventy-one days. Three main objectives, it was hoped, would be accomplished. These were: to erect a fort at the junction of the Mississippi and the Ohio which was to constitute a "bridle" on American trade, and prevent the shipments of powder by Pollock from New Orleans to the "Rebel forts"; to get control of the mouth of the Missouri River with the hope of underselling Spanish traders and thus gain favor with the Indians of that region; and by dislodging the rebels from

---

[6] *Mich. Pioneer and Hist. Coll's.*, IX, 478.

the Illinois, to regain the Mississippi trade, which otherwise would be entirely lost. It was stated, also, that the expedition would contribute to the security of the Floridas.[7]

Advancing with great difficulty by Lake Erie, and the Maumee River across the portage to the head-waters of the Wabash, holding conferences and gaining recruits, Hamilton reached Ouiatanon where he was joined by a number of Wabash chiefs who had previously sworn allegiance to the American cause.

A reconnoitering party sent out by Captain Helm was captured and thus he was uncertain of the whereabouts of the enemy, increased in number by Indian accessions to about five hundred, until they were within three miles of Vincennes. At first sight of this formidable force, the French were panic-stricken and deserted, leaving Helm but a single American soldier to guard the fort.[8] Following the surrender, the inhabitants when summoned to the church renewed their oath of allegiance to the British—"We the undersigned, declare and acknowledge to have taken the oath of allegiance to Congress, in which we have forgotten our duty to God and have failed in our duty to man. We ask pardon of God and we hope from the goodness of our legitimate sovereign, the King of England, that he will accept our submission and take us under his protection as good and faithful subjects, which we promise and swear to become before God and before man. In faith of which we sign with our hand or certify with our ordinary mark, the aforesaid day and month of the year 1778." [9]

Had Hamilton pushed on by a forced march, it seems probable he would have regained control of the Illinois

[7] Haldimand to Clinton, November 10, 1778. *Draper MSS.*, 58J2. "Hamilton's Report," *Clark Papers*, p. 182.

[8] The story of the loaded cannon related in Mann Butler's *History of the Commonwealth of Kentucky*, 2nd ed. (Louisville, 1834), p. 80, note, is *not* referred to in any of the sources and probably did not occur. See Roosevelt, *The Winning of the West*, II, 63, note, and Reuben G. Thwaites, *How George Rogers Clark Won the Northwest*, p. 41.

[9] "Hamilton's Report," *Clark Papers*, p. 183. The population of Vincennes numbered 620.

towns, but the season was too far advanced, he thought, for such a venture. Most of the Indians were sent to their villages. Ninety whites were retained as the garrison for Fort Sackville, which was put in a better state of defense. Scouting parties were sent to the mouth of the Wabash and toward the Falls of the Ohio and Kaskaskia. Messages were forwarded to Stuart, urging him to prepare the warriors of the Southern tribes for a joint attack the following spring upon Kentucky and Illinois.

Shortly after the capture of Kaskaskia, Clark learned of the proposed march of General McIntosh from Pittsburgh against Detroit. Not before December was he informed that such an expedition had been abandoned. First information came to him about that time of the expedition under Hamilton which was supposed to be aimed at Kaskaskia. A short distance from the village, while on a journey to Cahokia, he narrowly averted capture by a party of Indians under white leaders. At Prairie du Rocher, while attending a ball in his honor, Clark received a report that Hamilton's entire force was within three miles of Kaskaskia. With his usual unconcern in the face of grave danger, he dissipated the general confusion of the company by ordering the dance to go on until his horses were saddled.

At Kaskaskia, he encountered the greatest consternation over the attack which seemed imminent. Confident of the success of the British, the French resolved to become neutral. Coolly preparing to withstand the attack, Clark determined to burn that part of the town commanding the fort. The suspense was ended when a scouting party returned with the news that "the great army" was a small party of raiders then rapidly retreating. The incident was convincing evidence, however, of Hamilton's success at Vincennes and an attack on Kaskaskia, Clark now knew, was only a question of time. While uncertain how to proceed, timely information brought by Colonel Francis Vigo caused him to decide upon the course he would follow.

Vigo, in his capacity of trader, had gone to Vincennes with provisions and powder for Captain Helm. During the preceding fortnight, these had been collected through drafts drawn on Pollock in favor of Vigo and of French creditors. It was suspected by Hamilton that Vigo, who was made a prisoner, had come in the interest of the Americans. As a Spanish subject, however, he was released and returned to St. Louis, having agreed not to do anything injurious to British interests on his way to that post. This agreement fulfilled, he hastened to Kaskaskia and on January 29 gave Clark "every intelligence that I could wish to have." [10] The day following, an additional order of $1,452, drawn on Pollock, was accepted by Vigo.

Clark's position was desperate, when he resolved to undertake the venture of marching immediately upon Vincennes.[11] This is evidence of genius associated only with a born leader. "It was at this moment," he declared, "I would have bound myself seven years a slave to have had five hundred troops." [12] The wish was vain, for not only had he received no Virginia reinforcements, but for nearly a year he had not received, as he said, "a scrape of a pen" from Governor Henry. He writes:

We now Viewed ourselves in a very critical Situation, in a manner cut off from any Intercourse between us and the continent. That G. Hamilton in the Spring by a Junction of his Northward and Southern Indians which he had prepared for would be at the Head of such force that nothing in this Quarter could withstand his arms. That Kentucky must amediately fall and well if the desolation would end there. . . . We saw but one alternative which was to attact the Enemy in their Quarters. If we were fortunate it would save the whole if otherways it would be nothing more than what would Certainly be the consequence if we should not make the attempt. . . . The Season of the year being so favourable as the Enemy could not suppose that we should be so mad as to attempt to march 80 leagues through a drownded Cuntry in the Debth of Winter—that they would be off their Guard and probably would not think it worth while to keep out spies.

[10] "Mason Letter," *Clark Papers*, p. 138.
[11] "Memoir," *Ibid.*, p. 267.
[12] "Mason Letter," *Ibid.*, p. 138.

THE FATE OF THE WEST

His confidence that the expedition would prove successful inspired his men and "in a day or two the Country seemed to believe it, many anctious to retrieve their Characters turned out, the Ladies began also to be spirited and interest themselves in the Expedition, which had great Effect on the Young Men."

With this enthusiasm, provisions and ammunition were quickly collected. Once more, Pollock was the magic word which induced French leaders to share in the burdens of preparation. The fate of the West was dependent upon this timely aid. Charles Charleville, Datchurst, and Rapicault are names of men again appearing and receiving orders, on Pollock, exceeding $1,000 each. Within sixty days, bills amounting to some $9,000 had been drawn in favor of Vigo. They were to be made payable by Pollock at thirty days sight, or at a time not specified, in specie, or its equivalent. In like manner, Joseph Plassy, a former captain under the British, who was rated among the richest of the Kaskaskians, furnished Clark on the day preceding his departure for Vincennes with flour, buffalo-meat, and other supplies amounting to $1,565.

On the fourth of February, the *Willing,* a row-galley, with a crew of forty-six men commanded by Lieutenant John Rogers, set off under orders to anchor a short distance below Vincennes and prevent any boat descending the Wabash. This, the first armed boat on the Ohio River, mounted two four pounders, a nine pounder and four swivels and carried a store of provisions and of ammunition, a portion of a shipment by Pollock.

"I shall march across by land myself with the Rest of my Boys on this forlorn hope," Clark writes his friend George Mason. "You must be sensible of the feeling that I have for those brave officers and soldiers that are determined to share my fate. . . . No time is to be lost. Was I shoer [sure] of a Reinforcement I should not attempt it. Who knows what fortune will do for us. Great things have been affected by a few men well conducted. Perhaps we may be fortunate. We have this consolation that our cause is just and that our Country will be grateful and not con[demn] our Conduct in case we fall through if so this Country as well as Kentucky I believe is lost."

On February 5, 1779, eight days after Clark learned of Hamilton's success, the little force of 172 men, nearly one-half of them French volunteers under their own colors, were "conducted out of the town by the Inhabitants," and took up their march toward Vincennes. The expedition thus begun proved to be one of the most heroic and dramatic undertakings of the entire Revolution. It has been well characterized as a stroke of inspiration found only on rare occasions in history.

From the outset, they encountered trials which became daily more extreme as they dragged themselves over the 180 miles to their goal. The weather was mild for mid-winter, but on account of frequent rains the trail was miry and in the lowlands the water stood several inches deep. At night, with no tents for shelter, Clark had great difficulty in keeping up the spirits of his followers who were worn out with fatigue. They gathered around the great camp-fires and feasted on buffalo and other game, each company taking turn in hunting and cooking. Diversions followed, such as singing and dancing. On the thirteenth, they came to the junction of the two branches of the Little Wabash. Because of the floods, they constituted a single stream five miles wide and three feet deep in the shallowest places. "This," writes Clark, "would have stop'ed any set of men that was not in the same temper we was." [13] Two days were consumed in building a canoe and ferrying the men and stores across the river. On the evening of the fifteenth they came to an elevated spot upon which they encamped. Through the acts of a "little Antick Drummer who floated on his drum," Clark was aided in diverting the minds of his men, then greatly fatigued. Their trials had only begun, for their provisions were almost gone and all game had been driven off by the floods. Late in the evening of the

[13] "Memoir," *Ibid.*, p. 271.

seventeenth, they came to the Embarrass River which could not be forded. Upon a knoll of ground from which the water had but recently receded, they passed the remainder of the "drizzly and dark night." The next morning they heard Hamilton's morning-gun at Fort Sackville, then only nine miles distant.

Still unable to ford the river, they marched downstream and early on the afternoon of February 18 came to the Wabash River. Here they remained during the two following days. Three attempts were made to get men across to the vicinity of Vincennes in order to gather information and secure boats. These efforts failing, the despairing men were set to building boats. Many of the volunteers talked of deserting. For two days they had gone without food of any sort. Writing of their condition, Clark says: "If I was sensible that You would let no Person see this relation I would give You a detail of our suffering for four days in crossing these waters, and the manner it was done; as I am sure that You would Credit it, but it is too incredible for any Person to believe except those that are as well acquainted with me as You are, or had experienced something similar to it." [14] To his followers he talked of the victory soon to be gained, laughed at their fears and by his air of confidence inspired courage in those who were faltering. Five hunters descending the river were captured and from their story it was gathered that the approach of the Americans was not suspected and that the inhabitants would be found well disposed. The diarist of the expedition writes: "One of our men killed a deer which was distributed in camp— Very acceptable." [15] From daybreak to late afternoon of the 21st the two canoes plied back and forth to the eastern bank of the river where the troops were landed on a small hill called the Lower Mamelle. All thought of bringing the pack-horses across was abandoned. The men, plunging into the water at times up to their necks,

[14] "Mason Letter," *Ibid.*, p. 140.
[15] "Bowman's Journal," *Clark Papers*, p. 158. Original in *Draper MSS.*, 49J9.

advanced three miles to another hill, and there, as we learn from Bowman's Journal, they encamped. "Rain all this day, no Provisions," he continues. "We came one league farther to some sugar camps, where we staid all night heard the Evening and Morning Guns from the Fort— No provisions yet, lord help us."

In crossing the Horse-Shoe Plain, on the morning of the twenty-third, still greater difficulties were encountered. This plain of four miles was covered with water, breast high. Hardships already undergone now began to tell on the weakest. As they fell in the ranks, they were picked up by the canoes and carried to an island about ten acres in extent. "Never," Bowman relates, "was men so animated with the thoughts of revenging the wrongs done to their back Settlements as this small army was."

Resuming the march, with the icy water up to the shoulders of the tallest, they came to a small "grove." Many, worn out, clung to the trees and floating logs until they were picked up by the boats. Fires were built and a sort of broth was made from a half-quarter of buffalo which was taken from some squaws who chanced to be passing in a canoe. Slightly refreshed and cheered with warmth from the fires and the beauty of the day, they resumed their march with renewed courage. At one in the afternoon they came to a slight elevation of dry land covered with trees, called Warrior's Island. Here, for the first time, they got a view of the town and fort scarcely two miles away. From a duck-hunter who was taken prisoner, they learned that their coming was not suspected in that season of the year. The walls of the fort, he informed them, had been completed and two hundred Indians had just arrived.

What course was to be taken at this crisis? Clark was aware that the number of his followers was much smaller than the combined force of the enemy and their Indian allies. Moreover, there were two hundred Frenchmen of military age in Vincennes. Their decision to aid either party would determine the result.

Some of the leaders, Clark knew, were lukewarm in their allegiance to the British. A bold stroke would serve to confuse any who might oppose him. Accordingly he prepared a letter which was carried to the village by the hunter who had been kept in ignorance of the size of the American force. "Gentlemen," he wrote: "Being now within two Miles of Your Village with my Army determined to take your Fort this night and not being willing to surprize you I take this step to request of such of you as are true citizens and are willing to enjoy the liberty I bring you to remain still in your house, and those (if any there be) that are friends to the King will instantly repair to the fort and join the hair Buyer General and fight like Men and if any such as do not go to the fort, shall be discovered afterwards, they may depend on being well treated and I once more request they shall keep out of the streets for every person I find in arms on my arrival I shall treat him as an enemy." [16] The villagers quickly gathered in the public square to hear this message. Overcome with surprise, no one dared to carry the information to Hamilton.

About sunset, Clark ordered an advance with "drums braced" and colors flying. By marching around a slight elevation of ground which obstructed the view so that only the flags could be seen from the town, the impression was made that a thousand men were approaching.[17] Their real numbers were not known, because of the darkness, as they reached the village marching in two divisions, one led by Clark and the other by Captain Bowman. With drums beating, they marched up the principal street, the inhabitants receiving them joyfully. Major Bosseron and Colonel Legras had secreted supplies of ammunition, procured from Pollock, and these were now freely given to Clark, whose stock was nearly exhausted. The British Indians fled upon the approach of the

---

[16] "Bowman's Journal," *Clark Papers*, p. 159.

[17] This statement follows the account given by Clark in his *Memoir*. Evidence for the ruse, characterized as childishness by Theodore Roosevelt, is to be found in the *Life of Clark*, pp. 484, 485. For the discussion on the authenticity of the *Memoir, see Ibid.*, pp. 474-494.

Americans. A chief of a Wabash tribe tendered Clark the assistance of one hundred warriors, but this offer was declined.

Meanwhile, Hamilton had been completely surprised when a few Americans under orders from Clark opened fire on the fort located at the outer edge of the town. He attributed the shots to drunken Indians, but on investigation it was learned that Clark had come. The siege of the fort quickly followed, the Americans and Frenchmen having thrown up an intrenchment within two hundred yards of the gate. In the darkness, small squads of men under cover of the houses were able to advance to within thirty yards of the walls. The firing continued throughout the night. The British cannon were located on the second floor of the block-houses, so high as to afford but slight protection. So accurate was the aim of the backwoodsmen firing through the port-holes that a number of gunners were killed or wounded.

At daybreak a "very smart fire of small arms" was begun on the American works and one man was wounded. At nine o'clock, Clark sent a messenger to the fort demanding its surrender and while awaiting the reply his followers ate their first regular meal within a week.

"They were not disposed to be awed into action unworthy of British subjects," was Hamilton's answer, and the firing was resumed. At the end of two hours Lieutenant Helm approached the American lines under a flag of truce. The British, he was instructed to say, were prepared to capitulate under honorable terms. The reply could not be misinterpreted: "Col. Clarks compliments to Mr. Hamilton, and begs leave to inform him that Col. Clark will not agree to any other terms than that of Mr. Hamiltons surrendering himself and Garrison prisoners at discretion. If Mr. Hamilton is desirous of a conference with Col. Clark he will meet him at the Church with Capt. Helm!" [18]

At this meeting, epochal in its effects on our national history, Hamilton strove for modification of the ultimatum. But Clark proved obdurate. Terms were quickly drawn by which

---

[18] "Bowman's Journal," *Clark Papers*, p. 161.

the fort with all stores was to be delivered up and the garrison was to march out as prisoners-of-war. On the morning of the twenty-fifth, the garrison of seventy-nine men was received at the fort entrance by two companies of troops drawn up under Captains Bowman and McCarty.

As Clark entered the fort the American flag was run up and a salute of thirteen guns was fired. Clark was surprised to find that this fort, now renamed Patrick Henry, mounting twelve guns, with ample stores of ammunition and garrisoned by trained soldiers, had been surrendered so readily. Its capture marks the climax of one of the most heroic achievements in history. The boldness of the plan, the skill with which it was executed, and the perseverance manifested in overcoming obstacles seemingly insurmountable, excited the admiration even of Hamilton.[19]

Courage born of desperation was manifested by men and leaders alike, for all were fully conscious that failure would mean the loss not alone of the Illinois but of the entire trans-Allegheny country. Within a year, the authority of Virginia over the region stretching from the Ohio to the Illinois River and 140 miles up the Wabash had been established by conquest.

The goods captured from the British were divided among Clark's followers, the officers receiving nothing except a few articles of clothing, the soldiers getting "almost rich." Included in the large quantity of military stores, much needed by Clark, were a 6-pound brass field-gun, two iron four pounders and two swivels.

Fifty men, most of them French militia under Captain Helm, were sent up the Wabash with the object of intercepting a party of British bringing stores from Ouiatanon. Seven boats heavily laden with provisions and Indian supplies valued at $50,000 were captured and the forty men constituting the crews were made prisoners.

Four days after the capture of Fort Sackville the *Willing* arrived. A messenger from Williamsburg who was on board

---

[19] Hamilton's report, July 6, 1781, *Clark Papers*, p. 207.

brought to Clark and his men the thanks of the Virginia Legislature for their victory at Kaskaskia and a promise of some suitable reward. Twenty-six of the prisoners, including Hamilton and seven of his officers, were sent under guard to Williamsburg where, because of his alleged incitement of the Indians to take scalps, Hamilton was kept in close confinement. Toward the end of the Revolution he was exchanged for Captain Willing.

In his treatment of the French volunteers who had accompanied the British, excellent judgment was shown by Clark. Great was their rejoicing upon finding that instead of being imprisoned they were to be given their freedom after taking the oath of neutrality. For their return to Detroit they were provided with boats, arms, and provisions. Any property remaining was to be sold for their benefit. Thus, French interest in the American cause was advanced. "I after this," Clark writes, "had Spies disguised as traders, constant to and from Detroit. I learnt they answered every purpose that I could have wished for, by prejudicing their friends in favour of America." The hope for American success was openly expressed and a celebration lasting three days followed the announcement of Hamilton's defeat.

In fact, the capture of Detroit was the next step contemplated. To the paroled prisoners Clark asserted that he would arrive at that post nearly as soon as they. In his message to Captain Richard Lernoult, officer in command, he writes: "I learn by your letter to Govr Hamilton that you were very busy making new works, I am glad to hear it, as it saves the Americans some expense in building."

Two British subordinate expeditions in the West likewise failed as a result of Vincennes. One of these from Michillimackinac, led by Captain Charles Langlade, on its way to attack the Illinois posts, upon arriving at "Milwakee" was forced to return. Gautier, with a force of two hundred Indians, advancing over the Fox-Wisconsin route in order to join Hamilton, after the taking of Kaskaskia, had reached the mouth of

THE FATE OF THE WEST

Rock River. Learning of Hamilton's defeat, he made his way back to Green Bay as rapidly as possible.

At Detroit there was great consternation on the part of the British due to the expectation of Clark's early arrival.[20] Request was made for reinforcements from Niagara. Provisions were scarce owing to the large quantities used for the Vincennes expedition. Indians tributary to Detroit were panic-stricken as shown in their demands for troops and cannon for their protection. "So situated," wrote General Haldimand, Commander of Canada, "it will require great judgment and temper to preserve the Indians in our interest after so glaring and recent a proof of our want of strength or want of conduct. . . . Whenever they do quit us the valuable Fur Trade will immediately be lost to Great Britain." "I find the burthen heavy without assistance," writes Captain Lernoult, commander at Detroit. "It requires, I confess superior abilities and a better constitution. . . . I beg leave to repeat to you the necessity of reenforcement being sent, as the consequences may be fatal." Major Arent de Peyster was convinced that Michillimackinac, poorly defended as it was, would be surrendered with the capture of Detroit although a single man should not be sent to take it. He was mystified by a report in which Clark declared that he was preparing also for an advance against that post.

The Indian problem now claimed Clark's attention. Chiefs of the Piankashaw, Kickapoo, and Miami who had remained faithful to the American cause came early to assure him of their fidelity. He "Extol'd them to the skies for their manly behavior and fidelity." In council, he gave due regard to ceremonial, strengthened the chain of friendship by smoking the sacred pipe, exchanged belts of wampum, and provided provisions and taffia with which they were "to make merry" at their frolics. With cleverness, he disabused them of the thought which had been implanted by Hamilton that in the event of victory by the Virginians the lands of friends and foes

[20] *Draper MSS.*, 58J9.

alike would be taken. To show the falsity of this position, Clark refused to accept from them a present of land two and one half leagues square. "I made," he states, "a very long speech to them in the Indian manner. . . . Told them that we claimed no Land in their Country; that the first Man that offered to take their Lands by Violence must strike the tomahawk in my head; that it was only necessary that I should be in their Country during the War and keep a fort in it to drive off the English, who had a design against all People." [21] The treaty was then concluded to the satisfaction of both parties.

In conference with the Chippewa and other Indians who had accompanied Hamilton and who came to beg for mercy, Clark was the complete master. "The capture of Hamilton," he said, "was a sufficient confirmation to the Indians of everything I had formerly said to them and gave the greatest weight to the speeches I intended to send them; expecting that I should shortly be able to fulfill my threats with a body of troop sufficient to penetrate into any part of their Country; and by reducing Detroit bring them to my feet."

Messages sent the tribes immediately tributary to Detroit were well calculated to neutralize any effort which might be made on the part of the British to induce them to undertake new expeditions. Whether they chose the peace-belt or the war-belt was of little consequence, they were told, "for the Big Knives' greatest glory was in war and they were in search of enemies since the English were no longer able to contend against them."

British leaders, in like fashion, strove to arouse the Indians for defense. The appeal of Major de Peyster before a council of chiefs, he afterward formed into a lengthy rhymed chronicle in which he says:

> I know you have been told by Clark,
> His riflemen ne'er miss the mark;
> In vain you hide behind a tree,
> If they your finger's tip can see,—
> The instant they have got their aim

[21] "Mason Letter," *Clark Papers*, p. 147.

Enrolls you on the list of lame.
But, then, my sons, this boaster's rifles,
To those I have in store, are trifles;
If you but make the tree your mark
The ball will twirl beneath the bark,
'Till it one-half the circle find,
Then out and kill the man behind.

. . . .

Suppose awhile his threats prove true,
My children! What becomes of you?
Your sons,—your daughters,—and your wives—
Must they be hacked with these big knives?
Sure you have heard the aged tell,
How Ferdinand and Isabelle
Their empty coffers filled with gold?
The story makes my blood run cold!—
Their war-chiefs hunted down with hounds,
And covered o'er with ghastly wounds
All such as did not dare oppose
The first invasion of their foes.[22]

Such were the preliminaries in a movement which Clark confidently anticipated would result in the gaining of Detroit, his main objective.

[22] *Wis. Hist. Coll's.*, XVIII, 377–390.

CHAPTER XI

DETROIT LOST FOR WANT OF A FEW MEN

THE area of Clark's activities had been extended by Governor Henry beyond that defined in his original instructions so as to include the "Enemy's Settlements above or across," as he might think best. With Detroit in his possession, the whole Northwest would be under his control and in the execution of this objective, as Clark later declared, "My very soul was wrapt." Indeed, he did not doubt the success of his plans for taking that post. The time seemed ripe, for his followers, including the French militia, were eager for the expedition—"We could now augment our forces in this quarter to about four hundred men as near half the Inhabitants of St. Vincens would join us. Kentuck we knew could immediately furnish perhaps 200 men as there was a certainty of their receiving a great addition of settlers in the spring." News had been received also of the arrival at Kaskaskia of Captain George from New Orleans with Willing's followers and additional contributions from Pollock.

Before setting out for Kaskaskia Clark provided for a government at Vincennes through the appointment of Captain Helm to take control of all civil matters and to serve as Superintendent of Indian Affairs. The garrison of forty men, carefully selected, was commanded by Lieutenant Richard Brashears. A message was forwarded to John Bowman, county lieutenant in Kentucky, urging him to begin the immediate enlistment of men and the collection of provisions for the drive against Detroit.

Six boats, on March 20, bearing the eighty men accompanying Clark, pushed off down the Wabash for their return to Kaskaskia. The thought among the villagers who had gathered to wish them a "good and safe passage" found expression by one of their number: "Although a handful in comparison to other armies, they have done themselves and the cause they were fighting for, credit and honor, and deserve a place in History for future ages; that posterity may know the difficulty their forefathers had gone through for their liberty and freedom. Particularly the back Settlers of Virginia may bless the day they sent out such a Commander and officers, men." [1] When the boats reached Kaskaskia, "Great Joy" was manifested by the garrison, then commanded by Captain Robert George. The villagers were no less gratified at the return of Clark, for although at times they became restive under his stern discipline, he was the one American who gained and continued to hold their confidence.

The problems and disappointments he was to meet during the ensuing three months were among the most trying of his entire career. He found the people greatly excited over the recent conduct of some Delaware warriors. Learning also of depredations committed at Vincennes by another party, as a warning to the other tribes, he ordered a ruthless war against the marauders. In the attacks upon their villages, no mercy was shown except for the women and children, and the chiefs soon sued for peace.

Now he was to learn, in a communication from Pollock, that his credit at New Orleans was exhausted. "I am sorry to inform you that all the last Bills you drew upon me which came down by Monsieur Perreau [Perrault] & others is under protest for want of funds. This I Suppose cannot surprise you when I assure you I have never received a Single Dollars worth to pay them or even a Scrap of advice from yourself; the Hon[ble] Congress or the State of Virginia about them. This being the case you'll Naturally Conclude its out of my power to pay such heavy Sums without Money particularly now having already advanced every Dollar I could Raise. . . . Therefore it is in Vain for you to draw any more bills untill you are assured I have received Funds from some quarter to pay them." [2]

[1] *Clark Papers,* p. 611.
[2] *Draper MSS.,* 49J6.

Twenty-five thousand dollars in orders drawn on Pollock, by Clark, were under protest at New Orleans. They represented, in part, the expense incident to fitting out the expedition against Vincennes, and in furnishing supplies for the Kaskaskia garrison. While borrowing money on his own credit, Pollock had promoted the shipment of arms, Indian goods, taffia, and sugar to the Illinois country, hoping to receive, in exchange, cargoes made up of flour, and deer, beaver, and otter skins. Continental currency had but recently appeared in the West and in his efforts to sustain this money at par, Pollock continued, until July, 1779, to pay "Boatmen and Traders silver dollars for Paper Currency Dollar for Dollar." In this process, he became the possessor of currency amounting to $8,470, which because of its worthlessness at New Orleans he kept under seal.

Aware of the situation, traders from the East rushed to the Illinois country where goods might be procured with these certificates at their face value. They brought such large sums and distributed the money so liberally in trade, especially in securing provisions which they hoped to dispose of to the army, that merchants became alarmed and then refused to accept it. Describing the problems with which he was confronted growing out of depreciated currency, Clark declared: "There is one circumstance very distressing, that of our own moneys being discredited, to all intents and purposes by the great number of traders who come here in my absence each outbidding the other, giving prices unknown in this country by five hundred per cent, by which the people conceived it to be of no value, and both French and Spaniards refused to take a farthing of it."

Washington at the same time was urging that some effectual method should be found to restore the credit of the Continental currency—"The depreciation of it is got to so alarming a point that a wagon-load of money will scarcely purchase a wagon-load of provisions." [3]

By July, 1779, Pollock was in dire distress. His letters, num-

[3] Jay, *Correspondence and Public Papers*, I, 208.

bering twenty-one, to the Committee of Congress, had brought no response. "No accounts from your quarter," he writes, "excepting new demands from above [Illinois] . . . tho' in the height of these disappointments there's nothing gives me pain or uneasiness but that of not hearing from you, particularly on hearing of Capt. Bethell & Capt. Wilson being the other day at Havana direct from your place and not honored with even a line." [4]

A few days preceding the date of this letter, the Committee had broken silence but their message brought little reassurance to Pollock—"It gives us pain when we reflect on the many difficulties you have labored under by your exertions for the public Cause, and be assured Sir, our utmost endeavor shall be used for your speedy relief." [5]

They were powerless to assume this obligation, however, until, as they wrote, the

new wheat is manufactured of which we have had this season the finest Crops, both as to quality and quantity, that has been known for many years. Indeed the crops of the preceding Year were not only scant, but the wheat of Maryland and Virginia was infected by a fly, that rendered a great [part] thereof unfit for use. This added to the great supplies for our armies, together with the necessity we were under of largely supplying the Count D'Estaings, [fleet] at Boston, obliged the States to lay an Embargo on all provisions, which we now expect will soon be removed upon the arrival of new flour at our Market, when we shall exert ourselves in shipping large quantities to New Orleans, and we think with you that it will be safest via Havanna where it may be reshipped to you in Spanish bottoms, provided there is no rupture between that Court and Great Britain, and that it be admitted by the Spanish Governor, whose permission it will be necessary for us previously to obtain.

Immediate relief through any funds which were then available to the Committee was even more hopeless. In fact, the utter helplessness of the general government is well portrayed in this same communication—"By your Letter of the 15th.

[4] July 27, 1779. *Pollock Letters.*
[5] July 19, 1779. *Ibid.*

December, we learn that you had purchased the Brigantine Minerva for 2000 pistoles for which you have drawn on us in favor of Captain Joseph Faribault. This bill has not yet appeared, and when it does it will not be in our power to honour that, as well as that drawn in favour of Captain Joseph Connand and Joseph Calvert, for the reasons already assigned unless they will receive our Current Paper Money at the present governing Exchange, i. e. Six paper dollars for one Spanish, and this they declined, as the Paper Money is of no use to them out of these States; we must therefore desire you to settle with them at New Orleans." [6] Because of a lack of vessels available for the use of the general government, Pollock had not only assumed the burden of purchasing the *Minerva,* but he paid 2,100 pistoles to fit her out for sailing. He provided also for a cargo of sugar, salt, and taffia consigned to the Committee to be taken on at Havana at a cost of 1,378 pistoles. He was then obligated to pay, within a month, $56,000 for the United States, "a sum which it will be impossible for me to clear without Some Speedy Relief."

In spite of what Pollock calls his old story, "that he has no funds or orders from his Court for that purpose," Galvez advanced an additional $11,000. Thus Pollock's immediate needs were, in part, satisfied. For this loan, he was forced to pay 10 per cent interest and to allow the Spanish treasurer an additional 6 per cent. "You may imagine how agreeable I am situated," Pollock wrote on receiving an ultimatum from the governor, "that I shall not call upon him for any more."

How futile, likewise, had been his appeals for assistance from Virginia may be gathered from his numerous messages to Governor Henry. In one we find: "But now I am obliged to stop, having thoroughly exerted my abilities in every circumstance whatever that offered in this part of the world since the beginning of the war, particularly since the arrival here of Capt. George Gibson in October 1776 down to this day of which I have frequently wrote you. But am sorry to be

---

[6] The bills in favor of Calvert and of Connand, amounting to $4,000, represented purchases of supplies for the United States.

obliged to inform you that I have never been honored even with a single line from the Executive Power of your State. However I hope there is a good time coming." In another letter, he asserts that it would take some volumes to describe how he had hitherto supported the credit of Virginia.

At this time he was enabled, by mortgaging a part of his landed estate, to meet a further order from Governor Henry for goods amounting to $10,000. Flour and meal which had been promised had not been forwarded and he had already met bills drawn on Virginia to the amount of $33,000. Thus he described the situation:

> Being already drained of every shilling I could raise for the use of your's and the rest of the United States, I went first to the Governor of this place, and then to every merchant in it, but could not prevail upon any of them to supply said goods, giving for their reason the few goods they had here imported, would in all probability become double the value of what they were just now, particularly at this juncture as war between Spain and Great Britain was daily expected, and the little probability there was of getting paid from your Quarter in any reasonable time, by depending only on the Letter of Credit & Mr. Lindsay's Contract. In fine, finding it impracticable to obtain any by that means, and at the same time being fearfull of the bad consequences that might attend your being disappointed in those goods, I have voluntarily by mortgaging part of my property for the payment at the latter end of this year, purchased the greatest part of them from a Mr. Solomon. You have therefore Invoice & Bill of Loading amounting to 10,029 Dollars 1 Rial.[7]

In corroboration of this statement, we find the messenger from Virginia declaring: "Government goods cannot be had here [New Orleans], on any terms whatsoever without the Cash laid down and then they are extremely high. I should not have been able to obtain one Bail of Blankets in this place from any Merchant here had not Mr. Pollock mortgaged his own Property." In due time, the cargo arrived at Kaskaskia.

Was Pollock to charge the bills drawn on him to the United States or to Virginia? No instructions had been received, but

[7] *Draper MSS.*, 49J60.

still hopeful after the lapse of three years, he writes, in no spirit of the cynic, however, "I suppose I shall be fully instructed in due time."

The twelfth of May, 1779, was a red-letter day in the annals of the old Northwest, for on that day Clark assembled the villagers of Kaskaskia at the door of their church to hear the proclamation of the new government. During the previous December, the legislature of Virginia passed a noteworthy act establishing the county of Illinois, which included all the inhabitants of Virginia north of the Ohio River. The establishment of some form of government was thought expedient, for, as stated: "From their remote situation, it may at this time be difficult, if not impracticable, to govern them by the present laws of this Commonwealth, until proper information, by intercourse with their fellow citizens, on the east side of the Ohio, shall have familiarized them to the same." [8] This type of government had already been brought into general usage by Virginia in the process of westward expansion.

The formalities of the occasion must have been viewed with astonishment by the French inhabitants. Clark, as presiding officer, assured them that they were to become partakers in the liberty enjoyed by Americans and that the new government was one of such kindliness that they would bless the day they had decided to favor the cause of America! [9] He then introduced his good friend, Colonel John Todd, Jr., with whom he had been intimately associated in Kentucky and who was now to assume the office of county lieutenant for Illinois. In the instructions issued by Governor Henry, all Virginia troops in the county were to be under the command of Clark, while Todd was to be in control of civil affairs. They were to cooperate in using their best efforts in cultivating and conciliating the affections of the French and Indians. The rights of the inhabitants were to be secured against any infractions by the troops and any person attempting to violate the property of the Indians was to be punished. Particularly, they were solic-

---

[8] Hening, *Statutes at Large*, IX, 552. Act of Establishment.
[9] For Clark's introductory remarks, *see Life of Clark*, p. 160.

DETROIT LOST

ited to prevent all Indian raids on Kentucky and to maintain friendly relations with the Spaniards.

John Todd was well prepared to assume the duties of county lieutenant. Beyond having a good general education, he had studied law; had seen service in Dunmore's War; and had served as delegate from Kentucky in the Virginia House of Burgesses. The well-chosen language used in his inaugural address was full of promise for the success of the new government and served to renew the enthusiasm of his hearers for the French-American alliance:

> Gentlemen [he said], I am sent by the government of Virginia to exercise the duties of chief magistrate of this county. The Republic of Virginia has had only noble motives in coming here. It was not moved by the love of conquest but has come to invite you to participate with her citizens in the blessing of a free and equal independence and to be governed and judged by officers who shall be placed in power by the people.
>
> Your great distance from the Capital, gentlemen, does not permit you to send representatives to the assembly; but if in the future it happens that for your welfare or to avoid loss you prefer such representation, I have it in my instructions to assure you that it will not be refused you.[10]

Under this form of government, the county lieutenant, who was the chief executive, was empowered at his discretion to appoint deputy commandants, militia officers, and commissaries. Civil officers, whose duties were to administer the laws already in vogue, were to be chosen by the citizens of the several districts. Officers with new duties were to be supported by the State, others by the people. Pardoning power was vested in the county lieutenant in all criminal cases save murder and treason. The inhabitants were to be protected in all of their religious, civil and property rights.

In the election of the six judges, which followed, the voters exercised, for the first time, their rights as citizens of a republican government. Two members of the court were also selected at Prairie du Rocher and one at St. Philippe. Gabriel Cerré,

---

[10] *Cahokia Records,* p. lix.

outstanding French leader, who had, as we have seen, generously assisted in furthering the American cause, was placed at the head of this court. "From the great Confidence reposed in your Judgment and Integrity by the good people of Kaskaskia and its dependencies and agreeably to an act of the General Assembly of Virginia," so their commission reads, "you are hereby constituted and appointed Justices of the Peace for the District of Kaskaskia and Judges of the Court of the said District in cases both Civil and Criminal."[11] Todd likewise appointed a sheriff and a states attorney. Elections of judges for the districts of Cahokia and Vincennes followed shortly and resulted, as at Kaskaskia, in the selection of Frenchmen. French law was retained, although it was slightly modified by the law of Virginia. Trial by jury was permitted and seems to have been required in criminal cases.

Within a few days, the clash of interests appeared, when Todd was called upon to hear a recital of French grievances formulated by the Kaskaskia magistrates.

The soldiers, he was informed, had been killing the plow-oxen and milch cows for food without the consent of their owners. They protested that, contrary to French custom, liquor was being sold to the Indians and trade carried on with Negro slaves. The attitude of some of the Virginia officers made the administration of government more difficult. Captain Richard McCarty, who was in charge of the garrison at Cahokia, wrote a friend: "Colo. Todd's Residence here will spoil the people entirely for the Inhabitants no more Regard us than a parcel of Slaves. . . . I think it would be a happy thing could we get Colo. Todd out of the Country for he will positively sett the Inhabitants and us by the Ears."[12]

Conflicts between these two types of people could scarcely have been averted. They differed in language, in manners, and in religion and such fundamental differences would have produced clashes even in a better-organized society. Moreover, the American troops and the French people were suffering

[11] *Cahokia Records*, p. lxi.
[12] *Ibid.*, p. 616.

from a lack of necessary food and clothing. At Kaskaskia and Cahokia, the dissatisfied troops were daily deserting and the garrison at Vincennes was without salt.

Fearful that adventurers and speculators would get possession of the rich bottom lands as they had done in Kentucky through violation of the Virginia land laws, Todd decreed that no new settlements should be made on the flat lands "unless in manner and form as heretofore made by the French inhabitants." Little heed was paid to this legislation by some of the Americans who flocked to this region, and within a short time it was completely nullified. Grants of land were easily procured from the Indians by adventurers, representing merchants in Philadelphia, London, and Virginia. One of the smaller grants procured in this fashion contained a million acres.[13]

The value of the currency was uncertain and rapidly decreasing. Prices of provisions were trebled within two months. This problem was made more complicated because of counterfeit money which despite drastic legislation was in general circulation.[14] French merchants began also to make formal protest of bills of exchange drawn by Clark on Oliver Pollock, but the proposal to take them up in Virginia paper money was refused. Discontent, under these conditions, grew steadily worse, and Todd after three months of continuous turbulence wrote Governor Henry: "I expected to have been prepared to present to your excellency some Amendments upon the form of Government for Illinois, but the present will be attended with no great inconveniences till the Spring Session, when I beg your permission to attend and get a Discharge from an Office, which an unwholesome air, a distance from my connexions, a Language not familiar to me, and an impossibility of procuring many of the conveniences of Life suitable, all tend to render uncomfortable."[15] During the fall of 1779,

---

[13] *Clark Papers*, p. 357.
[14] For Todd's plan to meet the emergency, see *Life of Clark*, pp. 166, 167.
[15] *Chicago Hist. Soc. Coll's.*, IV, 319.

Todd returned to Kentucky, where he continued to be active in public affairs, serving as delegate from the County of Kentucky in the Legislature of Virginia and later becoming Colonel of Fayette County through appointment by Governor Thomas Jefferson.[16]

In the meantime, with Detroit uppermost in the minds of Clark and Todd, they were pushing preparations for an expedition against that post. "The Inhabitants of Illinois must not expect settled peace and safety," Todd's instructions read, "while their and our Enemies have footing at Detroit and can interrupt or stop the Trade of the Mississippi. If the English have not the strength or courage to come to war against us themselves, their practice has been and will be to hire the Savages to commit murder and depredations. Illinois must expect to pay in these a large price for her Freedom, unless, the English can be expelled from Detroit." [17]

The Detroit garrison consisted of scarcely one hundred men, and the fortifications were unfinished. The town and adjacent country contained some 2,500 inhabitants, two-thirds of them being males. In a survey, 138 slaves were enumerated, likewise 413 oxen, 779 cows, 664 horses, 313 sheep, 1,076 hogs, 619 steers and 141,500 pounds of flour besides wheat, Indian corn, oats and peas in goodly quantities.

Great enthusiasm for the expedition against Detroit was manifested on the part of officers, troops, and the French militia. At no time does Clark appear to better advantage than in the appeal which he made to the young men, many of whom had accompanied him against Vincennes, returning, as he said, "covered with laurels." Even the old men volunteered. Like enthusiasm was prevalent at Vincennes and supplies were soon collected.

In a letter to Pollock, Clark acknowledged that he was not surprised at finding his credit at New Orleans exhausted. "As for drawing any more bills on you," he said, "I have thought

---

[16] Kentucky territory was, in 1781, divided into the three counties; Kentucky, Fayette, and Jefferson.
[17] *Clark Papers,* p. 84.

it fruitless. Virginia State will never let you suffer long for what you have done." But faith in Pollock on the part of Vigo, Charles Gratiot and others among the French led them, in the emergency, to accept bills drawn on him by Clark to the amount of $5,000.

The arrival of Colonel John Montgomery from Virginia with a mere handful of men, not one-third the number expected, was Clark's first disappointment. He was still confident that Colonel John Bowman would join him at Vincennes with his Kentuckians. A company of cavalry under Captain Godfrey Linctot was dispatched up the Illinois River to secure the neutrality of the Potawatomi at St. Joseph and to cover the design of the main expedition against Detroit. Toward the end of June, Clark with another party of horsemen which British informants magnified to one or two thousand, marched to Vincennes, the place of rendezvous. The arrival of only thirty Kentucky volunteers was a severe blow to Clark. Colonel Bowman, desirous of winning honors for himself, had led an expedition numbering some three hundred men in a raid on some Shawnee villages in Ohio, which proved a failure.

To attempt the taking of Detroit with his available force of three hundred and fifty men, Clark knew would be futile. His disappointment found expression in these words: "Never was a person more mortified than I was at this time, to see so fair an opportunity to push a victory; Detroit lost for want of a few men."

But preparations for such an expedition proved of great significance. Evidence is clear that the conquest of the West would have been fully accomplished by July of 1779, immediately following the capture of Hamilton, had Clark's call for men been complied with. "If," exclaimed Joseph Bowman, second in command, "we could have had more men here then what we had there is no telling what we mought have done. But I am afraid that the Assembly has not thought this Country of so Great Importance as what it Raley is."

Over and again in face of such opposition and hardships as

they were compelled to meet, there must have come to these leaders, as well as to Pollock, the inquiry whether after all the sacrifice was not too great. But interpreting their most intimate letters, we find no hesitation on their part in making the choice between the cause for which they had enlisted and their own aggrandizement. "There mought," Bowman writes Clark, "have been a final Peace settled with the Indians by this time; and nothing but that alone Induces me to continue as long as what I have done, as I am Sensible that the acting in a Publick Capacity interfairs too much with our Private affairs."

Master of propaganda, Clark dispatched messages to the French at Detroit containing copies of the articles of alliance between France and the United States. "And no doubt," he said, "they will produce the desired effect." [18] It was reported by couriers that an army of two thousand well-armed Americans and French was prepared to march on that post. "Every effort is making to strengthen and complete our new Fort, as we are not, equal to oppose the passage of such numbers to this place," a Detroit officer declared. "Our ditch and glacee will be in a very good state the end of this week. An abatte [abatis] is afterwards to be thrown round. The barracks will be ready at the same time. I wish to God I could say the same of our well; it is now upwards of 60 feet below the level of the river and no appearance of water. . . . Could we only rely on the inhabitants or had they either the inclination or the resolution to defend their town there would be nothing to apprehend on that Head as we might then take the field."

French and Indians at Detroit were in a panic over the report which had been broadcast that the English, unable to withstand the effect of the alliance of the Americans, French, Spanish, and Germans would be driven out of America. Two expeditions sent from Michillimackinac to intercept the Americans, one comprising a force of some three hundred regulars, traders and Indians; the other numbering six hundred made up mainly of Indians; and a third of two hundred Indians led

---

[18] *Clark Papers*, p. 174.

DETROIT LOST

by Detroit officers, retreated in haste upon receiving the report that Clark was marching toward Detroit. A campaign against Vincennes and another against Fort Pitt were also abandoned. British control over the Indians was weakened, some of the tribes declaring their attachment for the Americans, and the Wabash tribes made overtures to Clark.

Washington had now recognized the necessity for taking Detroit and advised an expedition for that purpose either during the winter when the lake was frozen over or to delay until spring and meanwhile to collect supplies and information.

Clark resolved, for the time being, to take up a position at the Falls of the Ohio. From this post, he would be able to defend his conquests and at the same time could protect Kentucky where swarms of new settlers were arriving as a result of his successes. He further contemplated establishing a fort near the mouth of the Ohio River. This, as we have seen, had been advocated by Patrick Henry and was favored by Galvez as a means of facilitating intercourse with Pollock. From this post, the Chickasaw Indians might be controlled and deserters escaping down the River might here be apprehended. To protect American trading boats and stop the great "Concourse of Toryes and deserters that pass down the River to our Enemies," Clark had stationed an armed patrol at the junction of the Ohio and the Mississippi.

From the outset, Clark had found desertions one of his chief problems. His small force gathered at Corn Island for the march on Kaskaskia was depleted because of the escape during the night of the Holston men, stampeded through contemplation of an advance into the enemy country. In one of his early appeals to De Leyba, he writes: "I need not mention to you how great the encouragement for desertion when a soldier has only to cross the river to free himself from the service of his Country, without there is a stop put to it. I know that I am at Liberty to give up a deserter if I chuse, I doubt it is not the case with you which I expect will be detrimental to me as mine are Raw troops and must be often corrected. I don't suppose it will require much deliberation to give me an answer on that head." [19]

Officers at Fort Pitt were protesting the escape of men, enlisted as regulars, to New Orleans. We find one officer appealing to Pollock to serve as intermediary with Governor Galvez for the return of a purchasing agent who had made his escape with a horse, a Negro and eleven thousand pounds of currency. Clark urged upon Pollock that arms and clothing, the property of the States, should be taken from the deserters at Natchez and "other settlements in your Quarter." Among these requests, one calls for the arrest of soldiers who had brought a flat-boat loaded with corn, intended for the garrison, to New Orleans where the cargo was sold. Following Pollock's representation, Galvez was pleased to give all Spanish commandants orders "not to protect such American deserters for Reasons quoted in my Letter to his Majesty." [20]

Leaving small garrisons at Kaskaskia, Cahokia, and Vincennes, Clark set out for the Falls of the Ohio, arriving about the middle of September. Here he found that settlement on the mainland had gone forward rapidly. This region had been described by travelers as the richest under the sun. The soil it was said could not be surpassed; vast natural meadows furnished a range which seemed inexhaustible, and great herds of buffalo, elk, and deer were common. The impulse to secure land was so great that people in Virginia were reported to be "running mad for Kentucky."

By order of the county court, local government for the town, named Louisville, was established through the selection of trustees, seven in number. Magistrates were elected who were "to regulate the many Villanys and bring to justice all offenders." A clerk and a sheriff were elected and militia officers appointed. Trial by jury was likewise provided for. The town was to be laid off with regularity and rules for buildings were prescribed.

Had the plan submitted by Clark to the surveyors who were

[19] "Clark MSS.," *Va. Archives*.
[20] Pollock to Don Pedro Piernas, Copy in "Clark MSS.," *Va. Archives*.

engaged in planning the town been adopted, Louisville, we are told, would have been the most beautiful city on the continent.[21] There was included a reservation of land along the river-front to be used as a public park. The court-house lot was to contain two whole squares and from this center was to radiate a park half a square in breadth extending the whole length of the town.

In general, Kentucky hamlets comprised a stockade and one-story log cabins, with their clapboard roofs, puncheon floors, and small windows usually without glass, and chimneys carried up with "cats and clay" to the height of the ridge pole. Corn bread and hominy were the chief food, but turnips, beans, potatoes, pumpkins, and melons were grown. The corn was ground with great labor in hand-mills or was pounded in the cavity of a stump with a pestle attached to a sweep. Toward the close of 1779 a log dam was built at Harrodsburg and a pair of large hand-mill stones were placed in what was known as a tub-mill for grinding corn. Flax was grown, and the clothing made therefrom was in part substituted for that made from the skins of animals.

Among the pastimes were hunting, horse-racing, and wrestling. Drinking liquor was common and coarse jocularities were not frowned upon. Militia musters offered occasions for all sorts of sports. Religious forms other than teaching the catechism were generally neglected. While there was preaching in some of the communities earlier than 1783, that date marks the founding of a Presbyterian Church, the first in Kentucky. The Baptists, the Methodists, Episcopalians, and Roman Catholics established places of worship about the same time.

As the settlements increased in number, confusion arose over conflict of titles to the lands. Actual settlers petitioned the Virginia legislature for relief against the encroachment of speculators. "A constant war of four years," they declared, "has reduced many of us so low that we have scarce cattle enough amongst us to supply our families and many of us that

---

[21] *Draper MSS.*, 35J47.

brought good stocks of both horses and cows now at this juncture have not left so much as one cow for the support of our families. We have thought it proper to present you with a just estimation of our losses in settling and defending this extensive country. In the late act of the assembly in opening and establishing a land office many of the petitioners are not able to get as much as one hundred acres. Unless there is some redress, this must be the unhappy event that we must lie under the disagreeable necessity of going down the Mississippi to the Spanish protection or becoming tenants to private gentlemen who have men employed in this country at one hundred pounds per thousand for running round the lands." [22] By November, 1779, Kentuckians, having lost their fears of Indian raids, were again venturing to build cabins and take possession of their small tracts of land.[23]

Clark, in council with his officers, again took up the question of preparing for an expedition against Detroit. The reduction of West Florida was also a favorite topic for consideration since Pollock was continuously urging Clark to lead such an expedition. "The inhabitants at the latter [Natchez] is chiefly in our favour," he writes, "and in all probability will join you when an oppty offers. I heard of your departure for Detroit and fully and most sincerely wish you Success. I hope you'll do the business there time enough to pay us a Visit this fall, as that will be a fine time for your men to come down." [24] With the bearer of this letter, he sent two swivels ready for mounting.

In early October, the West suffered a disaster which strengthened the British and greatly affected warring tribesmen. Colonel David Rogers had come to New Orleans, as we have seen, with important messages from Governor Henry.[25] Assisted by Pollock, he was enabled with his men to make the perilous journey overland to St. Louis, the River being under the control of the British. At this post, he secured the goods

[22] *Draper MSS.*, 14S31.
[23] For a more extended account of economic and social conditions in Kentucky, see *Life of Clark*, pp. 177–183.
[24] *Draper MSS.*, 49J64.
[25] *See ante.*, p. 153.

and munitions which had been sent up by Pollock, consigned for the use of Virginia. Upon arriving at the Falls of the Ohio, Clark detailed an escort for the boats. A little beyond the present site of Cincinnati, they were surprised by a band of Indians under the renegade leader, Simon Girty. Thirteen men only of the seventy constituting the company escaped the massacre and among the victims was Colonel Rogers. In addition to the booty procured from two of the boats, important messages from Clark and Todd were taken. The third boat returned to Louisville, with its cargo of clothing, blankets and ammunition, thus giving much needed aid to Clark's troops.

A retaliatory expedition was demanded by Kentucky leaders, but owing to the more aggressive policy of the enemy, necessary supplies could not be collected before the coming of winter.

Kentucky annals refer to this as the hard winter—with snow covering the ground for three months and with the rivers frozen to the bottom. Thousands of buffalo, deer, and turkeys perished from the cold. Many settlers and numbers of immigrants on the Wilderness Road died of starvation and cold. "If we was only now in Old Virginia," a settler exclaims, "we could have something good to eat and drink but here we have nothing to eat in this dreary wilderness and we dont know when we shall have."

Suffering of the garrisons at the Illinois posts was equally severe. Colonel Montgomery wrote of Kaskaskia: "Everything animate and inanimate groans under a most unseportible Burden of a severe winter. Inhabitants has lost almost all their stocks for want of corn to feed them."[26] Fortunately, relief was furnished the troops through a further order drawn by Montgomery on Pollock to the amount of $6,400 and through the opportune arrival in the fall of a large bateau loaded with merchandise and taffia. This cargo had been forwarded by a friend of Pollock to his son with orders that he "should give all assistance and succor to any army or detachment belonging to the United States of America which he might meet with on

---

[26] "Clark Papers," *Missouri Historical Society* (St. Louis).

the Mississippi." [27] In keeping with this advice, Montgomery procured merchandise to the amount of $12,000 and in turn was enabled to obtain provisions for this amount. From the same source, John Todd supplied his troops with provisions, liquors, and "other necessaries" to the amount of $30,000. The arrival of a messenger dispatched by Pollock, brought the good news that American independence had been proclaimed at New Orleans; that a declaration of war between Spain and Great Britain was daily expected, and that an expedition, which he was to accompany, was about to set out against Manchac, Natchez and Pensacola. Such information served once more to arouse the enthusiasm of Clark and his associates for an advance against Detroit, the key to British operations in the Northwest.

"I make no doubt that he [Galvez] will soon reduce the British Troops, Tories and Savages, in this part of the World," was Pollock's optimistic message to Congress. What its effect must have been may be conjectured as we consider the crisis in Eastern affairs described by Washington two months earlier: "If Britain should be able to make a vigorous campaign in America this summer, in the present depreciation of our money, scantiness of supplies, want of virtue and want of exertion, 'tis hard to say what may be the consequence." [28]

While Clark was urging upon Virginia authorities the necessity for an advance against Detroit, conditions in the New Orleans sector were becoming of increasing importance.

[27] "Clark MSS.," *Va. State Archives, Auditor's Reports*, p. 46.
[28] Jay, *Correspondence*, I, 210.

CHAPTER XII

CONTROL OF THE LOWER MISSISSIPPI

BRITISH leaders, from the opening of the Revolution, were aware of the attitude of Spain toward the colonial cause, but they waited for some overt act. "Though I have no doubt this minute of the existence of a Spanish as well as a French war," Hamilton wrote while in possession of Vincennes, "yet I have as yet, no accounts by which I may venture to act on the offensive against the subjects of Spain, which I ardently desire, as there would be so little difficulty in pushing them entirely out of the Mississippi." Three weeks later, he wrote Galvez protesting against the sale of gunpowder to the Rebels and orders were to be enforced for intercepting, at Natchez, all supplies for Americans which might be sent up the River from New Orleans.[1]

The prize ultimately sought by Spain was not the trade of the Mississippi alone, so generously proffered by Governor Henry, but the possession of the entire valley. Pollock was fully aware of this attitude. Over and again he appealed to the Committee of Congress, to Patrick Henry and to George Rogers Clark for an expedition against the British possessions on the Mississippi and the Gulf of Mexico. Had his advice been heeded, there need not have followed those years of diplomatic controversy between Spain and the United States relating to the free navigation of the Mississippi River and the possession of West Florida.

Engaged in fitting out in warlike manner the prize ship *Morris,* so named in honor of his friend Robert Morris, a vessel of which he was justly proud, Pollock writes:

[1] *Canadian Archives* (1882), p. 26.

She will mount 16 six pounders upon one deck, 2 Bow and 2 stern chasers, 8 four pounders upon her quarter deck with swivels etc. She sails well and I expect to have her completely fitted out with about one hundred and fifty men on board in about two months ready for sea by which time I expect your orders with respect to her destination or cruize from this place. But my present view is to keep her in readiness to take Sylph sloop of war which is now about twenty leagues above this town on her way to Manchac at which place I am informed she is to stay to protect them. This will be absolutely necessary to have done in order to keep the navigation of this River clear particularly if you have a demand for more goods up this River and should make the expedition against it and Pensacola, she may become a valuable acquisition.[2]

He urged the Committee to send an expedition against Natchez, defended at that time by a force of 200 men, and against Manchac, having only one half that number. From 800 to 1,000 men, including Indians, constituted the British defense. One thousand Americans would be adequate, he thought, to clear the River of the enemy, and with 3,000, Pensacola could be captured—"But Pensacola is the principal object and if you should determine on this, lose no time in acquainting me that I may have everything wanted ready for that Purpose. I shall have letters lodged for the Commanding Officer at the Arcansas acquainting him with every particular for his Government."

Clark's expedition against the Illinois posts was interpreted by Pollock as a stage toward the conquests to be made on the lower Mississippi. Indeed, rumors were current that three hundred men were descending the River for an attack on Natchez. With Manchac also in the possession of the Americans, Pollock would be free to continue supplying goods for Clark's use.

"I hope," he writes Clark, "on or before the arrival of this Party you'll have it in your Power to open the communication on the Mississippi to this place. . . . Should this or the Expedition against Pensacola take place I hope you'll give me the

[2] July 8, 1778, *Pollock Letters*.

CONTROL OF THE LOWER MISSISSIPPI 193

earliest Intelligence possible for my Government here as I have it in my power to be of infinite Service on the Occasion, provided I have only timely notice." [3] His advice by special messenger was of similar import: "Acquaint the commanding Officer [Clark] of the necessity of opening the communication on this River and taking possession of the country immediately before war should be declared between Great Britain and Spain by which the latter will save us that trouble and in consequence we will lose a valuable conquest which might now be easily obtained." [4] Following the capture of Vincennes, Clark replied that while an expedition against the Floridas had been contemplated, it was not then possible because of the small force under his command.

Early in 1779, the offer of Spain to mediate had been unceremoniously rejected by the British ministry. The Spanish ambassador quit London without formal leave-taking and the Spanish king, in spite, as he claimed, of countless efforts to preserve peace and his attempts to maintain rigid neutrality, determined to join his nephew, the King of France, in the struggle against Great Britain. Great Britain was accused of insulting the Spanish flag and seizing Spanish ships; of exciting the Indians to attack Spanish settlements, and of attempting to get possession of the Bay of Honduras. Contraband goods had been carried by English traders, and since no satisfaction could be gained for these acts, the protection of Spanish subjects as well as the dignity of Spain demanded that such insults should be repelled. A treaty between France and Spain having been agreed upon, the formal declaration of war quickly followed. Among the Spanish objectives specified in the treaty were: to regain Gibraltar, acquire the river and fort of Mobile, Pensacola, and all the coast of Florida along the Bahama channel; the expulsion of the English from the Bay of Honduras, and the restitution of the Island of Minorca.

Frequent reports had come to Galvez that the British posts on the lower Mississippi were being strengthened by the ar-

[3] *Pollock Letters*, August 8, 1778.
[4] *Ibid.*, August 20, 1778.

rival of veteran troops.⁵ Toward the close of July he learned that war had been declared by Spain. "By beat of drum," on August 20, the independence of the American States was proclaimed at New Orleans. Nine days later, specific directions were received by the Spanish governor for driving the English from the Gulf of Mexico and the neighborhood of Louisiana, "freeing us by that means from the disadvantages which are caused to our commerce and the continued dangers in which their ambitious designs hold us." ⁶

Appointment as the leader of the Spanish forces was welcomed by Galvez. The selection was a wise one, for he possessed an intimate knowledge of the country and was energetic and self-confident. Moreover, he had, from the outset, established, as we have seen, friendly relations with Pollock and through him with the Committee of Congress, and had won the good-will of the Indians accessible to New Orleans. A plan for operations against Pensacola was already in hand. It was based on knowledge recently secured by his adjutant major, Captain Panis, while on a visit to that post.⁷ While his mission was ostensibly to discuss the points at issue with Governor Chester, Panis proceeded to carry out the secret and more important part of his mission which pertained to the investigation of the resources of the British at Pensacola. At both Mobile and Pensacola, he found the fortifications to be in a state of decay, but at Pensacola because of the Willing raid there was feverish haste to put everything in condition for defense.

In submitting his plan for a campaign, Galvez followed in principle the report of Panis which recommended the sending from Havana of four thousand troops and a naval force comprising two ships of the line together with six frigates, a number of small armed boats in addition to necessary transports.

⁵ Supplement to the *"Madrid Gazette"* del Viernes 14 de Enero de 1780. The original is in possession of the Chicago Historical Society.

⁶ Kathryn T. Abbey, Doctoral Dissertation, *Florida as an Issue During the American Revolution*, MS., p. 105.

⁷ On March 2, 1778, Captain Panis arrived at Mobile and a few days later proceeded to Pensacola. By July 5, he was back in New Orleans and submitted his report to Galvez.

CONTROL OF THE LOWER MISSISSIPPI

One thousand men were to accompany him from New Orleans.

Meanwhile, in spite of an adverse decision by his Council which recommended preparations for defense only, Galvez determined, with such a force as might be available, to carry out immediately his secret design against the Mississippi posts. Manchac was his first objective.

Preparations were well under way when a hurricane swept over New Orleans and along the River with such destructiveness as to cause general consternation throughout the whole province. In the wake of the storm were the wrecks of many dwellings in the town, and up and down the River, on both banks for a distance of forty miles, crops were ruined and stock killed.

Unfortunately for the plan of Pollock, the *Morris,* now ready to be sent against the enemy, was sunk. Of this blow, he writes:

> I am extremely sorry to inform you of losing the ship Morris at this levée by a hurricane that happened here and which has destroyed a great part of this town and sunk several of the King's galleys and other vessels in this River. In short the scene was too distressing for me to describe on paper. I and my family as well as many others had a narrow escape for our lives. I saved all my books and papers which were the only articles in my house I could keep dry. All the ship's crew (except eleven who were unfortunately drowned) got saved on the wreck and were picked up about three leagues below this Town. This is a most unlucky circumstance for this Government and particularly to myself after all my trouble and vexation of mind, and expense in fitting out this ship, and just now, when I had her ready and a channel opened to commence hostilities against the English at this Place, to lose her in the critical moment.[8]

In the midst of this desolation, and with New Orleans defenseless, Galvez demonstrated his capacity as a leader. He determined to renew preparations for attacking the British posts on the River, which had not suffered from the storm. His appeal to the inhabitants convened in the Place d'Armes met

[8] To the Committee, August 25, 1779. *Pollock Letters.*

with enthusiastic approval. As interpreted by Pollock, the response was due to the announcement of "our Independancy" and as a token of their confirmation of Galvez as governor. "Gentlemen," said Galvez, "I cannot avail myself of my commission, without previously swearing before the Cabildo, that I shall defend the province; but although I am disposed to shed the last drop of my blood for Louisiana and for my King, I cannot take an oath which I may be exposed to violate, because I do not know whether you will help me in resisting the ambitious designs of the English. Shall I take the oath of Governor? Shall I swear to defend Louisiana? Will you stand by me, and conquer or die with your governor and your King?"[9] "For the defence of Louisiana, and for the service of the king, we tender you our lives," was the enthusiastic response, "and we would say our fortunes, if we had any remaining."

With his designs still secret, having provided for the defense of New Orleans, Galvez set out for Manchac on the morning of August 27, 1779. His force consisted of 170 veterans and 330 recruits. Nine American volunteers "under the banner of America," with Pollock serving as personal *aide* to Galvez, accompanied the expedition. Eighty free Negroes and Mulattoes were taken along to assist in artillery service and engineering. On the march, recruits of various conditions and colors, including 160 Indians, were gained at the German and Acadian settlements, at Point Coupeé, and elsewhere. Thus, a force of some 1,400 was ultimately marshaled. Because of disease and the fatigue of the march, not more than two-thirds of this number were fit for duty.

A surprise assault upon Fort Bute (Manchac) was begun on the morning of September 7th. There was no defense since the main force of the British had withdrawn to Baton Rouge, which was regarded as a more advantageous position.[10]

After a rest of six days, Galvez resumed the march toward this post sixty miles distant. Here the enemy was well fortified and defended by a force of four hundred regulars and one hun-

---

[9] Gayarré, *op. cit.*, III, 124.
[10] *La. Hist., Quart.*, XII, 263, 264. Caughey, *op. cit.*, 155.

CONTROL OF THE LOWER MISSISSIPPI 197

dred militia. Approaches from the River, offering the possibility of aid, were cut off. Of two possible courses, starvation of the garrison or an immediate assault, Galvez chose the latter. After an artillery duel lasting many hours, the fort was dismantled and articles of capitulation were submitted, September 21. The terms of surrender included giving up Fort Panmure and Natchez.

That Natchez had been surrendered without sign of resistance was accomplished through the mediation of Pollock. A month earlier, he had written Clark: "The inhabitants at the latter [Natchez] are chiefly in our favor and in all probability will join you when an opportunity offers." [11]

Fort Panmure, difficult of access on a steep hill and defended by eighty regulars and a number of militia, might readily have withstood attack by a considerable force. Pollock's message to the inhabitants declares:

> Well knowing the glorious cause of the United States, I cannot express the joy and happiness I feel when I come to acquaint you that his Catholic Majesty, the King of Spain, has declared their Independence and also war against our Tyrannical Enemy, Great Britain. His Excellency, Don Bernardo de Galvez at the head of 1500 brave men is now in possession of this Fort and means to continue his route to your settlement. The Canal is now become common freedom and Liberty. All the subjects and well wishers of the American Cause are in Duty bound to give every assistance to his Most Catholic Majestys arms to reduce the Enemy and particularly those on this River who have been protected on every occasion by Governor Galvez since his arrival at New Orleans.[12]

They were assured of protection from the Indians by an adequate garrison and were to have full enjoyment of their religion. The subjects and friends of the United States were to receive the same price for their crop of tobacco as that paid to the inhabitants of Louisiana. In the event that it should ultimately remain Spanish territory, any individual disposed to leave the country to return to the United States was to be

[11] August 6, 1779. *Pollock Letters.*
[12] *Ibid.*

granted full permission to dispose of his lands and effects and go without molestation.

The inhabitants were now in a dilemma. A proclamation from General John Campbell, commanding officer at Pensacola, was received at the same time inviting them together with the Indians of the region to take up arms immediately in favor of the British. Colonel Dickson, officer in charge, agreed to surrender the fort and garrison and a special messenger sent by Pollock accompanied the Spanish officer to whom the fort was to be delivered.

During the progress of these events, General Campbell, with a force numbering one thousand men, one-third of them Pennsylvania and Maryland Loyalists, remained at Pensacola. His orders to make an attack on New Orleans and advance to Natchez where he was to be joined by troops from Canada were disregarded. As an excuse, the vessels at his disposal, it has been asserted, were sufficient to transport only a force of two hundred and fifty men. The coöperating force, as we shall see, was turned back at St. Louis.[13]

Summarizing the outcome, Galvez wrote: "It had so fortunate a result that with the loss of only one man and of two wounded, we have taken all the English settlements which they had on this river, with the three forts of Manchack, Baton Rouge, and Fort Panmure at Natchez, the first by assault, the second by capitulation and the third by evacuation in which we have killed men enough and made prisoners of about 550 men of the regular troops, including Colonel Dickson and 27 other officers, eight ships with various supplies and various smaller boats." As viewed by Pollock, these victories which gave control over 430 leagues of territory would facilitate the taking of Mobile and Pensacola.

Suitable rewards were granted the Spanish leaders who had rendered distinguished service, Galvez receiving the title, brigadier general. To Pollock was proffered by Galvez the title colonel in the Spanish Army, which he declined to accept.

[13] *Wis. Hist. Coll's.*, XI, 145, 147.

Before setting out on the expedition, Pollock had hurriedly arranged to transfer the officers and crew of the ill-starred *Morris* to a Spanish armed schooner assigned him as a good-will offering by Galvez. A number of English vessels, loaded with military stores destined for Manchac, were on Lake Pontchartrain. An English ship mounting sixteen guns was lying at Ship Island. The order given Captain William Pickles, who was placed in command of the schooner by Pollock, was to engage the enemy wherever possible. His captures, it was hoped, would make up for the loss of the *Morris*. An armed privateer of seventy tons, the *West Florida,* was taken after a brief engagement. "The taking of this vessel is an infinite advantage to this place [New Orleans]," writes a friend of Pollock, "as she prevented all communication by the Lakes to Manchack and Pensacola."

Of significance also was the capture by Captain Pickles of a British settlement on the north side of Lake Pontchartrain for, as will appear, the articles of capitulation acknowledging the subjection of the inhabitants to the United States were to be submitted by Pollock, and, on his representation, by the Committee of Congress, in support of the claim of the United States to West Florida and to the right of the free navigation of the Mississippi River.

Returning to New Orleans, Galvez proceeded to marshal his resources for an attack on Mobile and Pensacola. These objectives had been embodied in a royal order of May 18, 1779. The inhabitants of New Orleans, with confidence in their governor, entered enthusiastically into the preparations. While the plan provided for a joint movement from New Orleans and Havana, Navarro, Governor of Cuba, was slow to respond, since he favored a combined attack on St. Augustine by a joint American and Spanish force.

Navarro, in conference with his advisers, decided that the number of troops asked were not available. In place of ships and troops for a joint expedition against Mobile, a proposal from Havana looked toward a combined attack upon Pensacola. After much delay, a Junta, which was composed of Navarro and his military advisers finally acquiesced in the plan of Galvez to send a force for an attack on Mobile.

Confident of success, Galvez could brook no further delay, and having embarked his force of some seven hundred and fifty men made up of regulars, militia, including twenty-six Americans, and a few companies of free Negroes, he dropped down the River, January 14, 1780.

Pollock's brief military career was evidently to his liking, for although he declined the official honor tendered by Galvez, he sought shortly after an appointment by Congress.[14]

Why, then, did he not accompany Galvez on this expedition, for his letters indicate marked interest in every phase of the movement? It seems probable that he remained at New Orleans as a measure of precaution. Mobile, with its garrison of three hundred men, could, it was assumed, offer little resistance, but in the event of failure before Pensacola, American reinforcements would be necessary. Responsibility for procuring such assistance rested alone with Pollock. "There is no Intelligence yet arrived of the Havana Force joining him," he writes, "and if that should fall through and the enemy reinforce Pensacola from the Continent we shall in all probability, stand in need of your assistance from above next Summer." [15]

Particulars of the expedition were to be dispatched, by express, to Philadelphia. Procuring a boat for this purpose, at his own expense, Pollock issued to the captain instructions as follows: "Agreeable to your promise you'll not fail in touching at Mobile or Pensacola or thereabouts whenever you may find Governor Galvez with his Expedition and you'll deliver this

---

[14] "And the War, in all appearance, is not over in this part of the World," he wrote the President of Congress. "It is likely I shall soon have an opportunity in action again. In consequence, I beg your Excellency will honor me with a commission in the Rank your Excellency may judge proper, for my services and abilities, as this is highly necessary particularly in case I should have the misfortune to fall into the hands of the enemy." July 22, 1780. *Pollock Letters.* The application was not granted by the Board of War, but no reason for refusal is stated. *Jour. of the Cont. Cong.,* XVIII, pp. 1072, 1086.

[15] February 22, 1780. To the Committee of Congress. *Pollock Letters.*

Inclosed letter and learn from him as near as you possibly can the true State of that expedition as well as the Situation of the Enemy." That there was a complete understanding between Galvez and Pollock is evident, for to any representative whom Pollock might send was to be delivered in writing "their whole Menuovres."

For his actions in critical situations Pollock alone was responsible. "I am unfortunate enough," he wrote the Commercial Committee, "never to receive a Line from you but what I am oblig'd to send Express for. . . . Pray look back Sirs, it gives me pain to mention it, but perhaps you may be unacquainted with the Circumstances. I have gone early and voluntarily to work in the public Cause, and tho then distant from the Scene of Action yet I freely risqued My Person and Property in the face of the Enemy in West Florida, in consequence of this, and the very disagreeable Situation I am launched into I expected a little more attention would have been paid to my Letters than what I have yet experienced. . . . I am led to think that some Method might have been fallen upon before now for my Relief, at least (if not the whole) part would satisfy my hungry Creditors, and do pleasure to the Governor (from whom I have received many favors for the United States.")[16] Moreover, since the opening of the War, he had not received "a single line from the Council" of Virginia. Such discouragements were to him only spurs to new endeavor. A few days earlier he had called in Clark's unaccepted bills to the amount of $40,000. These creditors, "in great want of their money," were insisting vehemently on payment by Pollock. At the same time, he was employing boatmen and sending supplies and powder to the Illinois country.[17]

[16] *Pollock Letters*, March 3, 1780. He refers particularly to the $74,087 borrowed from Galvez on account of the United States.

[17] *Draper MSS.*, February 22, 1780. Letter addressed to John Todd, Jr.: "You have now inclosed bill of lading for ten barrels of Gunpowder containing 1000 pounds which I hope will arrive safe and in good time. . . ."

"As I am much afraid Mr. Lindsay's Goods may have suffer'd by

The *West Florida,* provisioned and equipped for sixty days, by Pollock, was directed to join the Spanish fleet. Captain Pickles, her commander, under Pollock's orders was to take part in the reduction of Mobile and Pensacola, "for the space of twenty days or longer, if necessary, or as requested by the Spanish Commander-in-Chief." [18] This accomplished, he was to proceed to Philadelphia, having taken on a cargo of taffia and sugar at Havana. In the event of failure to procure these articles, costing from two to three thousand dollars, with an order on Congress, the captain was to draw on Pollock, "at so long a sight as you care, and I will do honor to your drafts. But as you know my situation, of this you must be as tender as possible particularly if you find there have no vessels with flour from Congress touched at Havanna for this place." [19]

Pollock on no occasion lost sight of the possible effect of his contributions on the future claims of the United States and in a notable dispatch to the Committee of Congress, five days after Galvez set out for Mobile, he writes: "I am still at a loss respecting who is to possess the province of West Florida but at all events I strongly presume you'll not give up that part of it on the Mississippi with the free navigation of the River. . . . You know the Court of Great Britain puts a great Value on the post of Pensacola and be assured the Court of Spain puts no less, therefore should you think proper to give up your

---

laying so long at Point Coupée; I have employed the bearer Stephen Gooding to go up there to receive them, and see them put on board of Monsieur Lafonds Bateau in good order as also to take care of said goods until their arrival at the Illinois."
To the Committee of Congress, February 22, 1780. *Pollock Letters.* His account general with the United States showed a balance in his favor of 85,770 pistoles. "You'll no doubt observe by my different letters," he writes the Committee, "the difficulties I have laboured under for those heavy advances, as also the Interest I have, and am still obliged to pay."

[18] *Pollock Letters,* January 20, 1780. The *West Florida,* after her capture by Captain Pickles, had been used to patrol the lakes and thus prevent a possible attack on New Orleans by the British from Pensacola.

[19] *Pollock Letters.*

pretensions to that Post you may add some other valuable acquisition in place of it." [20]

Upon entering the Gulf, the Spanish fleet of twelve vessels was overtaken by a storm which caused the loss of some of the vessels but no loss of life. At the entrance to Mobile Bay, a fresh storm broke and the entire expedition was in danger of being wrecked. Five ships were stranded on a sand-bar. The men on board were safely landed but military stores and provisions were greatly reduced.

Fortunately, five ships of the expected Havana fleet arrived with some six hundred troops and supplies on board. With the information that additional reinforcements were to follow, Galvez decided to attack Fort Charlotte, a well-built structure having a garrison of three hundred men.

As a preliminary, Galvez demanded immediate capitulation, "for to-morrow perhaps nothing will be left to you but the sterile repentance of not having accepted my proposition in favor of the unfortunates who are under your command." That he did not think it compatible with his duty as a British officer to surrender without a battle, was the reply of Captain Durnford.[21]

After an assault lasting two days, the British agreed to accept the proposed terms of capitulation, which included the surrender of the troops and Mobile with the surrounding territory.[22]

Reinforcements, 1,100 in number, arrived from Pensacola

---

[20] *Pollock Letters*, January 20, 1780.

[21] March 1, 1780. Note addressed to Captain Elias Durnford, Commanding officer. "If I had fewer than two thousand men under my command, and if you had more than one hundred soldiers and a few sailors, I would not ask you to surrender, but the great inequality of forces compels us—you to yield immediately, or I to make you bear all the extremities of war if a useless and uncalled for resistance irritates the patience of my troops, too much annoyed by some accidents." *La. Hist. Soc'y.*, Publications I, Part III (1896), pp. 31, 32. The total force under Galvez was probably 1,400. *See* Caughey, *Galvez, op. cit.,* 184. Dr. Caughey gives an extended account of the capture of Mobile.

[22] *Pollock Letters.*

in time to have prevented the taking of the fort, but General Campbell feared to attack and after the capitulation made a hurried retreat.

In the attack upon Mobile, the *West Florida* captured a small prize. After the surrender, she was taken to Philadelphia and sold, her crew having been assigned to other Continental vessels.

Galvez waited anxiously for aid from Havana sufficient to enable him to carry out his plan for taking Pensacola. The officer in charge of a force which arrived from Cuba a few days after the capture of Mobile refused to coöperate and Galvez prepared to return to New Orleans. "Governor Galvez is returned with the expedition intended against Pensacola," Pollock wrote the Committee, "not being able to make the attack for want of a sufficient sea-force which he expected from Havana; however, he has left 1200 men in possession of Mobile which I hope will keep us quiet here until there's a reinforcement arrives." [23]

[23] *La. Hist. Soc'y.*, Pub's., I, Part III, pp. 32, 33. Members of the garrison were to remain prisoners until the end of the War. Many of them were sent to Louisiana. The inhabitants who had assisted the British were permitted to remain after taking the oath of allegiance to Spain.

CHAPTER XIII

WERE AMERICANS TO RETAIN THE WEST?

WHILE preparing for the capture of Detroit, Clark, during the spring of 1780, began the construction of Fort Jefferson, twelve miles below the mouth of the Ohio at a spot known as the Iron Banks. Some months earlier, he had advocated building this fort, for on account of a failure of crops in the Illinois country, some location nearer the frontier settlements would make the sustenance of his troops more feasible. Moreover, he argued that this should be made the center for the other Western posts; that it would become, at once, the key to the trade of the Western country and furnish a good location for the Indian department.[1] The continuance of American control over the Illinois country, as Clark believed, would depend on the concentration of his available force at the new fort. By this striking move, the Indians would be so mystified that they would refuse to join the British. There is no suggestion, however, of abandoning any territory north of the Ohio. Governor Jefferson had adopted the views of Clark and Todd on the practicability of a concentration of troops at this new fort which would, as he said, facilitate trade with the Illinois and be near enough to furnish aid to that territory; protect the trade with New Orleans; and together with other posts to be established would constitute a chain of de-

---

[1] Settlers were to be drawn to this location through a promise of 400 acres of land to each family at a price to be fixed by the Virginia General Assembly. The French, in 1702, built a fort at the mouth of the Ohio with the aim of keeping the English from the Mississippi. After three years, it was abandoned. Governor Hamilton planned to construct a fort at the same place. Clark, too, preferred this location, but found the land on the south bank of the Ohio subject to inundation. His proposal to bank them out, as at New Orleans, was thought too expensive.

fense for the Western frontier. In pursuance of this project, the troops were withdrawn from Vincennes, leaving only a company of twenty-three Virginians and the French militia to guard that post. But before the retirement of the troops from the Illinois villages took place, it was learned that an attack by the enemy was imminent.

By March, 1780, Clark was aware that the British were once more winning control over the Northwestern tribes and that they contemplated some such plan of action as that attempted by Governor Hamilton. Not only must this attack, which threatened the total loss of western control by the Americans, be checked, but an advance by the Spaniards east of the Mississippi, who, as John Todd said, "Have a fondness for engrossing territory," must likewise be met.

The British plan which included: gaining control of the Mississippi by attacking New Orleans and the other Spanish posts; the recapture of the Illinois country, Louisville and the other Kentucky posts and finally Forts Pitt and Cumberland, was one of the most striking military conceptions of the whole Revolution. If successful, the region west of the Alleghenies must have become and doubtless would have remained British territory, for all communication between West and East would have been cut off. Large numbers of British rangers and Indians would then be free to take part in the war on the coast.

To carry out this plan, five simultaneous movements were projected and three assaults were to be made at widely separated points. General John Campbell was to proceed from Pensacola and capture New Orleans.[2] His strength was to be increased by the addition of white troops and Indians from Michillimackinac, this force having come down the River after taking St. Louis. A third detachment assembled by Detroit officials under Captain Henry Bird, was assigned "to amuse" Clark at the Falls of the Ohio.[3] A subsidiary force consisting of a chosen band of Canadians and Indians under Captain Langlade, was directed to proceed from "Chicago and

[2] For the failure of General Campbell, see ante., p. 198.
[3] *Mich. Pioneer and Hist. Coll's.*, X, 395.

AMERICANS TO RETAIN THE WEST? 207

Make an attack by the Illinois River."[4] Another party was ordered to watch Vincennes and the plains between the Wabash and the Mississippi.

Such a campaign was possible only through lavish expenditures for Indian presents. Bands of braves are said to have stripped themselves upon approaching a post and demanded that their British father again clothe and outfit them. The refusal of a trifle, if not done with caution, it was asserted by De Peyster, might turn a whole war-party.

The command of the expedition against St. Louis and the Illinois villages was entrusted by Governor Patrick Sinclair of Michillimackinac to Captain Emanuel Hesse. This force, made up of regulars, traders, and Indians, numbering nine hundred and fifty, set out the second of May from the junction of the Wisconsin and the Mississippi.[5] Various motives had been adduced to stir up enthusiasm for the expedition. To the Northern Indians this was an opportunity to fall on their hereditary foes, the Illinois tribes.[6] Traders who aided in securing the Spanish posts were to be granted exclusive right to the Missouri trade for the ensuing winter.

Conspicuous among the Menominee, Winnebago, and Ottawa warriors was a body of two hundred Sioux under the leadership of Wabasha, their illustrious chief. While the capture of Governor Hamilton had weakened the hold of the British on the Northwestern tribes, the Sioux, as stated by Sinclair, were "undebauched, addicted to war and jealously attached to His Majesty's interest." To Matchikuis, Ottawa chieftain who was flattered by the title of general and with the privilege of wearing the scarlet coat and epaulets of the British, was given the chief command of the Indians.

St. Louis contained a population of about eight hundred—

---

[4] *Wis. Hist. Coll's.*, XI, 151.

[5] Reports on the number in the expedition differ. Governor Sinclair stated there were 750. There were, in addition, 200 Sioux warriors, thus making a total force of 950. According to the Spanish report, there were 300 whites and 900 Indians. *George Rogers Clark Papers, 1771–1781,* p. CXXVIII, N. 3.

[6] Sinclair to Haldimand, *Wis. Hist. Coll's.*, XI, 151; III, 150, 154, 157.

mostly French. It was the capital of upper Louisiana and a leading center for the fur-trade. In no condition to offer defense, great alarm was produced over the report that the enemy was descending the Mississippi for an attack. Intrenchments were hurriedly thrown up and were manned by a force made up of twenty-nine regulars and 281 villagers. On May 26, the attack on St. Louis was repulsed and the British withdrew to Cahokia, where their attack likewise failed.

Meantime, Clark, who had been engaged in constructing Fort Jefferson, responding to the urgent call that he come to the relief of St. Louis, hastened with a small body of troops to Cahokia. The statement has often been made and as frequently denied that he crossed the River to St. Louis and that it was the knowledge of his presence which caused the precipitate retreat of the British.[7] Clark claimed for his men and himself the honor of having saved St. Louis and the rest of Louisiana for the Spanish.[8]

The main body of the enemy retreated rapidly in two divisions—one up the Mississippi, the second directly across country to Michillimackinac. As a counter-stroke, Clark sent Colonel Montgomery with a small force against the villages of the Sauk and Fox at Rock Island, but the Indians had fled.[9]

---

[7] "He continued only about two hours in St. Louis when he returned to Coho [Cahokia]." Stipp, *Western Miscellany*, p. 54. This writer prepared his sketches from notes which were furnished him by Clark and other contemporaries.

[8] Clark to Genet, February 5, 1793. *Draper MSS.*, 55J1. Colonel Montgomery, February 22, 1783, claimed that Clark had not rendered assistance to Governor de Leyba. *Cal. Va. State Papers*, III, 443. For the attack on St. Louis, *see Life of Clark*, pp. 204–207. William A. Meese, "Rock River in the Revolution," *Transactions of the Illinois State Historical Society*, XIV (Springfield, 1921), 97–103. A factor in the outcome was that De Leyba had been warned of the approach of the enemy and provided for the defense of the town by throwing up intrenchments which were manned by twenty-nine regulars and 281 villagers. Sinclair declared that failure was due to the treachery of Calvé, an interpreter, and Ducharme, a trader, both of whom commanded companies of the Indians. *See* James, "The Significance of the Attack on St. Louis, 1780," *Proceedings of the Mississippi Valley Historical Association*, II, 208–210.

[9] *Wis. Hist. Coll's.*, IX, 291.

AMERICANS TO RETAIN THE WEST? 209

The third offensive was likewise a failure. For weeks, Major De Peyster lavished what his superiors characterized as amazing sums on the "over indulgence" of the Indians tributary to Detroit in enlisting them for the expedition against Louisville. With a well-equipped force of 1,100, one thousand of them Indians, Captain Henry Bird, one of the best types of British leaders, descended the Maumee and the Great Miami to the Ohio. Notwithstanding his possession of two pieces of light artillery, he decided not to hazard an attack on the fort at the Falls. He was also aware of the arrival of reinforcements from Virginia. He knew, too, that the expedition against the Illinois posts and St. Louis had failed and Indian leaders were terrorized lest Clark should return. Instead of an attack on Louisville they insisted on a raid against two small stockaded posts, Ruddle's and Martin's Stations. Resistance was hopeless against the British artillery. Satisfied with this slight success, Bird set out for Detroit with about three hundred and fifty prisoners, some of them reported to be loyal to the Crown. So rapidly did they retreat that they abandoned their cannon at one of the Miami villages. The movements against Vincennes were also barren of lasting results.

At no time in his career, did Clark show to better advantage his power as a leader. No obstacle deterred him from his decision to deliver a counter-stroke which would prevent the enemy from making a similar advance. It was his opportunity to overcome the Shawnee, the most warlike of the Ohio tribes, "a nest of hornets" as they were called. Because of their ascendancy over the other tribes, no agreement could be lasting without their assent. Learning of the designs of Bird, Clark set out from Cahokia, with a few men, for Fort Jefferson, barely escaping capture on the way. Unmindful of dangers, he struck off with two companions through the wilderness for Harrodsburg, where he began the organization of a retaliatory expedition. With characteristic decision, in spite of protests from the crowd of investors in land, he closed the land office. By August 1, seven weeks after leaving Cahokia, he had succeeded, "by every possible exertion," in forcing the mustering of one thousand volunteers at the mouth of the Licking River.[10] Among the officers accompanying him on the expedition were Colonel Benjamin Logan, serving as second in command, Colonel James Harrod, Daniel Boone, and Levi Todd.

When the limited supplies were divided, each man had received a pound and a half of meal, nine quarts of parched corn, and a small amount of buffalo meat. On the second of August, they crossed the Ohio and set out for Old Chillicothe, the Shawnee capital. Due to the necessity of cutting a roadway, four days were taken for this march of seventy miles. Warned of the approach of the Americans, the Indians fled. A plentiful supply of green corn and string beans gave Clark the occasion, as he remarked, "for feasting and recruiting" his followers. The crops and buildings of the Indians having been destroyed, the march was resumed.

For some time, careful preparation had been under way at Piqua to meet this invasion. A new stockade had been built and Indian families and effects were removed to a place of safety. Early on the afternoon of August 8, when within two miles of the village, Clark was forced to meet the first onset of a combined force of three hundred Shawnee, Mingo, Wyandot, and Delaware warriors. Additional British reinforcements arrived during the progress of the battle.

Clark wrote, a few days later:

> I had scarcely time to make those dispositions necessary before the action commenced on our left wing, and in a few minutes became almost general, with savage fierceness on both sides. The confidence the enemy had of their own strength and certain victory, or the want of generalship, occasioned several neglects, by which those advantages were taken that proved the ruin of their army, being flanked two or three different times, drove from hill to hill in a circuitous direction, for upwards of a mile and a half. At last [they] took shelter in their strongholds and the woods adjacent, when the firing ceased for about half an hour, until necessary preparations were made for dislodging them. A heavy firing again commenced, and continued severe until dark, by

---

[10] Clark's account of the expedition, August 22, 1780, *Clark Papers*, p. 451.

which time the enemy were totally routed. The cannon playing too briskly on their works they could afford them no shelter. . . . This would have been a decisive stroke to the Indians, if unfortunately the right wing of our army had [not] been rendered useless for some time by an uncommon chain of rocks that they could not pass, by which means part of the enemy escaped through the ground they were ordered to occupy.

No pursuit was ordered by Clark, since the excessive heat and lack of food were telling on the strength of his men. "Having," as he wrote, "done the Shawanese all the mischief in our power, after destroying Picaney [Piqua] settlements, I returned to this post [Louisville] having marched in the whole 480 miles in 31 days."

Some idea of the suffering of his men on this return march may be gotten from the following statement written some years later by one who took part in the expedition:

The roasting ears got on their return at Chillicothe had given out. Camped, no supper that night—left next morning. Some of them well nigh starved before reaching the settlements. . . . Day after day without a particle of food, or if any but a sorry pittance of jerk, parched meal or green corn, snaps or pumpkins—these were the conquerors of the West.

Had Clark failed, it seems reasonable to assert that King's Mountain, decisive battle that it was, with the resultant renewal of patriotic zeal, the turning of the tide of war in the South and the checking of Cornwallis, would not have been fought.[11] "Back Water Men" under Isaac Shelby and John Sevier would have been hard pressed to protect their settlements against an overwhelming force of British and Indians such as had been thrown back by Clark.

It was but a few months later, in making his striking appeal to Kentucky lieutenants for a new army with which to advance for the reduction of Detroit, that Clark declared:

. . . but I know and always knew that this Department was of more real Service to the United States, than half of all their

[11] For King's Mountain, *see Life of Clark*, pp. 217-220; *see also* Lyman Draper, *King's Mountain.*

frontier posts and have proved of great importance by engaging the attention of the Enemy that otherwise would have spread slaughter and Devastation throughout the more interior Frontier, deprived them of giving any assistance to our Eastern armies, and more than probable, the Allegany [Mountains] would have been our boundary at this time. . . . It was our Interest on the Ouabache that has preserved your Settlements; Otherways, Holdston, New River, Greenbrier etc. must long since have been depopulated by the Indians or rendered incapable of performing those Services they have done against the British forces in Carolina and elsewhere.

That Clark's success was in no small part due to the contributions made by Pollock, cannot be questioned when we read the correspondence for the first six months of 1780. John Todd, Jr., Lieutenant Colonel, applied to him for powder and clothing for Kentucky militia although he must have been aware of the financial distress of Pollock. In his reply, Pollock declares: "I cannot negotiate a bill here just now for a single dollar upon any part of the world, partly owing to the scarcity of specie as the Treasurer here has been giving out bills of credit for all their payments for this three months past, and must continue so until they get a supply of dollars from the Havanna." [12] Nevertheless, five hundred pounds of powder and a stock of medicines were shipped by him on the *Grace of God* in good order and well conditioned. In due time, the farewell invocation, "and so God send the good Ship to her desired Port in Safety. Amen," having been fulfilled, the cargo was delivered to Clark or to Todd.

Unaccepted bills of Clark, amounting to $60,000, Pollock had called in. While "straining every nerve" to negotiate new bills drawn by Clark, he succeeded in sending for his use 1,200 pounds of powder, seven hogsheads of whiskey and a supply of goods to be used in negotiations with the Indians. "I have paid several of your bills, since I wrote you last," was his message to Clark, "and shall do all I can to get in the remainder as soon as possible. Though I am sorry to inform you I am much afraid I will not be able to get any Cash here. But in order that you

[12] May 4, 1780. *Pollock Letters.*

AMERICANS TO RETAIN THE WEST? 213

may not be distress'd for the necessaries you may want just now I have strongly recommended your Bills which I have agreed to accept at three months sight, but I beg that you'll be as frugall in drawing as possible." [13]

Among the numerous bills drawn to the amount of 39,000 hard dollars, were those of Clark and Montgomery for the recruiting service; for provisions and merchandise for the troops; and for an Indian agent and an interpreter.

From Governor Henry, Pollock received notice to draw on Penette, De Costa, Freres and Company, of Nantes, for $65,-814, the amount of his disbursements for Virginia. "I accordingly drew for that Sum," he writes, "and the bills came back protested producing thereby the addition of damages to my other Distresses." A year earlier, he had received an order from the Commercial Committee to draw on Samuel and J. H. Delap of France and have no concern over the outcome. In due time, these bills came back protested.[14] "This stroke," he said, "has obliged me now to put my land and negroes for sale to pay them off with the interest and damages which come high, and in all probability my dwelling house will come next upon the carpet and in consequence of not hearing from you on this subject, although there are many opportunities from your place to Havanna. This has laid me under more obliga-

---

[13] May 26, 1780. *Draper MSS.*, 50J40.

[14] *The Writings of Benjamin Franklin*, ed. Albert H. Smyth (New York, 1907), VII, 405. Franklin to the Commercial Committee, October 21, 1779. "Gentlemen,—I received the honor of yours dated the 21st of July containing an extract from Mr. Pollock's letter to you, in which he mentions his drafts on Mr. Delap for 10,897 dollars, and his expectation that in case of any difficulty I will see those Bills paid. I should certainly do everything in my power to support the credit of the States, and every Person acting under their authority but I have been so exhausted by great and unexpected drafts and expenses, that I am glad those bills have never been proposed to me, as I could not have taken upon myself to pay them. And I beg that you would not in future have any dependence of that kind upon me without knowing beforehand from me that I shall be able to pay what is desired. I hope you will excuse my giving this caution, which is forced from me by the distress and anxiety such occasional and unforseen demands have occasioned me."

tions to this Governor than I would wish and from the little notice you have hitherto taken of his and my letters, has rendered my obligations still more disagreeable."

The summer of 1780 was a most trying period for Pollock. Continental currency had reached New Orleans. Worthless in trade, the holders offered it to Pollock whom they knew as an agent of the general government. Describing this situation, he wrote: "In order to support its credit, which would have been instantly ruined by a refusal on my part, not only at New Orleans but everywhere on or near the River I received and exchanged it for specie."

But the demands of hungry creditors could not be met with promises to be fulfilled in an indefinite future. Once more he was forced to turn to his friends for relief. His success was merely another indication of the reputation he had won. Describing these days of gloom he declared: "I must then have sunk under the load if I had not prevailed on Don Bernardo de Otter Contador of Louisiana, to lend me 40,000 dollars. My application to him was for money out of the Publick Treasury, but having no orders to warrant it, that could not be done. His friendship however for me and his regard for the interest of the United States induced him to make the advance from his own private fortune." [15] Another friend, Daniel Clark, entrusted his whole fortune of 40,000 Mexican dollars to Pollock. Bills for this amount, drawn on Virginia were accepted in exchange. According to Clark's testimony, this contribution was applied toward meeting the necessities of troops under Clark and Montgomery. They were, as we have seen, preparing for the drive against the Shawnee strongholds.

While Clark was engaged in the expedition against the Shawnee, an attack was made on Fort Jefferson by a force made up of Chickasaw and Choctaw warriors. For some unknown reason, the instructions of Governor Jefferson ordering the purchase of the site for this fort from the Indians had been disregarded. Six days and nights the onslaughts continued and

[15] Pollock to the President of Congress, September 18, 1782. *Pollock Letters*.

were met in sheer desperation by Captain Robert George and his small force. While the garrison numbered sixty, only one-half of this number were, on account of sickness, fit for service. Their supplies of food, water, and ammunition were almost exhausted when the Indians withdrew.

During the remaining months of 1780, this post was menaced by attacks from various quarters, but according to the testimony of American officers, it was saved only through timely aid by Pollock: Colonel Montgomery wrote Governor Jefferson:

... had it not been for the Assistance of Mr. Oliver Pollock, with whom I am now present, we must undoubtedly evacuate that Post. He well knowing that Govern't. having to heart the Setling a place of so much Consequence and from those good principles he hath always Shewn Sent us Relief from time to time both Ammunition and Goods in our Greatest distresses until he has Sent his All & is Still Striving to send us further supplies. I am fully Convinced it will not be in his Power to Send further Supplies without Relief. I am in hopes you will take the Speediest Method of Sending him remittances or providing a Fund for our future Relief, as I can see no other Method for the Preservation of the Illinois Country.[16]

On his journey to New Orleans, Montgomery met Philip Barbour, a trader, who, following the advice of Pollock, was bringing a cargo of goods to be disposed of in the Illinois country. To Clark, Pollock wrote: "This will be handed you by Capt. Philip Barbour whom I beg leave to recommend to your protection. . . . He carries some cloathing and other Articles with him for Sale, which I hope you'll find usefull for your Troops." [17] Once more Pollock manifested his faith in the cause by sending to Clark five cases of guns and five hundred pounds of powder.

Before quitting Kaskaskia, Montgomery had secured sundries and provisions for his troops, with the usual orders on Pollock amounting to $11,600. His successor continued this

[16] January 8, 1781. *Clark Papers*, p. 498.
[17] August 10, 1780. *Draper MSS.*, 50J52.

practice "for the sustenance of his company." One of these orders is indorsed by Pollock, "accepted to pay when I receive funds for that purpose." But to boatmen engaged in carrying messages and taking supplies up the River for Clark's use, Pollock was compelled to pay wages in "hard" money.

As winter approached, the condition of the troops at Fort Jefferson was desperate. Sickness was still prevalent among them and the suffering of the inhabitants of the village through the loss of their crops and stock was most acute. Their melancholy situation was thus described by Captain Leonard Helm: "Sitting by Capt. George's fire with a piece of Lightwood and two Ribs of an old Bufaloe which is all the meat we have seen this many days, I congratulate your success against the Shawanahs [Shawnee] but this never doubt when that brave Col. Clarke Commands. We will know the loss of him at the Illinois. . . . Excuse haste as the Lightwood just out and mouth watering for want of the two ribs." [18]

The coming of Captain Barbour at this crisis was described in a message to Pollock as follows: "When [he] heard of our Distresses the season was far spent and the Enemy [Indians and English] surrounded us on every Quarter, but notwithstanding he broke through fire and ice and came to our assistance. The necessaries he has brought us supply our Immediate wants and articles to purchase provisions for some time which our paper currency would by no means do. . . . Capt Barbour will give you all the news we have in this Remote hole." [19]

Possession of these goods, consisting of sugar, taffia, soap, coffee, tobacco, writing-paper, saws, carpenter's tools, rum, swords, gun-flints, and powder enabled the quartermaster to procure in trade, necessary provisions and clothing.[20] "And had not the purchase been made," Colonel Montgomery writes, "a great part of the Troops must undoubtedly have perished as so many of them were so sick that it was impossible

---

[18] *Clark Papers*, p. 466.
[19] Letter of Captain George. *Clark Papers*, p. 496.
[20] From an inventory. "Clark MSS.," *Va. State Archives*.

AMERICANS TO RETAIN THE WEST? 217

for them to have evacuated the place without those supplies." [21] To Pollock was accorded the credit by Captain George for saving Fort Jefferson and for winning the friendship, "of the neighboring savages whose minds were wavering." Demands, "from almost every quarter" were likewise met, including the drawing of supplies from the Illinois villages, the furnishing of liquors and ammunition for the use of the Indian department at Vincennes and the sending of a small force to assist in protecting that post.[22]

That soldiers, in spite of the great need for the defense of Fort Jefferson, were spared to go to Vincennes indicates how critical the situation was at the latter post. During the autumn of 1780, a number of French leaders in this village had petitioned the Spanish governor at St. Louis to come to their protection against frequent Indian attacks. Disregarding their oath of American allegiance, they appealed to Governor Cruzat, as "good citizens of France" and therefore the allies of Spain. In his expression of sympathy for their grievous situation, the governor made the significant declaration that since

[21] Certificate of Colonel Montgomery, "Clark MSS.," *loc. cit.*

[22] February 15, 1781. *Clark Papers,* p. 506. Prompt payment for the cargo in gold or silver amounting to $237,320 was urged upon Pollock by Captain George and his officers as an incentive to Barbour to bring further supplies. Upon this amount, Pollock paid $32,500, although he protested that too high a price had been paid for the goods. Some months later, Capt. George writing the Governor of Virginia asserted: "You will thereby perceive that it was my intention the above sum should be paid in current Money instead of Specie, altho I must acknowledge the Bills were expressly directed to be paid in Gold and Silver. . . . Acknowledge myself unacquainted with the Nature of Bills of Exchange. . . . My Ignorance of such matters 'tis true have laid me open to imposition; but I am happy to hear the Bills have been protested as nothing was ever further from my intentions than to have drawn for such an enormous sum to be actually paid in Specie." This transaction was to bring criticism upon Pollock, as we shall see, in the final adjustment of his accounts. It was claimed that he had assisted Barbour in a scheme to defraud the government. Upon the presentation of the evidence, however, these accusations were withdrawn. This amount was finally charged against Virginia. "Clark MSS.," *Va. State Archives,* Auditor's Report, 44. Letter of Pollock to George, April 2, 1781, *Pollock Letters.* Letter of George to the Governor of Virginia, October 6, 1781, "Clark MSS.," *Va. Archives.*

he regarded them as subjects of the United States by *right of conquest,* their relief should come from their superiors at the Illinois.[23]

The significance of this interpretation is seen as we consider its relation to an occurrence some months earlier, known as the La Balme Expedition, and shortly after to the so-called capture of St. Joseph.

While the real purpose of the La Balme expedition is something of a mystery, the leading facts connected therewith are known.[24] Disaffection from the American cause at Vincennes, due, in the main, to the exactions of Virginia officers, became more open upon the arrival at Kaskaskia of a French officer, Augustin Mottin de la Balme. With recommendations from Franklin and Silas Deane, American agents at the Court of France, he came to the United States and during the summer of 1777 received a commission from Congress as inspector general of cavalry. The appointment proving unsatisfactory, with credentials from Luzerne, French minister to the United States, he came West and by July, 1780, was at Vincennes. Here he was enthusiastically welcomed, "being received by the Inhabitants as the Hebrews would receive the Messiah." [25] At Kaskaskia and Cahokia also he won support through the promise of assistance from France. In recognition of their antagonism to Virginia, he declared that the troops of that colony had carried on the western expedition against the will of the other States and in spite of the protests of the United Colonies. He urged that they should demand the withdrawal

[23] December 15, 1780. The originals of this petition and the reply are in the *Bancroft Collection,* University of California. Copy in *Wis. Hist. Coll's.,* XVIII, 429, note 39.

[24] It has been suggested that this expedition was undertaken for the purpose of giving France control over their former colonial possessions in the trans-Allegheny country. Frederick J. Turner, "Policy of France towards the Mississippi Valley," *Am. Hist. Rev.,* X, 255. There is evidence to show that La Balme was attempting to carry out a plan of which Washington and Luzerne, the French minister, were cognizant, namely; to gain the aid of the Illinois French in winning Canada. *Washington's Writings,* ed. Sparks, VIII, 44, 72.

[25] *Kaskaskia Records,* pp. 163-168.

AMERICANS TO RETAIN THE WEST? 219

of Virginians from their lands. He called upon them for an immediate expedition against Detroit, which, as he said, "will win the confidence of the honorable Congress and convince the King of France of the real interest which you take in a cause for which he has already made great sacrifices and which will procure for you in a little while all imaginable assistance from him." [26] La Balme, having enlisted a company of about eighty Frenchmen in the Illinois villages, and some Indians, set out under the French flag for Detroit. Fort Miami was captured and plundered but a few days later the expedition was attacked and La Balme and thirty of his men were killed. Another detachment which he had sent from Cahokia succeeded in taking St. Joseph, a small but important trading-post.[27] Returning, they were overtaken near Chicago and cut to pieces by the Potawatomi.[28]

Early the following January, an expedition which was made up of some 40 militia from St. Louis, 20 Cahokians, and 60 Indians, took St. Joseph and raised the Spanish flag. For twenty-four hours they were in possession, but fearing a counter-attack by the British, they returned to St. Louis. Before retiring, Captain Eugene Pouré, leader in charge, drew up a document taking possession, by right of conquest, in the name of the King of Spain, of St. Joseph and its dependencies and of the River Illinois.[29] The expedition was highly commended by

[26] *Kaskaskia Records,* XCII.
[27] Located near the site of Niles, Michigan.
[28] *Mich. Pioneer and Hist. Coll's.,* XIX, 591.
[29] "I annex and incorporate," the proclamation states, "with the domains of his Very Catholic Majesty, the King of Spain, my Master, from now on and forever, this post of St. Joseph and its dependencies, with the river of the same name, and that of the Islinois, which flows into the Missicipy River." Quoted by Dr. Lawrence Kinnaird, "The Spanish Expedition against Fort St. Joseph in 1781, A New Interpretation," *Miss. Valley Hist. Rev.,* XIX, 182.

According to the American account, the expedition consisted of 30 Spaniards, 20 Cahokians and 200 Indians. Clark planned to capture this post in September, 1779, but volunteers could not be secured for the expedition. *Clark Papers,* p. 366.

A number of diverse views have been advanced as reasons for this expedition. As seen by Edward G. Mason, it was an effort to extend the

the King of Spain and in the peace negotiations carried on at Paris the following year this "conquest" was made the basis for the Spanish claim to territory north of the Ohio River.

For the future of the United States, it was fortunate, indeed, that Clark, with the assistance of Pollock, had been able to conquer the British posts and, notwithstanding Spanish aggression, to maintain his control over the Illinois country. At

claims of Spain to territory east of the Mississippi River. "How little did those light hearted soldiers and their red allies know that they were but the pawns in the great game whereof the players were at Paris and Madrid." Edward G. Mason, "March of the Spaniards Across Illinois," *Magazine of American History with Notes and Queries* (New York, 1886), XV, 464, 469. The attack on St. Joseph, according to Professor C. W. Alvord, was undertaken by the Cahokians with assistance from St. Louis, "to avenge the loss of their friends" in the La Balme expedition. "The Conquest of St. Joseph, Michigan, by the Spaniards in 1781," *Missouri Hist. Rev.*, II, 195–210. Dr. Alvord accepted the interpretation of Arthur C. Boggess, in his volume, "The Settlement of Illinois, 1778–1830" (Chicago, 1890), p. 38. Dr. F. J. Teggart, who had access to new documentary evidence in the Bancroft Library of the University of California, maintains that Francisco Cruzat, lieutenant-governor at St. Louis, was responsible for the expedition and that it was undertaken as protection for St. Louis against an impending British attack. Frederick J. Teggart, "The Capture of St. Joseph, Michigan, by the Spaniards in 1781," *Mo. Hist. Rev.*, V, 214–228.

New evidence on this expedition has been presented by Dr. Kinnaird. His conclusion is based on a letter of Cruzat to Governor Galvez discovered by him in the Louisiana Collection of the Bancroft Library. Cruzat wrote: "The urging of the Indian Heturno, both on his own account and in behalf of Naquiguen, both chiefs, that I should make an expedition against the English of the Fort San Joseph . . . compelled me to arrange for the departure from this town . . . a detachment of sixty volunteers under the orders of Don Eugenio Puré." He gave as reasons for this step that refusal on his part might have caused these Indians to desert the Spaniards for the English; that if St. Joseph were captured by this force the Indians friendly to the English would be terrorized and the expedition against St. Louis in the spring would be prevented; and that it was good strategy to send the Indian allies of the Spanish against the enemy Indians. Kinnaird, *op. cit.*, 188, 189. Dr. Kinnaird has presented an exhaustive study of this problem and his conclusions are satisfactory. Dr. Caughey connects the capture of St. Joseph with the campaign of Galvez from New Orleans. Caughey, *op. cit.*, 169, 170.

the close of the campaign against the Shawnee, Clark was free, once more, to develop plans for the capture of Detroit. He had been assured that an expedition under his command, for this purpose, was to be undertaken in 1781.

CHAPTER XIV

THE NORTHWEST: CONQUEST OR GIFT?

BY CHRISTMAS TIME, 1780, Clark, who had been engaged, under the direction of General Steuben, in the campaign against Benedict Arnold, was called to Richmond. Governor Jefferson was aware that a formidable expedition from Detroit was planned against the frontier posts with the opening of spring. He determined to put the enemy on the defensive and adopted the original plan of Clark to send an expedition for the reduction of that post. The results hoped for through such an offensive were stated by the Governor as follows: "If that Post be reduced we shall be quiet in future on our frontier, and thereby immense Treasure of blood and money be saved, we shall be at leisure to know [turn] our whole force to the rescue of our Eastern country from subjugation, we shall divert through our own country a brand of commerce which the European States have thought worthy of the most important struggles and sacrifices and in the event of peace on terms which have been contemplated by some powers we shall form to the American Union a barrier against the dangerous extension of the British Province of Canada and add to the Empire of Liberty an extensive and fertile country, thereby converting dangerous enemies into valuable friends."[1] At the opening of the year 1781, therefore, there was no evidence of final territorial demands for territory, less in extent, than the whole of the Northwest.

Promise of success was greater for Washington looked upon Clark's plan with favor. In keeping with this spirit, he ordered Colonel Daniel Brodhead, at Fort Pitt, to give the enterprise every possible assistance by furnishing supplies and a detach-

[1] *Clark Papers*, p. 490.

THE NORTHWEST: CONQUEST OR GIFT? 223

ment of Continental troops. "I do not think," Washington wrote Brodhead, "the charge of the enterprise could have been committed to better hands than Colonel Clark's. I have not the pleasure of knowing the gentleman; but, independently of the proofs he has given of his activity and address, the unbounded confidence, which I am told the Western people repose in him, is a matter of most importance." [2]

Clark was advanced by Jefferson to the rank of brigadier general.[3] The force was to consist of two thousand men, including the Illinois battalion, a regiment of regulars under Colonel Joseph Crockett and militia recruited from the three Kentucky and other frontier counties. From Pittsburgh, the expedition was to proceed down the Ohio to the Falls. By March 15, all was to be in readiness to advance up the Wabash on the way to Detroit, where Clark was to establish the "authority of this Commonwealth in all instances in lieu of that of his Britannic Majesty." Such, in outline, was the plan which was formulated with great detail by Jefferson.

From the outset, Clark experienced the greatest difficulty in securing men and supplies. County officials refused to cooperate in furnishing their quotas of militia. Recruiting officers wrote of their efforts to carry out the draft in Berkeley County: "We are sorry to inform your Excellency that we have the greatest reason to believe that those whose Turn it now is from this County will suffer any punishment rather than obey our orders for their march." [4] An effort to enforce the draft in Hampshire County resulted in the mutiny of seventy men. Confronted with a like spirit in other counties, Jefferson finally yielded to the suggestion that a call for volunteers should be issued. A regiment of two hundred regulars at Pittsburgh

---

[2] *Writings of Jefferson*, ed. Sparks, VII, 345.

[3] Jefferson had urged Washington to assign Clark a Continental commission, but this was not possible under the rule which forbade his granting such a commission to officers in state regiments.

[4] This County was to furnish 275 men. Seventy men from the County were then serving in the Southern army. Sixty-eight were to join Washington's army. To complete the quota for Clark's army would have meant bringing into service one-half the men available in the County.

under Colonel John Gibson was ordered by Baron Steuben to join Clark.

At first, Colonel Brodhead gave assurance of complete coöperation. But jealous of Clark, and desirous of winning laurels for himself by an expedition against Detroit, he refused to honor the request for Gibson's regiment. In appealing to Washington, Clark writes: "If you should approve of the troops in this department joining our forces tho they are few the acquisition may be attended with great good consequences as two hundred might turn the scale in our favor. . . . For in part it has been the influence of our posts on the Illinoise and Ouabash that have savd the frontiers and in great measure baffled the designs of the enemy at Detroit. If they get possession of them they then Command three times the number of Valuable warriors they do at present and will be fully Enabled to carry any point they aim at Except we should have a formidable force to oppose them." [5] To Clark's disappointment, Washington permitted Brodhead to determine the number of Continentals which might be detached on this expedition and he refused to coöperate.

Notwithstanding the desire of President Reed of Pennsylvania to render all the assistance within his power, volunteers were secured only by the use of strong-arm methods, due, in the main, to the dispute over the boundary between Pennsylvania and Virginia. Some of the leaders accused Clark of being a Virginia trader and a land-jobber and protection to those opposing the draft was proffered by some of the Pennsylvania county lieutenants.[6] Finally, early in August, despairing of accomplishing his designs against such deep-seated opposition, he set out for Louisville with only four hundred men. This force was scarcely adequate to guard the boats containing supplies for fully two thousand.

Clark's preparations had served, however, as a defense for the frontier. Efforts were redoubled to put Detroit in condi-

---

[5] *Clark Papers*, p. 553. Gibson agreed with this interpretation.

[6] For boundary disputes and other problems with which Clark was confronted, see *Life of Clark*, pp. 235–240.

THE NORTHWEST: CONQUEST OR GIFT? 225

tion to withstand such an attack. Demands for presents by the Indians drawn there for councils, increased "amazingly." [7]

An extended list of articles intended to keep favor with tribesmen, in addition to "vermilion," always indispensable, were: Ruffled and plain linen shirts, cotton trousers, scarlet coats, quantities of tinsel lace, cotton, linen, and silk handkerchiefs, finger-rings, watch-chains, combs, looking-glasses, Jew's harps, and other evidences of the desire to expose the red-men to the outward forms of civilized life. But 136 dozen scalping-knives were also included in the inventory. In justifying bills amounting to some £36,000, characterized by General Haldimand as wasted, De Peyster declared: "The Indians in this country must be looked upon as a large body of Irregulars, Fed and Cloathed to prevent the inroads of the Virginians into this Country." [8]

By the end of May, the fears of the British were increased by the report that Clark was descending the Ohio with one thousand men and that this force would be increased by a like number from Kentucky.[9] British officers were ordered to act at once in order to prevent further strengthening of the frontier settlements. Such an order meant war on combatant and non-combatant alike.

One hundred rangers and three hundred Indians, under Captain McKee, advanced to the Ohio with the intention of waylaying Clark, but arrived too late. Captain Joseph Brant, an Iroquois, ablest leader employed by the British in the West, with a body of rangers and Indians lay in wait for a company of 107 picked men from Westmoreland County under Colonel Archibald Lochry. Arriving at Wheeling a few hours after Clark's departure, this force descended the river, hoping to overtake him. Brant's surprise attack was successful and one-third of the Americans, including Lochry and six other officers, lost their lives. The others were made prisoners. Shortly after, the force under Brant united with that under McKee

[7] *Mich. Pioneer and Hist. Coll's.*, X, 465.
[8] *Ibid.*, X, 548.
[9] *Ibid.*, p. 478.

and the pursuit of Clark was kept up. Notwithstanding their known superiority in numbers, the Indians, fearing Clark's name, refused to attack and broke up into small raiding parties. The rangers insisted on returning to Detroit.[10]

Arriving at the Falls early in September, Clark found that Fort Nelson, so-named in honor of the Governor of Virginia, had been completed. Soldiers in the garrison were suffering from the lack of clothing and food. "My men," Captain Slaughter declared, "have no shirts, hats, blankets, or Breeches, not having drawn Cloath for that purpose, shoes, Stockings, moccasons, so that they are totally unfit for duty."[11] For months these troops had received no pay; desertions were common; the credit of Virginia was exhausted and provisions could not be procured with Continental currency.

The distress of the troops and settlers at Fort Jefferson had become continuously more acute. Relief from Pollock was exhausted except as he was able to negotiate loans from individuals, Spanish merchants and American traders. He writes Captain George of this Post:

> Your favours I have now before me. As I have no Funds belonging to the State of Virginia or indeed any other State in consequence I have forwarded Copy of your draft to Government and am in hopes funds will be provided for that and other purposes of the same nature now much wanted— But as all commerce and communication is so very uncertain there is no dependance upon what time those Funds may arrive Notwithstanding I have done everything that can be done for that intent and have reason to believe something favourable will soon turn up, but in the mean time you must have a little more patience and be as frugal as possible, and make the last supply run as far as you can. The expedition against Pensacola is now getting ready to embark the third time and I hope it will fall next month.[12]

Meantime, he had shipped a supply of medicines to Fort Jefferson. Two drafts drawn on him by Captain George for liquors and clothing to the amount of 32,500 and 5,400 Span-

---

[10] *Mich. Pioneer and Hist. Coll's.*, X, 516.
[11] *Draper MSS.*, 50J79.
[12] February 17, 1781. "Clark MSS.," *Va. State Archives.*

THE NORTHWEST: CONQUEST OR GIFT? 227

ish milled dollars were likewise accepted. He had recently paid bills drawn on him by Clark when preparing for the march to Vincennes in favor of Vigo for $921 and another for $1,452. Other creditors finally made their appeals for payment through the Spanish courts. That the debtor in one case was given due consideration, may be implied, inasmuch as the trial took place in Pollock's home. The document relates:

On the first of April one thousand seven hundred and eighty-one, in the city of New Orleans before me Notary in the house of Mr. Oliver Pollock appeared Juan Vaucher and entered a demand on said Pollock with a bill of exchange drawn by the Commander of the American troops of the post of Illinois, Mr. Clark, against said Pollock and transferred to said Vaucher by Juan Maria Legras in favor of whom the bill was drawn at Kaskaskia, February the second of the past year 1780 for 1752 piastres.

Demand being made on the aforementioned Pollock in my presence, he replied to the said Vaucher that he did not have funds to meet the bill. Therefore the latter protests once, twice, thrice and the rest required by law that all losses, delays, damages, injuries, occasioned be not at the risk of the protector and I affirm that with the said Pollock came witnesses resident of this city—present J. Vaucher and Oliver Pollock before me, in testimony of truth,
LEONARDO MAZANGE— *Notary Public.*

In this dilemma, Pollock turned to the Commercial Committee for relief. "I shall depend upon you," he writes, "for this and my other advances. The necessity of supporting the credit of the bills from above (otherwise the Posts in the Illinois Country must inevitably have fallen long ago) obliged me to take this method and if you will examine the heavy advances and the long time they have been due (exclusive of the service done) I hope you will upon the whole find the charges reasonable." [13] In the same communication he speaks of the seizure of a cargo of gunpowder by a British force at Natchez, which he was forwarding for the relief of Fort Jefferson. Pollock's sky seemed to clear with the taking of Pensacola.

As long as this post, defended by 1,300 regulars and sailors,

[13] May 17, 1781.

under General Campbell with inhabitants and Negroes numbering an additional 1,200, was in the possession of the British, Galvez recognized that his control over the lower Mississippi region was menaced. Throughout the year, after the capture of Mobile, he strove to carry out the demand of the king that Pensacola should be attacked. In a council of officers held at Havana, with Galvez, now a Field Marshal, present, it was decided to furnish him with a force of 3,800 men and equipment for carrying out this objective by the middle of October. Notwithstanding adverse weather predictions, the expedition sailed.[14] Within forty-eight hours, the transports were overtaken by a hurricane lasting five days, of such terrific force that the vessels were scattered, some of them finding shelter at Mobile and New Orleans, while others returned to Havana.

Preparations, hastened by the report that Pensacola was being reinforced, were again under way by the first of the year 1781. Overcoming all opposition and in spite of his ill health, Galvez was prepared to set sail from Cuba by the last of February. On March 9, "At the hour of Prayer the convoy came to anchor at a distance of one cannon shot from shore." That night the troops were landed on the Island of Santa Rosa at the entrance to the harbor of Pensacola. A battery was constructed for the protection of the ships while crossing the bar into the harbor.

The inhabitants took refuge within the fort and preparations for a siege, which lasted a month, were soon under way.[15]

---

[14] October 16, 1780, "Diary of Bernardo Galvez on the Operations against Pensacola," *La. Hist. Quar.*, Vol. I, No. 1, pp. 44–84.

[15] For the preliminary correspondence between Galvez and Campbell, see *ibid.*, pp. 53–58. These letters are of special interest, in contrast with twentieth-century usage since they are concerned with the protection of buildings and of women and children and the disposal of prisoners.

Galvez to Campbell

"MOST EXCELLENT, MY DEAR SIR:

The English in Havana intimated with threats that none of the ships or buildings of the King and private parties is destroyed, burned or torn down under pain of being treated with the utmost rigor. The same warning I give to your Excellency. . . . God keep your Excellency many

THE NORTHWEST: CONQUEST OR GIFT? 229

Meantime, additional troops from Mobile and New Orleans arrived, increasing the number of men under Galvez to 3,500. Three weeks later, the Spanish force was greatly strengthened by the arrival of a squadron of eight ships and 1,600 troops from Havana.[16] The last hope for the besieged garrison was now gone.[17] On the morning of May 8, a shell exploded an English powder magazine, causing a breach in the wall of an advanced redoubt.[18] That afternoon a flag of truce was run up over Fort George and the following day articles of capitulation were agreed upon. Under the terms, not only Pensacola, but all of West Florida was to remain in Spanish hands.[19] As a reward for this brilliant achievement, Galvez was promoted to the rank of lieutenant general in the army and was named Governor of West Florida and Louisiana. He was, likewise,

---

years. March 20, 1781, Most Excellent Sir. Your most attentive servant kisses your Excellency's hands.
BERNARDO DE GALVEZ"
Campbell to Galvez
". . . that neither the City nor buildings of Pensacola, nor any part or portion of it, will be occupied or employed by any of the parties to attack, preserve or defend themselves, nor for any other purpose whatever, but that it shall be an asylum for the sick, women and children, who may remain there without malicious injuries, harm, or molestation on the part of the English, Spanish troops, or their allies. March 21, 1781. Most Excellent Sir, Your most attentive servitor kisses your Excellency's hand.
JOHN CAMPBELL"

[16] The number of men under Galvez was 7,000. Caughey, *op. cit.*, 208. Dr. Caughey gives an extended account of the operations at Pensacola, *Ibid.*, 200-214.

[17] Originally the garrison contained 1,600 men. Three hundred and fifty had made their escape to Georgia, sixty deserted.

[18] One hundred defenders lost their lives.

[19] One hundred women and 123 children were to accompany the prisoners who were to "embark as soon as possible in ships in good condition and provided with provisions at the expense of His Catholic Majesty to be taken to whatever ports of Great Britain General Campbell may select, except the ports of the island of Jamaica and St. Augustine, Florida." The troops and sailors were "not to serve against Spain or her allies until exchanged for an equal number of Spanish prisoners, or of the latter's allies."

awarded the title, count, and granted a salary of 10,000 pesos annually during the continuance of the War.

Information on the capture of Pensacola was transmitted immediately to Congress by Pollock. With the Mississippi thus reopened for trade, he counted on the inauguration of some plan for his financial relief. Flour, he suggested, would find a ready market at from $35 to $40 a barrel in New Orleans and Pensacola. Evidently there was a surplus in the Pittsburgh market for the commander of that post, at the opening of navigation in 1782, reported that he gave permits to ten boats, each carrying ten tons, loaded with flour for New Orleans and Kentucky. Another fleet, even larger, was then preparing for the same markets.[20]

Once more, early in May, the garrison at Fort Jefferson was saved through an order drawn on Pollock to the amount of 5,420 pistoles. From this time, desertions by the soldiers and settlers became so general that the fort was finally evacuated.[21]

Throughout the year 1781, Pollock was still hopeful that his claims against the United States and Virginia would be approved. After consideration by a committee of the memorial presented by his agent, Congress directed the Treasury Board to pass $37,836 in specie to his credit.[22] But there were no funds to meet this obligation. A second agent appeared with a memorial pertaining to the advances made to Pollock by Governor Galvez. Upon this appeal $21,419 were passed in his favor to the books of the Treasury. Six per cent was stipulated as the interest rate in both cases. One of the agents to whom Pollock finally gave full power of attorney in presenting his claims before the Committee of Congress and also to the Governor of Virginia was Daniel Clarke, who, as we have seen, had made large advances in money to meet the wants of Clark's troops.

Colonel Clark, he declared, was without supplies from Vir-

---

[20] General Irvine to Washington, April 29, 1782. C. W. Butterfield, *Washington-Irvine Correspondence* (Madison, 1882), p. 202.

[21] June 8, 1781. *Clark Papers*, p. 585.

[22] This memorial was presented by his agent, John Henderson, January 24, 1781. *Draper MSS.*, 43J149, 150.

THE NORTHWEST: CONQUEST OR GIFT? 231

ginia. His necessities were procured from the inhabitants of the French villages. Bills, therefore, were drawn on the treasury of the State. In Clarke's words:

> To give value and credit to these bills, Mr. Pollock did with more zeal than prudence exert himself,—he expended his own fortune which was respectable in honouring those Bills and borrowed money on his own Credit for the same purpose to a very considerable amount. To my knowledge, Mr. Pollock owes at this hour upwards of eighty thousand dollars, which he borrowed for the service of this State. . . . Unless your Excellency will be pleased to take Mr. Pollock's case into consideration, and to order an immediate adjustment of his accounts, his Creditors will no longer forbear with him. As soon as I return to New Orleans, if I should be unsuccessful in my application to your Excellency on his behalf, he will most assuredly be deprived of his Liberty. If his accounts are now settled, though payment be deferred a year, or longer, it will in some measure appease his clamorous creditors, and keep him from experiencing the miseries of a loathsome prison. . . . I wish for no more, than to see justice take place between Virginia and her servant Pollock, who, to my knowledge when the event of ye War was doubtful, and the independence of America uncertain, virtuously and like a true Whig advanced his fortune in support of her Cause. Ruin from a victorious British Enemy, Pollock might reasonably expect, but from a victorious friend, from Virginia, to whose service his Life and Fortune have been devoted, he had reason to expect a just, if not a generous acquital.[23]

To Governor Harrison, Clarke wrote:

> The balance in favor of Mr. Pollock appears great. But as the whole has been an expenditure for the purpose of supporting your army to the Westward, which could not possibly subsist, or continue in that Service had not Mr. Pollock generously exerted himself in their behalf.[24]

The tide of war had now turned against the British. With the surrender of Cornwallis at Yorktown, October 19, 1781, the Revolution east of the mountains was really at an end. Instructions issued to Sir Guy Carleton as he was setting out

---
[23] *Calendar of Va. State Papers,* III, 25–29.
[24] "Clark MSS.," *Va. State Archives,* January 17, 1782.

to take command in America contain evidence of this fact. He was directed to transfer the garrison at New York to Halifax and the garrisons at Charleston and Savannah were to be withdrawn.

But during the last months of 1781, and for a year thereafter, control over the West was still in the balance. Early in December, the numerous recommendations from Western officials were taken up by the Legislature of Virginia. While the members were fully aware of the critical situation, they were powerless to assume the burdens of an offensive warfare with an empty treasury and with paper money depreciated to the ratio of 1,000 to 1.[25] Legislative regulations and the imposition of additional taxes were resorted to with the hope of restoring lost credit. But contributions for the support of the army under General Nathanael Greene and the campaign against Cornwallis had drained the State of its resources. The extended territory from which collections were to be made rendered immediate relief through taxation well nigh impossible. Governor Harrison was forced to answer the appeal of General Greene for relief as follows: "The credit of the State is lost and we have not a shilling in the Treasury. The powers formerly given to embody and march the militia of the State are no longer continued to us, nor can we impress what may be necessary for you or even for ourselves. Invasion has nearly drained us of our Stock of Provisions and Refreshments of all kinds necessary for an army. As this is not an exaggerated but a true state of our situation I leave you to judge whether any great Dependance can for the present be placed on this State." [26]

In council with his officers and the three Kentucky County lieutenants early in September, Clark clung to his immediate objective to march against the Indians by way of the Wabash or the Miami and then to Detroit. While insisting upon the maintenance of the garrison at the Falls, the county lieutenants recommended that a fort should be built at the mouth of the Kentucky, and urged the assembling of a strong force for

[25] *Draper MSS.*, 51J98.
[26] *Harrison Letter Book*, 1781, p. 32. January 21, 1782.

THE NORTHWEST: CONQUEST OR GIFT? 233

the reduction of Detroit in the spring. Clark still advocated an expedition up the Wabash against the Indian tribes, for it was among them that British emissaries seemed to be most strongly intrenched. He saw in such a movement the capture of Detroit and the possession of Lake Erie; control of the savages and preservation of the Kentucky settlements; retention of power over the Illinois, both Spanish and American; and ultimate influence on the terms of peace.[27] It seems probable that he had in his possession the message from Colonel Arthur Campbell, written a month earlier, in which he stated that peace might be expected within a few months. This message concludes with language strikingly resembling that of Benjamin Franklin in the peace preliminaries, seven and a half months later: "I wish we could carry our arms to the banks of Lake Erie, before a cessation would take place; to attempt it farther, might be risking too much. For Canada confined to its ancient limits may serve our present turn, although every true American must acknowledge the advantages that would accrue, could Canada be added to the Union." [28]

During the fall and winter, British leaders renewed their efforts to gain control of all the Northwestern tribes. Clark's preparations, his evasive answers to their inquiries and messages to the enemy, had caused more than one-half of the tribes to make overtures for peace.[29] Typical of these reports was one sent to the court at Kaskaskia, early in December, calling for a thorough enforcement of the laws. Peace, he said, was shortly to be expected since Cornwallis with his entire army had surrendered and Clinton had lost three thousand men. "Charleston," he declared, "is, besieged and I think by this time it has surrendered with all the English troops; so that there will scarcely remain an Englishman on the continent except those who are prisoners." [30]

Late in February, 1782, chiefs of the Shawnee, Wyandot,

[27] Clark to Governor Nelson, Oct. 1, 1781. *Clark Papers*, pp. 605–608.
[28] Campbell to Clark, Sept. 3, 1781. *Clark Papers*, p. 595. Colonel Campbell was stationed at Washington, Pa.
[29] "Draper MSS.," Shane Papers, XVI, 37.
[30] *Mich. Pioneer and Hist. Coll's.*, X, 548.

Delawares, and ten other tribes, were brought to Detroit. They were instructed to make no attack until toward spring. As a feint, small parties were sent forward to steal horses and commit minor depredations, in order to put settlers off their guard until the coming of the main expedition, which was to capture Fort Nelson and the other posts and at a single blow lay waste the whole frontier. As expressed by Clark, "the designs of the Detroit Gentry is reduced to a certainty. They have their eye on this and the Spanish Illinois." [31] Promise for the success of such a plan was greater because of the arrival at Detroit of Rocheblave, Lamothe, and other captured leaders who were all anxious to retrieve their former disasters by recapturing the Illinois country and Vincennes.[32]

Fully aware that the task was one of the most difficult he had undertaken, Clark pushed his preparations vigorously for foiling this attack which he was assured would be directed against Fort Nelson. "If we should be so fortunate as to repel this invasion without too great loss to ourselves," he wrote while strengthening the various means of defense, "the Indians will all scatter to their different countries and give a fair opportunity for a valuable stroke to be made among them."

Assuming a portion of the expense himself, Clark gave special attention to the construction of four armed galleys with the design of using them to control navigation at the mouth of the Ohio. By the end of May, one of these boats with a 73-foot keel was completed. When fully equipped, it was to be manned with 110 men and was to carry a six pounder, two fours and a two pounder. Obstacles in carrying out his plans were continuous.[33]

Clark's preparations had in the usual manner been magnified by British leaders. Kaskaskia, Vincennes, Piqua had familiarized them with his penchant for the seemingly impossible. It was reported that he was about to march with a large

---

[31] Letter to Governor Harrison, May 2, 1782. "Clark Papers," *Ill. Hist. Coll's.*, XIX, p. 64.

[32] For the Lamothe plan, *see* Butterfield, *Washington-Irvine Correspondence* and *Mich. Pioneer and Hist. Coll's.*, X, 546, 547.

[33] *See Life of Clark*, pp. 261, 262.

THE NORTHWEST: CONQUEST OR GIFT? 235

army for the capture of Detroit. To add to their alarm, the first intelligence reached them, in early April, of the surrender of Cornwallis. It was rumored, also, that the Iroquois were about to make peace with the Americans. There was no hope for assistance from Montreal since British authorities were aware that any troops to be spared would be needed for the reinforcement of Clinton at New York. General Haldimand, anticipating the necessity for holding Detroit, in the event of peace, ordered the collection of sufficient provisions to enable the garrison to withstand a formidable assault. Immense treasure was granted the Indians by officials and discipline was relaxed, for as stated, Indians must be used to prevent the inroads of the Virginians and they must be "delicately managed to prevent their favoring those rebels."

In early June, 1782, occurred the defeat of Colonel William Crawford, a friend of Washington, who was advancing from Pittsburgh at the head of 480 mounted men against the Wyandot and Shawnee villages on the Sandusky River. So leisurely had they advanced that upon arrival at the first of the towns, spies having dogged their footsteps, they were confronted with a force of rangers, volunteers, and Indians hurriedly brought to the defense by Captain William Caldwell. After a two days' battle, the Americans, under the mistaken impression that the enemy was greatly superior in numbers, began a retreat which ended in hopeless confusion. Among the fifty men killed or missing was Colonel Crawford. He, with others, was put to death with the extreme of torture.[34]

By the middle of August, Captains Caldwell and McKee with a force of three hundred Indians and rangers, eluding the vigilance of John Todd, succeeded in crossing the Ohio and bringing on the disaster of the Blue Licks.[35] Todd lost his life

[34] The Delawares justified their fiendish performances as a retaliation for the cruelties their relatives had undergone at the hands of backwoodsmen in the Moravian Massacre. See *Life of Clark*, pp. 263, 264. For a more extended account of conditions on the upper Ohio, see Ralph C. Downes, "Indian War On the Upper Ohio, 1779–1782," *Western Penna. Hist. Mag.*, XVII, No. 2.

[35] For this battle, consult *Life of Clark*, pp. 268–75.

in this ill-starred affair. Other leaders, in petitioning Governor Harrison, strove to shift the blame to Clark for his failure to build other fortified posts in addition to Fort Nelson. Replying to a rebuke from the governor, Clark maintained that the completion of this fort had saved the Western country, and that the disaster of the Blue Licks was due to the conduct, "extremely reprehensible," of leaders who were attempting to offset their former neglect of duty.

Early in September, Caldwell was again at the upper Sandusky, where he awaited the coming of a rumored expedition from Fort Pitt. Detroit officials, anticipating that he would be forced to retreat before so formidable an enemy and that the Shawnee would be unable to withstand an attack by Clark, prepared a second line of defense which would cover the retreat. As usual, Major De Peyster, overcome with fear at the rumor of the approach of the enemy, was ready to sacrifice his Indian allies. He wrote Captain McKee as follows: "By the accounts of their force, in the present sickly state of the Rangers, and the Indians being so much distressed, I fear you will be obliged to retreat at least until you are joined by the Miamies. I have sent all the Indians I could muster, particularly the Ottawas of the Miami River. . . . You must be sensible that my soldiers are little acquainted with wood fighting and ill-equipped for it withall. I have therefore only ordered them to take post where they can secure ammunition and provisions and support you in case you are obliged to retreat, which I hope will still not be the case." [36]

Once more, using tactics made familiar in modern warfare, a grand attack by the Americans was to be launched following a desperate defensive. Clark was to attack the Shawnee strongholds. General Irvine was to advance from Fort Pitt against Sandusky. Nine hundred men were to be sent also against the Genesee towns.

Kentuckians responded quickly to Clark's call for a retaliatory expedition. Parched meal and buffalo beef were readily collected, but other supplies were procured with difficulty.

---

[36] October 1, 1782, *Mich. Pioneer and Hist. Coll's.*, X, 651.

THE NORTHWEST: CONQUEST OR GIFT? 237

The credit of the State was worthless and creditors who had already advanced all of their property were then beseeching Clark to aid them in adjusting their claims. Among them was Pollock, whose agents had gained but slight consideration from Virginia.

"I am heartily sorry that you should meet with such disappointments in the settlement of your accounts," Clark writes Pollock. "I have already taken every step in my power to get the Creditors of the State paid to no effect. . . .

"Except what the state owes me am not worth a Spanish dollar, I wish it was in my power to follow your proposition to step forth and save my country from the disgrace that is likely to fall on her. If you could point out the means nothing would give me such pleasure, and fully Recompense all the uneasiness I have suffr'd on account of those persons, Many whom I know have advanced their all on the faith of Government." [37] Clark finally exchanged 3,500 acres of his own land for the flour necessary for the expedition.

On November 4, 1782, at the head of 1,050 mounted men, he set out from the mouth of the Licking for Chillicothe, the Shawnee stronghold. During a march of six days, rigid discipline was maintained.[38] A plan of attack in minute detail had been worked out by Clark. Three miles from the town, Colonel Floyd was dispatched with three hundred men to make the assault. His approach was discovered and the inhabitants, warned by the alarm cry, made good their escape. Chillicothe and five other Shawnee villages were burned and great quantities of corn and other provisions were destroyed. Colonel Logan with a detachment of one hundred and fifty men captured the British trading-post at the head of the Miami and burned such stores as they were unable to carry away with them. After vainly attempting, for four days, to bring on a general engagement, Clark returned with his troops to the mouth of the Licking, where the divisions separated.

By this blow, virtually the last during the Revolution, Clark

[37] October 25, 1782. "Clark Papers," *Ill. Hist. Coll's.*, XIX, p. 144.
[38] *Draper MSS.*, 11J24.

had not only saved the frontier settlements from danger of attack but he had once more offset the designs of British authorities to bring about a union of the Northwestern and Southwestern tribes. This plan was closely akin to that of 1780 and was well calculated to win support from the Indian chiefs. A large force from Detroit was to advance against Fort Pitt, and, after taking that post, was to capture the Illinois country.[39] Thus, Kentuckians, it was said, would be driven across the mountains and the "other inhabitants into the sea."

But Clark had again carried out his favorite policy of convincing "the Indians that they were inferior to us, that the British assertions of our weakness were false, and that we could at all times penetrate into their Country at pleasure." The redmen were panic-stricken. Their winter supplies were destroyed. The policy of retrenchment on the part of British officials cut down the quota of presents. As interpreted by the Indians, this was a step toward their complete abandonment. Further demands by them for protection from Detroit were refused.[40]

From this review of events up to the close of 1782, it is seen that Clark had extended his radius of menace toward Detroit and had thrown the enemy into confusion. Sickness still pervaded the ranks of the British rangers. Regulars, it was claimed, were not suitable nor were they equipped for winter campaigning. Said Major De Peyster: "The few Rangers of this Post prevents my doing anything essential for the relief of the Indian villages, it is therefore to be hoped that when the enemy have done all the mischief possible they will retire." [41] He was aware that the road to Detroit was open and foretold an attack by the Americans in the spring. Indian leaders were again ordered to act solely on the defensive. In demanding reinforcements, De Peyster declared: "Light troops are therefore what we want and believe me there will be amusement for a good number of them the ensuing campaign without acting

[39] February 2, 1783, *Clark Papers*, p. 189.
[40] *Mich. Pioneer and Hist. Coll's.*, I, 320, 321.
[41] November 21, 1782, De Peyster to Haldimand, *Ibid.*, XI, 322.

THE NORTHWEST: CONQUEST OR GIFT? 239

on the offensive." So thoroughly had Clark carried out his policy of intimidating the Indians that, as stated by Boone: "The spirits of the Indians were damped, their connexions dissolved, their armies scattered and a future invasion [was] entirely out of their power." [42]

Messengers sent by General Irvine informed Clark that the expedition against Sandusky was assured. As they were about to set out from Fort McIntosh, the place of rendezvous, letters were received from the Continental Secretary of War countermanding the order. Washington had been assured, on British authority, that all hostilities were suspended and that the Indians were directed to commit no further depredations. Nevertheless, reports were still sent out by Irvine that he was about to march with a large force. These were intended to deceive the Wyandot and prevent their coöperation with the Shawnee against Clark.

Combatant and non-combatant alike at Detroit and all the other posts awaited the passing of winter with anxious foreboding. British officials fully expected the coming of the Americans, with the design of pushing their frontier-line in the Northwest forward as far as possible, and thus, in the event of peace, securing control of the fur-trade.[43]

Clark's threats to march against other unfriendly tribes as he had against the Shawnee increased the turmoil among the Indians. Once more, he had been able to procure supplies amounting to $750 with an order drawn on Pollock. He proposed enlisting a force of 1,500 troops which was to march against the Indian stronghold at the head of the Wabash. In this way, he would convince the Indians that their very existence depended upon preserving peace with the Americans. A garrison of regular troops was to be stationed at Vincennes with supplies sufficient to equip an army which might be brought together at any time for the purpose of penetrating

---

[42] Testimony of Daniel Boone before a Committee of Investigation, December 20, 1787. "State Department MSS.," *Bureau of Indexes and Archives.*

[43] *Mich. Pioneer and Hist. Coll's.*, XI, 351.

"into any Quarter of the Enemy's Country at Pleasure." No further effort was made to carry out these plans, for by the middle of April, 1783, official announcement of peace preliminaries had reached the frontier. By the terms of the treaty, concluded in Paris, September 3, 1783, the Old Northwest was ceded to the United States.[44]

Since no specific reference is made in the diplomatic proceedings to the conquest by Clark, the question has long been a mooted one as to how far Clark was in military control of the Northwest and what effect it had in winning this great empire for the United States. Two views have been advanced.

Ten months preceding Clark's final drive against the Shawnee, an agent, in presenting Pollock's claims for relief before the Governor of Virginia, referred to the great expense incident to carrying on war in the West and Pollock's participation therein, declaring: "But great as they [expenses] are, yet greater are the benefits you have and will derive from them. You have, Sir, taken possession, and I hope secured the remotest part of your territorial Claim, and perhaps the finest Country on Earth. You have made yourselves respectable among the Indians of that Country, and secured their friendship. You have prevented the British and their Indian allies from taking possession of that Country and thereby opened and secured a communication to New Orleans where your back Settlers on the Ohio will always meet with a friendly reception and a good market for their Produce. And you have, Sir, in all human probability prevented the British of Detroit and their Indians from joining Lord Cornwallis, while he was in the full career of a successful invader, over-running this Country. Such a junction, Sir, at that time, would have been fatal to Virginia." [45]

This view was likewise advanced in a letter by Governor

[44] The present States of Ohio, Indiana, Illinois, Michigan, and Wisconsin were included. For the events leading up to the definitive treaty and the terms agreed upon, *consult* Edward Channing, *History of the United States*, III, 346-373.

[45] January 17, 1782. Daniel Clarke to Governor Harrison. *Cal. Va. State Papers*, III, 25-29.

THE NORTHWEST: CONQUEST OR GIFT? 241

Harrison to Clark, in which he states that since an offensive war against the Northwestern Indians has been given up, Clark's services in that region will no longer be necessary—"But before I take leave of you, I feel myself called on in the most forcible manner to return my thanks and those of my council for the very great and singular services you have rendered your Country, in wresting so great and valuable a territory out of the hands of the British Enemy, repelling the attacks of their savage allies, and carrying on successful war in the heart of their country." [46]

Two of the three commissioners who were selected to adjust the claims of Virginia against the United States for debts contracted by Pollock and others in carrying on the Revolution in the West, confirmed this view.[47] "It appears to me," David Henley writes, "from the knowledge I have of the Illinois account and papers . . . that your [Pollock's] exertions in behalf of General Clark and the troops under his command, was a means of enabling him to hold the country and support his army." William Heth in a letter to Pollock declared: "There is no circumstance of which I am more convinced than that the conquest of the Illinois country could not have been maintained by Virginia and that consequently that it would not now form a part of the United States if it had not been for your assistance and very liberal advance." [48]

In speaking of the sacrifice of his fortune and the debts he had contracted "for the support of the service," Pollock asserts: "Having no other person in that Quarter of their Country to Supply their forces, the Troops must [have] quit the Country which would now be in possession of the British or the Spanish Monarck." [49] The testimony of Clark himself con-

---

[46] July 2, 1783.

[47] The three commissioners were William Heth, representing Virginia; John Pierce, representing the United States, and David Henley, who was selected as the third commissioner.

[48] William Heth to Oliver Pollock, April 22, 1788. Printed pamphlet, *Va. State Archives.*

[49] July 16, 1782. "Executive Communications to the Virginia Assembly," October 21–December 28, 1782. *Virginia Archives.*

firms this argument, when he says: "The service Mr. Pollock rendered upon all occasions in paying those bills, I considered at the time and now to be one of the happy circumstances that enabled me to keep possession of that Country." [50]

But John Pierce, who represented the United States in the adjustment of the claims of Virginia, declared that by leaving the territory with his forces, Clark relinquished the defense of it "and he cannot, I think, be said to have maintained or defended a Country beyond him in which he retained no garrison and from which he was at such a distance as to afford no immediate assistance." [51]

Similar divergent views have been advanced by historians. In one of his last published statements, Professor Frederick J. Turner speaks of Clark as "the conqueror of the Illinois country." [52] "We were in reality, given nothing more than we had by our own prowess gained," Theodore Roosevelt declares. "The inference is strong that we got what we did get only because we had won and held it." [53]

Arguments in support of the opposite view may be summarized as follows: "The summer of 1779 marked the zenith of Virginia's power north of the Ohio; from that date there was a steady decline. . . . For a year more, there were a score of soldiers in those posts, acting as scouts; but even these were recalled in the following winter, and the villages were left to shift for themselves. . . . Virginia had really only weakened the hold of the mother country on a small corner of the disputed territory." "The basis for the success of American diplomacy," Dr. Alvord continues, "had been laid, not by the victory of the arms of Virginia, not through the boldness of George Rogers Clark in winning the Old Northwest for the

[50] July 2, 1785. "Clark MSS.," *Va. Archives.*
[51] Report of the Commissioners.
[52] Frederick Jackson Turner, *Sectionalism in American History* (Henry Holt and Company, 1932), p. 55.
[53] Roosevelt, *The Winning of the West*, II, 38. For a similar view, see Reuben G. Thwaites, *How George Rogers Clark Won the Northwest*, p. 72; Claude H. Van Tyne, *American Revolution* (American Nation Series), IX, 284.

THE NORTHWEST: CONQUEST OR GIFT? 243

United States, but in the liberal principles held by a British statesmen."[54]

In support of this view, the argument has also been advanced that the Earl of Shelburne had probably never heard of Clark, "and his operations or would have been influenced by them if he had."[55] But in the files of the British Public Record Office have been found quotations from a Philadelphia newspaper of July 3, 1779, giving extracts from the well-known letter of Clark to Governor Henry, which describe the defeat of Governor Hamilton at Vincennes. It follows, therefore, that Lord George Germaine and probably other British leaders were aware of this victory by October, 1779.[56] The testimony of Hamilton is likewise proof of this statement. He says: "In

---

[54] Clarence W. Alvord, "Virginia and the West," *Miss. Valley Hist. Rev.*, III (1916, 1917), p. 34. Dr. Alvord writes: "Most western writers, anxious to magnify the importance of their own region, have been inclined to give Clark the credit of securing for the United States this important acquisition; the easterners have had too little information on the subject to express an authoritative opinion, but many have allowed their skepticism to become evident. . . . It is possible that the American commissioners may have felt that their position in claiming the West for the new republic was somewhat strengthened by the knowledge of the success of Clark, but it is unbelievable that they would have demanded less, even had he failed, since the first boundaries proposed by Benjamin Franklin included all Canada as well as the West." *Ibid.*, p. 35.

[55] Solon J. Buck, *Minnesota Historical Quarterly*, X, p. 65. "The appraisal of Clark's services by contemporaries and historians has been beclouded by the erroneous assumption that his objective was the conquest of territory for the United States or Virginia. His campaign was rather in the nature of an offensive defense of Kentucky, which was just beginning to be settled, and even his plans for the capture of Detroit had the same end in view. When the available forces proved insufficient for the continuance of this type of operations he fell back to the Ohio and devoted his energies to guarding the frontier and making occasional raids into the enemy's territory. Despite the fact that bands of Indians at times got across the border and attacked the Kentucky settlements, Clark's tactics were successful to the extent that they made possible the continued influx of settlers, with the result that at the end of the Revolution Kentucky had a population of fifteen or twenty thousand. That was the real achievement of George Rogers Clark. Thus Clark's operations may have had an indirect influence on the negotiations."

[56] These extracts were enclosed in a letter of General Clinton to Lord Germaine, No. 62, July 26, 1779. Public Record Office (new classification), Colonial Office, Class 5, Vol. 98 [old A. W. I.], p. 273.

the month of June, 1781, I returned to England. Lord Sackville, Mr. Ellis, and finally the Earl of Shelburne had the condescension to attend to my situation, and from their favor and protection am happy to think they did not attribute my failure to negligence or want of zeal for His Majesty's Service." [57]

The fact that Clark concentrated his available force at Fort Nelson after 1779 does not prove that he relinquished his hold on the Northwest. His own testimony warrants another conclusion for he wrote: "I see but one probable method of maintaining our authority in the Illinois which is this by evacuating our present posts and let our whole force center at or near the mouth of the Ohio." [58] The results of his campaigns of 1780 and 1782 demonstrate his wisdom in selecting Fort Nelson as his base for operations. In his appeal to the Virginia Commissioners for assistance in organizing an army which should by the summer of 1783 "penetrate to the head of the Wabash," he claimed that Virginia was in control of the territory which had been conquered. His expression was: "The Illinoise Settlements like to be lost to the State through inattention that will nearly double the Enemy." [59] Judged by the statement of a well-known British leader, the Illinois country was under the control of Clark in April of the previous year. "If the expedition succeeds in taking the Illinois," Lamothe writes in submitting his plan of operation, "then the small army will embark & go to reduce the Post of St. Vincennes and continue its route to come to Detroit by the Wabache." [60] Plans for the campaign to be carried out by the British in the spring of 1783, comprehended, as we have seen, "an expedition against Fort Pitt, the Falls of the Ohio and Kentucky and thence to the Illinois." [61]

Fort Nelson was, as Clark wrote on a number of occasions,

---

[57] *Draper MSS.*, 45J69.

[58] He refers to the concentration at Fort Jefferson. The same argument obtained relative to Fort Nelson.

[59] February 25, 1783, *Clark Papers*, p. 204.

[60] Lamothe was then, April 24, 1782, at Detroit. *Mich. Pioneer Coll's.*, X, 571.

[61] Feb. 2, 1783, *Clark Papers*, p. 189.

THE NORTHWEST: CONQUEST OR GIFT? 245

the key to the Western country. This was well-known to the British. They were aware that it dominated trade on the Ohio and that it was the center for operations against Detroit. From this base, it was possible for Clark to reach Vincennes and Kaskaskia by a much shorter march than could have been accomplished by the British from Detroit. The report of any advance by the enemy was quickly imparted to Clark. Moreover, warriors of the tribes on the Miami River and the Wabash, chief dependence of the British, could not be induced to engage in any expedition which would leave their villages exposed to attack by an enemy so readily brought against them.

After a review of these facts, I again state, in answer to any criticism of my use of the expression "conquered territory," that Clark was really in military control of the greater part of the Northwest when negotiations for peace were begun.

The American commissioners could have had no doubt on this point. Was it not the foundation for the demand that the Great Lakes and the Mississippi were to constitute the boundaries? Indisputable right to this territory had been asserted as an offset to any Spanish claims. American ministers at Versailles and Madrid were informed through a letter prepared by a Committee of Congress, "that if a right to the said territory depended on the conquests of the British posts within it, the United States have already a more extensive claim to it than Spain can acquire, having, by the success of their arms, obtained possession of all the important posts and settlements on the Illinois and Wabash, rescued the inhabitants from British domination and established civil government in its proper form over them." [62] In fact, as we have seen, the Spanish governor at St. Louis in December, 1780, defined the status of the inhabitants as "subjects" of the United States by right of conquest.[63]

That this claim constituted the background for the attitude of the American commissioners in Paris is definitely confirmed by the correspondence of John Jay. In a letter to Robert R.

[62] Oct. 17, 1780, *American State Papers, Foreign Relations,* VI, 868.
[63] *See ante.,* p. 218.

Livingston, November 17, 1782, two weeks before the signing of the peace preliminaries, Jay referred to the proposed territorial claim of Spain as defined by a line extending from the "confluence of the Kanawha with the Ohio, thence round the western shores of Lakes Erie and Huron, and then round Lake Michigan to Lake Superior." This suggested boundary, likewise approved by the French representative, was declared to be "utterly inadmissable" by Jay. "Dr. Franklin joined with me," he wrote, "in pointing out the extravagance of this line; and I must do him the justice to say that in all his letters to me, and in all his conversations with me respecting our western extent, he has invariably declared it to be his opinion that we should insist upon the Mississippi as our western boundary." [64] Franklin, beyond question, knew of the military accomplishments of Clark, and it must be inferred that he gave this information to the other commissioners.[65]

Any claim by Great Britain to the territory had been disposed of in the report of a special committee of Congress which declared: "From a full confidence that the western territory now contended for lay within the United States, the British posts therein have been reduced by our citizens and American government is now exercised within the same." [66] Even

[64] Jay to Robert R. Livingston. *The Correspondence and Public Papers of John Jay* (New York, 1891), II, 390. In a letter to Livingston, April 12, 1782, Franklin declared: "I see by the newspapers that the Spaniards having taken a little post called St. Joseph, pretend to have made a conquest of the Illinois country. In what light does this proceeding appear to Congress? While they decline our offered friendship, are they to be suffered to encroach on our bounds and shut us up within the Appalachian Mountains?" Wharton, *Dip. Corr.*, V, 300.

[65] In a letter written to him by Petre Sargé, from La Rochelle, France, July 6, 1779, Franklin was informed of the capture of Kaskaskia and Vincennes by Clark and of the assistance given by Pollock. Sargé sailed from New Orleans, April 20 of that year. "Franklin Papers," *American Philosophical Society*, Philadelphia. This letter was called to the author's attention by Dr. Lewis J. Carey. For this letter and its significance, *see* Carey, "Franklin Is Informed of Clark's Activities in the Old Northwest," *Miss. Valley Hist. Rev.*, XXI, No. 3, pp. 375-378.

[66] *Jour. of the Cont. Cong.*, XXIII, 476. The report of the committee was based upon a communication submitted by the Massachusetts

THE NORTHWEST: CONQUEST OR GIFT? 247

more definite was the declaration of a second committee which met the approval of Congress. This was committed to the Secretary for Foreign Affairs, "to be by him digested, completed and transmitted to the ministers plenipotentiary of the United States for negotiating a treaty of peace." "The very country in question," it asserts, "hath been conquered through the means of the common labours of the United States." [67] Is there not warrant for the conjecture that Franklin was referring to this phase of their instructions when he wrote: "After some weeks, an under-secretary, Mr. Strachey, arrived, with whom we had much contestation about the boundaries and other articles, which he proposed and we settled; . . . We spent many days in disputing, and at length agreed on and signed the preliminaries. . . . They wanted to bring their boundary down to the Ohio, and to settle their loyalists in the Illinois country. We did not choose such neighbors." [68]

The suggestion has been made that because of the great expense incurred in keeping control of the Indians, Great Britain was willing to transfer her claim over the Northwest to the United States. But the policy of buying Indian friendship did not cease with the signing of the treaty of peace.[69] British negotiators at the Treaty of Ghent, which brought the War of 1812 to a close, strove in vain to induce the American diplomats to accede to their desire to regain control over the North-

---

delegates in Congress which contained the statement: "The very country in question hath been conquered through the means of the common labors of the United States. . . . From a full confidence that the western territory now contended for lay within the United States the British posts therein have been reduced by our citizens and American government is now exercised within the same." This, in substance, was the content of an act of the Massachusetts Legislature, Oct. 27, 1781. It was submitted to Congress Nov. 17 of that year, and was reported on by a special committee, January 8, 1782.

[67] August 16, 1782. *Jour. of the Cont. Cong.*, XXIII, pp. 517, 524.

[68] John Bigelow, *The Life of Benjamin Franklin* (Philadelphia, 1875), III, 199–201. This communication to Livingston was dated Dec. 5, 1782.

[69] *See* Louise Phelps Kellogg, "Indian Diplomacy During the Revolution in the West," *Transactions of the Illinois State Historical Society*, No. 36 (Springfield, 1930), p. 12.

west. This accomplished, an Indian reservation was to be created which should serve as a permanent barrier between the United States and Canada west of Niagara.

Chief Black Hawk, as late as 1832, is known to have received yearly presents from British officers at Malden and felt secure of a retreat to Upper Canada if he failed in his rebellion against the authority of the United States.[70]

But the accomplishments of Clark, impossible without the contributions of Pollock, have even greater significance in the development of our nation. That there was a vision of the significance of these events on the part of the contemporaries of Clark and Pollock may be seen as we read: "Two very important events are presumed to have depended in a great measure on these very services of Mr. Pollock: By means of them, the conquest of the Illinois Country was made and secured; and it consequently now forms a part of the United States . . . and Louisiana also has become a part of the United States. From this resolution, and these spirited exertions, in this quarter in the dawn of the revolution, of which Mr. Pollock was the life and soul, the most important effects are at this very day arising." [71] This view has been stressed by one of the leading interpreters of our history [72] as follows: "But if the Northwest had not been acquired by the heroic

---

[70] Louise Phelps Kellogg, *Indian Diplomacy*, p. 12.

[71] From *The Case of Oliver Pollock*, December, 1803.

[72] J. Franklin Jameson in the hearing before the Joint Committee on the Library, Congress of the United States, Sixty-ninth Congress, second session, on Senate Joint Resolution 139 and House Joint Resolution 307. "Joint Resolution Providing for the Participation of the United States in the Celebration in 1929 of the One hundred and Fiftieth Anniversary of the Conquest of the Northwest Territory by George Rogers Clark, Authorizing an Appropriation for the Construction of a Permanent Memorial in the City of Vincennes, State of Indiana, and for other Purposes." An appropriation of $1,796,650 was made by the Federal government for this purpose. An additional sum of $794,259 was granted by the State of Indiana and by Vincennes and Knox County. It is one of the most noteworthy memorials in the United States. Through appropriations made by the legislatures of Indiana and Illinois, a monumental bridge has been erected across the Wabash River which is commemorative of the crossing by the Lincoln family, at this point (1830), from Indiana into Illinois.

THE CLARK MEMORIAL AT VINCENNES

THE NORTHWEST: CONQUEST OR GIFT? 249

action of George Rogers Clark, all the territory to the westward, which the map shows to be more than half of the United States, would never have been acquired; but if the *cribs and cabins* of the United States, to use an old phrase, had been confined to the Allegheny Mountains, it could never have had that career of imperial greatness that we see before us now."

CHAPTER XV

"THE NAVIGATION OF THE MISSISSIPPI RIVER MUST BE FREE."—OLIVER POLLOCK

NO OTHER man, during the decades 1775–1795, understood, as fully as Pollock, the ultimate effect on American interests of the Spanish possession of West Florida and the control by Spain of the navigation of the Mississippi River.[1] For years, as we have seen, he had been carrying on trade with the Illinois country. He knew, personally, the leading traders of that district, such as Gabriel Cerré and Francis Vigo. Some of them, as William Murray and James Rumsey, had taken up their residence in New Orleans and were closely associated with him in business. His vision of the significance of the West was gained also through correspondence with George Rogers Clark and John Todd, Jr., with Francis Bosseron of Vincennes and General Edward Hand of Pittsburgh. Moreover, he was intimately associated with and had the confidence of Spanish officials.

On no occasion does Pollock indulge in expressions such as were in vogue among Eastern leaders relating to Western affairs. Governor Patrick Henry, in 1777, declared in a letter to a Spanish official: "You must be too well acquainted with the nature of our States to entertain any jealousy of their becoming your Rivals in trade, or overstocked as they are with vast tracts of land, that they should ever think of extending their territory."[2] John Jay was opposed to protracting the War for the sake of conquering the Floridas, "to

---

[1] By the definitive treaties between Great Britain, France, Spain, and the United States, September, 1783, Louisiana and the Floridas were ceded to Spain.

[2] October 18, 1777. To the Governor of Cuba. "Clark MSS.," *Va. State Archives.*

which we had no title, or retaining the navigation of the Mississippi which we should not want this age." ³

Pollock's numerous recommendations, throughout the year 1778, on these problems, took different forms. He appealed to the Committee of Congress, after the Willing expedition, on the necessity of establishing posts on the Mississippi for the support of trade up that River since the sea-route had become most hazardous.⁴

No time is to be lost, Pollock asserts, "in sending troops to take Natchez and Manchac." This accomplished, "a regular supply of goods, up River, would be possible." His plan likewise comprehended the capture of Pensacola which would assure control of "all the Indians." For the conquered territory, Spain would be ready to grant advantageous terms.⁵ Such appeals could not fail of a hearing by Robert Morris, whose confidence had been gained by Pollock and who was a member of the Congressional Committee.

Not only was Congress furnished full information regarding events on the lower Mississippi, but communications were forwarded to General Hand at Pittsburgh and to Benjamin Franklin, who since December, 1776, had been at the French Court. Pollock urged upon Clark the necessity of freeing the River communication and of capturing West Florida before Spain should declare war against Great Britain. In that event, a valuable conquest would be lost.⁶ "The free navigation of this River," he again writes Congress, "for many reasons is much wanted for the general good of the Cause and may just now be very easily accomplished." ⁷

Colonel David Rogers, special agent for Virginia, who had been favorably received by Governor Galvez, through the mediation of Pollock, wrote Governor Henry: "I am humbly of opinion, Congress ought immediately to send a sufficient

³ Jay, *Correspondence and Public Papers*, I, 329. Statement made during the fall of 1778.
⁴ March 6, 1778. *Pollock Letters*.
⁵ May 7, 1778, *Ibid*.
⁶ August 20, 1778, *Ibid*.
⁷ August 18, 1778, *Ibid*.

force to retake Natchez and Manchac, and capture Pensacola. They are of great importance to us and should a war break out with Spain and England, the former will immediately possess themselves of these posts and as far as England claims, which would be a prodigious loss to us. At present the communication that way is entirely shut up. Three hundred men would effectually do the business as we have many friends among them." [8]

This appeal bears a close resemblance, as was natural, to that previously used by Pollock. It is not surprising, therefore, to find the same sentiment expressed in a letter to General Washington by Patrick Henry, which states: "Forts Natchez and Morishac [Manchac] are again in the enemy's hands, and from thence they infest and ruin our trade on the Mississippi, on which river the Spaniards wish to open a very interesting commerce with us. I have requested Congress to authorize the conquest of these two posts, as the possession of them will give a colorable pretence to retain all West Florida when a treaty may be opened, and in the meantime, ruin our trade in that quarter, which would otherwise be so beneficial. I can get no answer to this application, although it is interesting to our back settlements, and not more than four hundred men required for the service." [9]

Early in 1779, Pollock was appealing to the Committee as follows: "I cannot imagine what has deterred you from sending an expedition this way before now as it surely must come sooner or later. I shall live in hopes as I make no doubt you know the value of West Florida too well ever to give it up either by treaty or otherwise to any Power upon Earth." [10] With Natchez, Manchac, and Pensacola under the control of the United States, he asserts in a letter to Patrick Henry: "The inhabitants of Kentucky and Illinois country would have a free navigation to come down the River with their produce

---

[8] Rogers to Patrick Henry, October 4, 1778. *Pollock Letters.*

[9] William Wirt Henry, Patrick Henry, *Life, Correspondence and Speeches* (New York, 1891), II, 25.

[10] February 17, 1779, *Pollock Letters.*

to this place [New Orleans], where there is a good market or at our own establishments Manchac and Pensacola which will soon be preferable to this, as we can import our supplies of Goods immediately from Europe and dispatch them up to the back settlements quicker than from here. This being done the Country would get completely settled and flourishing commerce immediately take place after the war." [11] Moreover, in not one of his numerous letters, twenty addressed to the Committee prior to May, 1779, is there to be found the slightest yielding on this primary issue. Such recommendations could not fail of a favorable hearing on account of the intimate relations existing between Robert Morris and Pollock and the confidence in him on the part of Patrick Henry and Thomas Jefferson.

But, in Congress, the problem was made more perplexing because of the united Bourbon interests of France and Spain. There was a faction of congressmen who were prepared to yield the control of the Mississippi in order to gain the adherence of Spain to the Franco-American alliance. Their purpose was, as expressed by Richard Henry Lee, "Nothing but a studied depreciation of our back country."

During July of 1778, there came to Philadelphia "a Spanish merchant" from Havana, Juan de Miralles, who entered upon his task as official observer. Evidence seems to show that he was the originator of the views held by the Spanish Government regarding the Mississippi River. On December 30, 1778, he wrote José de Galvez:

Having arranged to confer in my house and in that of the French Minister [Gérard] with the new President of Congress [John Jay] and various members of it, I have explored (and the said plenipotentiary conspired to the same end) the idea which they hold as to the territory which the Americans have taken from the English in the interior of the Province of Louisiana, Illinois, etc. and in Florida in case they make conquest of it. In regard to the first we discovered, that it is that of encouraging, by means of a company already established, the settlement and cultivation of

[11] July 17, 1779, *Ibid.*

that vast and fertile country, promising that there will be twenty thousand souls there inside of four years, and more than five thousand ready to bear arms, and that the population will increase proportionately in the future. That the right which they have acquired from the English by conquest would give them the facility of exporting their produce by the Mississippi River which flows into the Gulf of Mexico; and as to Florida [they intend] to make another province out of it and add it to the rest of the confederation.[12]

For some weeks, the French minister had been zealously striving to gain the favor of a number of members of Congress for the Spanish cause. "Mr. Girard," Jay wrote, "used very frequently to spend an evening with me, and sometimes sat up very late. As the evening advanced he often became more open, and spoke without reserve on the subject of the views of Spain, and the interest of America with respect to her. He pressed our quitting to her the Floridas and Mississippi as indispensable prerequisites to a treaty, and urged a variety of reasons to support his opinions."[13]

Should Spain, by treaty, acknowledge the independence of the United States, defend it with arms, and grant an annual subsidy for a term of years, Jay would favor surrendering any claims we might have to the Floridas. The navigation of "her river below our territories," that is below the line of 31°, should be conceded to Spain "on her giving us a convenient free port on it."[14]

Gérard suggested to Gouverneur Morris that Spain should be conceded the exclusive navigation of the Mississippi and the possession of St. Augustine, Pensacola, and Mobile. Convinced of the necessity of limiting the Confederacy especially at the South and West, Morris was prepared to sacrifice the

---

[12] Samuel Flagg Bemis, *Pinckney's Treaty*, p. 22.
[13] These advances were made during the fall of 1778.
[14] "Such a policy on the part of Spain would, as Jay believed, bring about general peace and Great Britain rather than hazard the loss of Canada, Nova Scotia and the islands by continuing the war, would yield the Floridas to Spain and independence to us." Jay, *Correspondence and Public Papers*, I, 329-330.

FREE NAVIGATION OF THE MISSISSIPPI

navigation of the Mississippi below the mouth of the Ohio. In this way, the growing, somewhat lawless, population between the Ohio, the St. Lawrence and the Mississippi, might be kept under control of the Confederation.[15] Early in September, 1779, Congress was definitely informed by the French minister that Spain had declared war against Great Britain.[16] Since the middle of March much time had been consumed by Congress in wrangling over possible terms of peace. There was extended debate on the navigation of the Mississippi River and the boundaries. With the knowledge that Spain had declared war, the discussion turned to the question of instructions to be given a minister plenipotentiary who was to endeavor to consummate a treaty of alliance between Spain and the United States.[17] The terms of a possible treaty finally adopted by Congress, September 28, 1779, provided that should Spain accede to an offensive and defensive alliance with France and the United States, the King of Spain should not be precluded from securing to himself the Floridas— "On the contrary, if he shall obtain the Floridas from Great Britain these United States will guarantee the same to his Catholic majesty, provided always that the United States shall enjoy the free navigation of the river Mississippi into and from the sea." [18]

John Jay, recently President of the Continental Congress, was selected to carry on negotiations at Madrid. "He was

[15] Edward S. Corwin, *French Policy and the American Alliance* (Princeton, 1916), 249.

[16] Francis Wharton, *Revolutionary Diplomatic Correspondence of the United States* (Washington, 1889), III, 310.

[17] *Ibid.*, 311.

[18] *Ibid.*, 344. On October 13th, Witherspoon of New Jersey moved, and it was seconded by Gouverneur Morris, that Jay be privately instructed to recede from the claim of "a free navigation of the Mississippi below the 31st degree of latitude" if the obtaining it "be found an insuperable bar to the proposed treaties of amity and commerce between these states and his Catholic majesty." This motion was defeated. The States voting aye, were New Hampshire, New York, New Jersey, and Maryland. Six states voted no. The vote of Massachusetts was divided. *Jour. of the Cont. Cong.*, pp. 1774-1789 (Washington, 1904-), XV, 1168-1169.

particularly to endeavor," his instructions further declared, "to obtain some convenient port or ports below the thirty-first degree of North latitude on the river Mississippi, for all merchant vessels, goods, wares, and merchandises belonging to the inhabitants of these states." Because of the distressed state of our finances and the great depreciation of our paper money, failing to secure a subsidy, he was to solicit a loan of five million dollars at not more than 6 per cent interest.[19]

There was little prospect of success for this mission when, on account of the presence of English cruisers, Jay was forced to disembark at Cadiz on January 22, 1780, after what he described to Benjamin Franklin as a terrible voyage. He was without letters of credit or recommendation to anyone in the city, and had no money except what had been loaned him by two of his fellow-passengers.[20] "I too have had my hair-breadth escapes," wrote John Adams, who had recently arrived in Europe for the purpose of negotiating for peace. But, he continues: "Happy, however shall we be if all our hazards and fatigues should contribute to lay the foundation of a free and prosperous people."

William Carmichael, Jay's secretary, was soon after sent to Madrid with instructions as follows: "In speaking of American affairs, remember to do justice to Virginia and the western country near the Mississippi. Recount their achievements against the savages, their growing numbers, extensive settlements, and aversion to Britain for attempting to involve them in the horrors of an Indian war. Let it appear also from your representations that ages will be necessary to settle those extensive regions. . . . It would be advantageous to know whether Spain means to carry on any serious operations for possessing herself of the Floridas and banks of the Mississippi." [21]

On April 4, Jay arrived at Madrid prepared to open negotiations with Count Florida Blanca. At no time, however,

---

[19] *Wharton, op. cit.*, III, 363.
[20] Jay, *Correspondence*, I, 254.
[21] *Ibid.*, I, 266–268.

FREE NAVIGATION OF THE MISSISSIPPI 257

during the two years he remained, was he given official recognition. As a result, he was excluded from the Court and was studiously neglected by officials and in society. The Committee of Foreign Affairs added to his embarrassment by drawing on him for 100,000 pounds sterling. Writing of such a policy, he said: "I would throw stones too with all my heart if I thought they would hit only the Committee without injuring the members of it. Till now I have received but one letter from them and that not worth a farthing, though it conveyed a draft for one thousand pounds sterling on the bank of hope." [22]

In an extended conference, May 11, 1780, Florida Blanca, with greater hospitality than Jay had anticipated, assured him that while it was the intention of Spain to give America all the assistance within their power, a loan was not possible.[23] It was clearly evident that the ambitions of Spain were, as already shown, unalterably opposed to the interests and aims of the United States. Franklin aptly expressed the situation when he wrote: "As yet they know us too little and are jealous of us too much." The one obstacle in the way of making a treaty arose, it was intimated, from "the pretensions of America to the free navigation of the Mississippi. The United States, the prime minister asserted, had at one time relinquished all right to the use of the Mississippi and was now making it an essential point of a treaty. Jay replied that many of the states were bounded by the River and were greatly interested in its navigation. It was made clear to Jay, however, that "this was an objective that the King had so much at heart that he would never relinquish it." [24]

At a conference in September, Florida Blanca taking the same position, declared, "with some degree of warmth, that unless Spain could exclude all nations from the Gulf of Mexico they might as well admit all; that the King would

[22] Jay, *Correspondence*, I, 440.
[23] A complete account of this conference is given in Jay, *Correspondence*, I, 276, 277, 316–326. Jay was finally able to secure, as a result of his efforts, a loan of $150,000.
[24] *Wharton, op. cit.*, III, 724.

never relinquish it; that the minister regarded it as the principal object to be obtained by the war; and *that obtained,* he should be perfectly easy whether or not Spain procured any other cession; that he considered it far more important than the acquisition of Gibraltar, and that if they did not get it, it was a matter of indifference to him whether the English possessed Mobile or not." [25] But West Florida, with Pensacola and Mobile, he was determined to secure for Spain in order to exclude all foreigners from the Gulf. To that end, also, he insisted on the exclusive navigation of the Mississippi.

A few days earlier, Jay had expressed, in a conference with Don Diego Gardoqui, member of a wealthy firm of Bilbao, a view similar to that advanced by Pollock. This, no doubt, prompted the statement of Florida Blanca.[26] Gardoqui observed that the Americans would not need this navigation during their generation and that future generations could take care of themselves. "Aids" would no doubt follow an offer by Jay to surrender the navigation of the Mississippi.

> I told him [Jay replied], that object could not come in question in a treaty for a loan of one hundred thousand pounds; that the Americans, almost to a man, believed that God Almighty had made that river a highway for the people of the upper country to go to the sea by; that this country was extensive and fertile; that the General, many officers, and others of distinction and influence in America were deeply interested in it; that it would rapidly settle; and that the inhabitants would not readily be convinced of the justice of being obliged either to live without foreign commodities, and lose the surplus of their productions, or be obliged to transport both over rugged mountains and through an immense wilderness to and from the sea when they daily saw a fine river flowing before their doors and offering to save them all that trouble and expense and that without injury to Spain.[27]

"Our affairs here go on heavily," Jay wrote Franklin. "The treaty is impeded by the affair of the Mississippi." In con-

[25] Jay, *Correspondence,* I, 424–425.
[26] Conference Notes, September 3, 1780. Gardoqui was the agent of Florida Blanca in this conference.
[27] Jay, *Correspondence,* I, 394–395.

gratulating Jay on the stand he had taken, Franklin said: "Poor as we are, yet as I know we shall be rich, I would rather agree with them to buy at a great price the whole of their rights on the Mississippi than sell a drop of its waters. A neighbor might as well ask me to sell my Street Door." [28]

The Comte de Lucerne, French minister to the United States, was also using his influence to further the Spanish position. Because of a pleasing personality, good nature and good sense, he "acquired a personal ascendancy over Congress in matters touching the common cause of France and the United States that had never fallen to the lot of the acrid and pedantic Gérard, even in the honeymoon days of the alliance." [29] As viewed by the French foreign office, the United States possessed no title to lands bordering on the Mississippi; these lands were subject to conquest by Spain; Americans probably never had a right to the navigation of the Mississippi; and the Floridas did not belong to the United States under any title.[30]

During March, 1780, the news reached Miralles of the Spanish successes on the lower Mississippi. When published in Philadelphia, the report aroused great excitement especially over the intimation that Spain would continue to hold the territory.

To what extent the protests of Americans emanated from the reports by Pollock, cannot be definitely stated. To the Committee of Congress the last day of September preceding, he wrote of his happiness at being able to inform them of the "Success of His Catholic Majesty's arms and Ours in this part of the World." "I thank you very much for what you, with your influence, have contributed in favor of the Common Cause," Galvez wrote Pollock.

It is to be recalled that it was Pollock's letters, carried by his special agent, that won the capitulation of Natchez, not-

---

[28] Jay, *Correspondence*, I, 431–433.
[29] Quoted from Corwin, *op. cit.*, p. 265.
[30] *Jour. of the Cont. Cong.*, XVI, 114–116.

withstanding the proclamation of General Campbell, demanding "all those Inhabitants and Indians to embody and take up arms immediately in favor of the British." Spain has acknowledged the independence of the United States, they were informed. Everyone well affected toward the common cause should give all possible assistance to Governor Galvez.

Some months earlier, Pollock had referred to the inhabitants at Natchez as Americans and friends to America. Shortly after, in a second communication, he wrote: "The Spirit of Liberty, the protection which every American has received on this River from Governor Galvez his generous behavior towards all the inhabitants with the advantages which must now arise from uninterrupted commerce with New Orleans, where you will meet with a good market for all your produce and the necessary supplies for your families, will I hope be sufficient inducement to you to render all service in your Power to his Catholic Majesty's arms." [31]

Early in September, Captain William Pickles, commanding a schooner in the service of the United States, following an order from Pollock, entered Lake Pontchartrain and after a severe battle captured the *West Florida,* a British armed sloop. For two years this vessel had controlled the lakes. Following this success, Captain Pickles secured the submission of the inhabitants of that district. "We therefore," the capitulation reads, "consider ourselves belonging to the said States and are willing to remain here and enjoy our property and privileges under the said United States." [32] The relation of these events to the claims of the United States had but one interpretation as viewed by Pollock.

In the West, the report was current that the Spaniards were to possess both the Floridas as soon as they were captured.[33]

---

[31] September 22, 1779, *Pollock Letters.*

[32] October 16, 1779, *Pollock Letters.* This agreement was also forwarded to Congress. The signatures are those of persons either English, Irish, or American.

[33] *Frontier Retreat,* ed. Louise Phelps Kellogg, p. 131.

FREE NAVIGATION OF THE MISSISSIPPI

But we find Pollock asserting, six days after Galvez had set out for the attack upon Mobile:

> I am still at a loss respecting who is to possess the Province of West Florida, but at all events I strongly presume you'll not give up that part of it on the Mississippi (with the free navigation of the River) which has already been reduced by Capt. Willing, and consequently guaranteed by the Treaty with France, as also from the pass of Regulus to the pass of Manchaque which runs along Lake Pontchartrain, and was taken the 21st of September last by Capt. Pickles, as you'll see by the enclosed copy of capitulations made with the inhabitants which if there is not Treaty previous, you have an undoubted right to. Your possession of the Illinois Country down to the river Yazoo, can only in my opinion be supported by the free navigation of this River, and that still more solidly by the possession of the North side from the Sea up, but at least from Manchac upwards, which is as already mentioned guaranteed by the Court of France agreeable to the capitulation of the inhabitants with Captain James Willing, the original of which lies in my hands.[34]

That these communications weakened the position of those members of Congress who were disposed to compromise on Spanish demands, cannot be questioned. In a report submitted by a special committee, we find, in the main, the arguments of Pollock.

After a statement relating to the submission of the inhabitants on Lake Pontchartrain to the United States, there is a second paragraph in the committee report which accepts Pollock's statement: "That it also appears to your Committee by the Letters of the Governor of Louisiana, that Captain Pickles in the Sloop West Florida, by joining the force of those States under his command with that of Spain greatly facilitated the reduction of West Florida which acknowledgement on the part of his Excellency Governor Galvez together with the submission of the inhabitants of Lake Pontchartrain may in the opinion of your committee serve to strengthen and support the claim of the United States to the free navigation of

[34] July 10, 1780, *Pollock Letters.*

the River Mississippi and to a Port or Ports on said River." [35] These facts were embodied in a resolution which was dispatched to Jay at Madrid.[36]

Meanwhile, Luzerne had been striving to win adherents in Congress to the French-Spanish party. He pictured the great migration which would inevitably set out from the East to these fertile valleys of the West. The possession of the Mississippi Valley, he declared, instead of being a source of strength to the United States, would cause constant friction with Spain. So telling was his appeal that he gained favor with Samuel Huntington, President of Congress, and his friends. The support of the delegates from New York, Pennsylvania, New Jersey, and Delaware, he counted on, for they were only slightly interested in western lands. Since the County of Kentucky had declared its independence, Virginians, he thought, were not hostile to the proposal. Maryland, a landless state, with delegate Jenifer, leader of the French-Spanish faction as spokesman, was favorable to Spanish interests.

Opponents to the schemes of Luzerne were led by Burke of North Carolina, who denounced the ambitions of Spain as overbearing, unjust, and prejudicial to the rights of the States.[37] Finally, it was agreed that no declaration should be made before the arrival of a report from Jay.

During June, 1780, news of the capture of Mobile reached Spain. The liveliest expressions of joy were everywhere manifested. This proved disastrous to any advances by Jay, and thereafter the claims of the United States were treated with even less favor on the part of Florida Blanca.

On August 14, Jay's dispatches, giving an account of his trying experiences, arrived at Philadelphia. The pretensions of America to the free navigation of the Mississippi were, he observed, the one obstacle which prevented procuring a treaty with Spain.[38]

[35] *Jour. of the Cont. Cong.*, XVII, 600.
[36] *Phillips, op. cit.*, 165.
[37] *Ibid., op. cit.*
[38] Wharton, *op. cit.*, 724.

FREE NAVIGATION OF THE MISSISSIPPI

The new instructions which were drawn up for Jay's guidance (October 4, 1780) manifested no disposition to yield to the Spanish demands. It was provided: "that the Minister adhere to his former instructions, respecting the right of the United States of America to the free navigation of the river Mississippi into and from the sea; which right, if an express acknowledgement of it cannot be obtained from Spain, is not by any stipulation on the part of America to be relinquished." [39]

Alarmed at the success of the British in the South and the capture of Charleston during the early summer of 1780, delegates in Congress from Georgia and South Carolina proposed to yield to Spain the exclusive navigation of the Mississippi below the thirty-first parallel as the price of an immediate alliance. Virginia delegates were instructed to favor such a proposal but they were to endeavor to secure free ports for American traders on the Mississippi. Congress, helpless and in despair, prepared new instructions for Jay (February 15, 1781). He was to recede from the demand for the free navigation of the river below the thirty-first parallel. He was also to yield on the issue of free ports, "providing such cession shall be unalterably insisted upon by Spain and providing the right to the free navigation of the river above that line should be recognized." [40]

Americans were convinced that this spirit of liberality would lead to an early treaty with Spain. Luzerne, in the belief that Spain would now agree to a treaty of alliance, ceased urging concessions upon Congress. Huntington wrote Jay: "You will not only be able without further delay to conclude the proposed alliance with his Catholic Majesty, but the liberality and friendly disposition manifested on the part

---

[39] *Ibid.*, IV, 78. James Madison, member of a committee of three, drafted a letter to Jay setting forth in masterly fashion the defense for the principles asserted by the United States. For his observations, consult *Jour. of the Cont. Cong.*, XVIII, 935–947.

[40] *Jour. of the Cont. Cong.*, XIX, 152–153. Delegates from Massachusetts, Connecticut, and North Carolina voted no. The vote of New York was divided. All of the other States voted yes.

of the United States by such a cession will induce him to afford them some substantial and effectual aid in the article of money." [41] Robert Morris, recently appointed superintendent of finance, was hopeful that Spain would be prepared to relieve the financial stress by granting large sums of money, either as subsidies or loans, five million dollars being suggested as an amount sufficient for "our present emergencies." [42] As compensation for such generosity Spain might anticipate, on the return of peace, in addition to repayment of the loan and protection of Spanish-American dominions, a large increase in exports to the United States of wine, oil, fruit, silk, and cloth, and remittances in return of wheat, corn, fish, and naval stores. The United States, he urged, would never be a dangerous neighbor, for "the attention of this country for a century past has been, and for a century to come most probably will be, entirely turned to agriculture and commerce."

In attempts at negotiation, continuing for months, Jay's patience was sorely tested. As he said: "Delay is their system; when it will cease, I can not conjecture." Florida Blanca was too sick or too busy and Del Campo, his secretary, who was appointed to carry on the negotiation, claimed that he was without instructions and that he, likewise, was much indisposed. In fact, Jay was not informed of the change in negotiator until three months after the appointment had been made.[43] Moreover, Jay's letters by post were uniformly opened, and were, at times, suppressed. His instructions of February 15 became known to him, after the lapse of three months, through the letter of a friend.[44]

[41] Jay, *Correspondence*, II, 35.
[42] July 4, 1781. *Ibid.*, II, 40–51. Jay referred to this letter as excellently well calculated for being shown entire to the Spanish minister, and it was later submitted to him. *Ibid.*, 102, 103, 107. This wish was a vain one, for Jay two months later stated that the Spanish treasury was low, and that "much of the money for the expenses in this war costs them between thirty and forty per hundred, by bad mismanagement and want of credit."
[43] *Ibid.*, II, 235, 238.
[44] *Ibid.*, II, 79.

The reply to Jay's arguments uniformly took the form, often reiterated, that the "King had always been accustomed to consider the exclusive navigation of the Gulf of Mexico as a very important object to Spain, more so indeed than even Gibraltar, and he was persuaded that his Majesty would never be prevailed upon to change his ideas on that subject." On May 19, Jay waited on the Minister but was unable to make any progress toward securing a treaty. Efforts at negotiation, equally fruitless—called, by Jay, painful perplexities and embarrassments—continued until early October, when he made an extended report to Congress.[45]

While using an honest effort to carry out his instructions, it is evident Jay was not in sympathy with the proposal on the navigation of the Mississippi, which he styled ungenerous concessions on the part of Congress. As he wrote: "The cession of this navigation will in my opinion render a future war with Spain unavoidable, and I shall look upon my subscribing to the one as fixing the certainty of the other." [46] Nevertheless, one of the articles which he submitted as the basis for a treaty of amity and alliance, September 22, 1781, contained the following statement: "The United States shall relinquish to his Catholic Majesty, and in future forbear to use, or attempt to use, the navigation of the river Mississippi from the thirty-first degree of north latitude—that is, from the point where it leaves the United States—down to the ocean." [47] As usual, the proposal was not acceptable to Spain.

Jay's advances during the remainder of the year 1781 were met, continuously, with evasion and delay on the part of the Spanish representative. As he expressed the situation— "I have not been able to obtain anything more than excuses for procrastination." [48]

Meanwhile, Congress was called upon to consider the view-

---

[45] Jay, *Correspondence*, II, 69–134.
[46] *Ibid.*, p. 86.
[47] Wharton, *op. cit.*, IV, 761.
[48] February 6, 1782. Jay, *Correspondence*, II, 177.

point of men of the Western waters as defined by Pollock. Once more he called attention to the importance of securing the free navigation of the Mississippi: [49]

> There's many, no doubt, has wrote on the subject, but perhaps few have felt the consequences. Therefore as in all probability a negociation for Peace, will soon come about, I would wish to acquaint your Excellency that the preservation and support of all that most promising Western Circuit, depends on the free navigation of the Mississippi and to compleat or perfect that navigation, it is highly necessary that the United States of America should obtain the late English Side of the River, [say] from Manchaque upwards. But if circumstances should operate contrary to that idea, then in fault thereof, to obtain on this Island the Houmas Village which is about twenty-two leagues above the Town [New Orleans] on this side of the River, containing about one league in front of the River, and six or seven in depth, fine high land back to the Lakes and an excellent Place for vessels to lay with a very good landing in the River just opposite this Tract of Land.[50]

As an alternative, he proposed that a league of land should be secured:

> in the front of this River with the depth back to the Lakes as near to this Town [New Orleans] as possible. [This, he continued], may do for a Fort for our own Vessels and a deposit for our own Goods, otherwise without some Place, of this kind, it will be impossible to carry on the Commerce of this River to advantage or satisfaction, and that taking place, the Country above will flourish and nourish this Place with her produce and commerce and the contrary will only prevent the Country above from being so directly settled. But at all events for the mutual Benefit and good Understanding of both Powers, I think it absolutely necessary that the Navigation of the River Mississippi should be equally free to both Nations. And in consequence some Place on said River should be agreed upon or appointed to establish a Custom House

[49] Pollock to the President of Congress, October 15, 1781. *Pollock Letters.*

[50] The villages of the Houmas, as described by Iberville, were made up of 200 cabins surrounding a temple made of upright logs. At this spot, Tonty deposited a glass bottle as a sign of possession. Later on, the French raised a cross on the same site. Justin Winsor, *The Mississippi Basin, The Struggle in America Between England and France, 1697–1763* (Boston, 1895), p. 38.

of our own, for which, provided the whole of the English Side cannot be obtained (which however I think the United States have a claim to) the next most proper and convenient Place on this River, is the Houmas Village . . . for the deposit of the Produce, Wares or Merchandize belonging to the Subjects of the United States, in order that Vessels and Goods should not by any Ways or Means, be liable, either to visit, duty or seizure upon any Pretence whatever while in our Bottoms, or in our Landing, and in order that both Nations may still reap a mutual and advantageous Benefit from this arrangement, I think a free Commerce may also be agreed upon betwixt Spain and the United States upon the Mississippi, as the inhabitants of this place has petitioned their Court strongly for that Purpose.[51]

A letter from Jay, April 28, 1782, was convincing in its evidence that Spain was ready to make no concessions on the questions at issue. Congress, with Pollock's communications in hand, then adopted the significant resolution that "the American Minister at Madrid be instructed to forbear making any overtures to that Court or entering into any stipulations in consequence of overtures which he has made; and in case any propositions be made to him by the said Court for a treaty with the United States, to decline acceding to the same until he shall have transmitted them to Congress for approbation." [52]

Upon receiving an urgent message from Franklin that the American commissioners were desirous of his assistance in negotiating peace with Great Britain, Jay set out for Paris, reaching that city on the twenty-third of June. "You may make a journey for health or pleasure, without retarding the progress of a negotiation not yet begun. Here you are greatly wanted," Franklin wrote. "Spain has taken four years to consider whether she should treat with us or not. Give her forty and let us in the meantime mind our own business." [53] Carmichael, secretary of legation, remained in Spain, but

---

[51] *Pollock Letters.*
[52] August 7, 1782. Jay, *Correspondence*, II, 209.
[53] April 22, 1782. Jared Sparks, *Writings of Benjamin Franklin* (London, 1882), IX, 211, 212.

Florida Blanca instructed Count d'Aranda, Spanish minister to France, to continue negotiations with Jay.

Thirteeen more years in diplomacy and intrigue, big with events, were to elapse before agreement was reached on these problems so closely related to the development of American union and expansion. Throughout this period, the policy, nowhere else as clearly defined as in the letters of Pollock, was the only one which could appease frontier discontent.

CHAPTER XVI

POLLOCK'S FORTUNE ANNIHILATED; HIS FAMILY DEPENDENT ON FRIENDS

BY THE close of the year 1781, Pollock was fully aware of the seemingly hopeless financial muddle into which he had been thrust. Suits against him multiplied. Even in this crisis, he was saved from imprisonment through loans to the amount of $36,000 from a number of Spanish citizens. Virginia was then attempting, in vain, to assume the burdens of war, East and West. Her treasury was empty, her paper money was practically worthless. "Our paper money is at an end," wrote Governor Benjamin Harrison, "and from the redundancy of that baneful medium which has hitherto circulated amongst us, the credit of the State is at a very low ebb." [1] Even worse than inability to pay, was the refusal of officials to accept the bills for which Pollock had become responsible. They claimed that he had not been appointed their agent and consequently had no right to draw bills against the State. Advances he had made on behalf of Clark and his officers amounted at the close of the year 1781 to $139,739. Six months later, by his own testimony, Pollock was in debt at New Orleans for an additional sum of $92,199. He writes the Committee:

> But I can only look up to the United States (which was pleased to honor me with their agency early in the War for the support of which let my operations and conduct announce for themselves), for the money which I have laid out in their service by their order and approbation in consequence of which I have taken the liberty to desire Mr. [Daniel] Clarke to lay the aforementioned accounts before your tribunal in full confidence your Excellency and the

[1] "Harrison Letter Book, 1781," *Virginia State Archives*, p. 31.

Honble. the Members will see me immediately reimbursed, in order that I may be able to pay the money borrowed (by order of the Commercial Committee as per their letter dated the 24th. of October 1777) from his Excellency General Galvez and others of this Place for the different supplies made the United States.[2]

Galvez had recently been transferred to Havana, as general and commander-in-chief of the Spanish troops. Here he was preparing for a formidable expedition against the enemy, undertaken, as a representative from South Carolina was informed,

in a great measure at our request and to favor our trade. . . . In the course of our conversation [the letter continues], he frequently mentioned as proof of his friendship for the United States the many things he did for our people while he commanded at New Orleans, and in particular his having advanced upwards of one hundred thousand dollars to different American agents. And what hurts him exceedingly is that Congress never have honored him by acknowledging it, or even writing him a line during five years, tho' frequently solicited and should his King call on him for the expenditure of this sum which he advanced without orders he has not anything to produce to justify his conduct. . . . It will make him very happy to find Congress take notice of these matters and a line expressive of their knowing and considering him as a friend to our Country may be attended with pleasing consequences to America as well as every individual who have anything to do here [Havana]. You must be fully sensible of the consequences arising from the connection with those people even in a mercantile point of view, and how much more so on the general political scale.

Pollock's confidence was strengthened through the knowledge that Robert Morris had been made Superintendent of Finance. This proved but a momentary hope, however, for Morris, writing the President of Congress, October 18, 1781, declared: "When I say that I cannot command more than one-twentieth of the sum necessary for the current services of the year, I am within the strictest bounds of truth."[3]

---

[2] October 30, 1781. *Pollock Letters.*
[3] Quoted from Oberholtzer, *op. cit.*, p. 124.

POLLOCK'S FORTUNE ANNIHILATED

In keeping with the recommendation of Pollock, recognition was at last given by Morris for the service rendered the American cause by Galvez. "I am now Sir directed by the United States," he wrote, "to express to your Excellency the grateful sense they entertain of your efforts in their favor. These generous efforts gave them so favorable an impression of your character and that of your Nation that they have not ceased to respect you and to wish for an intimate connection with your Country. Conceiving it to be for the mutual interest of Spain and North America they have one earnest wish that as the Cause is one and the enemy one, so the operations against him may be combined in such manner as to answer the great Purpose all have in view." [4]

A note of optimism which dominates his language was a result, doubtless, of the surrender of Cornwallis. Galvez was assured that the sums he had granted in the service of the United States should be accredited to him on a proper assignment from Pollock—"Payment will be made both of Principal and interest as soon as the situation of our Finances will admit of it which from the present prospect of things, may happen in a shorter space of time than the public creditors have been led to expect."

By the first of the year 1782, Pollock's resources were exhausted. The credit of his friends was no longer available; supplies promised him by Congress were not sent; and the demands on the part of his creditors, many of them in desperate straits, that he meet his obligations were growing daily more insistent.

Very modern in tone is the message of Don Joseph Foucher, Treasurer-General of Louisiana: "In mine of the 2nd. Instant," he wrote, "I begged you would make all speed in paying the sum due from you to this Treasury under my direction —as you offered to do by the end of the last year—but I fear you have not been able to comply or have not attended to my said notice, wherefor I must inform you that if you do not immediately take the most proper steps to pay this sum into

---

[4] November 21, 1781, *Pollock Letters*.

the Royal Treasury I must have Recourse against you to the jurisdiction of the Country. God send you many years." [5]

To meet these demands, notwithstanding the hardships to which his family would be subjected, Pollock volunteered to dispose of his store and stock of goods, his dwelling and furnishings, his indigo works, his agricultural implements, his plantation slaves and some of his domestic slaves. While a portion only of his indebtedness could thus be liquidated, the proffer was accepted.

Confronted with financial disaster, he determined to make his appeal, in person, before the authorities of the United States and of Virginia. The latter, he had been informed, did not deem it expedient even to examine his accounts covering the advances he had made in assisting their troops in the West. "The feeling human heart will readily conceive the anguish of my tortured soul," Pollock writes, "at parting with my wife and numerous family, whom I reduced to extreme misery and distress by imprudently giving these tortures to serve a country whose gratitude and justice I had too much confidence in." Before setting out for Philadelphia, he also met the harsh condition, in keeping with the Spanish law, of securing a respectable American citizen, who was to serve as hostage for his return. He carried a letter from Governor Stephen Miró addressed to Thomas McKean, President of the Continental Congress. In it, reference was made to the service rendered by Pollock on behalf of the common cause through securing the surrender of Natchez. His zeal for the cause of the United States and of Virginia was likewise highly commended.

Arriving at Havana, he was waited upon by sixty American captains "who were lying there under great distress; their vessels rotting (chiefly armed for the defense of their country) their men imprisoned under an embargo, which had continued in some cases for five months." This was a phase of the arbitrary procedure of Spanish authorities who had for years been endeavoring to hold their American possessions as markets for a small group of Spanish monopolists. As we have

[5] January 15, 1782. *Pollock Letters.*

POLLOCK'S FORTUNE ANNIHILATED

noted, Pollock, notwithstanding this policy, had been free to develop his trade relations. Other Americans seized the opportunity to engage in clandestine trade.

When Spain, in 1779, became the ally of France, communication with her colonies was rendered hazardous through the activity of the British fleet. In order to supply Cuba with bread, a royal order was issued which granted limited trade relations with the United States. Acceding to a request of the Cuban Captain General, Congress lifted the food embargo by permitting the export of three thousand barrels of flour to that island. Robert Morris, then Superintendent of Finance, undertook the task of filling the order through his firm and sent Robert Smith as a special agent to supervise the arrival of the ships at Havana. Other merchants to whom concessions had been granted by the Cuban representative in Philadelphia likewise sent their agents, and thus was begun an American commercial colony in that port. Even then, no business might be carried on except through the mediation of a Cuban agent and the payment of import taxes amounting, at times, to 30 per cent and export duties of 10 per cent. Rumor of the appearance of a hostile fleet caused the harbor of Havana to be closed without warning, thus entailing great losses to American shippers. With the hope of remedying these aggravations, Morris induced Congress to grant a commission to Smith as special agent of the United States. Little was accomplished, however, before the opportune arrival of Pollock.

In his vigorous appeal to the governor, Pollock showed that enforcing the order was virtually striking at the resources of the United States. "It would," he declared, "affect the fleet and armies of our allies and particularly that grand expedition now forming at Cape Francois against the island of Jamaica, commanded by his Excellency General Galvez, which in all probability may be distressed just now for want of provisions to carry it into execution and the inconsistency of this continued embargo, without even the appearance of answering any public good to the common cause, to which all those individuals are most strictly attached still increases their grievances, and cannot fail to alarm the United States (whom I have the honor to represent) if not immediately redressed by granting the necessary papers and passports to one and all of them to proceed to their intended destination."

So effectively had the delicate situation been presented, that within a few days, the vessels sailed for their several ports. Writing of the incident, Pollock said: "By a providential coincidence of circumstances, these vessels arrived in safety during the most fatal season which our commerce has experienced. I came in one of them and tho' reduced to Poverty myself yet I had a Heart-felt satisfaction in accompanying a Treasure so important, to the Country in whose service I had labored so long." [6]

Landing at Wilmington, Pollock made the journey to Richmond only to find that the Virginia Assembly was not in session and that the governor had no authority to act independently. Before his departure for Philadelphia, where he hoped to have his claims recognized by Congress, Pollock issued two statements in which he appealed to the governor for relief and defined the motives which governed his course of action during the Revolution. In his letter to Governor Harrison, he met the charge, which was current, that since he had no positive appointment as agent from the State of Virginia, he was not justified in assuming the office. Granted that the appointment

[6] September 18, 1782, *Pollock Letters*. The British fleet was making inroads upon American commerce. In a letter of September 11, 1782, an English officer reported that off the east end of Cuba they had captured several rich prizes. The day following, a report showed the capture of fifteen prizes engaged in the West India trade. Four days later, the toll was several American and three Spanish vessels: "Among the numerous arrivals of trading vessels at different ports on this Continent as reported on October 9, ten have lately got safe into Baltimore from the West Indies. It is a pleasing reflection, that notwithstanding the powerful fleet of the enemy now on our Coast, they cannot prevent our receiving the supplies necessary for the public use or the necessities of the people." An English report of October 19 states that: "His Majesty's ships have made deep impression upon the fortunes of the Baltimore merchants by their late successful cruises." *Pennsylvania Journal and the Weekly Advertiser.*

POLLOCK'S FORTUNE ANNIHILATED 275

was neither formal nor direct, Pollock maintained that his services on numerous occasions had been sought indirectly. As we have seen, there were no misgivings on the part of George Rogers Clark that he had been authorized by Governor Henry to draw bills on Virginia which would be accepted by Pollock. In fact, Governor Henry had specifically informed Clark that his wants would be supplied by Pollock. The merchants of St. Louis were given assurance through the following message of Clark: "Mr. Pollock is agent for the United States, and for the State of Virginia, also my orders are from the Executive Power of Virginia at the same time a Continental Charge agreeable to an act of Confederacy. . . . To Say that the bills will positively be honored at Orleans its what I cant do but from the nature of my commission and Mr. Pollock's Contract I dont think he can refuse them with propriety either drawn payable by the Continent or the State of Virginia."[7] In substance, Governor Harrison could not have failed to know the facts which had been presented by Governor Jefferson in which Pollock was specifically recognized as the agent of Virginia. ". . . for the Smaller Force we have hitherto kept up at Kaskaskia," Jefferson wrote Galvez, "we have contracted a considerable Debt at New Orleans with Mr. Pollock, besides what is due to your State for the Supplies they have generously furnished, and a number of bills from Col. Clark now lying under protest in New Orleans. We learn that Mr. Pollock is likely to be greatly distressed if we do not immediately make him remittances. The most unfavorable harvest ever known since the settlement of this country has put it out of our power to send flour, obliging us for our own subsistence, to purchase it from the neighboring states of Maryland and Pennsylvania to whom we have until this year furnished large quantities. The want of salt disables us from preparing beef and pork for your market. In the situation of things we can not but contemplate the distress of that Gentleman, brought on him by services rendered us, with the

[7] Addressed to Lieut.-Governor De Leyba, Dec. 17, 1778.

utmost concern." [8] In the event that the proposal made for a loan by Governor Henry had been granted, he advised that $65,814 should be advanced "for us" to Mr. Pollock.

In the appeals of Virginia officers, in the West, that he accept the bills which they drew on him, Pollock was assured that Virginia would pay "with gratitude." Moreover, his conduct had been formally approved by a regularly constituted Board, and, in reimbursement for his advances, he had been ordered by Governor Jefferson to draw on the firm of Penette, Da Costa, Freres, of Nantes. As an accepted agent of the United States, "who would not," he declared, "conceive that it was his duty to attend to the particular service of this Commonwealth as well as to the services of the United States. And, if in the opinion of the Virginia authorities, his services were no longer indispensable to their cause, would they not have ordered him to desist from making further advances of money. Sir this is what I had a right to expect and what they would have done. . . . They were silent and permitted me to go on advancing my own fortune and to contract debts to the full extent of my credit in Louisiana for the support of this service."

He set forth the injustice of the demand that he be forced to present his claims before a commission in the West which was then engaged in the investigation of the conduct of all officers, agents, contractors and other persons who had "disbursed public money in the Western Country." [9]

In reply to this request, Pollock writes: "It is at New Orleans, at my own place of Residence, you had my fortune, and

[8] Jefferson to Galvez, Nov. 8, 1779. "Executive Papers 1777 to 1779," *Va. State Archives.*

[9] The first Western Commission appointed by Virginia was made up of the following men: Colonel William Fleming, Colonel Thomas Marshall, Judge Samuel McDowell, and Judge Caleb Wallace. Three had authority to act for the Commission. Their first meeting was held in Harrodsburg, November 1, 1782. April 16, 1783, having collected all possible data, they returned to Virginia "with a horse-load of papers." Their journal is published in "Clark Papers," 1781–1783, *Ill. Hist. Coll's.,* ed. James, Vol. XIX, Virginia Series, Vol. IV (Springfield, 1924), pp. 290–464.

the whole extent of my credit, and it is at New Orleans I ought to be paid what I so disinterestedly advanced for you, can it be conceived just or generous that I should after having exposed myself already to a dangerous voyage from New Orleans expose myself still further by going throu' a Country abounding with hostile savages, to supplicate a liquidation of my accounts, from commissioners who know not or can know but little of them." He suggested, if approved by his creditors and if payment were not then possible, that one-fourth of the indebtedness should be paid in October and at the end of each six months thereafter one-fourth of the balance. These securities, bearing 6 per cent interest, he proposed to turn over to his creditors. In this manner, he would be able to return "in peace, tho' in poverty to his unfortunate family."

But since nothing was to be accomplished before the convening of the Assembly, Pollock set out for Philadelphia where he hoped to get a hearing before Congress on his claims against the United States. Before leaving Richmond, he appealed to George Rogers Clark. "I presume you are acquainted," he writes, "with the difficulties I met with in liquidating my accounts in monies advanced for the Service of the Commonwealth to you and the other officers who commanded the Virginia troops on the Mississippi.

"And as you Sir have been a chief instrument in leading me into the dilemma I am now in I conceive that you are called upon by honor and justice as well as by me to endeavor to facilitate an arrangement of my accounts and to extricate me from the entanglements I find myself in." In place of receiving payment from Virginia, "with gratitude," he asserted, "they are as destitute of inclination as of the means of paying me. . . . Step forth rescue your Country from the eternal disgrace that must attend their iniquitous reward of my exertions, as you have by [your] exertions when on the Mississippi saved and preserved that valuable country for the State you serve." [10]

Clark was then on the eve of his retaliatory drive against

[10] July 24, 1782, *Pollock Letters*.

the Shawnee, following the defeat at the Blue Licks.[11] Pollock's available resources were exhausted. Many of his other creditors were entreating him to aid in the adjustment of their claims. "I am heartily sorry," was Clark's reply, "that you should meet with such disappointments in the settlement of your accounts, I am sensible that you have no drafts on the State from me but what ought to be paid. . . . If I was worth the money I would most chearfully pay it myself and trust the State. But [I] can assure you with truth I am entirely reduced myself by advancing everything I could raise except what the State owes me am not worth a Spanish dollar. I wish it was in my power to follow your proposition to step forth and save my country from the disgrace that is likely to fall on her." [12]

Returning to Philadelphia, Pollock was happy to learn that Morris, in submitting a memorial to a special committee of Congress, had recommended favorable action on his claims. "In addition to what is contained in all these documents," Morris advised, "I have frequently been informed by persons from that quarter of the world of Mr. Pollocks good conduct. I am myself therefore fully persuaded that Oliver Pollock late Commercial Agent of the United States at New Orleans having manifested great zeal, integrity and abilities during his residence at that place is entitled to the most favorable notice and attention. I doubt not that the Committee will on a full examination find sufficient reason to present him in the most favorable manner to Congress." The finding of the committee, which was submitted to Congress, was equally promising. They referred to the zeal and industry which he had manifested. Large sums, they declared, had been advanced by him out of his private fortune. Large debts, with Spanish creditors, he had also contracted, "that public faith, justice, and humanity require that the sundry accounts should be liquidated and the balance paid, or at least security given

---

[11] *See Life of Clark*, pp. 273–278.
[12] *Clark Papers*, 1781–1783, p. 144.

POLLOCK'S FORTUNE ANNIHILATED

for payment of the same whenever the state of our public funds shall render it practicable." [13]

How indefinite such an adjustment was to be, may be understood from the portrayal of the national financial crisis by Morris. A year earlier, he had declared: "When I say that I cannot command more than one-twentieth of the sum necessary for the current services of the year, I am within the strictest bounds of truth." [14] For the year 1782, $8,000,000, payable in specie or its equivalent, was demanded from the States. One-fourth that amount fell due on April 1. A month later, $5,500 was received from New Jersey as a portion of its quota. Not another State had made a contribution. Of this situation, Morris writes: "The habitual inattention of the States has reduced us to the brink of ruin."

Owing to complications in his accounts between the United States and Virginia, Pollock must again make the journey to Richmond. In a letter to the governor, delivered by Pollock, Morris appealed for an early adjustment of these accounts. Once more he expressed his opinion on the service rendered by Pollock: "The act is couched in such favorable terms that it might be unnecessary to say anything personally relating to that gentleman. But the many reasons I have to entertain the most favorable opinion of him would convert my silence into injustice. I feel it my duty to assure your Excellency that a variety of evidence has occurred to convince me that Mr. Pollock, with much abilities to serve his country, has joined unwearied industry to disinterested zeal, I must add also that he has been essentially useful in those moments when an extreme distress gave double value of every office of friendship." His reception by Governor Harrison and the Assembly was gratifying to Pollock: "When I undertook the agency of the United States and conceived it my duty to act for Vir-

---

[13] Reported to Congress, October 22, 1782.
[14] To the President of Congress, October 18, 1781. Quoted from Oberholtzer, *Life of Morris*, p. 124.

ginia also," he wrote the governor, "my credit was extensive, my fortune equal to 100,000 Dollars. At this day my credit as a merchant is injured, my fortune annihilated, and my numerous family become pensioners on the bounty of my friends." [15]

A balance of $136,466, it was agreed, was a just claim against Virginia. Of this amount, they obligated themselves to pay $10,000 within a year. The residue, with interest, was to be paid in four annual installments. The promise was illusory, for a succeeding legislature reversed this decree. Nor is this surprising, for the governor had declared shortly before that the credit of the State was lost and that there was not even a shilling in the treasury.

Upon presenting this scrap of paper from the Virginia Legislature, Pollock declared to the President of Congress:

> I am constrained then further to have recourse to Congress and rely on their justice not only for a speedy settlement of my account with the United States, but also for such reimbursements as will enable me to discharge those heavy incumbrances in which I have become involved by my zeal and attachment to the cause of America.
>
> Congress have my accounts now inclosed. My whole fortune has been expended in the Cause of the United States. I am oppressed by a heavy load of debts and involved in difficultys and totally deprived of the means of pursuing a plan of business for the support of myself and family.
>
> Under circumstances of distress more easy to conceive than express, an appeal is now made to the Justice of the United States (with which Congress can not be unacquainted) and it is earnestly that I solicit their speedy attention to him who has devoted himself, his fortune and every prospect in life to their Cause. [16]

Weeks of waiting for a reply to his memorial followed. Again, he was forced to turn to his friends for a bare subsistence for his family, consisting of Mrs. Pollock and their six children. Day after day he was haunted by the appeals of his personal creditors. Others besought him to intervene

---

[15] July 16, 1782. *Executive Communications to the General Assembly.*
[16] February 24, 1783. *Pollock Letters.*

with Morris on their behalf, since, following his counsel, they had made advances to the government and were, like himself, reduced to a condition of penury.

One agent writes:

> Mr. Nash is quite uneasy about his bill as he has much need of the money. The bill drawn by Mallett and Jukes on you for one hundred and seventy Odd Dollars in favor of myself which I showed you before you left this, was sent me by Mr. Henry Toomer to raise money to assist his brother Anthony Toomer with his family home (to the Southward) as I believe I told you when I presented it and I have been obliged to advance him that and a larger sum to enable him to leave this place.... By the last post I received another bill drawn on you for 535 dollars at thirty days sight.... I am informed that I have another set of Bills drawn on you for 535 dollars which have been on their way to me since September and I am in hourly expectation of receiving them—I shall have quite as much need of the sum as of the other two.

The significant service rendered by Captain Pickles and the crew of the *West Florida* on Lake Pontchartrain is readily recalled. This vessel, taken over by the government, was assigned as a dispatch boat to European service. Members of the former crew made known their grievances because of the non-payment of prize money, in the following letter to Pollock:

> After waiting in vain upwards of two years for the Honbl., the Congress to make a settlement with us for the West Florida, we are at last obliged to apply to you for the same purpose. We would wish not to injure you, but when men are left to do themselves Right they ought not to neglect any opportunity or means in their power to accomplish it.
>
> We therefore think that as you employed the West Florida in the service of the United States, and disposed of her at last to Congress, that you are accountable to the Crew for her and we on our parts are determined to try a regular course of Law to obtain payment from you and leave you to settle the affair with Congress.

The inability of the Federal government to meet its financial obligations, as well as the helpless state of its creditors during this period of depression, are set forth in the petition for relief of another member of the crew of the *West Florida* who had furnished medical supplies for the equipment of the *Morris:* "Agreeable to your indication," he writes Pollock, "I apply to Capt. Haigei to interest himself in my behalf with Mr. Morris, but to no Purpose and have apply'd myself (Both to no purposes). . . . I need not point out to you my distresses, you are acquainted with 'em. If you can be of any services to me, Ither by letter to Mr. Morris or otherwise you'l render me more than life, for I am in a most desponded Situation. . . . I depend intirely on you doing honor to this small part of my advances on the Ship Morris acct. for Medicine."

After Daniel Murray had written of the loan made to him by Pollock which relieved his distress, he asked for an extension of time in which to cover this obligation, saying: "You may be assured that I will honorably pay you the first remittance I send from the Illinois. The Gentleman who fits me out does not act towards me with any Generosity otherwise I might have been gone from here long ago and have had it sooner in my power to Discharge my obligations. However I hope you will with your wonted goodness have a little patience."

Nine days later, the recurrence of what he called "my bad state of Health rendering me peevish," or "madness at my disappointments," induced Murray to join the pack of suppliants closing in upon Pollock. "I enclose you account of the Expenses incurred in my several services for the United States, chiefly transacked within your Department as their Agent at New Orleans, and all by your particular desire and appointment. You are well acquainted with a great part of the Expenditures, and the Views that led to the whole; and you must be perfectly sensible that you are bound by every tye that can bind Mankind to reimburse me these Expenditures made upon the most disinterested principles."

But there was no promise for early relief in the report submitted by a special committee of Congress. His claims which they were called to pass upon amounted to $58,735. In the treasury books, Pollock had already been accredited to the amount of $60,255. Of the claims considered by the committee, the largest pertained to three invoices of goods which were shipped for the account of the United States but were used by Clark in the Illinois country. William Murray had been sent from New Orleans by Pollock with special dispatches to Congress. But since he did not come on a specific order from Congress, there was no disposition to include his expenses as a legitimate claim on the government. In order to support the honor of the United States, Pollock held $11,-133 in Continental money for which he had advanced specie. This sum, together with a charge of $5,000 covering his expenses as Continental agent, were to be passed upon by Congress.

Another item submitted to the committee grew out of the sale of Pollock's property at New Orleans to the amount of $45,000. Upon this claim, the report states: "The Committee can only remark that it appears clearly that the said Pollock was a man of considerable property in the Country where he resided and that the United States are largely indebted to him. They have reason to believe (from information) that he has been under the necessity of selling his property. If Congress shall be of opinion that he is intitled to this compensation they will so direct."

Moreover, no part of the $74,087, the loan made by Galvez during the year 1778, had been paid. Pollock was now urging that responsibility for this obligation should no longer be his.

The committee proclaimed his "zeal and his sufferings" which entitled him to the favorable consideration of Congress and stated "that a considerable payment ought to be made to him as soon as the situation of the public finances will permit." Without means for resuming trade, and with the bare necessities of life for his family contributed by friends, Pollock gained little hope from the resolutions, often repeated, on the service he had rendered.

At this crisis in his affairs, he was induced to accept the office of commercial agent for the United States at Havana, succeeding Robert Smith, recently deceased. This appointment was more pleasing to him for he would be in position to coöperate with his friend Galvez, who had been appointed Governor-General of Cuba.[17]

His twenty years of intimate association with Spanish officials admirably fitted Pollock to undertake the duties of an office which promised great possibilities for the promotion of American commerce. "Confidence in your ability and training," his credentials state, "we appoint you as our agent of commerce during our pleasure in the City and Port of Havana, to manage what occasions the interests of Congress and to assist the American merchants with your counsel and solicit their business with the Spanish Government and governing yourself to conform with the orders which you will receive from time to time from the United States in Congress assembled." [18]

---

[17] His official title was Don Bernardo de Galvez, Knight of the Royal and distinguished order of Charles III, Commander of Bolanos in the order of Calatravo, Lieutenant General of the Royal Armies, Inspector General of the troops in America, Governor and Captain General of the Provinces of Louisiana and the two Floridas, and also Governor and Captain General *protempore* of the Island of Cuba and city of St. Christoval de la Havanno, Judge Protector of his Majesty's tobacco revenue, of the packets and Couriers of the Royal Company, etc., etc. In recognition of the services rendered the United States by Galvez, Pollock had secured a portrait of him which he presented to Congress. The acceptance included the provision that it should be placed in the hall in which Congress met.

[18] His appointment bore the date, June 2, 1783. *Pollock Letters.*

CHAPTER XVII

OUR FLAG INSULTED; POLLOCK IMPRISONED

LOADING two vessels with merchandise, since he had been granted special permission, by an accredited Spanish agent, to carry provisions to the Cuban market "at a handsome profit," Pollock set out for Havana.[1] On August 6, he presented his commission to Governor Unzaga, for Galvez had not arrived. As he stated in transmitting his credentials, he had come with the design of cultivating that harmony and friendship necessary for the promotion of commerce.

But with the coming of peace, all Spanish favors heretofore granted to American traders ceased and the port of Havana was closed to all foreign vessels. The question of recognizing Pollock, who came "to promote the reciprocal interests" of both nations, could not be decided in routine fashion. Moreover, he had won favors from Governor Unzaga during his first years as a trader in New Orleans.

A special commission of three was constituted "for the purpose of treating, conferring, or coming to an agreement on what is most suitable in reason of admitting or not admitting Don Oliver Pollock." Acknowledging the exceptional nature of the case, the commission decided that, notwithstanding the credentials presented, he should not be recognized until formal instructions therefor should be received from Madrid.

To mark time was not agreeable to a man of his decision of character, and he assumed the exercise of certain of his official functions. Grievances of American merchants and captains were his chief concern. By order of the governor, all

---

[1] As an economy measure, it was recommended by John Jay, September 20, 1785, that consuls should be granted permission to carry on trade. They were to receive no salary from the government. *Jour. of the Cont. Cong.*, XXIX, 723.

American merchants residing in Havana after February 23, 1784, "without their knowing why or wherefore," were subject to arrest. Some of them were confined "in the worst gaols." Applications for a hearing before a court of justice had been treated with silent contempt. As creditors, they were helpless in collecting sums due them through the evasions of debtors. Their goods were disposed of at forced sales. Appeals for relief were disregarded by the governor. "This is the mode he chooses to pursue," one writes, "to drive the Americans from this country where he is determined not to leave one of them, and as to their debts and effects he declares he cares nothing about them. They are of no consideration with him, they may go and find them where they please; that further remonstrance will bring even heavier punishments." Such conduct, they maintained, was wrong upon every principle of honor and honesty and contrary to all the rules of even the most uncivilized nations upon Earth.[2]

Protests from Pollock to the governor on account of these abuses followed in quick succession. "Therefore I the said agent," he declares, "at the request aforesaid, do in the most solemn manner protest against the unjust proceedings of Governor Lewis Unzaga and his tribunal aforesaid as the sole and only occasion of all loss, detriment or damage that has or shall be sustained by any person or persons whomsoever concerned." [3]

The harsh treatment accorded officers and crews likewise symbolized disregard for the rights of American citizens on the part of Spanish authorities. Official permission to captains to refit their vessels in the port of Havana after they were driven in by gales, was disregarded. For reasons unknown, vessels were boarded, crews and officers "were abused and beaten, colours were struck" and at times officers were taken off and imprisoned. As interpreted by Pollock in his letters to the governor, such acts were "so glaring an insult to the Flag of the United States, that I cannot in justice to my masters

[2] *Draper MSS.,* 43J137–139.
[3] *Ibid.*

or your government, pass it over in silence, not doubting but your Excellency will do the needful for the harmony of both nations and honor me with the result; which shall be communicated to Congress to prevent any misrepresentation that might otherwise happen on a matter of such importance."

More drastic was the order issued early in the summer of 1784, whereby, "No admittance, succour or relief is to be granted or given to any American vessels should they be even sinking at sea or in sight of Havana." The plague (yellow fever) then raging in the United States was advanced as the reason for this order. In language strikingly under control, Pollock declares in a letter to Morris: "Yet the treatment of Contempt and Injustice upon all occasions is most cordially handed down by this Government to the Americans here in general and only those who have seen and felt can form a true idea of their abuses. . . . I may with propriety conclude this subject, that whether the Plague is with you or not, the unprecedented conduct of this Government towards the Americans here is equal to any plague upon Earth." [4]

Based on these communications, the report of a Committee of Congress, of which Thomas Jefferson was chairman, gives evidence that more positive ideas were evolving in the minds of leaders regarding the attitude then prevailing of foreign Powers toward the United States. The sudden arrest and indiscriminate imprisonment "in a common dungeon (with felons and persons of the vilest condition) of merchants and men of character, citizens of the United States who were resident at the Havana, by permission, to solicit and receive monies due from the Spanish Government and the subjects of Spain," was to be construed as "an insult too serious to be overlooked or submitted to by a free people." [5]

In substance, the report of this committee was adopted by a committee of the States, representing Congress during the summer recess. In his representation of the "outrage complained of," Minister Carmichael was directed to state to the

[4] July 7, 1784. *Pollock Letters.*
[5] *Jour. of the Cont. Cong.*, XXVII, 384.

Spanish Government that Congress "do not entertain a doubt but that satisfactory explanations will be had and ample satisfaction given to the parties . . . and that orders will be issued to prevent in future any violence or injuries to such of the citizens of these United States as may happen to be within any part of his Catholic Majesty's dominions."[6]

American trade with Havana disappeared. During the year 1783, twenty-two vessels cleared from that port for Philadelphia and eighteen sailed from the latter city for Havana. In 1785 only one cleared for Havana and not a single vessel entered the United States from that port.[7]

Even Pollock was to become the victim of arbitrary usage on the part of officials. Before quitting the United States on his mission, the Legislature of Virginia voted that a certificate of indebtedness amounting to 3,000 pounds sterling was to be paid him on January 1, 1784, with interest at the rate of 6 per cent. He was to receive a like amount one year later and two years thereafter he was to be paid 17,469 pounds. Scarcely had he reached his destination before an order of the Assembly forbade the issuing of further warrants or payment on those certificates already granted him. Bills on Penette, Da Costa, Freres, and Company, of Nantes, which, as we have seen, had been drawn to secure supplies for Clark amounting to $65,814, were returned protested, since Virginia had failed to ship the tobacco necessary to cover the order. Of this amount, Pollock was able to make up $20,000 out of his own resources.

With the knowledge that Virginia had forbidden further payments to Pollock, his creditors at New Orleans petitioned Governor Unzaga to detain him until these debts should be paid "to the uttermost farthing." In compliance with an order from the governor, a non-commissioned officer and two soldiers entered Pollock's home with fixed bayonets and "then and there seized upon his chariot, together with a pair of

---

[6] *Jour. of the Cont. Cong.*, XXVII, 602, 607.

[7] Roy F. Nichols, *The First United States Consuls and Trade Relations with the Spanish American Empire, 1779–1809.* MS. Paper presented before the American Historical Association, 1934.

mules, harness, his negro coachman, etc." They were taken to the house of the Depositor-General, an act held by Pollock to be contrary to Spanish law. Moreover, debts incurred by Havana bakers amounting to $9,574 for flour supplied them by Pollock were attached for meeting the demands of New Orleans creditors.

With all of his property confiscated, "with nothing left in this country" for the subsistence of his family, it was his hope to quit Havana. But in this he was to fail, for, as he wrote: "Thus disagreeably situated, I have been labouring hard for this month past with all the interest and influence I could possibly make to procure permission of this Governor to get away from this place but sorry I am to inform you it avails not." [8]

Payment of the passage money for himself and family had been accepted by a ship captain bound for Philadelphia. To Pollock's consternation, after all their baggage had been placed on board, the ship departed leaving them "without a second change of cloaths or scarce a bed left to lay on." Assisted by a loan from a friend, stores necessary for the voyage were again collected and placed on board another vessel. Lacking the written permission from the governor, Pollock and his family were refused passage.

Some understanding of his despair may be gained from his communication to the governor: "Thus reduced and Harassed with a large family to support which since the creditors lay their heavy hands upon my property, I have been under the disagreeable necessity of recourse to a friend whom I have now tired out, and in consequence I am obliged to call upon Your Excellency for support, otherwise grant me your passport to leave the country, the want of which has caused all the heavy expenses, disappointments and delays that has happened to me. Therefore to avoid any more of the same nature I request that your Excellency will let me know what I have to depend on." [9]

[8] *Pollock Letters*, August 28, 1784. To the Governor of Virginia.
[9] *Ibid.*, to Governor Unzaga, August 17, 1784.

As viewed by Unzaga, judicial appeals made by creditors were to be enforced literally although he was fully aware that the case of Pollock was exceptional. His final decision was expressed in a letter addressed to the President of Congress in which he states: "In my judgment, I have not been able to concede to anything other than to permit Mr. Pollock to send his wife and family, he remaining detained until he finds a way to cover his debts. . . . As this person came here recommended by your Excellency under the authority of Congress, it has seemed proper to me to notify your Excellency of the cause of his detention." [10]

"With nothing left in this country to subsist on," there was now no choice left for Pollock. Having borrowed $3,000 from a friend, he again procured passage for his family on a boat bound for Philadelphia. He was now penniless, virtually a prisoner, "harassed by public officers of justice beyond description," and exposed to the resentment of incensed creditors. He was in no condition to procure relief for himself or to afford either advice or protection to the other citizens of the United States. His bondman was still a prisoner at New Orleans. "Such," he declared, "was the disagreeable predicament in which my Amor Patria had involved me." But he was confident that through a presentation of his claims by Robert Morris to Congress there would come speedy relief for his family, always his chief concern, who were now wholly dependent upon friends, and freedom for himself.

Nothing was to come, even from this appeal, for Morris writes: "With respect to this Gentleman's application for money I found my hands tied up by an act of Congress, and therefore neither his services nor his suffering nor a view of those distresses to which a helpless family are reduced, could induce me to grant that relief which justice and humanity did equally demand. I persuade myself, however, that it will be among the earliest objects calling for the attention of Con-

[10] *Pollock Letters*, August 26, 1784. To Thomas Mifflin, President of Congress. The reply to Pollock was similarly worded.

gress to alleviate sufferings which in their attending circumstances are equally severe and extraordinary." [11]

Meantime, Pollock was receiving full information regarding the critical situation growing out of the closing of the Mississippi River to American traders. We have seen with what persistence, before the close of the Revolution, he was urging upon Congress that the fate of the West was dependent upon the free navigation of that River.

According to the terms of the treaty of peace between Great Britain and the United States, it was provided that the navigation of the Mississippi from its source to the gulf should forever remain free to the subjects of these two nations. The thirty-first parallel east from that River was to constitute the Southern boundary of the United States. But a secret article in the treaty stipulated that in the event that Great Britain continued to possess the Floridas, the boundary should be 32° 30', or a line extending east from the mouth of the Yazoo River. It was maintained by Spanish officials that this line, which had been established by Great Britain in the treaty of 1763, should constitute the northern boundary of West Florida. Unless, they demanded, the United States should assent to the unconditional surrender of the territory between these two lines, no treaty on commercial subjects between the two nations could be considered, and moreover, the Mississippi River below Natchez was to be closed to all American commerce. This was soon to become a reality. With the determination to convert the Gulf of Mexico into a Spanish lake and to close the Mississippi to all foreign commerce, a royal order early in 1784 provided that no American vessels were to be admitted to the port of New Orleans. Soldiers guarded the entrance to the River at the Balize.

To control all communication from upstream, the commandant at Natchez was directed to detain all boats until orders for their disposal were received from the governor at

[11] *Pollock Letters,* addressed to the President of Congress, September 30, 1784.

New Orleans.[12] Spanish customs officers boarded every American boat attempting to pass Natchez, compelled the owners to pay heavy tolls, forced them needlessly to delay, and in other ways subjected them to petty annoyances. Boats from Pittsburgh, it was reported, were held at Natchez for as much as fifty days, some of the crews dying of starvation.[13]

"I cannot conceive of the reason for so doing," Pollock's agent declared, "unless the treaty of commerce has debarred us from the privilege of trading in this river, if so, the whole American Possessions on the Mississippi will be totally useless for want of a communication to sea. It is strange to me that after having a full right to the navigation of the Mississippi (as granted to us in the definitive treaty of Peace) it should be thus suddenly stopped, and not the least tolerance to enter even the mouth of the river! There is one American vessel here from Rhode Island which has been here upwards of two months and now is ordered away together with her cargo. Perhaps you may be acquainted with the reason for this very unexpected turn." [14]

In due time, the protests of Pollock on the conduct of Spanish officials were transmitted to Congress and to Carmichael, in whose abilities, firmness, and integrity Robert Morris expressed the utmost confidence. Morris did not disguise the fact that such representations from the agent of a weak government would be futile. "It would be weakness in us," he asserts, "not to see that the usual Delays of that Court will be protracted to the utmost extent. The event like most others of the sort, must depend materially upon the degree of energy which shall prevail in the government of America and with respect to that there is but too much cause to wish and too little ground to hope." [15]

Early in February, 1785, Pollock's hope revived upon the coming of Galvez, who was to assume the office of Governor

[12] Miró to Galvez, March 12, 1784. *Ayer Coll.*
[13] "Draper MSS.," *William Clark Papers*, I, 98.
[14] Thomas Paterson to Oliver Pollock, May 1, 1784. *Pollock Letters.*
[15] To the President of Congress, September 30, 1784. Morris resigned his office November 1 of that year.

of Cuba. In a congratulatory message, Pollock thanked the governor for his early services to the United States and for his justice, protection, and politeness shown at all times to American citizens. He included a statement on the abuses which had heretofore been permitted. Specifically, he asked for an impartial hearing on the claims of American merchants who had been driven out of the island. He urged that his surety at New Orleans should be released; that he himself might be freed from his "gloomy confinement and tedious detention for debts contracted on account of the United States, and to go forward to the United States, to procure the necessary funds to discharge the debts due to his Catholic Majesty and his subjects, for the speedy discharge of which depend everything in my power shall be executed." [16] As on earlier occasions, Galvez was ready to contribute to the "personal service" of Pollock and "whatever might be advantageous to the Americans."

"But," as Pollock wrote, "before he had time to effect my release by a regular course of law, he was appointed Vice Roy of Mexico. This became an impediment to the obtaining my liberty but this generous nobleman touched with my situation and being witness to the exertions and sacrifices I had made at New Orleans for the service of the United States during the late war, generously stepped forth and became my surety to the attornies of my creditors for the amount of $132,764."

Recognition was accorded him, such as permission to attend the Governor's Court and to wear "his sword and cane in like manner as persons the most distinguished." Moreover, as a further mark of distinction, he again appeared on festive occasions in his coach drawn by mules, Galvez having ordered the return of this property to him. Upon leaving Havana, he sailed in company with "the Spanish Envoy, Mr. Diego Gardoqui," on a "frigate of the King." [17] In recognition of Pollock's efforts, American seamen held as smugglers in Havana were granted their freedom and were permitted to return

[16] March 1, 1785. *Pollock Letters.*
[17] *Dip. Corr. of the United States*, III, 176.

with him to Philadelphia.[18] Such efforts on the part of Galvez to promote harmony and friendship between Spain and the United States were seconded by Gardoqui. Upon landing at Chester, Gardoqui supplied the American seamen with the money necessary to enable them to return to their homes. "These marks of liberality and respect," John Jay declared, "have made a very agreeable impression on Congress, and they have ordered me to signify to your Excellency the sense they entertain of them. . . . I am also directed to request the favor of your Excellency to mention this circumstance to the Count, and to assure his Majesty, that as such acts of justice and kindness not only become civilized nations, but also tend to conciliate and confirm mutual friendship, the United States will omit no opportunity of acknowledging and returning them."[19]

Accurate information upon conditions in Cuba became known, probably for the first time, upon Pollock's return to Philadelphia, and Jefferson, because of his intimate relations with Pollock, thus became familiar with the facts.

Beyond the knowledge Pollock had acquired through frequent visits as a trader and as a resident in Havana for some months before the Revolution, he had during the period of his "tedious detention" collected information "from the archives and other unquestionable authorities without exposing myself to the suspicion of jealousy which pervades every branch of the Spanish government." His purpose in initiating this investigation was that it might prove of "some service to my country in forming the basis of the Treaty to be proposed by the Spanish Envoy," or that it might "at a future period convey some new and useful information."[20]

Under normal conditions, the imports to Cuba, excluding dry goods, would, he estimated, amount to $800,000 annually. Among the necessary importations were flour, beef, pork,

---

[18] *Dip. Corr. of the United States,* III, 179.
[19] Jay to Florida Blanca, September 10, 1785. *Ibid.,* p. 176.
[20] *Draper MSS.,* 43J158. June 3, 1785, addressed to the President of Congress.

apples, potatoes, codfish, beer, cider, masts, iron, and steel. Exports, he remarked, would, because of her fertile soil and happy climate, be increased many fold providing the inhabitants were permitted to purchase slaves in proportion to their ability to pay for them—"No industry is to be expected from the exertion of the white inhabitants of that region of sloth." [21]

For protection, there were two regiments of regular troops at Havana. In addition, there were four regiments of white, colored, and black infantry, numbering some five thousand men. Put to the test, he asserts, they would conduct themselves with little honor. Little assistance was to be expected from the country militia even at a time of emergency. A seventy-four gun-ship and two frigates, in good condition but poorly manned, constituted the naval protection. Labor on another one hundred gun-ship was discontinued because of lack of money. At the entrance to Havana harbor were Moro and Cavanas, two strong fortifications, and St. Theresa at its head, but Fort del Principi, the strongest fort of the land side, was not occupied.

To the subjects there was due from the government "about four million dollars. The inhabitants of the whole island of Cuba may without any exception be pronounced universally dissatisfied with the heavy yoke imposed by their despotic system of government, and they doubtless will at some future period, eagerly embrace the earliest favorable opportunity to shake off the galling chain, nay, even the military part are far from being pleased with their situation." [22]

Was not this information on Cuban affairs to influence the thinking of American leaders during the next century?

Following the invasion of Spain by Napoleon in 1808, which resulted in the paralysis of Spanish power in the Americas, the attention of European and American Statesmen was directed toward the naval and commercial importance of the "Ever faithful island of Cuba." Jefferson, then President, was

[21] *Ibid.*
[22] *Pollock Letters.*

vitally interested in the question, and, according to the instructions to agents of the United States in Cuba and Mexico, they were to express unauthoritatively to persons of influence: "If you remain under the dominion of Spain, we are contented, but we should be extremely unwilling to see you pass under the dominion or ascendancy of France or England. In the latter cases, should you chuse to declare independence we cannot now commit ourselves by saying we would make common cause with you but must reserve ourselves to act according to the then existing circumstances." [23]

To President Madison, early the following year, Jefferson declared: "Napoleon might consent to our receiving Cuba into our Union to prevent our aid to Mexico and the other provinces." [24] From this time, Americans were prepared to assert reversionary interest in the "Pearl of the Antilles." [25]

[23] Jefferson, *Writings*, ed. Ford, V, 443.
[24] *Writings of Thomas Jefferson*, ed. H. A. Washington, V, 443.
[25] J. B. Moore, *Digest of International Law*, VI, 380.

CHAPTER XVIII

POLLOCK CHARGED WITH MISCONDUCT IN OFFICE

AFTER a brief visit with his family in Philadelphia, Pollock hurried to New York. No time was to be lost in bringing his claims before Congress. He was obligated to pay Gardoqui, upon arrival in the United States, all claims held against him by Spanish creditors amounting to $151,696. Almost one-half this sum represented the original loan made by Galvez.[1]

To secure such an amount from a government, virtually bankrupt, seemed a task too great even for a man possessed of the ability and influence of Pollock. His statement to the President of Congress indicates the necessity for his summoning all the perseverance of which he was possessed. "The distressed situation of my family and affairs," he writes, "urges me to trouble your Excellency once more respecting the report that lays before Congress. My long sufferings for my zeal to the United States, is too much for my pen to describe, let it suffice that I am a prisoner on parole, and my attorney, Mr.

---

[1] A report of Louis Serrano, notary in Havana, shows the following amounts due the several creditors for which Pollock had become responsible: "To His Majesty, 13,112 dollars; to His Excellency Count de Galvez, 74,087 dollars; to Don Joseph Foucher, 21,035 dollars; to Mr. Beauregard, 3000 dollars; to Mr. Mausy, 3000 dollars; to Mr. Santiago Mulen, 12,200 dollars; to Mr. Cardel Sardet, 15,155 dollars; to Don Marcos Olivares, 2000 dollars; to Don Narcis de Alva and Company, 8,107 dollars. Which sums are the Sums due to all the creditors which are pending in the Court of the Intendant General of the army and Royal treasury and on which the Trusts are suspended by virtue of his having engaged to pay them in the said provinces to the Said Signor Commissario Ordinador on condition that out of the debt due to the Royal treasury are to be deducted 1875 dollars which he asserts he has paid, and for which Sum he is not credited in the proof for which reason he is to produce to the Said Commissary competent vouchers for the payment of that Sum." May 2, 1785. *Pollock Letters.*

Thomas Patterson detained at New Orleans for the debts of the United States. Whilst I am reduced from affluence to the last extremity to support a small numerous family, from whom I don't know the moment—the injured creditors may once more force me to part and leave them to the bounty of strangers for support." [2]

He urged especially that the sum due Galvez should be immediately placed to his credit. Shortly before he had been advised that the committee report on his distressed situation could not, because of other business, be taken up for consideration by Congress. Then he plead for the advance of a pittance, on account, for the support of his family. As a further step in meeting his obligations, he urged that Congress should recommend to the Government of Virginia the speedy discharge of moneys due him from that State by such "measures as may be necessary to relieve me from the incumbrances I am involved in, on behalf of the Publick."

To his surprise, he now learned through conversations with Virginia delegates that the assembly had refused to ratify the report of a committee which provided that out of the revenue collected during 1784, the treasurer should be instructed to pay the balance due on warrants issued to Pollock early in 1783 and "that a settlement of other accounts with him be adjusted." [3]

At the same time, he was confronted with a report which delayed action by Congress. His statement was as follows: "Understanding to my great surprise that some aspersions have been cast on my character and that some things have been suggested even to some of the members of that honble. body who honored me with their commission, which have tended to place my sufferings on account of my engagements for these States in a disadvantageous light, I cannot in justice to myself and to the commission with which I was honored forbear to mention this to you and request your interposition

[2] September 22, 1785, *Pollock Letters*.
[3] This report was submitted by the committee, December 4, 1784. "Clark MSS.," *Va. State Archives*.

POLLOCK ACCUSED

that a fair inquiry may be made into my conduct and agency."[4]

Jay was directed by Congress to investigate the report. In conference with Gardoqui, Jay learned that there was a rumor in Havana that "on unloading a cargo said to be flour from a vessel in which Pollock either came himself as a supercargo or which was consigned to him, the casks were placed on the wharf and that on removing them from thence to a storehouse, one of the casks giving way, it appeared to contain contraband goods. That this circumstance made much noise and that the Intendant was obliged to take notice of it."[5]

In conference with Jay, Pollock denied the charge and as proof submitted a testimonial from Governor Galvez bearing on his conduct as agent for the United States. It was asserted that Pollock had served the soldiers and citizens of his country with all the zeal and love which becomes all true patriots and that he spared neither pains nor trouble to obtain the end he proposed to himself. Since Galvez had but recently come to Havana, this certificate of good character refers, primarily, to the service rendered by Pollock at New Orleans. The assumption seems warranted that Galvez had no knowledge of any dereliction on the part of Pollock at any time and paid no heed to the rumor.[6]

Four days after the conference between Jay and Pollock, a Committee of Congress recommended that the debt of $74,087 due Pollock because of the loan from Galvez should be discharged as soon as the state of the treasury should permit and that the accrued interest on this sum should be paid without delay.

On numerous occasions, Pollock asserted that he had paid the bills drawn on him in specie dollar for dollar. But because of the large sums he had advanced in meeting the demands for carrying on the War in the West, suspicion was aroused on

[4] July 7, 1785. Addressed to John Jay, Secretary of the Department of Foreign Affairs. *Pollock Letters.*
[5] *Jour. of the Cont. Cong.,* XXIX, 522.
[6] This certificate was dated May 1, 1785, shortly before Pollock sailed for the United States.

the part of Federal officers that at least one of these bills actually represented transactions in depreciated paper money. Pollock replied:

> But those bills express no such depreciation. Is it to be supposed or will common sense admit that Spanish subjects would receive those bills at a depreciated state, to carry them 500 leagues down the Mississippi and then cross the seas with them in war time to come here and receive paper money, which paper money they had positively refused on the spot from those officers that drew the bills? No, if any of those bills ever had been intended to have been paid in a depreciated state, the poor Spanish traders (who risqued their lives and property up that river) have been grossly imposed on. But the fact stands thus, those traders were informed by Genl. Clark and every officer under him, that proper funds were lodged in the hands of their agent O. Pollock.
>
> Upon the whole, those officers and soldiers were sent by this State to conquer that vast western Country, without funds or without credit depending upon my support. Under those disadvantages, in that remote part of the world where they were to be supplied in war time at that immense distance from the sea and inexperienced troops as well in discipline as in economy, has all combined to increase the expense of the expedition far beyond the ideas of Government. This begot suspicions in the mind of Government and those suspicions have fallen in proportion to the sums I advanced, heavily in both instances on my shoulders! So that my greatest misfortune has been in doing too much.[7]

Fortune was now in his favor, for he learned that George Rogers Clark was in New York. More than any other man, Clark possessed full knowledge of Pollock's transactions. Upon the one in controversy, he had been outspoken in his condemnation of the supposed questionable deal of Pollock, growing out of the sale of the cargo of goods by Philip Barbour to Captain George at Fort Jefferson. As we have seen, the goods came in time to relieve the great distress of the soldiers and inhabitants of that post. As related by Clark in a letter to Governor Nelson, Barbour agreed to accept Virginia currency but con-

---

[7] This statement was prepared by Pollock for the use of his agents in Richmond, November 21, 1785. "Clark MSS.," *Va. State Archives.*

trived to get a bill drawn for gold or silver for the entire amount—"Consequently supposed he secured at least fifteen times the sum he asked for his cargoe. It appears to me that it was a scheme between Messrs. Pollock and Barbour before Barbour left Orleans, as per the enclosed copy that accidentally fell into my hands. . . . I understand they have already demanded payment. I make no doubt Pollock has Barbour's receipt for the payment of that number of hard dollars, but the premeditated fraud, if so (otherwise I ask their pardon) by no means excuses Capt. George, as soon as the auditors arrive he must account for this cargoe." [8]

On this bill, when it was presented by Barbour, Pollock actually paid $32,500. In a letter to Captain George, he states: "I am very happy to find that the supplies furnished your post by Mr. Philip Barbour has been of so much service particularly in turning your neighboring savages into firm Friends which formerly held out the hatchet against us. Notwithstanding this I think you paid too high for those goods." [9]

Clark, after a conference with Pollock, their first, prepared a new statement which was convincing to the commissioners. "These are to certify to all whom it may concern," he declares, "that all the bills I drew when I commanded the Virginia troops in the Illinois Country upon Mr. Oliver Pollock agent for the United States at New Orleans were considered by me to be for specie as the respective bills expressed in dollars." Because of this service, Clark claimed, it was possible for him "to keep possession of that country." [10]

But for many years, notwithstanding acceptance by Virginia of Pollock's statement, the rumor of misconduct was still current among a "class of people who know nothing at all of the nature of your disbursements and who are too apt to condemn without a hearing." In this wise spoke William Heth, a

[8] October 6, 1781. *Clark Papers*, 1781–1783, pp. 4, 5.
[9] The Western Commissioners fixed the value at $21,661 for the cargo which was delivered at Fort Jefferson. "Clark Papers," *Ill. Hist. Coll's.*, XIX, 322.
[10] July 2, 1785. "Clark MSS.," *Va. State Archives*.

Virginian who was one of the three commissioners appointed to adjust the claims between the United States and Virginia which emanated from the conquest of the Northwest.

To these commissioners Pollock made an appeal for a statement on the advances he had made on behalf of Virginia. The replies of two of them were explicit on the indispensable service he had rendered to Clark.[11] "The conquest of the Illinois country," the Virginia commissioner concludes, "could not have been maintained by Virginia and consequently that it would not now form a part of the United States, if it had not been for your assistance and very liberal advances; except indeed that your private fortunes were injured thereby, and that your character had been lightly spoken of by those, who are ever more ready to join in a popular clamor against a public servant than to examine minutely into his transactions."

Almost two more decades were to elapse before Pollock, through official recognition was to be free from the stigma attached to his name because of this transaction. Then it was to come through the testimony before the Court of Claims by this commissioner. In reply to Pollock's request for the evidence presented, Heth writes:

Respecting Mr. Pollock's claim against the United States, I certainly know nothing. . . .

It affords me much real pleasure to have it now in my power, not only to do away with such foul slanders, but to do ample justice to his character as a public agent, and to his great merits, as a true patriot, and also to make some amends, for the injury I once did him, by entertaining—though for a short time—similar opinions, in consequence of his name having been connected in certain reports—though no ways interested as I soon found—with that of a man who had certainly attempted the grossest imposition upon the state of Virginia through Mr. Pollock, as her agent, and in which he might probably have succeeded, had it not been for the honest integrity and firmness of Mr. Pollock in repelling a claim

---

[11] April 15, 1788. There was no statement from John Pierce, who was the commissioner representing the United States. Augustus B. Woodward, *A Representation of the Case of Oliver Pollock*, Washington, February 12, 1803.

of a most enormous size, which he had strong reasons to believe was unjust, though sanctioned by a bill of exchange, drawn upon him by proper authority, but whose ignorance of such negotiations, subjected him to the prey of an unprincipled speculating trafficker. Mr. Pollock saved the state against the designs of an intriguing character, in this instance, about $200,000. . . . It is known, if not to the whole of the committee, to two members, that I was the commissioner appointed on the part of Virginia, to ascertain the sum to be reimbursed that State, by the United States, which had been incurred in the conquest and protection of the Northwestern Territory. When I entered upon that duty, I felt as I have already said strong prejudice against Mr. Pollock. A thorough and most complete investigation of his account, about which so much has been said (and which has already been adjusted between the parties, by arbitrators in every respect competent thereto) dissipated these prejudices. . . . This investigation, with that of a variety of other documents and of the correspondence between Mr. Pollock and the different Governors of Virginia, Genl. Clark, and other subordinate officers proved to me that Mr. Pollock had been not only a much abused man, and most shamefully and ungratefully treated, but that, no one, scarce, at the seat of government then, seemed to know anything of his merits as a real patriot, of the uncommon services rendered by him in supporting and advancing the American cause, for with me there is no sort of question but that the United States are more indebted for the Northwestern Territory to Oliver Pollock, than to any man now living, or who did live at the time of its conquest—for the great enterprise of the brave Gen. Clark and the gallantry of his little army, could not have accomplished and maintained what he did, had it not been for the prompt, zealous and liberal advances of Mr. Pollock. With the fortunes and influence he then possessed—if he had remained to this day at New Orleans without having concerned himself with those agencies, he would be found to be among the most wealthy merchants in the United States. From the remarks which have been made upon Mr. Pollock's present claim, in the conversation which I have had with some members of this committee, I hope it will not be deemed improper for me to say here, that I believe him to be utterly incapable of exhibiting any charge against the United States, that he does not most religiously believe to be strictly just, and that, he never paid any claim or demand, as an agent, that he would not have paid in his private capacity. In one word, I believe him to be as honest a man as ever discharged any public trust; and certain it is, that his fortunes were ruined by that zeal to discharge the trust and confidence resposed in him, which he manifested upon every occasion. [12]

In the meantime, Congress again demanded a reëxamination of Pollock's accounts and ordered particularly that there should be taken up for consideration those claims emanating from the expenditures for Virginia. It was proposed by Pollock that the adjustment of this balance should be undertaken by two commissioners who should meet in New York. One of them was to be appointed by the United States and the other by Virginia. This was met by a counter-proposal by Governor Patrick Henry, and accepted by Pollock, that he should once more come to Virginia.

Evidently the generosity of his friends enabled him to make this journey, since no response seems to have been made to his request to the President of Congress for the payment of four or five thousand dollars on account. This amount, he estimated, would cover his expenses for travel, would permit him "to pay off some money I borrowed during my detention at Havana and provide the necessaries for my distressed family at Philadelphia." [13] "Feeling sensibly for Mr. Pollock's distress," as expressed by the Governor of Virginia, evidently brought no response to the request of Pollock for an advance of one hundred pounds to provide for his expenses while in Richmond.[14]

Following the advice of Governor Henry, two arbitrators were named for a final adjustment of the claims due Pollock. According to their award, the amount still due him was fixed at $92,321 in specie, including interest. Among these claims were a number based on drafts which were executed during the early months of the Revolution. The report to the legislature included also the recommendation that a commission of 5 per cent, named by Pollock, should be granted to cover the

[12] "Clark MSS.," *Va. State Archives.*
[13] September 23, 1785. *Pollock Letters.*
[14] Letter of Governor Henry, October 12, 1785. "Letter Book of Benjamin Harrison," *Va. State Archives.*

expenses of his journeys to Richmond; to provide for the agents whom he had employed; for the remuneration of his hostage in New Orleans; and for the inconvenience to which he had been exposed through "a ruined fortune, a distressed family and an injured credit."

The act passed by the legislature was in harmony with these findings and provided that Pollock was to be granted any favor which might be accorded foreign creditors of the State. As a measure of protection, a large portion of the indebtedness was not to be paid until Pollock should produce receipts from his creditors in proof that the State would be "exonerated from all claimants on account thereof."

Convinced that his claims against the United States could now be satisfactorily adjusted, Pollock returned to New York and once more made his appeal to Congress. In describing his seemingly hopeless financial status, he wrote: "And it is a very heavy additional misfortune, that for several years past, the incumbrances of the large and many debts I had contracted for the Public totally destroyed my credit and rendered me incapable of pursuing the smallest commercial business. For what merchant would consign to or intrust his property in the hands of a man who was involved in such heavy debts and until my Country, by rendering the justice which is due shall remove these obstacles I must continue to languish in the same inactive and helpless situation."

Out of the sums procured from Virginia, however, it became possible for him during the years 1786 and 1787 to ship to New Orleans, consigned to his agent, Daniel Clarke, Negroes from the West Indies and flour from Philadelphia. So profitable were these ventures, that he was enabled to cancel a portion of his indebtedness.

As at all times, with the welfare of his family, comprising Mrs. Pollock and eight children, uppermost in his mind, he made an advance payment upon an estate, the well-known Silver Spring near Carlisle, Pennsylvania.[15] This was to be his

[15] Silver Spring is situated about ten miles from Carlisle and eight miles from Harrisburg. Lucetta Adelaide Pollock was born in New

home for twenty years.[16] In this community where he had lived before he entered upon his career as a trader, he had previously acquired a farm, a portion of which was in the hands of a tenant. Judged by a communication from his sister Mary, but little income was to come from the remainder of this property, then her home. She writes, in language describing the economic depression then prevalent even in the best rural communities:

> And for my own Part, I foresee so much trouble and expence under the present situation of afairs and comparing whats past with whats to come I think we are not equal for the task. I do indeed long to see this place flurish and would think no trouble two much was we abel in pocket to carry on even in a midlar way. . . . My dear brother you make a demand of a sum of money, Lord bless you, if we could make five times as much it would not be sufficient to answer the demand hear. . . . I think we had better make room for some stranger that has a heavy pocket if such can be found that can lay out a deal of money and wait till it comes out of the ground for you know we cannot reap before we sow.

Orleans, September 9, 1782. Bernard Galvez Pollock was born in Philadelphia, June 3, 1785. His sponsor at the time of his baptism was Don Diego de Gardoqui. The names of the other children were: Procopiers, Charles, Christine, Jerret, Marie, Antonia, and James.

[16] At Carlisle, during 1788, Francis Vigo conferred with Pollock relative to the claims of Vigo against Virginia. *Ill. Commissioner's Report*, Vol. 10 (1834), p. 94B. Various statements have become current relating to the value of the goods furnished by Colonel Vigo for the use of Clark's troops. The usual expression is: He threw his "entire fortune" into the cause. But no amount is indicated. According to the testimony of Vigo himself, made before John H. Smith, Virginia Commissioner in 1834, the advances made by him amounted to "nearly $12,000." On this sum, he had received payments from Pollock and from other sources, $3,256 (1788). When he visited Pollock at Carlisle, he presented a draft for payment covering the balance, $8,616. Pollock declared that "he had no funds of Virginia in his hands, although it was due and should long since have been paid; that Virginia would sometime or other pay it with interest." *Illinois Regiment Commissioner's Report*, MS., Vol. 10 (1834). The draft and vouchers were lost and thus Vigo was unable to establish a legal claim. After his death, March 22, 1836, the prosecution of this claim dragged on for another forty years, when a decision was reached to pay his heirs the sum in controversy, $8,616 with interest for ninety-eight years (1778–1876), a total amount of $49,898.

POLLOCK'S RESIDENCE AT SILVER SPRING

This has been a hard winter, nothing astir but poor travelers. When one spends a shilling there is another to beg Logens and breckfast or a Diner, for Godsaik.¹⁷ Notwithstanding the man that could hold out until he could rais grain of his own and rais stock might do well hear, or if we were abel to Punch [produce] a large quantity of grain that we might do very cheap for reday money we could make something cleaver in selling it to the roming travelars as the road will be full of them. But people can do nothing without money. . . . My mind is very much perplext.¹⁸

¹⁷ Carlisle was on the main traveled route from Philadelphia to Pittsburgh. There it was customary to transfer goods from wagons to the backs of horses.
¹⁸ *Pollock Letters.*

CHAPTER XIX

FATE OF THE WEST IN THE BALANCE

DURING the four years in which Pollock was striving to bring about the settlement of his claims against the United States and Virginia, Gardoqui was carrying on negotiations with John Jay over the points at issue between Spain and the United States. Because of his familiarity with the facts and his friendly relations with Gardoqui, Pollock's advice on a solution which would be most desirable for the future interests of the United States was invaluable.

We have seen how persistently he urged upon Congress that the fate of the West was dependent on the free navigation of the Mississippi River. How much greater this need since, with the advance of westward migration, the population of Kentucky in 1785 was estimated at 30,000. The Cumberland settlements numbered 3,500 inhabitants.

Moreover, Western demands for protection were becoming more insistent. "Pray let me know," wrote a trader at Natchez, "if you can explain a quible they make here about the line being at the Northermost part of 31° for my part I am not Geographer enough to do it. If they meant anything why did not they write it 32 at once or 31 or whatever number of miles they lik'd then a body would know what to be at. I want to be assured about the Natchez, for if it should be ours and that we maintain our navigation of the Mississippi I shall make it my residence. . . . Why don't government send commissioners to have the line run?"[1] "What in the name of God," he again writes, "are Congress about that they let their subjects be so vilainously treated in this place and suffer the treaty to be so notoriously violated?"[2]

---

[1] July 22, 1784, "Draper MSS.," *William Clark Papers*, I, 89.
[2] *Ibid.*, p. 95.

FATE OF THE WEST IN THE BALANCE

Washington, who had made a tour of the upper Ohio country, writes of the critical situation as follows:

> The western states (I speak now from my own observation) stand as it were upon a pivot. The touch of a feather would turn them any way. They have looked down the Mississippi, until the Spaniards, very impolitically I think for themselves, threw difficulties in their way, and they looked that way for no other reason than because they could glide gently down the stream, without considering, perhaps, the difficulties back again, and the time necessary to perform it in, and because they have no other means of coming to us but by long land transportations and unimproved roads. These causes have hitherto checked the industry of the present settlers; for except the demand for provisions, occasioned by the increase of population, and a little flour, which the necessities of the Spaniards compel them to buy, they have no incitement to labor.[3]

According to his credentials, Gardoqui was granted full power to regulate commerce and establish the boundaries of Spanish frontier possessions. But by his secret orders he understood that the exclusive navigation of the Mississippi River through Spanish territory and the boundaries were the most important subjects upon which he would have to treat. This information was imparted to the President of Congress by Pollock, who had held several conferences with Galvez and

---

[3] September, 1784. *Writings of Washington,* ed. Sparks, IX, 63. Washington hoped that the negotiations between Gardoqui and Jay would lead to a settlement advantageous to both nations. In a recently discovered letter from Washington to an unknown correspondent in Moscow, we find an expression of his views, as follows: "Sir; I am greatly obliged to you for the several communications of your letter— I wish disagreeable consequences may not result from the contentions respective to the navigation of the river Mississippi. The emigrations to the waters hereof are astonishingly great and chiefly of that description of people who are not very subordinate to law and good government.

"Whether the prohibition from the Court of Spain is just or unjust— politic or otherwise, it will be difficult to restrain people of this class from enjoying natural advantages. It is devoutly to be wished that Mr. Gardoqui would enter into such stipulations with Congress as may avert the impending evil and be mutually advantageous to both nations." Mount Vernon, June 21, 1785. Moscow Historical Museum.

Gardoqui in Havana and had come with the latter as a fellow-passenger to Philadelphia.

Further inside information gained by Pollock through these conversations, which were doubtless divulged to Jay, he referred to as follows:

> That though they are very sanguine in their expectations from what they call right of conquest, as well with respect to territorial limits, as the exclusive right of navigating on the Mississippi, as far as their assumed rights extend, yet they are very diffident of the advisability of their claim on the part of the United States, and notwithstanding the full powers to treat which Mr. Gardoqui will produce to Congress, I am well authorized to affirm that in case of the expected difficulty in determining the limits he is instructed to correspond with General Galvez previous to a final adjustment of those limits, who I believe is fully empowered by his Court to conclude ultimately with the United States.

The view advanced by Galvez that the settlement at Natchez was included within the province of West Florida, and therefore that Great Britain had no right to cede any portion of that province to the United States or to grant them any right of navigating the Mississippi within the same, Pollock stoutly opposed. He asserted, as he had in his numerous communications to Congress five years earlier, that while the claims of the United States might reasonably extend to the whole of West Florida, there should be no yielding on the thirty-first degree of latitude as the southern boundary and that the prosperity of the West was dependent on the free navigation of the Mississippi River.[4]

But free navigation was of little commercial value unless there should also be secured a place of deposit where produce brought down the River might be transferred to ocean-going vessels. Upon this point, Pollock once more declared: "I doubt not Congress must be well informed that the navigation of the Mississippi must always be impracticable (supposing it acceded to on the part of the Court of Spain) unless a reciprocal liberty be reserved to both Nations to land occasionally upon

[4] *See* pp. 252, 253.

FATE OF THE WEST IN THE BALANCE

either side of the River, and this must in a certain proportion be equally necessary to the subjects of Spain as to the Citizens of the United States settled in the interior parts of that Country." [5]

"Don Diego Gardoqui is arrived," Jay wrote, "and has been received so much in the spirit of friendship that I hope his master and himself will be well pleased." That he thought the situation serious may be seen in his further statement: "Our negotiations with him will soon commence, and I sincerely wish that the issue of them may be satisfactory to both countries. To prepare for war, and yet be tenacious of peace with all the world is I think, our true interest." [6]

Pollock's favorable report on the generous treatment which had been accorded Americans by Galvez served as pretext for withdrawal of the demand by Congress for satisfaction on the conduct of Governor Unzaga toward American seamen. "As that man is now out of office," Jay wrote, "and does not appear to have acted by orders of his Court, as no direct commerce between these States and Spanish American Ports is probable and as Count de Galvez who succeeded Unzaga shewed a degree of kindness to Americans, in some degree proportionate to the harshness they experienced from the latter, the expediency of such Remonstrances, appear very doubtful to your Secretary." [7]

Jay was specifically directed to secure a treaty which should guarantee to the United States the free navigation of the Mississippi from its source to the ocean, as defined in the treaties with Great Britain.

With the opening of negotiations, the fundamental questions which received consideration were the reopening of the Mississippi to American traders, the boundary of West Florida, and a treaty of commerce. A satisfactory treaty of commerce could be obtained, Gardoqui contended, only on condition that the United States should abandon all claims to

[5] Philadelphia, June 3, 1785. *Draper MSS.*, 43J160.
[6] *Writings of Jay*, III, 160.
[7] *Jour. of Congress*, XXIX, 714, 715.

the right of navigating the River below Natchez. The concession made in the treaty with Great Britain, he held, was a specific grant and this she had no power to transfer to another country. Nor was he prepared to accept the argument advanced by Jay that the United States possessed a natural right to follow to the ocean all rivers on which any of its territory bordered.

A treaty of commerce was demanded by the commercial interests of the coast, for out of it would come, as they believed, business prosperity. To that section, therefore, Gardoqui directed his appeal: "No one is ignorant of the great advantages," he stated to Jay, "which the United States derive from their trade with Spain from whence they yearly extract millions as well by their productions as by their navigation which so much promotes the growth and maintenance of their marine." [8]

Speaking on behalf of this section, Rufus King writes: "Our Fish and every article we sell in Spain is sold upon the Footing of the most Favored Nation in that country. This is favor and not right: Should we embarrass ourselves in the attempts of imprudent men to navigate the Mississippi below the northern boundary of Florida we can expect no favors from the Spanish Government. England is our rival in the fisheries, France does not wish us prosperity in this branch of commerce. If we embroil ourselves with Spain what have we to expect on this subject? The answer is too obvious or important to leave a doubt of the policy of forming a treaty of commerce between the United States and Spain." [9]

In general, Representatives in Congress from the South were equally insistent that the commercial interests of the West, as advised by Pollock, should be protected.

After a year of fruitless negotiation, Jay, on August 3, 1786, with the hope that a treaty of commerce might follow, recommended that the United States, without prejudicing her

[8] *Papers of James Monroe, MSS.* (New York Public Library).
[9] *Rufus King Letters, MSS.* (New York Historical Society).

rights, should forego the navigation of the Mississippi for twenty-five or thirty years. He declared that Spain would never willingly yield the navigation of the River, that force alone could bring it about, and that the United States was not prepared for war. The advantages to be derived from favorable commercial relations, Jay argued, were immediate, whereas the West would not need the much-desired navigation for a half-century. Moreover, the boundary question would be more easily adjusted, he thought, should Spain be conceded her demand on the Mississippi question.[10]

Meantime, Pollock was declaring that Spain was not justified in her claim, advanced by Galvez, that Natchez was to be included in the province of West Florida, since Great Britain in defining the boundary of the Colony of Georgia had "extended its southern limits to the thirty-first degree upon the Mississippi." [11]

> It may be proper [he writes], that Congress be informed that soon after the Peace of 1763, His Britannic Majesty in his charter to the province of Georgia extended its limits to the 31st. degree of North Latitude upon the Mississippi, and after Governor Johnston was appointed to the administration of West Florida, the Inhabitants of the Natchez district petitioned him to take them under the jurisdiction of his Province on account of the inconvenience they labored under from the Georgia Seat of Government being so distant from the settlements. The Governor and Council at Pensacola took into consideration the Natchez petition and transmitted a copy of their proceedings to the British Court, recommending the request of the petitioners, and that the limits of his Government should be extended to the River Yazoo, and in the meantime assumed the jurisdiction of that district, but this proceeding never was confirmed by the Court of Britain.

Thus Pollock showed a familiarity with documents which were of the utmost importance on the questions at issue. It is significant that this communication was unquestionably in

[10] "Secret Jour. of Congress," *Foreign Affairs*, IV, 81–84.
[11] Pollock to the President of Congress, June 3, 1785. *Draper MSS.*, 43J185.

the possession of the President of Congress and doubtless was known to Jay even before the formalities of the reception to Gardoqui had taken place.[12]

Pollock was familiar also with the Spanish claims to territory north of 32° 30′:

> I cannot positively ascertain the extent of their claims to the territory upon the east side of the Mississippi [he writes], but from an anecdote that happened in 1780, I conceive they mean to assume territorial rights far beyond the Natchez district, for when Colonel Montgomery of the Virginia Troops was at a place called the English Arkansas about 400 miles above the Natchez, on his way down to New Orleans, in order to get supplies from me for his men, he had planted the American colors at that place when a Spanish officer Captain Devillia [De Villiers] came over from their post and buried under ground in a tin box the colors of Spain as a symbol of his having taken possession of that part of the Country.[13]

That Georgia, through an appointed agent, Lt. Colonel Thomas Green, was demanding from the Spanish commander at Natchez the surrender of that post, upon the claim that it was within her territory, was likewise known to Pollock. Information that hostilities were imminent had been brought to him by one of his friends. This dispatch from Thomas Patterson, who was still held as Pollock's bondman in New Orleans, states that the Spanish governor was determined to resist any alleged claim on the part of Georgia. "The Governor of this place," he writes, "has ordered up all the troops here to the Natchez and a number of cannon, ammunition, intrenching tools etc. The militia of the town are this day to assemble and keep guard. . . . I am creditably informed that the Governor has sent to the Havana for a reinforcement

---

[12] The letter is dated Philadelphia, June 3, 1785. The reception took place on July 15. *Diplomatic Correspondence*, 1783-1789, VI, 66, 81.

[13] *Pollock Letters*. According to instructions given Gardoqui by Galvez, the Spanish claim was to extend to the Ohio River. But there was no claim made to territory north of this River, based on the capture of Fort St. Joseph. For maps showing Spanish claims to territory east of the Mississippi River, see Samuel F. Bemis, *Pinckney Treaty*, pp. 76, 77.

FATE OF THE WEST IN THE BALANCE

of troops to consist of about two thousand men. All this, together with the preparation of every warlike instrument in this place makes an appearance of hostilitys not being far off." [14] Accompanying this message was the familiar refrain of Pollock: "Should the United States be deprived of the free and uninterrupted navigation of the Mississippi, then America may bid adieu to the most promising part of her territory."

In Congress, the proposal of Jay aroused heated discussion, behind closed doors, continuing for three weeks. It became a sectional issue. New Englanders, desirous of procuring a commercial treaty and alarmed over increased migration to the West, demanded the acceptance of the proposed plan. "Should there be an uninterrupted use of the Mississippi at this time by the citizens of the United States," Rufus King of New York declared, "I should consider every immigrant to that Country from the Atlantic States as forever lost to the Confederacy." [15]

Southern members insisted that Jay should immediately break off all further negotiations. "Such an act if passed," Madison asserted, "would indicate to the people of the Western waters that they had been sold to the men of the coast. Might they not be justified in considering 'themselves ab-

[14] June 28, 1785. *Pollock MSS.*, Virginia State Library. It is noteworthy that the validity of Georgia's title to this territory was confirmed by the Supreme Court of the United States. "The very ground," the decision states, "on which she [United States] denied the capacity of Spain to conquer, or take by cession, the territory on the Mississippi was fatal to the pretensions set up by her against Georgia and South Carolina, to wit, that Spain could not acquire by conquest a territory within the limits claimed by an ally in the war. . . . There was no territory within the United States that was claimed by any other right than that of some one of the Confederated States, therefore there could be no acquisition of territory made by the United States district from and independent of some one of the States." *Harcourt vs. Gaillard,* 12 *Wheaton* 523.

A summary of the steps preceding the decision is given in C. H. Haskins, "The Yazoo Land Companies," *Papers of the American Historical Association,* V, 62, 63.

[15] August 13, 1786, King to Robert C. Winthrop. *Papers of Rufus King,* New York Hist. Soc'y.

solved from every federal tie and court some protection for their betrayed rights'?"[16] The attitude of the Eastern States was interpreted by Monroe as "an attempt to break up the settlements on the western waters and prevent any in the future. . . . To throw the might of population eastward and keep it there, to appreciate the vacant lands of New York and Massachusetts."[17]

But the rumor was widespread that Congress had agreed to the terms suggested by Jay. This still further aroused the distrust of the people of the West toward the dilatory policy of the Federal government and increased their antagonism toward Spain.

Western sentiment was expressed by a "gentleman" at Louisville to his friend in New England in the following spirited fashion:

> To give us the liberty of transporting our effects down the river to New Orleans and then be subject to the Spanish laws and impositions is an insult to our understanding. . . . The quantities of produce we now have on hand are immense . . . men of large means are already ruined by their policy. . . . Do you think to prevent the emigration from a barren Country loaded with taxes and impoverished with debts, to the most luxurious and fertile soil in the world? . . . Shall all this Country now be cultivated entirely for the use of the Spaniards? Shall we be their bondsmen as the children of Israel were to the Egyptians? Shall one part of the United States be slaves, while the other is free? . . . Preparations are now making there (if necessary) to drive the Spaniards from their settlements at the mouth of the Mississippi.[18]

The votes of seven States were counted in favor of Jay's plain. But nine votes were necessary to ratify a treaty. The Southern bloc was able to postpone ultimate decision for the new government under the Constitution.

To what degree the attitude of Pollock dominated Southern thought cannot be definitely stated. One "conversation"

[16] *Writings of James Madison,* ed. Gaillard Hunt, I, 1202.
[17] *Writings of James Monroe,* ed. S. M. Hamilton (New York, 1898–1903), I, 150.
[18] December 4, 1786. "Draper MSS.," *Trip* VI, 139–145.

FATE OF THE WEST IN THE BALANCE

which he held with the Virginia delegates is recorded. He was favorably known to Patrick Henry, Edmund Randolph, and Thomas Jefferson and was to become a recognized leader in the Democratic-Republican party. Early in 1786, he dined with Washington and spent the night at Mount Vernon.[19] Their friendly relations had been established nine years earlier.[20]

During the summer of 1787, Washington, then President of the Constitutional Convention, was Pollock's guest at dinner in Philadelphia.[21] It was during this period that Washington modified his views on the Mississippi question. During the summer of 1786, he wrote: "There are many ambitious and turbulent spirits among its inhabitants, who from the present difficulties in their intercourse with the Atlantic States, have turned their eyes to New Orleans, and may become riotous and ungovernable, if the hope of traffic with it is cut off by treaty. . . . It may be a more favorable time to speak decisively to them than when they have got stronger, but not sufficiently matured to force the passage of the Mississippi themselves." [22] Within a year, alarmed over the spirit of

[19] John C. Fitzpatrick, *The Diaries of George Washington*, III, 9.

[20] Pollock's assistance to the American cause was known to Washington and it has been declared that a portion of the powder which was procured by Captain Gibson (*see ante.*, p. 70), was forwarded to Washington's army. That friendly relations had been established between Washington and Pollock by the close of 1777 is evident from a statement in a recently discovered journal of Baron Passerat de la Chapelle, a French officer in the French and Indian War. This diary is now being edited by Dr. Louise Phelps Kellogg. Dr. Kellogg writes: "La Chapelle afterwards was stationed at Martinique. Thence in 1777 he says he was sent by Vergennes on a secret mission to the United States to see Washington and learn of conditions. He went to New Orleans and there got into touch with Oliver Pollock who gave him a letter to Washington. He went up the Mississippi and the Ohio, crossed to Bethlehem, where, October 6, 1777, he met De Kalb. Then went to Washington at Withe Plains (probably Whitemarsh), who received him kindly because of Pollock's recommendation. After three weeks he went back to New Orleans and left for Havana."

[21] Fitzpatrick, *Diary of Washington*, III, 233. Two days later Washington writes of being the guest of Chief Justice McKean. Four days later, he dined at the home of Robert Morris.

[22] *Writings of Washington*, ed. Ford, XI, 41.

hostility manifested in the West, he advised that Jay's proposal should be dropped.[23]

The impatience of the Westerners was further heightened because of the failure of Congress to deal effectually with their Indian enemies. Spanish officials, after the treaty of peace, continued their efforts, which had been markedly successful during the Revolution, to retain control over the tribes of the Southwest.[24] In the five leading tribes, Creek, Cherokee, Choctaw, Chickasaw, and Natchez, it was estimated there were some ten thousand warriors, a formidable buffer force which might be used for the defense of Louisiana and Mexico.[25] Several hundred Creeks, during July, 1784, returned to their villages loaded with presents following a treaty with Spanish agents. "They say, the Spaniards tell them that they expect a war with America shortly and that if their Red Brother will assist them, they will soon end it, for had it not been for them and the French, Great Britain would have subdued the Americans long ago."[26] To Alexander McGillivray, chief of this tribe, one of the most noted of Indian leaders, they paid a yearly pension of $600 in addition to a share in the profits from the Indian trade carried on at Pensacola. At Pensacola and Mobile, stores were established which furnished goods for traders frequenting the Indian villages. Trade in fire-arms was carried on secretly. "What I have seen lately is torment to bear," one letter states. "The Creeks have murdered a number of our friends in Georgia and immediately after the stroke

---

[23] *Whitaker, op. cit.,* 119.

[24] For Indian problems of the Northwest, *see Life of Clark,* pp. 347-362.

[25] Shaw, *British Administration of the Southern Indians,* 1756-1783, p. 195. During the summer of 1784, Creek, Chickasaw, and Choctaw chiefs signed treaties at Pensacola and Mobile in which they agreed to accept Spanish alliance; no white man should be received by them without a Spanish passport and Spanish traders should be protected. Creek and Choctaw bound themselves to aid in the defense of the provinces of Louisiana and West Florida. Jane Bury, "Indian Policy of Spain in the Southwest," *Miss. Valley Hist. Rev.,* III, 464.

[26] Colonel Martin to Governor Harrison, "Draper MSS.," *Trip* IV, 20, 21.

FATE OF THE WEST IN THE BALANCE

their King came here [with] 5 thousand Pounds of Ball and near as much powder and I believe some arms to enable them to stand against our country, this was done underhand but I found it out and am of opinion these people will do their utmost to encourage all the savages against us—this moment my very Blood calls for Vengeance." [27] According to a treasury report, Spanish presents amounting to $300,000 were made to the Indians during the eight years preceding 1788. Raids by Indian bands were frequent and Congress, as Westerners believed, was oblivious to their petitions for protection. As reported, a leading member of Congress from Massachusetts declared, in the course of debate, "that it would give him real pleasure to see the ocean wash the Western foot of the Alleghany hills." [28]

It is not surprising that men of the West came to the conviction that their future prosperity was dependent upon their own exertions. Since early summer, 1785, rumors were prevalent at the Spanish posts that expeditions were being organized for the purpose of capturing Natchez.[29] George Rogers Clark, it was said, had recruited twenty-four companies of sixty men each in Kentucky, Cumberland, and the other settlements, with the design of setting out in the spring for Natchez and New Orleans.[30]

Spanish officials were perceptibly alarmed over these repeated rumors. Their posts were poorly garrisoned and a force of only 695 men, two-thirds of them recruits, was available at New Orleans. They lacked artillery and their ammunition was almost exhausted.[31] Spies were kept on the lookout for the coming of the Americans.[32]

---

[27] "Draper MSS.," *William Clark Papers*, I, 136.
[28] William Littell, "Political Transactions," ed. Temple Bodley, *Filson Club Publications*, XXXI, 18.
[29] *Gardoqui Papers*, III, 262–267.
[30] McGillivray to Miró, May 16, 1785, *American Historical Review*, XV, 73. June 3, 1785, Peter Farrot to Miró, *Ayer Collection*, June 14, 1785, Miró to Galvez, *Ibid.*, July 24, 1785, Bouligny to Miró, *Ibid.*
[31] Miró to Galvez, June 14, 1785, *Ayer Collection*.
[32] June 16, 1786, *Ibid.*

But to the Spaniards, American frontiersmen were an ambitious class of people whose desires knew no bounds, who were not limited by a Sense of Justice and who would dare to commit any excesses against the Spaniards on the pretense of their right to secure the free navigation of the Mississippi.[33] Upon the presentation of the evidence by Gardoqui, Congress passed resolutions condemning all such irresponsible acts.

A new angle in the controversy was projected, on the second of July, 1787, when General James Wilkinson landed in New Orleans, bringing with him a cargo of Kentucky flour, tobacco and bacon. During the Revolution, he had been promoted to the rank of brigadier general. With the desire of improving his fortune, he came to Lexington, Kentucky, in 1784 and became a trader in skins and salt. Through his assistance in an Indian raid, he won the confidence of Kentuckians. Endowed with a mind notable for its versatility and cunning, and possessing ability as a public speaker, he entered upon a political career and soon became a dominating as well as a menacing force in Western affairs.

In Kentucky, he found the spirit of revolt rife over the high-handed methods of Spanish officials in closing the Mississippi. It was asserted by leaders that their security lay in separation from Virginia and admission into the Confederation as a separate State. Three conventions having paved the way for action, a fourth met in August of 1785, with the more radical element in control and Wilkinson in the saddle. Final action, he boasted, was delayed in order that the members might be guided by his views. A petition was adopted calling upon Virginia to sanction separation. An inflammatory statement to Kentuckians indicated the necessity therefor. An Act for Separation passed the Virginia Assembly, which was to become operative providing a Kentucky convention to be held in September, 1787, should accept the proffered terms. As a further condition, Congress was to consent to the admission of this new State into the Union.

[33] *Gardoqui Papers*, I, 65.

Meanwhile, a remonstrance against Jay's plan to close the River was prepared and published by John Brown, Benjamin Sebastian, Harry Innes, and George Muter. Conventions in the several districts were urged to the end that Congress might learn that "they would not tamely submit to an act of oppression which would tend to a deprivation of our just rights and privileges."

From the September meeting of delegates much was anticipated. They were aware that the Southern States were a unit in opposition to Jay's plan. Terms for separate statehood, as proposed by Virginia, were accepted and application was made to Congress for admission into the Union. December 31, 1788, was set as the date for the termination of Virginia's authority over them.

Wilkinson was in New Orleans during the time of the September convention. Because of his military and political reputation, although he came without a passport, his goods were not seized by Governor Miró, and he was permitted to dispose of his cargo free from the usual duty. Representing, as he claimed, the leading characters in Kentucky, he proceeded, in a lengthy *Memorial*, to make known the conditions in Kentucky to Miró and Navarro, and explained his objective in coming to New Orleans.

Because of the incompetence of Congress, he predicted the formation of "a distinct Confederation of the Western inhabitants." Once independent, Kentuckians would resort to any means to procure for themselves the free navigation of the Mississippi. With this their supreme desire, they were prepared to negotiate with Spain, but, in case they failed, they would, through alliance with Great Britain, secure their objective through the use of force. As a reward, Great Britain was to gain Louisiana and eventually Mexico. Spain, "if she attaches the Americans to her interest, may immediately deduce a vast Revenue from the connexion and establish a permanent barrier against Great Britain and the United States." [34]

[34] William R. Shepherd, *American Hist. Rev.*, IX, 499.

To this end, selected men of influence in the Western settlements were to be granted indulgence in trade. Becoming attached to the interests of Spain, they would become agents in procuring the independence of Kentucky and in forming an alliance with Spain. Successful in this step, the other Western settlements, he argued, would probably imitate Kentucky.

As an alternative, Wilkinson proposed the erection of a fortified post at a trading-station, L'Ance a la Grace.[35] Here, men from the West might settle and thus inaugurate emigration to Louisiana "as rapid as it ever was from the Atlantic States to the Western Country." [36] As a token of his good faith, Wilkinson took the oath of allegiance which made him a Spanish subject.

In characteristic fashion, he had declared that whoever imputed a different motive to human conduct than self-interest, "either deceives himself, or endeavors to deceive others." Proclaiming his readiness to receive instructions from the Spanish Government, he sought as a reward for his influence, permission to transmit to his New Orleans agent a cargo of Negroes, live stock, tobacco, flour, bacon, lard, butter, cheese, tallow, and apples to the amount of fifty or sixty thousand dollars. The proceeds therefrom were to be held as a pledge for his good conduct, "until the issue of our plans is known, or I have fixed my residence in Louisiana." [37] "If these secrets are divulged," so ends his appeal, "his Fame and Fortune would forever be destroyed." [37]

Impressed with the possibilities in the proposal, Miró and Navarro waited only a few hours before making their reply, in which they granted him permission to send Kentucky produce to New Orleans but not in excess of one-half the sum he suggested. The proceeds were to be deposited in the provincial treasury until the pleasure of their government should be made known. As interpreted by Miró, "the delivering up of

---

[35] Later became the site of New Madrid, Missouri.
[36] *Am. Hist. Rev.*, IX, 501. *See especially* note 1.
[37] *Ibid.*, 502.

FATE OF THE WEST IN THE BALANCE

Kentucky into his Majesty's hands, which is the main object to which Wilkinson has promised to devote himself entirely would forever constitute this province a rampart for the protection of Spain." [38] Enthused over his success, Wilkinson set out for Kentucky, going by way of Philadelphia.

Judged by their report, Miró and Navarro, while requesting instructions which would permit them to deal with any commissioners who might come from the Ohio country, were evidently more impressed with the suggestion for fostering immigration from that region to Spanish territory.

With the arguments favoring such a project they were already familiar. The Spanish Government, prior to the Revolution, attempted, as we have seen, to establish a barrier to British expansion through inducing immigrants to settle in Louisiana.[39] "There is no time to be lost," Navarro wrote his government, February 12, 1787. "Mexico is on the other side of the Mississippi, in the vicinity of the already formidable establishment of Americans. The only way to check them is with a proportionate population, and it is not by imposing commercial restrictions that this population is to be acquired but by granting a prudent extension and freedom of trade." [40]

Gardoqui was likewise interested in promoting a plan for inducing immigrants to settle in Louisiana.[41] Should they place themselves under the protection of Spain, Florida Blanca assured Gardoqui, there would be no difficulty in opening New Orleans to their commerce.[42]

To discontented persons in Kentucky, Tennessee, and Illinois, who were unable to pay the required one dollar an acre for land, such a proposal was heartily approved. "Some allowance should be made to them who have risqued their lives

[38] T. M. Green, *Spanish Conspiracy* (Cincinnati, 1891), p. 128.
[39] The number of Acadians who had settled in Louisiana by 1787 amounted to 1587. Gayarré, *History of Louisiana,* III, 185.
[40] *Ibid.,* p. 183.
[41] James, *Life of Clark,* pp. 385-390.
[42] *Gardoqui Papers,* IV, 242-246.

to settle in that country," a letter to the President of Congress declared. "If the price of land is not reduced, it is the determination of the people to go on the other side of the Mississippi or down to Natchez to settle; and such is the encouragement to people who will settle in the Spanish territory that a thousand acres of rich land is given to every person." [43] A number of well-known leaders, such as George Morgan, able adviser on Western affairs during the Revolution, Thomas Hutchins, geographer of the United States, and George Rogers Clark, entered into relations with Gardoqui for obtaining liberal grants of land.[44] Wilkinson, on behalf of himself and a small coterie of his henchmen, petitioned for a grant of six hundred thousand acres on the Yazoo for the establishment of a colony under Spanish jurisdiction.[45] Meantime, he proceeded to carry out his trade pact and to push the more radical part of his project to promote all indirect means to affect the separation

[43] The letter was written during the year 1787. "Draper MSS.," VI, 171.

[44] For this attempt to found a colony, see Max Savelle, *George Morgan, Colony Builder* (Columbia University Press, 1932), pp. 200–226. See also, *Life of Clark*, pp. 392–395. Clark refused to accede to certain of the terms proposed and his plan was given up. According to Morgan's plan, 2,000,000 acres opposite the mouth of the Ohio River were to be allocated for his colony. Generous concessions having been accorded him by Gardoqui, Morgan, on January 3, 1789, embarked at Pittsburgh in company with seventy farmers and artisans on four boats for New Madrid, which was to be developed as the leading city of his Utopia. The failure of Morgan was doubtless due to the opposition of Wilkinson.

[45] *Gardoqui Papers*, V, 59. By decision of the Spanish Council of State, generous concessions were to be allowed all settlers from Kentucky and the other settlements along the rivers flowing into the Ohio who might choose to migrate to Louisiana or who might be brought by Wilkinson. Their property was to be admitted free of the usual levy of 25 per cent, and they were to be accorded freedom of religion but not for the public observance of it. *Am. Hist. Rev.*, IX, 749. "It is the business of the states to take measures to stop them till their debts are paid," Thomas Jefferson wrote at a later time. "This done our citizens have a right to go where they please. I wish a hundred thousand of our inhabitants would accept the invitation. It will be the means of delivering to us peaceably, what may otherwise cost us a war." To President Washington, April 2, 1791. *Writings of Jefferson*, ed. Ford, V, 316.

FATE OF THE WEST IN THE BALANCE 325

of the Western settlements from the United States and to establish "a connection with Spain to the exclusion of any power, Kentucky enjoying the right of local self government." [46]

Early in June, 1788, Major Isaac Dunn, former military associate of Wilkinson, came to New Orleans in charge of flat boats loaded with tobacco, hams, and other Kentucky produce sent by Wilkinson. In his dispatches to Miró, Wilkinson referred to Dunn as "a fit auxiliary in the execution of our political designs" and worthy of every confidence. Returning to Kentucky, Dunn took with him goods valued at $18,000, which were to be sold, Miró urged, at fair prices in order that Kentuckians might through promise of commercial advantages be persuaded to adopt Wilkinson's ideas.

Early in 1789, twenty-five flat boats were sent to New Orleans with a cargo brought by Wilkinson's agents. Other Kentucky exporters were, through his influence, enabled to procure Spanish passports. Produce stored in Kentucky for three or four years thus found their way to market.

Prices advanced, tobacco selling for $9.50 a hundred pounds instead of $2.00 as formerly. Within a year, fifteen thousand barrels of flour were sent to New Orleans. Land values increased appreciably. Wilkinson's popularity was at its peak and he was regarded as an ambassador who had won great concessions from a foreign representative.[47]

To John Brown, delegate in Congress from Kentucky, was entrusted the task of presenting the petition to Congress for the admission of Kentucky into the Union as a separate State.[48] Consideration of the petition was referred to the new

[46] From Wilkinson's letter to Miró, September 17, 1789. This is known as his second "Memorial," *Am. Hist. Rev.,* IX, 753–766.

[47] Louis Pelzer, "Economic Factors in the Acquisition of Louisiana," *Miss. Valley Hist. Assoc. Proc.,* VI, 117; N. S. Shaler, *Kentucky,* p. 101.

[48] Wilkinson characterized Brown "as one of our deputies or agents," a young man of respectable ability, without political experience, timid, and with very little knowledge of the world. "Nevertheless, as he firmly perseveres in his adherence to our interests, we have sent him to the new Congress, apparently as our representative, but in reality as a spy on the actions of that body." Wilkinson to Miró, February 14, 1789. Gayarré, *op. cit.,* p. 241.

Congress, the first under the recently adopted Federal Constitution.

Brown was referred to by Gardoqui as a man upon whom he could depend.[49] The free navigation of the Mississippi would never be granted as long as Kentucky remained a part of the Union, Gardoqui informed Brown, but in the event that the people agreed upon separation from the United States, commercial concessions might be devised.

To Madison, Jefferson, and others in his confidence, Brown expressed his disappointment over the postponement of the decision by Congress, due, as he said, to the jealousy of Eastern members for the West. The only recourse for Kentucky, therefore, was independence.[50]

To Pollock, Brown made a statement, supposedly confidential, which was to be imparted to Governor Miró. Pollock was then about to sail for New Orleans with the design of resuming his activities as a trader, hoping thus to fulfill the promise of paying the debts which he had assumed on account of the Federal government and of Virginia.

[49] *Gardoqui Papers,* IV, 315, 363.

[50] "The ill-advised attempt to cede the navigation of that River had laid the foundation for the dismemberment of the American Empire by destroying the confidence of the people in the Western Country in the Justice of the Union and by inducing them to despair of obtaining possession of that Right by means of any other exertions than their own." *Documentary History of the Constitution,* V, 9. For Brown's statement to Madison, see *Ibid,* IV, 611, 612. The view of Jefferson is in the *Writings of Jefferson,* ed. Ford, V, 18.

CHAPTER XX

"POLLOCK MEETS ALL DEMANDS OF HIS CREDITORS"

THREE years had now elapsed since Pollock, upon leaving Havana, became personally responsible to Galvez for debts he had assumed on behalf of the United States and of Virginia. His decision to return to New Orleans was natural, for in that city he had achieved marked success in business. Leaving his accounts "to meet their fate," he fitted out a vessel and sailed from Philadelphia. At Martinique he disposed of the cargo and, having laid in another, proceeded to his destination.

That he would be received with favor by Spanish officials was assured for he had been intimately acquainted with Colonel Miró, now governor, who was second in command to Governor Galvez at the taking of Manchac and Baton Rouge. To Miró, Galvez had spoken favorably of Pollock, "and I continued to enjoy the same confidence," Pollock writes, "during the whole of his government."[1] Some years earlier, Miró had written a Spanish officer: "I must tell you of the great zeal which this person [Pollock] has always shown for the common cause, contributing in part to our first successes against the English establishments on this River. I am hoping that you will recognize the worth of his services."[2] Under orders from Miró, the commander at the Balize was directed to accord Pollock special marks of distinction and to bring him to New Orleans on the king's barge.[3]

Shortly before his arrival, New Orleans had been almost completely destroyed by fire. The Ursuline Convent, built of brick and located within a walled garden, "by a miracle," as

---

[1] Wilkinson, *op. cit.*, II, Appendix I.
[2] May 4, 1782. Addressed to Juan Manuel de Cajigal. "Dispatches of the Spanish Governors of Louisiana." Legajo 1304. *Ayer Coll.*
[3] *American Museum*, IV, 584.

stated in the convent records, was saved. A row of houses along the water-front also escaped. Included in the eight hundred and fifty buildings thus reduced to ashes were most of the homes.[4] Devoting himself to measures for relief, Miró called upon Gardoqui to ship from Philadelphia, provisions, medicines, nails, and other necessities which might be "resold at equitable prices."

Communicating with the governor, Pollock states that his purpose in coming was to pay his indebtedness in full, thus rendering justice to those creditors "who so liberally and nobly aided the United States in the most critical moments of her need and her exhaustion." He desired, also, to assist in procuring relief for the unhappy inhabitants who were sufferers from the recent fire.

While many years would probably elapse before the debt due the Spanish treasury could be assumed by the Government of the United States, Pollock proposed to obligate himself to cancel this indebtedness through the delivery of flour and tobacco "for the disposition of your royal treasury." Paying exorbitant prices for an inferior product would thus be prevented. Three thousands barrels of the very best flour from Philadelphia and four thousand barrels of good quality from Kentucky at the stipulated price of ten pesos a barrel were to be delivered annually. Two hundred casks of good leaf tobacco were also to be delivered. Payment for one-half of the net product of each cargo was to be made in silver, which might be exported free of duty. Any balance was to be accredited to his account—"until the entire amount of the debts named be settled."

The proposal, fully approved by Miró, was submitted to the Spanish Government. "I do not find," Miró wrote, "this prejudicial to Spanish commerce, nor to the freedom which

[4] The population of New Orleans was then about 5,000. Through the benefactions of Don Andres Almonaster y Roxas, a number of the public buildings, including a school, a cathedral, and the *Cabildo*, were rebuilt.

this province enjoys in the importation of flour and tobacco as he proposes to take in exportation silver, as there is no produce in this province adaptible for North America." [5]

The contract submitted by Pollock was essentially identical with the trade privileges accorded him by O'Reilly and by Galvez. Moreover, Miró, as we have seen, had granted permission to Wilkinson to dispose of Kentucky produce in New Orleans, and large shipments of tobacco had been sold by him to the government.

Disappointed, on ascertaining that the "exclusive privilege" of the tobacco trade was not to be his, Pollock was, however, awarded a special contract to supply the New Orleans and Havana markets with flour.[6] Thus, once more, he was enabled to demonstrate his business ability. Such was his success that, as stated by one of his contemporaries: "By diligence, perseverance, integrity and good fortune, he was able to settle and satisfy all the claims on him, from his private funds, without as yet deriving any aid from the United States excepting only the debt due to Don Galvez."

Thomas Patterson, who had for three years been held as hostage for Pollock, was granted his freedom. Powder and supplies used to equip the *West Florida* were paid for and the further claims of Spanish creditors to the amount of 59,442 pesos were canceled. Pollock regained possession of his Louisiana plantation and purchased a plot of ground in New Or-

---

[5] Miró, to A. Valdez, February 12, 1789. *Pollock Letters*. Miró wrote, in submitting Pollock's proposal: "In view then of the fact that payment in money is impossible because of the lack of it—a thing which is public and notorious—and quite unable to pay except with the productions of that continent, in view of the fact that this colony does not have any regular supply of flour, a product for which your Majesty and your subjects see the bitter necessity of paying exorbitant prices, many times for damaged flour, and obtaining it indirectly, an operation contrary to the interests and benign intentions of your Majesty and also extremely prejudicial to the public health of your subjects; to facilitate then the payment of debts, so sacred, and to cancel obligations, which he has contracted, he proposes" etc.

[6] Wilkinson, *Memoirs*, Appendix I. Testimony of Pollock.

leans.⁷ Payments were made also on his Silver Spring estate.⁸ To his nephew was assigned the task of supervising his Louisiana estate. It was stocked and "tools for working the place" were provided. Explicit directions were given by Pollock for keeping the levee in repair, without which you know by the laws of the country, it [the plantation] will be forfeited to Government." ⁹

Pollock had not neglected to deliver "the confidential message" from John Brown to Miró. In the words of the governor, this communication was as follows:

> He [Brown] saw clearly that the intention of his colleagues was, that Kentucky should remain under the jurisdiction of Congress, like the county of Illinois, and that a Governor should be appointed by them for that province as for the other; but as this was opposed to the welfare of the inhabitants of Kentucky, he was determined to return home (which he did before Pollock's departure from Philadelphia) and on his arrival, to call for a general assembly of his fellow citizens, in order to proceed immediately to declare themselves independent, and to propose to Spain the opening of a commercial intercourse with reciprocal advantages; and that to accomplish this object, he would send Pollock the necessary documents, to be laid before me and to be forwarded to your excellency. He requested Pollock to prepare me for it in anticipation.¹⁰

By any interpretation, there was nothing in this communication which might bring censure upon Pollock. Brown had already made known to a number of his correspondents that the only recourse for Kentucky was to secure absolute independence.

Jefferson had expressed to Brown the hope that "every meas-

⁷ *American Museum*, VIII, Appendix IV, 10. The bill of sale is dated January 30, 1789. According to the record, this lot, 60 feet by 120 feet, was situated on the corner of Royal and St. Louis streets.

⁸ He obligated himself to pay £5,500 sterling, with interest, for this property. Pollock to William Hamilton, agent, July 5, 1788, and June 1, 1789. MSS., *Penna. Hist. Society Coll.*

⁹ Pollock to Hamilton Pollock. *Spanish Records*, 1809. East Baton Rouge Parish Court House.

¹⁰ November 3, 1788. Dispatch of Miró to Valdez. *Gayarré, op. cit.*, III, 222.

ure should be taken which may draw the bonds of union tighter" between the Atlantic States and the West, and that the men of influence in the Western country should "defer pushing their right to that navigation to extremity as long as they can do without it tolerably." [11] To this, Brown replied that since Congress had rejected the application of Kentucky for admission as an independent State and the ill-advised attempt to cede the navigation of the Mississippi, the confidence of the men of the West in the justice of the Union had been destroyed. "Their vast increase in population (amounting to at least one hundred thousand souls in that district alone)," he further declared, "added to the great danger and difficulty attending a communication with the Seat of Government renders their connection with Virginia so burdensome that there is every reason to expect that immediately on hearing that Congress have refused to receive them they will assume their independence." [12]

Notwithstanding Miró's confidence in Pollock, he was not disposed to share with him inside information which he possessed regarding the Wilkinson plot. "Your excellency will, therefore, rest assured," Miró writes, "that Brown on his arrival in Kentucky, finding Wilkinson and his associates disposed to surrender themselves up to Spain, or at least to put themselves under her protection will easily join them, and it is probable, as Wilkinson has already foretold it, that, next Spring I shall have to receive here a deputation appointed in due form. I acted toward Pollock with a great deal of caution, and answered him as one to whom had been communicated some new and unlooked for information." [13]

That Pollock was acquainted with Wilkinson, his chief rival in business, is certain, for we learn from Pollock's testimony that on a number of occasions they were dinner guests together at the home of Governor Miró.[14] But in his deposi-

---

[11] May 26, 1788, *Writings of Jefferson,* ed. Ford, V, 16.
[12] *Documentary History of the Constitution,* IV, 9.
[13] Dispatch to A. Valdez, November 3, 1788. Gayarré, *op. cit.,* 222.
[14] Wilkinson, *Memoirs, op. cit.*

tion, Pollock asserted that while he was a resident in New Orleans he was not aware of any sinister relations between Wilkinson and Miró, "tending to affect his [Wilkinson's] honour or the interests of the United States." [15]

Information gained by Pollock from the governor was merely to the effect that permission had been granted to Wilkinson "to bring down tobacco, in hopes to pacify the Kentuckians and people of the Western country, to prevent a rupture between Spain and America, and in order to give time for negotiations between the two powers, relative to the navigation of the Mississippi."

Before Pollock's departure from New Orleans, the first phase of the "Spanish Conspiracy" had failed. In a communication to Miró, Wilkinson declared that it was his purpose in the Kentucky convention, July, 1788, to secure a vote in favor of Kentucky independence. In this he failed, but he succeeded in winning a postponement of the decision until it should be passed upon by a convention to be called the following November.

While Kentuckians were desirous of securing separate statehood within the Union and the free navigation of the Mississippi, they were opposed to forming a Spanish or any other alliance. Delegates, representing this view, dominated the November convention. An address to Congress was adopted which set forth their claim to the free navigation of the Mississippi and separate statehood.

By the opening of the year 1789, Wilkinson must have sensed the fact that his intrigue was on the rocks. In a letter to an agent of Wilkinson, General Arthur St. Clair, Governor of the Northwest Territory, wrote: "I am much grieved to hear that there are strong dispositions on the part of the people of Kentucky to break off their connection with the United States and that our friend Wilkinson is at the head of this affair. Such a Consummation would involve the United States in the greatest difficulties and would completely ruin this Country. Should there be any foundation for these re-

[15] Wilkinson, *Memoirs, op. cit.*

ports, for God's sake make use of your influence to detach Wilkinson from this party." [16]

That Wilkinson was a pensioner of the Spanish Government was unknown to Pollock. Moreover, evidence presented at the trial of Wilkinson indicates that between Pollock and Wilkinson there was at "no time a business nor any other connection." [17]

By the middle of July, 1790, Pollock was preparing to return to Philadelphia and had chartered a vessel for that purpose. For two years he had been absent and he desired "to see what revolutions time had effected in his favor." Unexpected business "perpetually presenting itself," he kept the vessel from sailing for two months.

From the beginning, as reported by one of the passengers, the voyage was a stormy one, and after two days at sea they encountered a hurricane which "almost drove us ashore into the bay of St. Bernards where it is said there is a race of cannibals who devour everyone they can lay their hands on. Luckily the wind came about to an opposite point and blew with as great violence as ever which carried us off the coast so it endangered the loss of the vessel. It however did not long continue so but came round to its old quarter and kept us beating about Cuba for several days and finally obliged us to put into Matanzas, a port about twenty leagues above the Havanna, where we continued a week and again ventured out but without experiencing any better fortune and were till the 5th. of November before the vessel reached Philadelphia." [18]

Pollock's sense of freedom may readily be imagined, as he read the message which he carried from Governor Miró addressed to Governor Edmund Randolph. After reference to the service rendered by Pollock as public agent for the United States and Virginia during the Revolution, Miró writes:

[16] Gayarré, *op. cit.*, 240. This letter, dated December 5, 1789, was addressed to Major Dunn and was forwarded by him to Wilkinson, January 15, 1789.
[17] Wilkinson, *Memoirs, op. cit.*
[18] Account by Andrew Bayard. It was addressed to Harry Innes. *Innes Papers*, XIX, 55.

Mr. Pollock in the execution of the orders he from time to time received from these states, contracted very considerable debts in this place, which he was unable wholly to discharge, altho' he disposed of all his estate real and personal in this Country, at a great disadvantage, for the purpose of fulfilling his engagements, with his creditors in this Province. Mr. Pollock has since his late arrival here very honorably and to the entire satisfaction of his Creditors in this Province, discharged all his remaining debts here, to a Considerable amount, which he owed on account of the United States and the State of Virginia. The great integrity evinced by this gentleman in the faithfull discharge of his engagements entered into for the service of his country, strongly interests me in his favour and induces me to pray you will have the goodness to take him under your protection, and that you will be pleased to give him your aid in obtaining as speedy reimbursement as may be for the moneys now due to him from the United States and the State of Virginia; which I shall esteem as a personal favour conferred upon myself.[19]

By the middle of December, Pollock was once more in Richmond and presented the letter of Miró to Governor Randolph as proof that he had met all the conditions which had been imposed by the Assembly, and he urged that he should be reimbursed for his advances without delay.

What was his surprise upon being confronted with a charge, emanating from two of his former creditors at New Orleans, that he had fraudulently met his obligation to them in depreciated currency. "To God, the Honor of Virginia and the President of Congress," they appealed, saying: "We submit our claim with humility trusting that the unconscionable and avaricious Pollock shall be compelled to pay us, a sum equal to that which Virginia on the same account and for the same purpose allows to him."

This claim, among others, grew out of the order on Penette, Da Costa, Freres, of Nantes, which, as agent of Virginia, Pollock had assumed. Nine years had elapsed since that transaction took place. Meantime, his agent at New Orleans, in disposing of flour and Negroes shipped by Pollock, received in

[19] *Cal. Va. State Papers*, V, 192.

POLLOCK MEETS ALL DEMANDS

payment the current money of the country. The claims held against Pollock by these creditors were in turn canceled, as shown by the receipts.

Their request that justice should be done them was addressed to President Washington. Pollock's "insignificance, poverty and the general dislike of the good people of this country towards him," they declared, "readily procured him a passport to quit this Country leaving us hopeless of our touching a farthing of the money he received of us for the aforesaid bills. . . . Individuals may rob States with impunity but they are seldom allowed to rob each other without being exposed." [20]

During his late residence in New Orleans, no such claim had been brought against Pollock, and Governor Miró's letter furnished ample testimony of his integrity. In a final review of this claim by Edmund Randolph, Attorney General of the United States, is found the statement: "But it may be added that Clark [Pollock's agent] altho he paid paper money, paid a money which was legitimated by the sovereignty of New Orleans. In short (if a dispute can be said to exist at all), it must lie between Beauregard and Bourgeois and Pollock. If he has deceived them, the laws of the United States afford redress." [21] No evidence has been found showing that this claim was ever revived.

Meanwhile, Virginia had surrendered her right to territory in the Northwest to the United States, upon condition that the Federal government would pay all the expenses of the conquest to the amount of $500,000.

Upon the advances made by Pollock, $300,000, an amount not equaled by that of any other person during the Revolution, payments had from time to time been made. As shown by the books of the Treasury, when the new government was in-

---

[20] October 14, 1789. Addressed to His Excellency George Washington Esq., President of the United States. MSS., Department of State, Washington, D. C.

[21] *Cal. Va. State Papers*, V, 109-111. February, 1790. Addressed to the Governor of Virginia or the President of the United States.

augurated there was then due him, including principal and accumulated interest, the sum of $108,605.[22] By the close of April, 1792, he had received this amount.

But there still remained unsatisfied claims amounting to $26,006. This sum was made up of charges, including interest for losses, damages, expenses, and commissions connected with Pollock's public agency.[23]

Throughout the period 1792 to 1803, he was a petitioner for this amount before the Committee on Claims of the House of Representatives.

While full praise was accorded him for the contributions he had made, his claim, it was maintained, was barred by an act of limitation which had been passed in 1793. This provided that "All claims upon the United States for services rendered or supplies furnished previous to the 4th. of March 1789, not presented before the first of May 1794 shall be barred." [24]

In reply, it was contended that with the exception of the expenses of his detention at Havana, the items enumerated

---

[22] The $74,087 procured from Galvez made up the greater portion of this amount. An analysis made by Pollock, December 6, 1782, of the amounts then due him were: the United States, $74,087; Virginia, $136,466. It may be assumed, therefore, that his contributions toward the Revolution in the West were almost double the amount he contributed to the general cause.

[23] Nine thousand, seven hundred fifty-four dollars of this amount represented the sale of flour to the Spanish bakers at Havana during the year 1784. For expenses connected with the detention of his family and his own imprisonment at Havana, he claimed $3,000. To Thomas Patterson, his hostage, and to a number of Spanish officers and subjects from whom supplies for "the conquest of the Illinois country" had been procured, he paid $1,740. There was also a claim which he had assumed for powder used to equip the *West Florida*. Commission on the loan of $74,087 borrowed from Galvez amounted to $3,704. Accumulated interest on these several items at 5 per cent made up the balance.

[24] Augustus H. Woodward, "A Representation of the Case of Oliver Pollock," February 12, 1803. Library of Congress. Woodward argued this case at the first regular session of the Seventh Congress, December, 1801. The brief was printed in 1802 and reprinted the following year. Woodward was a well-known lawyer in Alexandria, Virginia.

in the claim were not complete until after the fourth of March, 1789.[25]

"It is not for services he asks a compensation," his representative declared in an appeal in 1808. "He has yet interceded for no Charities, no gratuitous donations. Silent without a murmur when his country was distressed, he now requires what he conceives a matter of strict right." [26]

Finally, the justice of his claim won a decision in which it was maintained that since the principal items were incomplete on the fourth of March, 1789, they were not therefore "affected by the limitation." But even then payment did not follow, for at the close of the year 1803, Pollock was still a petitioner before the Committee on Claims.

[25] The sum awarded his bondman, Patterson, was agreed upon and paid by Pollock in 1790. Payment for the 500 pounds of powder was also made by him in that year. The commission on the money borrowed from Governor Galvez was covered in 1792.

[26] Woodward, *op. cit.* On August 21, 1793, $268,032.62 was paid Spain by the United States. This sum discharged the principal of the debt due on the twenty-first of March, 1782, amounting to $174,011.65 and accumulated interest at the rate of 5 per cent, to the amount of $99,007.89. See *Am. State Papers, Financial Affairs*, I, 672. For the loan of $150,000 procured by John Jay, *see ante.*, p. 257 and N. 23. No evidence has been found to account for the difference in the amount of the principal of $24,011. In addition to this loan, which does not include the $74,087 procured from Governor Galvez by Pollock (*see ante.*, p. 81), the United States received subsidies from Spain, including arms, ammunition, and clothing, amounting to $397,230.

CHAPTER XXI

"IN THE JUSTICE OF CONGRESS, I REPOSE THE FULLEST CONFIDENCE."—POLLOCK

A FEW statements only have been found which give some clue to Pollock's life during these years of anxiety. After 1791, he was evidently engaged in the supervision of his Silver Springs estate for he records the purchase of farming utensils, stock, and Negroes. Actively supporting the Democratic-Republican party, he served on a number of occasions as chairman of their local conventions. Preceding the election of 1798, he writes General Irvine of Carlisle in language as spirited as that he was wont to use in trade and diplomacy: "Since yours of the 12th. inst. I have been over and given a little necessary information in that quarter. I find the opposite side is to have what they call a general meeting at Carlisle, the 24th. inst. In fine, my friend, they are making every exertion and if we dont do the same and stick to one point all is lost. I will see the Whitehills tomorrow and make them do the needful. Keep close to [illegible] and I will bring forward all I can." [1]

Early in 1799, occurred the death of Mrs. Pollock. Her life was evidently one of self-sacrifice for her family, of devotion to her husband and to the causes he promoted. As a tribute to her memory, we find the following statement: "In her we saw the faithful and affectionate wife; a parent fond, indulgent and kind; a friend just, sincere and warm; a Christian engagingly pious, benevolent and liberal. She sought those in misery and relieved them. . . . She greatly aided her hus-

[1] To General William Irvine, Carlisle, August 15, 1798. Egle's *Notes and Queries*, I, 173.

THE JUSTICE OF CONGRESS

band in his patriotic work to serve his adopted country. . . . She appreciated his self-denial in the Cause of America and sympathized with him when the hours of ungratefulness came." [2] During the same year, their son James was fatally injured in a fall from his horse. That Pollock was then suffering, also, from financial embarrassment is certain. Having indorsed the note of an associate who failed in business, he was confined in a debtor's prison until bail was procured.[3]

The first days of December, 1803, found him in Washington urging, unsuccessfully, that his claim on the government should be met. Was he sharing party secrets with his friend Dr. Benjamin Rush, eminent physician of Philadelphia, when he foretold the early acquisition of Louisiana by the United States? He writes: "Much has been said and wrote respecting the Spanish Minister's protest about my old country Louisiana. The fact is that notwithstanding the protest was made, and the great Bonapart's name wove into it, I have no doubt but that we are in quiet possession of it before

---

[2] The Carlisle *Gazette*, January 23, 1799. St. Louis Cathedral, New Orleans, was destroyed by fire during the year 1777, and the record of the marriage of Oliver Pollock and Margaret O'Brien, along with other records, was lost. The baptismal register of Bernard Galvez Pollock, their youngest son, in St. Joseph's Church, Philadelphia, June 20, 1785, shows that his father was a Roman Catholic. The capital letter (P) following his mother's name, as Margaret (P) Pollock, is evidence, as interpreted by Catholic officials, that his mother was a Protestant. Mrs. Pollock and their son James were buried in the cemetery of the Presbyterian church near Silver Springs. A flat stone in St. Mary's Churchyard, Philadelphia, marks the burial place, March 26, 1804, of Lucetta Pollock, their youngest daughter. The marriage of their daughter Mary (Polly) to Dr. Samuel Robinson was performed by a Presbyterian clergyman, and the records of the First Presbyterian Church, Carlisle, show that a son, Jared (Jerret), and Mary Briggs were married by Dr. Davidson, pastor of that church.

[3] May 30, 1800. Rev. Horace Hayden, *A Biographical Sketch of Oliver Pollock, Esq., United States Commercial Agent at New Orleans and Havana 1776–1784*. The Court records are incomplete, and there is no evidence relating to his loss or sale of the Silver Springs Estate. One payment, only, seems to have been made by him on that property. See *ante.*, p. 305 note 3.

now; the official news of which is expected here before Xmas." [4]

It was at this time that Pollock decided to become a candidate in the forthcoming election for members to the House of Representatives. The Pennsylvania district from which two congressmen were to be chosen was composed of Cumberland, Dauphin, Mifflin and Huntingdon counties. General John A. Hanna and David Bard then represented the district and both of them were again the nominees of their respective home counties, Dauphin and Huntingdon. In the Cumberland County convention, Pollock and Bard were nominated but Robert Whitehill of that county chose to run independently. Since all of the candidates were Democratic-Republicans, the contest was virtually one of county rivalry.

The campaign was conducted by anonymous writers in the local newspapers. A gentleman of distinction lately arrived at Philadelphia from New Orleans writes an editor in support of the candidacy of Pollock:

This nomination is a mark of your public spirit and wisdom. Revolutionary merit is certainly among the most powerful testimonials of patriotism & in the selection & choice of public functionaries, this should always merit preeminency in our country's love, and mark the characters worthy of public confidence. The many important public services rendered by Mr. Pollock during the Revolutionary war with Great Britain, as agent at New Orleans, are well known and must ever endear him to the friends of American Independence. His person, his estate, his fortune, his all were on that occasion embarked in and pledged to the cause of national liberty; and he, by his purse, his sword & counsel eminently contributed, in the Southern department of our country, to rescue the then United Colonies from the domination of a foreign Prince, and place them among the great Nations of the world as free and independent states. In short, Mr. Pollock is a gentleman who justly ranks among the conspicuous benefactors of his country.

Another supporter writes:

[4] December 8, 1803. Letter in possession of The Library Company, Philadelphia.

THE JUSTICE OF CONGRESS 341

Remember that the love of country or of public good is among the essential qualifications necessary to constitute a representative and a statesman. . . . Oliver Pollock unites in himself, not only a love of country, but also a sufficient knowledge of it, together with most of its relations with foreign countries. His knowledge is of the more correct and best kind, since it is derived, not from theory alone, but confirmed by actual observation and experience. He has studied, not only written books, but the great book of the world; and without a knowledge of this, a man can be but illy qualified to participate in the great work of legislation. A man must first know man, before he can make wholesome laws to regulate the conduct of man.[5]

A "Farmer," appealing to his fellow-countrymen to rally to the support of Pollock, wrote of his uniform attachment to the Whig interests; of his zeal and love of National interests; of his patriotism at a time which tried the souls of men; of his unremitting efforts to procure the loans of foreign nations in the crisis of our Revolution, "after Continental paper money had reverted to its original state of nothingness and rags"; and of his sufferings in the cause of freedom.[6]

The statement of Governor Galvez that Pollock had acted in favor of the soldiers and citizens of his own nation with all the zeal and love which becomes a true patriot, was now made public, and, likewise, the testimony of Clark, who declared that through the advances made by Pollock, he was enabled to preserve the conquests he had made. This was a period in our history noteworthy for vehement attacks upon rival candidates for office by the press of the opposing party. In no statement is to be found any criticism on the candidacy of Pollock.

But since Pollock and Whitehill were residents of the same county, and since there was no outstanding issue in the election, the victory of their two opponents was inevitable. In one respect, the outcome was gratifiying to Pollock, for in his own county he led his nearest competitor by two hundred votes, and in Carlisle, his home district, his vote was greater

[5] Carlisle *Gazette*, September 28, 1804.
[6] *Ibid.*

than the combined vote of his three opponents.[7] In the next Congressional campaign he was again nominated but withdrew in favor of his friend Whitehill, in order to avoid a similar outcome.

Meanwhile, he had come to live in Carlisle, where Dr. Samuel Robinson, his son-in-law, was inviting the favor of the public "in the treatment of the various diseases of this climate, and was known to have been particularly fortunate in contending against the ravages of those which have become so prevalent under the form of bilious fever." He was to be consulted at the "house adjoining the one occupied by Oliver Pollock, Esq."

On November 2, 1805, occurred the marriage of Pollock to Mrs. Winifred Deady of Baltimore.[8] For the three following years, there appears in the directory of that city the name, "Oliver Pollock, gent."

To his children had been bequeathed by James Pollock, their uncle, interest in a number of partially improved Pennsylvania farms, some town lots in Carlisle, and sundry tracts of "valuable cotton lands" near Natchez. Serving as attorney for his children, Pollock devoted his time to the disposal of these holdings "either for cash or good negroes."

---

[7] *Carlisle Gazette,* October 19, 1804. The *Cumberland Register,* October 12, 1804, gives the following division of votes:

CUMBERLAND COUNTY		HUNTINGDON COUNTY	
POLLOCK	1367	POLLOCK	28
BARD	1168	BARD	804
HANNA	462	HANNA	1146
WHITEHALL	614	WHITEHALL	403
DAUPHIN COUNTY		MIFFLIN COUNTY	
POLLOCK	179	POLLOCK	108
BARD	942	BARD	333
HANNA	812	HANNA	611
WHITEHALL	34	WHITEHALL	463

[8] In the marriage register of the Pro-Cathedral of St. Peter, Baltimore, 1805, is the entry: "November second, 1805, with license the Rt. Rev. Bishop Carroll married according to the rites of the Catholic Church, Oliver Pollock, widower of Carlisle, Northumberland County, State of Pennsylvania, to Winifred Ann Deady widow of this city. Witnesses present, Gunning S. Bedford, Eliza Bedford, David Williamson, Juliet Williamson. FRANCIS BEESTON, *Rector,* St. Peter's."

By 1811, all of his claims against the Federal government and Virginia, except one for $9,574 with accrued interest, had been met. For this sum, he again memorializes the Legislature of Virginia—"He begs leave to be heard, with that dignified patience which belongs to the Representative of a free people, and that sympathy and feeling which is due to an old and faithful public servant, who risked more than his all, in that cause, the success of which secured to this happy land, the blessings of self-government." [9]

This petition grew out of the sale of his cargo of flour to the bakers in Havana when, as agent of the Federal government, he had been sent to that port. By an order of the Cuban authorities, any sums received on this account were to be held as security for debts which he had contracted with creditors in New Orleans.

Had Virginia made provision for meeting the bills, which, upon the order of Governor Jefferson, were drawn on Penette, Da Costa, Freres and Company, for Revolutionary supplies, or if the Legislature of that State had not rescinded the act whereby Pollock was to be reimbursed, his credit would have been reëstablished and his imprisonment at Havana would not have followed.

An appeal was made by Jefferson, as Secretary of State, to the two Spanish commissioners in Philadelphia, that since Pollock had met all claims against him, he was therefore entitled to full reimbursement for the money attached by the Cuban authorities. After an investigation, it was declared, "with great sorrow," that only one hundred and fifty dollars of this amount had ever entered the Cuban treasury. Any effort to collect the balance proved unavailing. For almost twenty years, Pollock had sought an adjustment of this claim. His last petition to the Legislature of Virginia was that of "a public servant, whose services, age, infirmities, and misfortunes might be offered as sufficient causes to ask even more than this, were he not authorized to prefer a claim upon the

---

[9] "Clark MSS.," *Va. State Archives.*

more substantial, though not more meritorious ground of right." [10]

Letters written to Pollock by Jefferson during the period the latter was serving as Governor of Virginia were lost. While Jefferson hoped, as he stated, that justice would be done, he was unable to give the "details of the correspondence." After a lapse of thirty years, he recalled only "that while Pollock was serving as agent of Virginia at New Orleans he paid out large sums for the State which enabled General Clark to carry on his expedition and was essential to his success." Failing to receive a settlement, Pollock again memorialized Congress, but also without success.

Following the death of Mrs. Pollock, in 1814, virtually a pensioner upon his family, he found a home with his eldest daughter and her husband, Dr. Robinson, in the State of Mississippi. No record of his life during the nine years which he spent in Pinckneyville, then the county-seat of Wilkinson County, has been found. "His private papers, miniatures, coat of arms, and commissions" were destroyed during the Civil War.[11] A country store and post-office at the cross-roads now mark the site of this otherwise deserted village.

Careful search has not revealed the exact place of his burial. But his life must be recalled as that of a patriot whose eagerness to serve and willingness to suffer and sacrifice for his country have not been surpassed in our history.[12]

Any memorial to his memory might well have carved upon it his own words which were written during one of his hours of deepest depression:

> It has not been my Fortune to move on a splendid Theatre, where the weary Actor frequently finds in the applause of his Audience, new motives to Exertion. I dwelt in an Obscure Corner of the Universe alone and unsupported. I have laboured without ceasing. I have neglected the Road to affluence, I have exhausted my all and plunged myself deeply in Debt, to support the Cause of

---

[10] "Clark MSS.," *Va. State Archives.*
[11] Hayden, *op. cit.*
[12] His death occurred December 18, 1823.

THE JUSTICE OF CONGRESS

America, in the Hours of her distress and when those who call'd themselves Friends were daily deserting her. But these things I do not Boast of, what I do boast of is, that I have a Heart Still ready (had I the means) to bear sufferings and make new sacrifices. I pray your Excellency to submit this Narrative to the indulgence of Congress. I am in their judgment and in their Justice I repose the fullest Confidence.[13]

[13] Pollock to the President of Congress, September 18, 1782. *Pollock Letters*, Library of Congress.

APPENDIX I

EVENTS IN THE PUBLIC CAREER OF OLIVER POLLOCK, 1776–1782, AS RELATED BY HIMSELF [1]

PHILADELPHIA 18.th Septr. 1782.

SIR:

Having been honored by Congress with an important and confidential employment, it becomes my duty to render an Account of my Transactions. This divides itself into two parts; The first is during the period, when I Obeyed only the dictates of my own zeal, & the request of a principal one of our Federal Union. The second after I became cloathed with the Character of Agent to the United States; I have the pleasure to reflect that from the beginning to the end I was deaf to evry motive except an ardent affection for our righteous Cause. And that having expended my all, in the service of my Country, the principal regret I feel, arises from this Reflection, that I am deprived of the means to shew that my ardor is still unabated.

My first effort was so early as in April 1776, at which time I laboured to persuade Governor Unzaga to take several American Vessells under the protection of his Guns, against a British Sloop of Warr (of whose approach I received information) on the principle that those Vessells were in a neutral Port, and entitled to the rights of Neutrality. My repeated applications on this subject were unavailing. The Vessells were seized and afterwards confiscated at Pensacola.

In August Captain Gibson with sixteen Men arrived with dispatches from the Executive authority of the State of Virginia, and from Major Genl. Lee. I translated their Letters, provided for the accommodation of the Party, & took effectual measures to conceal them & their Business from the many British Spies then in New Orleans; After many solicitations I prevail'd on the Governor to grant a Batteaux load of the Kings Powder, and then I purchas'd fitted out and dispatch'd a Vessel with the Powder, which to my very great satisfaction not only arrived in safety, but was a very signal and seasonable supply.

In October I dispatch'd a Vessell to Philadelphia with the Cap-

[1] Addressed to the President of Congress. *Letters and Papers of Oliver Pollock*, A. L. S., Library of Congress.

tains Gibson, Ord, & Bethel, by whom I wrote Letters to a Committee of Congress conveying such information as I was possessed of. The Honorable M^r. Morris who was of that committee can determine whether it was of importance.

My eagerness to seize evry Opportunity of serving my Country, had led me into such frequent importunities to Governor Unzaga that I had just reason to fear his displeasure. It was my good fortune however to have so far gained his good Opinion that when in January 1777 he was succeeded in Office by Don Bernardo De Galvez he presented me to that Gentleman as a faithful & zealous American, in whom he might repose implicit confidence; That worthy Nobleman immediately made a tender of his Services, and gave me the delightful assurance that he would go every possible length for the Interest of Congress. I shou'd be guilty of injustice did I not declare that this generous promise was honorably fulfill'd. And I should bely my own Heart, if I did not on this and on every proper Occasion express my grateful sense of the services he has rendered to the United States. The first instance of them was Retaliateing the Seizure of an American Schooner, in the Lakes, by the seizure & Confiscation of all British Vessels between the Balize and Manchac. Immediately on this circumstance I chartered a Vessell & sent her under the Command of Captain Lamere to inform Congress of the Governors favorable disposition, and of his assurances that the Port of New Orleans should be open & free to American Commerce and to the admission & Sale of Prizes made by their Cruizers;

The part I had taken marked me out as a victim to the Enemy, and therefore their application in May for Restitution of the Vessells seized by Order of Governor Galvez was accompanied by the demand of One Oliver Polock supposed Agent of the American Rebels. I had however the pleasure to see Col^o. Dickson & M^r. Stephenson return unsatisfied to the Govr. & Council of Pensacola by whom they had been sent on that errand.

In July 1777 I dispatch'd a Vessell to land Capt. Pickles on the Coast of Carolina & charged him with dispatches for Congress, by which I had the Honor to mention that the Goods formerly requir'd by the Executive of Virginia had arrived from Spain & waited their Orders. I prevaild also on the Govr. to write & Express those Friendly assurances which have been already mentioned, & I transmitted authentic intelligence (which I had with much difficulty Obtained) of the British strength at Pensacola.

In February 1778 I receiv'd intelligence of Capt. Willings approach, & immediately I waited on his Excellency the Governor & took evry necessary arrangement with him. I then laid a plan for taking a British Letter of marque of sixteen Guns lying then in the River, sent off all proper Intelligence to Capt. Willing, & dispatch'd my Nephew Thomas Pollock with fifteen Volunteers, & Capt Lafitte with Twenty Six arm'd Men to his assistance, On the third of March Lieu^t. McIntire brought the dispatches which had been entrusted to Capt. Willing and gave the agreeable intelligence that he had (with ten Men) surprised & taken the Letter of Marque. At ten OClock I sent him off with his Party in pursuit of other British Vessels which had gone down the River, one of which they captured. The Dispatches brought by Capt. Willing, Contain'd the appointment of Agent which Congress had been pleased to confer, This Honourable mark of their favor form'd in my Bosom a new Band of Duty, and became an additional spring to actuate my Conduct. I was therefore extremely solicitous to comply with the Orders I had received from The Honorable M^r. Laurens, M^r. Morris, & M^r. Smith a Secret Committee of Congress to Charter Vessels & Transport a large quantity of Merchandise by Sea, & also to send as much as possible up the River, for the use of the United States. Sensible of the necessities of my Countrey, which at that period were extreme the propriety of appropriating my Fortune to her Service would not admit of a moments deliberation. The misfortunes of America rendered her Cause still dearer than before to evry true American. And I was the more ready to repose confidence in the promises of Remittances which those Letters contained (and which have been since so often Reiterated) as I was determined to share the fate of my Countreymen if they should fall, and to rely on their justice if crown'd with success.

On the sixth of March I wrote to Congress my acknowledgments for their Appointment, and a Narrative of the Transactions in that quarter. I wrote again on the first of April, mentioning my intention to fit out the Prize Letter of Marque as a Cruizer and my having sent up the River (for the use of the United States) Goods imported from Spain for their Account to the Amount of 25,062½ Dollars & Goods supplied by myself to the Amount of 10,907¼ Dollars. I took the liberty also to point out the necessity of making me considerable remittances or lodging a Credit for me in Europe, that I might be enabled to execute my Orders with effect.

That no opportunity might be lost of serving faithfully in the Station to which I was call'd, I not only wrote to Doctor Franklin an account of all which had happen'd, but I also wrote to the Agents of The United States both at Charles Town and at the Cape every necessary information as to the benefits which would then Result from a commerce with New Orleans and I sent intelligence to Gen[l]. Hand, The Commanding Officer at Fort Pitt, of the situation of things on the River, Subsequent to the Conquest of those Countries by Cap[t] Willing.

In the Month of May I had the honor to address Congress by M[r]. Murray, & to recommend an expedition down the River to take possession of that immense Country which might have been effected by a small force, especially as M[r]. Murray (a faithful zealous American) was perfectly acquainted there, and wou'd have rendered signal services, as there were great numbers of true Americans who wou'd have Flock'd to our Standard, and as we could rely on evry assistance from Gov[r]. Galvez which he could possibly give without committing open Hostilities. I therefore recommended this Expedition in a pointed manner, and mention'd my persuasion that the Court of Spain wou'd give very advantageous terms for the Post of Pensacola, which also might have been taken with great facility, I have seen no Reason to change my Opinion on this subject, but I have good reasons to lament that the situation of things here wou'd not then permit of such an Expedition, or that it was thought unadvisable, for I must believe that by this decisive step some tedious discussions wou'd have been avoided, and some important questions prevented. By this conveyance also I inform'd Congress of the Sloop Virgo bound for & Laden on Account of the United States, and of my agreement for the Importation of Goods from France, requesting that the necessary Funds might be provided, as also that I might be enabled to fulfill my engagements for the Goods already sent. I further inform'd Congress of my application to the Governor of Havana, for opening a Trade between his Port & the United States, the advantage of which I was fully sensible of at that time, a happy experience has since demonstrated them. I wrote also to Governor Henry of Virginia respecting the Stores lodg'd at New Orleans, and a disposition of Governor Galvez to open a Commercial intercourse with this Country.

I shall not trouble Congress with the tedious & painful Detail with what pass'd with respect to Cap[t]. Willing and his Party. They continued at New Orleans until August, and were then (with much difficulty) sent up the River through the Spanish settlements, under the Command of Lieu[t]. George, a very considerable expence was incurr'd, and it was defray'd by the Publick Agent, who had however this consolation, that nothing but his unwearied efforts to surmount a variety of Obstacles could possibly have enabled them to return in safety.

On the 20th. of May I freighted a Sloop with more Goods for the United States, and wrote information to Congress of an Expedition set on foot by the Enemy against Manchac, which would prevent Capt. Willing & his Party from ascending the River.

In July I dispatch'd a Batteaux, under the Command of Capt. Cannon, for the Illinois, but I was Obliged to stop this Vessell, on being inform'd that a M^r. Robert Ross & a M^r. John Campbell had given advice of it to the Enemy, this information proving true, they were imprisoned by Governor Galvez; but I have since had reason to believe that in Obeying the dictates of my duty in this instance, I have occasioned to myself some personal disadvantages.

Early in August I informd Congress that I had been compell'd to borrow 6000 Dollars of the Govr. and that if supplies were not Granted to me, I was without Resources to perform my Engagements; I also wrote to them that their Agent at the Cape, M^r. Stephen Ceronio had seized and converted to his use, Peltries belonging to me, to the Amount of 14,445 Dollars. The reason of this Seizure was that the United States were indebted to him, and the Peltries were Shipped by their Agent. This was my first reward for serving America, & I am compell'd to add, that I have never yet been able to obtain any satisfaction for that seizure.

In September I informd Congress of a new Shipment of Goods, to the Amount of 7,230 Dollars. These were sent to Col^o. Clark, for the use of the Troops in the Illinois, or to be kept at the Order of Congress. In October I wrote to Governor Henry, on the subject of a Loan of 200,000 Pistoles propos'd to be Negotiated for the State of Virginia, and in the Success of which I obtain'd Govr. Galvez's Promise to interest himself. In the end of that Month I sent Capt. Willing with Lieu^{ts}. McIntire & Ellit in a Vessell Bound to the United States. I had then the honor to be in advance 42,434 Dollars.

In December I freighted a Vessell for the Havana to take on Board a Cargo for the United States, at that Place, and in a Letter by Her I stated my distresses for the want of remittances, which were become so great as to Oblige me to Sell off some of my Slaves at considerable Loss, to fulfill my engagements.

In January 1779 I sent to Col^o. Clark a supply of 500^{lbs}. Gun Powder with some Swivels, and wrote him an exact State of the Enemys force on the River, but lest the Boat shou'd miscarry I dispatch'd two Gentl^n. to him by Land, Express, who were possess'd of the necessary information. In February I had the honor to inform Congress of Genl. Campbells arrival at Pensacola, with 1500 Troops from New York, that I had sent Expresses with the Intelligence of Col^o. Clark, who was then continually drawing

Bills on me for his support. That to pay these Bills I had made a disadvantageous Contract for my remaining Slaves, & raised 10,000 Dollars at 12½ Cent Discount notwithstanding which, I was extremely distress'd to raise Moneys sufficient for discharging those Bills. This distress drove me, in April, to draw on Messrs. Delaps of Bourdeaux (at 90 Days sight) for 10,897 Dollars on the Credit of a Cargo which had been Shipped to their address. I informed Congress of this, & requested their Orders to Doctor Franklin to take up those Bills if Messrs. Delaps should not be possessed of the Property. I reiterated my Regrets for the want of Orders, as to the Letter of Marque Ship, which with her Outfits had Cost 23,500 Doll^s. exclusive of the Expences of Capt. Willings and Lieu^t. Georges Party, as well as the Illinois Officers Bills which then amounted to a very considerable Sum, I farther inform'd them that the Issue of a Suit I had commenc'd against Messrs. Ross & Campbell was their amercement for 6318 D^{rs}. damages, which were carried to the Credit of the United States in my Accounts. That I had been under the necessity of having Recourse to Govr. Galvez who having lent me 23,433 Dollars on Acco^t. of the United States, I had been compell'd to borrow of him 17,729 on my own Credit (including Interest) so that remittances became indispensible. In May I transmitted Duplicates of my Letters. Earnestly requesting Answers. In July I wrote to Governor Henry informing of a supply of Goods to the Amount of 10,000 Dollars delivered on his Letter of Credit. In August I wrote to Coll^o. Clark the Enemys force & Situation, and to Congress, mentioning the Loss of the Ship in a violent Hurricane, I also mention'd that it was my intention to get a Schooner for Capt. Pickles to Cruize in, that War was declared by Spain. And that Govr. Galvez had requested me to accompany him in his Expedition against Manchac Baton Rouge &c, I had that Honor, and was so happy (in my Military endeavours to please that Gentl^m.) that he Offerd me a Commission of Colonel in the Service of Spain. but I felt it my Duty to decline this Offer, the feeble services which (with nine Brother Americans) I had been able to render, were under the Banners of America, we took them with us into the Field. I made it however my request to Congress at this time that they would give me their Permission to serve in a Military line as one of their Officers.

On my return from this Expedition, I had the Honor to Receive a Letter from Congress of the 19th. July mentioning their Orders for Eventual Acceptance of my Bills on Messrs. Delaps; the pleasure which this intelligence gave me was but of short duration, as the Bills soon after came back Protested, with the Consequent Damages & Loss of Credit,

Capt. Pickles (who had sail'd on a Cruize in August) Captur'd in Septr. a Vessell of very superior force in Lake Ponchetrain, after a very severe conflict. In October Govr. Galvez requested he might continue to cruize there for the Protection of the Trade, which he did until the Month of Jany. 1780, and then proceeded to the Rendezvous of the force about to go against Mobile and Pensacola, In that Month I wrote a particular Account of things to Congress, and transmitted a Copy of the Capitulation made on behalf of the United States by Capt. Pickles, with the Inhabitants on the Lakes, I conceived this Capitulation to be a proper Ground on which to claim (at any convenient period) the Sovereignty of the Soil, and the allegiance of the Inhabitants.

In February I forwarded Powder & Goods to M^r. Todd, who had been appointed by the State of Virginia to act as Lieu^t Governor of the Illinois. In May I receiv'd and acknowledged a Letter from the Govr. of Virginia informing me to Draw on Messrs. Penet Da Costa & Co. for 65,8145/8 Dollars the Amount of my disbursements for that State, I accordingly Drew for that Sum, and the Bills came back protested producing thereby the addition of Damages to my other Distresses. In May I saw an Advertisement in the Pennsylvania Papers that Danl. Callaghan had Robbed John Whitzel of a large Sum of Publick Money, upon which I seiz'd the Robber (then at New Orleans, & secur'd 19,9951/2 Dollars Cont^l. Money, which are now in my Possession, ready to be delivered to the Order of Congress,

In July I again stated to Congress by a M^r. Henderson my accumulated difficultys & Embarrasments, Requesting relief, I must then have sunk under the load If I had not prevail'd on Don Bernardo de Otter Contador of Louisiana, to lend me forty thousand Dollars, my application to him was for Money out of the Publick Treasury, but having no Orders to warrant it, that could not be done. His Friendship however for me, and his regards for the Interest of the United States, induced him to make the Advance from his own private Fortune.

In the sincere attachment of M^r. Daniel Clarke to the American Cause I found an additional aid, who put the whole of his Fortune in that Country into my hands & took my Bills upon the State of Virginia for the Money, but as an increase of my own distresses, I have to lament that those Bills Still remain unpaid.

About this time the Cont^l. Money had found its way to New Orleans, and was daily offerd to me, as the Publick agent of our Nation. In Order to support its Credit which would have been instantly ruind by a refusal on my Part. nôt only at New Orleans, but every where on or near the River, I receiv'd and Exchanged it for Specie, by which Exchange I became possess'd of 8470 Dollars; those not being current at that place I seal'd up, and have them now in my possession.

In January 1782 I was press'd by Don Joseph Foucher Treasurer General of Louisiana to repay the Monies borrow'd of the Kings Chest, on account of the United States. I explain'd my situation & pointed out the only remaining resource in my Power, declaring my willingness to apply my remaining Estate if necessary, notwithstanding the hardships to which I must be subjected, it was accepted, and in consequence I sold my Indigo works, my House, my working Slaves, my implements of Husbandry, and some of my Domestic Slaves, for the Payment of a Part of the Debts, I had contracted on Account of the United States.

I then set out for the Havana on my way hither, In May last at the Havana, I had again the Opportunity of rendering a small service to America, by prevailing on the Governor at the request of several American Captains, to permit the Vessels there to depart, by a providential coincidence of circumstances, these Vessells arrived in safety during the most fatal Season which our Commerce has experienced, I came in one of them, and tho' reduced to Poverty myself yet I had a Heart-felt satisfaction in accompanying a Treasure so important, to the Country in whose Service I had labour'd so long,

It has not been my Fortune to move on a splendid Theatre, where the weary Actor frequently finds in the applause of his Audience, new motives to Exertion, I dwelt in an Obscure Corner of the Universe alone and unsupported. I have laboured without ceasing, I have neglected the Road to affluence, I have exhausted my all, and plunged myself deeply in Debt, to support the Cause of America, In the Hours of her distress, and when those who call'd themselves Friends, were Daily deserting her. But these things I do not Boast of, what I do boast of is, that I have a Heart Still ready (had I the means) to bear sufferings, and make new sacrifices. I pray your Excellency to submit this Narrative to the indulgence of Congress, I am in their judgment, And in their Justice I repose the fullest Confidence

With perfect Respect
I have the Honor to be
Your Exellencys
most Obedient
&
humble Servant
OL^r. POLLOCK (*rubric*)

APPENDICES 355

[Addressed:]
HIS EXCELLENCY THE PRESIDENT OF CONGRESS
[Endorsed on back:]
Letter 18 Sept 1782
Oliver Pollock
Read 23. 1782
Referred to Mr Clarke
Mr Duane
Mr Williamson

APPENDIX II

OLIVER POLLOCK AND THE DEVELOPMENT OF THE $ MARK

I AM indebted to Professor Florian Cajori, formerly of the University of California, for his studies on the "Evolution of the Dollar Mark."[1] The new evidence here presented, gained from a minute study of the correspondence of Oliver Pollock, serves to confirm the conclusion of Professor Cajori, namely; that "the modern dollar mark is a modification of the Mexican sign p^s for pesos, the chief alteration being the lowering of the letter s upon the letter p." The summary by Professor Cajori of the theories previously advanced relative to the origin of the dollar mark are likewise accepted. Chief among the dozen or more of these hypotheses is the United States origin of the $. But no evidence has been submitted to show that this symbol originated from the superposition of the S upon the U. For a like reason, the combination of HS or IIS, abbreviations for the Roman *Sestertius,* to produce the $ cannot be accepted.[2]

The leading argument of Professor Cajori, that the transition from ps to our dollar mark was made by the English-speaking people who came into contact with the Spaniards, was based on his study of a single communication from Oliver Pollock to George Rogers Clark, August 29, 1778.[3]

From a study of a large number of documents pertaining to the financial career of Pollock preceding the date, August 29, 1778, the one cited by Professor Cajori, the transition from ps to $ becomes clear.

In the letters addressed to Pollock by his correspondents in Philadelphia and Richmond, prior to 1775, we find the common forms to be the usual symbols for pounds, shillings and pence.

---

[1] Florian Cajori, *Popular Science Monthly,* 81: pp. 522–530; *The Scientific Monthly,* 29: 216; *Science,* N. S., 38: pp. 848–850. The Spanish dollar was known as "peso" and "piastre"; plural, pesos and piastres.

[2] For a complete statement, consult Cajori, "New Data on the Origin and Spread of the Dollar Mark," *The Scientific Monthly,* XXIX, pp. 212, 213.

[3] Professor Cajori was not correct in his statement that the $ was used *only a few times* in eighteenth-century documents and that *none of these* was earlier than the letter of August 29, 1778.

One of these early orders reads: "Inclosed you have Invoice and Bill of Loading, [sic] for 10 Baralls of Flouar amounting to £20—9—10." [4] This form was also used: "You have herewith Inclosed Invoice & Bill of lading for Sundreys amounting to One Hundred & Twenty four Pounds two Shill. & Sixpence which we desire you may dispose of at whatever Port you meet the best Market & as Soon as an oppty serves we desire you may send us a Remittance in Dollars or Johanna's." [5] Early in 1775, we find the abbreviations Dollrs, Dolls. drs, and ds commonly used by Pollock and by his correspondents on the lower Mississippi. "I shou'd be very glad you wou'd let Mr. James Rumsey have on my acc.^{t}," one of them wrote, "four Hundred dollrs. in negroes and I will pay you next Fall in Cash or Peltries." [6] In the statement regarding a land purchase, is found: "This Tract of 1000 Acres Capt Barbut proposes to Sell for 1000 Doll^{rs}. ready Money or rather than not dispose of it for 500 Doll^s. Cash, & the remaining 500 Doll^s. in Six Months." [7]

In the first formal statement of an account rendered on behalf of Pollock, January 9, 1775, is to be seen the use of *ps*, Figure 1 (page 358).[8] Thereafter, the symbol *ps* is commonly used in other accounts. It was made by a continuous motion of the pen, as in *p* with the *s* above.

In the next, Figure 2, is to be seen the same method of formation ending with the *s* being brought down on the *p* as in the mark preceding 165 of the first line. In the second line, preceding 252 there is the same formation as in Figure 1 (page 358), with the initial up stroke of the *p* appearing.[9]

By April 1, 1778, Pollock had adopted the use of the mark for the dollar which varies only slightly from the one now current. It is of significance to note that this, Figure 3 (page 358), appears in a bill rendered by Pollock for a consignment of merchandise, the value of which amounted to $1347. These goods were shipped to the Committee of Congress. The members of this committee were Robert Morris, William Smith, and Henry Laurens. If, as Professor Cajori declares, Robert Morris was the first "high official

[4] Philadelphia, July 3, 1767. Benjamin Harbeson to Oliver Polaoch [sic], *Pollock Letters*.
[5] Philadelphia, October 27, 1767. Wills C. Jackson to Mr. Oll^r. Pollock. *Ibid*.
[6] Natchez, February 16, 1775. Isaac Johnson to Oliver Pollock. *Ibid*.
[7] February 17, 1775. *Ibid*.
[8] The bill was evidently drawn as directed by Pollock.
[9] October 8, 1776. Oliver Pollock, debtor to John Jennings. Throughout the year 1777, there are numerous letters available from Pollock's correspondents in Manchac which show the transition from ps to $. *Letter Book of John Fitzpatrick*, 1768–1790, MSS. New York Public Library.

In Acco.ᵗ With Oliver Pollock .... Cr.

'775
Jan.ᵗ . By Cash Rec.ᵈ .... f.ᵗ 51.—

FIGURE 1

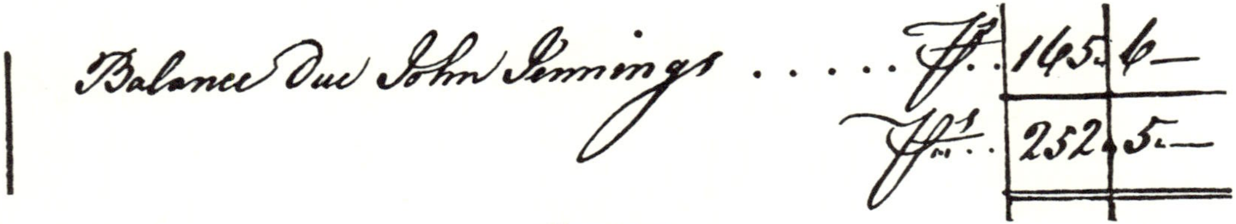

Balance due John Jennings ...... f.ᵗ 145. 6.—
                                  f.ᵗˢ 252. 5.—

FIGURE 2

f.ᵗ 1347" 7. ⅓

FIGURE 3

Carried over—

There are only a few remaining copies of the rare book that you have ordered. Rather than disappoint you, we are shipping you the best copy available. We expect this title to be out of stock within thirty days and we cannot guarantee its future availability.

We are supplying it in this condition for your inspection. Please feel free to return it to us within 30 days of delivery for full credit, if you find it unacceptable.

Returns MUST include this slip and the original invoice. The RMA# must be clearly marked on the outside of the package. To obtain an RMA# fax your request along with this slip to 1-603-669-7945 or mail it to:

AYER COMPANY PUBLISHERS
C/O RETURNS
300 BEDFORD STREET
BUILDING B SUITE 213
MANCHESTER, N.H. 03101

APPENDICES

of the United States Government" to use the dollar mark, it seems probable that he was induced to do so because of Pollock's influence.

This discussion has sought to emphasize the view that the $ mark was derived from the abbreviation *ps* for pesos and that Oliver Pollock in his correspondence and business forms contributed more than any other person of that period towards bringing this symbol into general usage. The dollar was adopted as the money unit by the Continental Congress in 1785. Its weight was modeled after that of the Spanish dollar then in circulation. The report of the Committee of Congress stated: "The most convenient Value of the Money Unit is a question not easily determined considering that most of the citizens of the U. S. are accustomed to count in Pounds, Shillings, and Pence; and that those sums are of different Values in the different States, hence they convey no distinct ideas. The money of the U. S. should be equally fitted to all." [10] On July 6, 1785, Congress took up the report of this Committee and the resolution: "That the money unit of the U. S. of America be one dollar," was passed unanimously.[11] The first United States dollars were coined in 1794. The dollar mark, $, first appeared in printed form in 1797.[12]

[10] *Jour. of the Cont. Cong.*, XXVIII, p. 355.
[11] *Ibid.*, XXIX, p. 500.
[12] *Report of the Commissioner of Education*, 1897-98, I, p. 812. The first use by Pollock of the mark $ where the single stroke is used, I found in the body of a letter from Pollock to George Rogers Clark, dated August 29, 1778 [$8550.4]. Dollars and ps are used interchangeably in this letter.

BIBLIOGRAPHY

UNPUBLISHED SOURCES

Archivo General de las Indies, MSS., Seville, Spain (transcripts in Ayer Collection, Newberry Library), 1777–1783.
"Draper MSS." (Wisconsin Historical Society Library), *William Clark Letters, George Rogers Clark Letters, Pollock Letters,* Draper, *Trips.*
Fitzpatrick, John, *Letter Book,* 1768–1790, New York Public Library.
Gardoqui Letters, Copy, Library of The University of Chicago.
"Haldimand MSS." British Museum, *Additional MSS.,* No. pp. 21, 844, 24, 322.
"Innes Papers," *Letters Relating to Kentucky Discontent,* 1789–91, National Archives.
MS., *Letters of Henry Knox,* Secretary of War, National Archives.
MS., *Letters of James Madison,* New York Public Library.
MS., *Letters of James Monroe,* New York Public Library.
George Morgan, *Letter Books,* 3 vols., Carnegie Institute, Pittsburgh.
MS., *Letters of Timothy Pickering,* Secretary of State, Massachusetts Historical Society.
Pollock, Oliver, "Letters," *Papers of Continental Congress,* National Archives.
"Public Record Office" (London), F. O. R. *America.*
"Rufus King Papers," *Navigation of the Mississippi River and Indian Relations,* New York Historical Society.
Spanish Records, 1809, East Baton Rouge Court-house.
Virginia State Archives, Executive Communications to the Virginia Assembly, October 21–December 28, 1782. *George Rogers Clark Letters, Pollock Letters, Letter Books of Benjamin Harrison, Letter Books of Thomas Jefferson.*

PUBLISHED SOURCES

ADAMS, JOHN, *Familiar Letters to his Wife* (New York, 1876).
ALVORD, CLARENCE W. (Ed.), "Cahokia Records, 1778–1790, *Collections Illinois State Historical Library,* II (Springfield, 1907), Virginia Series I.
——— "Kaskaskia Records, 1778–1790," *Coll. Ill. State Hist. Library,* V (Springfield, 1909), Virginia Series II.
——— and CARTER, CLARENCE E. (Eds.), "The Critical Period, 1763–65," *Coll. Ill. State Hist. Library,* XI (Springfield, 1916).
——— and CARTER, CLARENCE E. (Eds.), "The New Régime, 1765–67," *Coll. Ill. State Hist. Library,* XI (Springfield, 1916).

BIBLIOGRAPHY

American Archives 1st and 3rd series), ed. Peter Force (Washington, 1837–53).
American State Papers, *Foreign Relations*, VI (Washington, 1833).
—— *Indian Affairs*, I, II.
—— *Public Lands*, II.
BATES, ALBERT C. (Ed.), *The Two Putnams* (Connecticut Historical Society, 1931).
BECKWITH, H. W., *Collections Illinois State Historical Library*, I (Springfield, 1903).
BOSSU, N., *Travels* (1752).
BRACKENRIDGE, HENRY M., *Journal of a Voyage up the River Missouri; Performed in Eighteen Hundred and Eleven* (2nd ed., Baltimore, 1816). Reprinted in Reuben G. Thwaites, *Early Western Travels*, VI.
—— *Views of Louisiana* (Pittsburgh, 1814).
BRADBURY, JOHN, *Travels in the Interior of America, in the Years 1809, 1811; Including a Description of Upper Louisiana Together with the States of Ohio, Kentucky, Indiana and Tennessee, with the Illinois and Western Territories, etc.* (2nd ed., London, 1814). Reprinted in Thwaites, *Early Western Travels*, V.
BUTTERFIELD, CONSUL W. (Ed.), *Washington Irvine Correspondence* (Madison, 1882).
Calender of Virginia State Papers and Other Manuscripts, III, IV, V (Richmond, 1875–93).
Canadian Archives Reports, 1872–1921, 1882, (Ottawa, 1873–).
Carlisle *Gazette* (Kline's), 1804, 1805, 1806, American Archæological Society, Worcester, Mass.
Chicago Historical Society Collections, IV (Chicago, 1882–1908).
"Intercepted Letters and Journal of George Rogers Clark, 1778, 1779," *American Historical Review*, I (New York, 1896).
CLARK, GEORGE ROGERS, "Papers, 1771–1781," James A. James (Ed.), *Coll. Ill. State Hist. Library*, VIII (Springfield, 1912), Virginia Series, III.
CLARK, GEORGE ROGERS, "Papers, 1781–1784," James (Ed.), *Coll. Ill. State Hist. Library*, XIX (Springfield, 1926), Virginia Series, III.
"Correspondence of French Ministers to the United States, 1791–97," Frederick J. Turner (Ed.), *Report of American Historical Association*, 1903, II (Washington, 1904).
"Correspondence of George Rogers Clark and Genet," Frederick J. Turner (Ed.), *Am. Hist. Association Report*, 1896 (Washington, 1897).
CRAIG, NEVILLE B. (Ed.), *The Olden Time*, I, II (Pittsburgh, 1846–48).
Cumberland *Register*, 1804–1806, Wyoming County Historical Society.
DENNY, MAJOR E., *A Military Journal, Record of Upland and Denny's Journal* (Philadelphia, 1860).
Documentary History of the Constitution, IV, V.

DONIOL, HENRI, *Histoire de la Participation de la France a l'Etablissement les États-Unis D'Amerique*, I.
EGLE, WILLIAM HENRY, *Notes and Queries Historical and Geneological Relating to the Interior of Pennsylvania* (Harrisburg, 1891).
FITZPATRICK, JOHN C. (Ed.), *The Diaries of George Washington*, I–IV.
FRANKLIN, BENJAMIN, *Writings*, ed. A. H. Smyth, VII (New York, 1905–1907).
The Correspondence of General Thomas Gage, I, II, ed. Clarence E. Carter (Yale University Press, New Haven, 1935).
Journal of Captain Harry Gordon, 1766, ed. Newton D. Mereness (Macmillan Company, Publishers, 1916).
HENING, WILLIAM WALLER, *Statutes at Large, Being a Collection of the Laws of Virginia, 1619–1792*, IX (Richmond, 1819–23).
HENRY, WILLIAM WIRT, *Patrick Henry; Life, Speeches and Correspondence*, II (New York, 1891).
"Historical Manuscripts Commission," *Report on American Manuscripts*, I.
HOUCK, LOUIS, *The Spanish Régime in Missouri: A Collection of Papers and Documents Relating to Upper Louisiana, Principally Within the Present Limits of Missouri, During the Dominion of Spain*, I, II (Chicago, 1909).
JAY, JOHN, *Correspondence and Public Papers*, ed. H. P. Johnson, I, II (New York, 1890–93).
JEFFERSON, THOMAS, *Writings*, ed. P. L. Ford, V (New York, 1892–1899).
Journals of the Continental Congress, 1774–1789, II, IV, VI, VIII, XV, XVI, XVII, XIX, XXIII, XXVII, XXIX.
KELLOGG, LOUISE PHELPS (Ed.), "Frontier Advance on the Upper Ohio, 1778–79," *Wisconsin Historical Collections*, XXIII (Madison, 1916).
——"Frontier Retreat on the Upper Ohio, 1779–81," *Wisconsin Historical Collections*, XXXIV (Madison, 1917).
LITTELL, WILLIAM, "Political Transactions," ed. Temple Bodley (Louisville, 1926). *Filson Club Publications*, XXI.
Louisiana Historical Quarterly, I, IV, VI, IX, XI, XII, XIV, XXI.
"Diary of Frederick Mackenzie," I, II (Cambridge, Mass., Harvard University Press, 1930).
MASON, E. G. (Ed.), "John Todd's Record Book," *Chicago Historical Society Collections*, IV (Chicago, 1890).
—— "Rocheblave Papers," *Ibid.*
Michigan Pioneer and Historical Collections, IX, X, XI, XIX (Lansing, Mich., 1872).
MOORE, JOHN BASSETT, "Digest of International Law," *Pennsylvania Journal and the Weekly Advertiser*, 1783, 1784 (Philadelphia).
PIRTLE, HENRY (Ed.), *Colonel George Rogers Clark's Sketch of His Campaign in the Illinois in 1778–1779*, Ohio Valley Historical Series, No. 3 (Cincinnati, 1869).

BIBLIOGRAPHY 363

PITTMAN, PHILIP, *The Present State of the European Settlements on the Mississippi* (London, 1770), (ed. Frank H. Hodder, Cleveland, 1906).
POPE, J., *Tour in the Southern and Western Territories in 1790* (Richmond, 1792).
QUAIFE, MILO M. (Ed.), *The Capture of Old Vincennes. The Original Narratives of George Rogers Clark and of His Opponent, Governor Henry Hamilton* (Indianapolis, 1927).
ROBERTSON, JAMES A. (Ed.), *Louisiana Under Spain, France, and the United States, 1785–1807* (Cleveland, 1911).
—— "Spanish Correspondence Concerning the American Revolution," *Hispanic American Historical Review*, I, 299.
ROWLAND, MRS. DUNBAR, *Life, Letters and Papers of William Dunbar* (Jackson, Miss., 1930).
Secret Journals of the Acts and Proceedings of Congress, I, II, III, IV (Boston, 1921–).
SHEPHERD, W. R., "Wilkinson and the Spanish Conspiracy," *American Historical Review*, IX.
SPARKS, JARED (Ed.), *Diplomatic Correspondence of the American Revolution*, I.
STEINER, BERNARD C. (Ed.), *The Life and Correspondence of James McHenry*, Cleveland, 1907.
STODDARD, AMOS, *Sketches, Historical and Descriptive, of Louisiana* (Philadelphia, 1812).
THWAITES, REUBEN G. (Ed.), *Jesuit Relations*, LXIX (Cleveland, 1904).
—— and KELLOGG, LOUISE P. (Eds.), *Documentary History of Dunmore's War, 1774* (Madison, 1905).
—— *The Revolution On the Upper Ohio, 1775–77* (Madison, 1908).
TURNER, FREDERICK J., "George Rogers Clark and the Kaskaskia Campaign, 1777–1778," *American Historical Review*, VIII (New York, 1903).
Virginia Executive Communications to the General Assembly, 1777–1782.
VOLNEY, C. F. C., *A View of the Soil and Climate of the United States of America* (Philadelphia, 1804).
WASHINGTON, GEORGE, *Diaries*, ed. J. C. Fitzpatrick, I–IV (Boston, 1925).
—— *Writings*, ed. W. C. Ford, XI (New York, 1889–1893).
—— *Writings*, ed. Jared Sparks, V, (Boston, 1834–1837).
WHARTON, FRANCIS (Ed.), *The Revolutionary Diplomatic Correspondence of the United States*, I, II, V (Washington, 1889).
WHITAKER, ARTHUR P. (Ed.), "Documents Relating to the Commercial Policy of Spain in the Floridas," *The Florida State Historical Society Publications* (1931).
—— *The Mississippi Question* (New York, 1934).
WILKINSON, JAMES, *Memoirs of My Own Times*, I, II, III (Philadelphia, 1816).

Wisconsin Historical Collections, XI (Madison, 1855–).
WITHERS, ALEXANDER S., *Chronicles of Border Warfare,* ed. R. G. Thwaites (Philadelphia, 1816).
WOODWARD, AUGUSTUS H., *A Representation of the Case of Oliver Pollock,* 1803 (Library of Congress).

GENERAL MATERIAL

AITON, ARTHUR S. "The Diplomacy of the Louisiana Cession," *American Historical Review,* XXVI (1931).
ALDEN, GEORGE H., "New Governments West of the Alleghanies before 1780," *University of Wisconsin Bulletin,* II, No. 1 (Madison, 1897).
ALVORD, CLARENCE W., "Conquest of St. Joseph, Michigan, by the Spaniards in 1781," *Missouri Historical Review,* II (Columbia, Missouri, 1907).
—— "The Illinois Country, 1673–1818" (Springfield, 1920), *Centennial History of Illinois,* I.
—— *The Mississippi Valley in British Politics: A Study of the Trade, Land Speculation, and Experiments in Imperialism Culminating in the American Revolution,* I, II (Cleveland, 1917).
—— "Virginia and the West: An Interpretation," *Mississippi Valley Historical Review,* III (Cedar Rapids, 1916).
BEMIS, SAMUEL FLAGG, *Pinckney's Treaty* (Baltimore, Johns Hopkins University Press, 1926).
BENTON, E. J., "The Wabash Trade," *Johns Hopkins University Studies,* XXI.
BODLEY, TEMPLE, *Life of George Rogers Clark* (Boston, 1927).
BOGGESS, A. C., "The Settlement of Illinois, 1778–1830," *Chicago Historical Society Collections,* V, (Chicago, 1908).
BOYD, C. E., "The County of Illinois," *American Historical Review,* IV.
BRACKENRIDGE, H. M., *View of Louisiana* (Pittsburgh, 1814).
BROWN, JOHN MASON, *The Political Beginnings of Kentucky* (Louisville, 1889).
BUCK, SOLON J., "Review of Life of George Rogers Clark," *Minnesota Historical Quarterly,* X.
BUTLER, MANN, *A History of the Commonwealth of Kentucky* (Louisville, 1834).
BUTTERFIELD, C. W., *History of the Girtys* (Cincinnati, 1890).
CARSON, W. W., "Transportation and Traffic on the Ohio," *Mississippi Valley Historical Review,* VII (Cedar Rapids, 1920).
CAUGHEY, JOHN W., *Bernardo de Galvez in Louisiana, 1776–1783* (University of California Press, 1934).
—— "The Panis Mission to Pensacola," *American Historical Review,* X.
—— "Willing's Expedition Down the Mississippi," *The Louisiana Historical Quarterly,* XV.

BIBLIOGRAPHY 365

COFFIN, VICTOR, "The Province of Quebec and the Early American Revolution," *University of Wisconsin Bulletin*, 1 (Madison, 1896).
CORWIN, E. S., *French Policy and the American Alliance* (Princeton University Press, 1916).
COULTER, E. M., "The Efforts of the Democratic Societies of the West to Open the Navigation of the Mississippi," *Mississippi Valley Historical Review*, XI.
COX, I. J., "The Indian As a Diplomatic Factor," *Ohio Archæological and Historical Quarterly*, XVIII.
CRAIG, O. J., "Ouiatanon," *Indiana Historical Society Publications*, II.
DILLON, J. B. A., *History of Indiana* (Indianapolis, 1859).
DOUGLAS, W. B., "Jean Gabriel Cerré: A Sketch," *Illinois State Historical Society Transactions* (1905).
DOWNES, RALPH C., "Indian War on the Upper Ohio, 1779-1782," *Western Pennsylvania Historical Magazine*, XVII.
DOWNING, MARGARET, "Oliver Pollock, Patriot and Financier, "*Illinois Catholic Historical Review*, II.
DRAKE, DANIEL, *Pioneer Life in Kentucky*, ed. C. D. Drake (Cincinnati, 1870).
DRAPER, LYMAN, *King's Mountain* (New York, 1881).
DUNN, J. P., "Father Gibault," *Illinois State Historical Society Transactions* (1905).
—— *Indiana* (Boston, 1905).
DURRETT, REUBEN T., "Centenary of Louisville," *Filson Club Publications*, VIII.
ECKENRODE, H. J., *The Revolution in Virginia* (Boston, 1916).
ENGLISH, WILLIAM HAYDEN, *Conquest of the Country Northwest of the River Ohio, 1778-1783*, and, *Life of George Rogers Clark*, I, II (Indianapolis, 1897).
FORTIER, ALCÉE, *History of Louisiana*, I, II (New York, 1904).
GAYARRÉ, C. E. A., *History of Louisiana*, I, II, III (New Orleans, 1903).
GREEN, T. M., *The Spanish Conspiracy* (Cincinnati, 1891).
HALL, JAMES, *The Romance of Western History* (Cincinnati, 1857).
HAMILTON, PETER J., *Colonial Mobile* (Boston, 1897).
HANNA, CHARLES A., *The Scotch-Irish or the Scot in North Britain, North Ireland and North America*, I, II (New York, 1902).
HASKINS, CHARLES H., "Yazoo Land Companies," *American Historical Association Papers*, V.
HAYDEN, HORACE G., *A Biographical Sketch of Oliver Pollock, Esq., United States Commercial Agent at New Orleans and Havana, 1776-1784*.
—— "Oliver Pollock, His Connections with the Conquest of Illinois, 1778," *Magazine of American History*, XXII.
HENDERSON, ARCHIBALD, "Spanish Conspiracy in Tennessee," *Tennessee Historical Magazine*, III.
—— *The Significance of the Transylvania Company in American History*, October 12, 1935. Privately printed.

HOLMES, W. H., "Handbook of Aboriginal American Antiquities," *Smithsonian Institution, Bureau of American Ethnology, Bulletin*, 60 (Washington, 1919).

JAMES, JAMES A., "French Diplomacy and American Politics," *Report of American Historical Association*, 1911 (Washington, 1912).

—— "French Opinion as a Factor in Preventing War between France and the United States, 1795-1800," *American Historical Review*, XX (New York, 1925).

—— "Indian Diplomacy and the Opening of the Revolution in the West," *Wisconsin State Historical Society Proceedings* (Madison, 1910).

—— *Life of George Rogers Clark* (University of Chicago Press, 1928).

—— "Louisiana and American Diplomacy, 1795-1800," *Mississippi Valley Historical Review*, IV (1917).

—— "The Northwest, Gift or Conquest?" *Indiana Magazine of History* (1934).

—— "Oliver Pollock and the Free Navigation of the Mississippi River," *Mississippi Valley Historical Review*, XIX.

—— "Significance of the Attack on St. Louis, 1780," *Mississippi Valley Historical Society Proceedings, 1908–09* (Cedar Rapids, Iowa, 1910).

—— "The Significance of the Sesquicentennial Celebration of the American Revolution West of the Alleghany Mountains," *Illinois State Historical Society Journal*, XIX (Springfield, 1927).

—— "Significant Events during the Last Year of the Revolution in the West," *Mississippi Valley Historical Association Proceedings, 1912–1913* (Cedar Rapids, 1913).

—— "Some Phases of the History of the Northwest, 1783-86," *Mississippi Valley Historical Association Proceedings, 1913–1914*, VII (Cedar Rapids, 1914).

—— "Some Problems of the Northwest in 1779," *Frederick J. Turner Essays* (New York, 1910).

—— "Spanish Influence in the West during the American Revolution," *Mississippi Valley Historical Review*, IV (1917).

JOHNSON, CECIL, "Expansion in West Florida, 1770-1779," *Mississippi Valley Historical Review*, XX.

KELLOGG, LOUISE PHELPS, "Indian Diplomacy During the Revolution in the West," *Transactions of Illinois State Historical Society* (1930).

KING, GRACE, *New Orleans the Place and the People* (New York, 1928).

KINNAIRD, LAWRENCE, "The Spanish Expedition Against Fort St. Joseph in 1781, A New Interpretation," *Mississippi Valley Historical Review*, XIX.

MARSHALL, HUMPHREY, *The History of Kentucky*, I, II (Frankfort, 1824).

MARTIN, F. X., *History of Louisiana* (New Orleans, 1882).

MASON, E. G., "British Illinois, Philippe de Rocheblave," *Chicago Historical Society Collections*, IV (Chicago, 1890).

—— *Chapters from Illinois History* (Chicago, 1901).

BIBLIOGRAPHY 367

McCarthy, Charles H., "The Attitude of Spain During the Revolution," *Catholic Historical Review*, II.
Nichols, Roy F., "The First United States Consuls and Trade Relations with the Spanish American Empire, 1779-1809," MS.
Oberholtzer, E. P., *Robert Morris, Patriot and Financier* (New York, 1903).
Ogg, F. A., *The Opening of the Mississippi* (New York, 1904).
Pease, Theodore C. and Pease, Marguerite Jenison, *George Rogers Clark and the Revolution in Illinois, 1763-1787*, Illinois State Historical Library (1929).
Peck, John Mason, *A Gazetteer of Illinois* (Philadelphia, 1831).
—— *Annals of the West* (St. Louis, 1850).
Pelzer, Louis, "Economic Factors in the Acquisition of Louisiana," *Mississippi Valley Historical Proceedings*, VI.
Phillips, Paul C., "The West in the Diplomacy of the American Revolution," *University of Illinois Studies in the Social Sciences*, II (Urbana, 1913).
Priestly, H. I., *José de Galvez* (Berkeley, 1916).
Randall, James G., "George Rogers Clark's Service of Supply," *Mississippi Valley Historical Review*, VIII.
Reynolds, John M., *My Own Times, Embracing also the History of my Life* (Belleville, 1855).
Riley, Franklin L., "Spanish Policy in Mississippi," *Report of American Historical Association* (1897).
Rives, W. L., "Spain and the United States in 1795," *American Historical Review*, IV.
Roosevelt, Theodore, *The Winning of the West*, I-IV (New York, 1889-96).
Rowland, Kate Mason, *The Life of George Mason*, I-II (New York, 1892).
Savelle, Max, *George Morgan, Colony Builder* (New York, 1932).
Shaw, Helen Louise, *British Administration of the Southern Indians, 1756-1783* (Lancaster, Penna., 1931).
Shepherd, William R., "The Cession of Louisiana to Spain," *Political Science Quarterly*, XIX.
—— "Wilkinson and the Spanish Conspiracy," *American Historical Review*, IX.
Siebert, Wilbur H., "Loyalists in West Florida and the Natchez District," *Mississippi Valley Historical Review*, II.
Stipp, G. W., *The Western Miscellany* (Xenia, Ohio, 1827).
Tallmadge, Thomas E., *The Story of Architecture in America* (New York, 1927).
Teggart, Frederick J., "The Capture of St. Joseph, Michigan, by the Spaniards in 1781," *Missouri Historical Review*, V.
Thompson, Joseph J., "Catholic Statesmen of Illinois," *Illinois Catholic Historical Review*, III.
Thwaites, Reuben G., *Daniel Boone* (New York, 1903).
—— *How George Rogers Clark Won the Northwest* (Chicago, 1903).

BIBLIOGRAPHY

TURNER, FREDERICK J., "Diplomatic Contest for the Mississippi Valley," *Atlantic Monthly*, XCII.
—— *The Frontier in American History* (New York, 1921).
—— "Genet's Projected Attack on Louisiana," *American Historical Review*, II.
—— "The Policy of France toward the Mississippi Valley," *American Historical Review*, X.
—— "Western State-Making in the Revolutionary Era," *American Historical Review*, I.
VAN TYNE, CLAUDE H., "The American Revolution, 1776–83," I, II (New York, 1905). "American Nation Series," IX.
WHITAKER, A. P., *The Spanish American Frontier, 1783–1795* (Boston, 1895).
—— "The Spanish Intrigue in the Old Southwest," *Mississippi Valley Historical Review*, XIII.
WINSOR, JUSTIN, *The Mississippi Basin, 1697–1763* (Boston, 1895).
—— *Westward Movement* (Boston, 1897).

INDEX

Abbott, Lieutenant Governor Edward, 98, 99
Acadians, settlement of, 17
Alvord, Clarence Walworth, *Mississippi Valley in British Politics*, 34n.; American sympathizers at Kaskaskia, 102n., 136n.; interpretation of Clark's expedition by, 242, 243n.
American Bottom, location of, 21, 22; fertility, 25, 26

Bentley, Thomas, trader at Kaskaskia, 102n.; imprisonment and escape of, 103; testimony of Pollock on character of, 104
Big Knives, name for Americans, 93
Boone, Daniel, settles Boonesborough, 91; defender of Kentucky, 100
Bosseron, Francis, successful trader at Vincennes, 143, 144n.; assists Clark, 165
Bowman, Captain Joseph, enlists soldiers for Clark, 133; captures Cahokia, 138; Journal of, 163, 164
Bowman, Colonel John, leader of Virginia troops in defense of Kentucky, 100; fails to assist Clark, 183
British, surrender of New France to, 24; colonies of, in the West, 34-39; in the Southwest, 41-43; trade with the Indians, 45-52; and Revolution in the East, 71, 72; control in the West, 85-88, 92-94; dealing with the Indians of the Northwest, 94-98; expedition against Vincennes, 157-158; loss of Vincennes, 167
Brodhead, Colonel Daniel, orders to assist Clark, 222, 223; jealous of Clark, 224
Brown, John, delegate in Congress from Kentucky, 325; relations with Gardoqui, 326; confidential message to Governor Miró, 329-331

Cabildo, municipal government in New Orleans, 8
Cahokia, village in Illinois, 22, 23; capture of by the Americans, 138
Cahokia mound, 25n.
Camp Charlotte, treaty of, 87
Campbell, Colonel John, British leader at Pensacola, 129, 198, 206; surrender of Pensacola, 228
Capuchins, in New Orleans, 14, 15
Cerré, Gabriel, trader at Kaskaskia, friend of Clark, 139, 143
Chester, Peter, British governor at Pensacola, 40; reserved land for "Military Adventurers," 42n., 43; demands restitution of captured property and surrender of Pollock and Willing, 123
Clark, George Rogers, Virginia leader, 20; in Dunmore War, 87; explorer and surveyor on the Ohio River, 89, 90; visits Kentucky, 91; asks for powder from Virginia, 91; victory over Judge Richard Henderson, 92; military leader in Kentucky, 99-101, 104; proposed an expedition against the Illinois posts, 131; sets out on expedition, 132; enlistment of soldiers, 133; receives stores from Pollock at Pittsburgh, 134; number of followers, 134; equipment, 135; march to Kaskaskia, 135; capture of, 136; treatment of French, 137; Pollock to the rescue of, 140; aid of, by French, 142; troops destitute, 142; assisted by Pollock, 143-145; conciliation of Indians, 149, 151; appeals to Pollock, 150; prepares to recapture Vincennes, 161, 162; march to Vincennes, 162-164; message to the people, 165; capture of Vincennes, 166; terms of capitulation, 167; treatment of prisoners, 168; problem of Indians, 149, 169, 170; in-

369

INDEX

Clark, George Rogers (Cont.) structions on the capture of Detroit, 172; credit of Pollock exhausted, 173; new government organized at Kaskaskia, 178-181; plan to capture Detroit, 182; disappointed, 183; messages to French at Detroit, 184; effect of preparations, 185; at the Falls of the Ohio River, 185; plan for Louisville, 186, 187; resumes plan against Detroit, 188; constructs Fort Jefferson, 205; saves St. Louis, 208; prepares to attack British, 209-211; made Brigadier General, 223; problem of securing men and supplies, 223; new plans for attack on Detroit, 224, 233, 234; plan to attack Shawnee, 236, 237; effects, 238; "conqueror" of the Illinois country, 242, 243; memorial at Vincennes, 248, 249; in destitute condition, 278; reported that he would invade Spanish territory, 319; relations with Gardoqui, 324

Connolly, Major, British agent, 87, 88

Continental Congress, Commissioners sent by, to Indians of Northwest, 88, 89; policy regarding Indians, 96; Pollock agent for, 113, 114, 115; informed of capture of Mobile, 204; and problem of free navigation of the Mississippi River, 251-267; Robert Morris agent of, 270, 271; and financial crisis, 279; and financial distress of Pollock, 269-272; claims against, by Pollock, 277; letter about Pollock to, 278, 279; Pollock appeals to, 280-283, 297, 305

Corn, grown in lower Louisiana, 18

Cotton, grown in lower Louisiana, 18

Coureur de bois, 31, 32

Crawford, Colonel William, captured by the Indians, 235

Cuba, economic conditions in, 295; policy of the United States toward, 296

Dartmouth, Lord, policy of, 37

De Leyba, Fernando, lieutenant-governor at St. Louis, 138; and attack on St. Louis, 207, 208n.

De Peyster, Arent Schuyler, commander at Michillimackinac, 85; at Detroit, message to Indians, 170, 171; plan for expedition against Louisville, 209; feared attack by Clark, 236; on the defensive, 238

Detroit, important trade center, 85; key to British power in Northwest, 101; Clark plans to capture, 168, 171; fears of British at, 169; instructions on the capture of, 172; population of, 182; Clark makes further plans against, 188

Disease, remedies for in lower Louisiana, 18, 19

Dunmore, Lord, Governor of Virginia, 37; flees from Williamsburg, 63, 64; sends expedition against the Shawnee, 86, 87

Falls of Ohio, base of operations selected by Clark, 134, 185

Fire-arms, procured from British soldiers by Americans, 61, 62

Florida Blanca, Count de, Spanish prime minister, 109; opposed alliance with the United States, 110; suggested policy of, 113; defines policy of Spain, 257

Fort de Chartres, center of French influence, 22, 23; surrendered to the British, 25; troops withdrawn from, 36; abandoned, 37

Fort Gage, location of, 35

Fort Jefferson, constructed, 205, 208; attacked by Indians, 214, 215; distress relieved through aid from Pollock, 216, 217; evacuated, 230

Fort Nelson, Falls of the Ohio, 226; key to the Northwest, 245

Fort Pitt, center for operations on the upper Ohio, 86

Fort Sackville, at Vincennes, surrender to Clark, 67

Fort Stanwix, Treaty of, 38

Franklin, Benjamin, agent of Pennsylvania in London, 35; letter on Western settlement, 36; appointed commissioner to Spain, 109; information received from Pollock, 128; objects to claim of Spain for territory, 246; on boundary of territory gained by the United States, 247; on

INDEX

the free navigation of the Mississippi River, 259
Fur-trading, in Illinois and upper Mississippi region, 31, 32

Gage, Thomas, British General, policy on Western settlement, 39; views on Western trade, 47, 48n.
Galvez, Bernardo de, Governor of Louisiana, 74; tenders service to Pollock, 74; protects American privateers and trading vessels, 75; confidence in Pollock, 76, 77; differences with British leaders, 78; assures Pollock he will aid Americans, 78, 79, 128; orders seizure and sale of British vessels, 79; becomes more war-minded, 80; aids Pollock, 81, 83, 127; coöperates with Pollock, 83, 97; ready to coöperate with George Morgan, 106; influence of Pollock over, 106, 122, 260; writes Governor Henry, 153; leader of Spanish force, 194-199; captures Mobile, 203; captures Pensacola, 228; transferred to Havana, 270; letter from Robert Morris, 271; appointed Governor-General of Cuba, 284; frees Pollock, 293; appointed Viceroy of Mexico, 293
Gardoqui, Diego de, collects funds to aid America, 111; Spanish envoy at Philadelphia, 293, 294; credentials, 309; confers with Jay over terms of treaty, 311; negotiations, 312; and Western settlers, 323
George, Lieutenant Robert, leader of Willing expedition on their return, 146-148, 173; in charge at Fort Jefferson, 214, 215
Germans, settle on the lower Mississippi River, 17
Gibault, Father Pierre, village priest at Kaskaskia, 137; plan to assist Clark, 140, 141
Gibson, Captain George, Virginia agent at New Orleans, 61, 62; goes to Philadelphia with powder procured at New Orleans, 70
Girty, Simon, interpreter, 88
Grimaldi, Duke de, Spanish prime minister, gives assistance to Americans, 68, 110; succeeded by Florida Blanca, 109
Gunpowder, lack of, by Americans, 61; by Washington's army, 71

Habitans, 22, 29, 32
Hamilton, Henry, lieutenant-governor at Detroit, 92, 93, 94; dealing with Indians, 94, 97, 98; expedition against Vincennes, 157, 158; captured by Clark, 167; returns to England, 244
Hand, General Edward, Commander at Fort Pitt, 132, 133
Harrodsburg, first permanent settlement in Kentucky, 91
Havana, treatment of citizens of the United States by Spanish governor in, 287, 288; trade with United States, 294, 295; defense of, 295
Helm, Captain Leonard, enlists soldiers for Clark, 133; takes charge at Vincennes, 141; defense of Vincennes, 158; carries flag of truce to Clark, 166; captures British boats on the Wabash, 167
Henry, Patrick, Governor of Virginia, 91; asks aid from Cuba, 111, 112; suggests annexation of West Florida to the United States, 113; protection of Illinois, 131, 142; asks loan of Governor Galvez, 153; view of the West, 250
Hillsborough, Earl of, Secretary of State for the Colonies, policy of, 36
Hurricanes, on the Mississippi River, 12, 195

Illinois country, 21; trade in, 20; French inhabitants in, 27; social life, 28, 29; religion, 29; criminal offenses in, 29; land cultivated by habitans, 29; land holding in, 30; products of, 30; stock raising, 31; fur-trade, 31; produce shipped to New Orleans, 32, 33; government of, 178, 179
Illinois State Park Commission, 23n.
Indian Mounds, 25n.
Indians, in Illinois, 25, 26; of Northwest, 94-98; of the Southwest, 46,

372 INDEX

Indians (Cont.)
78, 318, 319; as slaves, 16, 26; neutrality asked by Americans, 89, 95, 96; allies of British, 95-99; conciliation of, by Clark, 149, 169, 170
Indigo, in lower Louisiana, 18

Jameson, J. Franklin, states results of Clark's victories, 248, 249
Jay, John, objections to Spanish claims, 246; and navigation of the Mississippi River, 251, 254; and Gérard, 254; appointed to carry on negotiations at Madrid, 255-258, 263-265; goes to assist Franklin in Paris, 267; appointed to confer with Gardoqui, 311; negotiations, 311, 312, 315
Jefferson, Thomas, member of committee of advisers to Governor Henry, 131; adopts plan of Clark for conquest of Northwest, 222, 223; and Pollock, 343, 344

Kaskaskia, Illinois village, 20, 21, 22; partly swept into the Mississippi River, 22n.; troops at, 37; militia company organized, 47; captured by Clark, 136; new government organized, 178-181
Kentucky, settlement of, 91; defense, 100; society in, 187, 188; hard winter in, 189; invasion of, 189; expedition from, against the Shawnee, 210; results, 211; separation from Virginia, 320; application for admission into the Union, 321, 325
King's Mountain, battle of, 211

La Balme Expedition, 218, 219
Laffont, Jean, accompanies Gibault to Vincennes, 140; assists Clark, 143
Langlade, Captain Charles, leads expedition against Milwaukee, 168; commander of expedition from Chicago, 206
Lee, Arthur, commissioner at Madrid, 110
Lee, General Charles, second in command to Washington, 62; takes command in Virginia, 64; foretells disaster to Spanish colonies if Americans are defeated, 67
Legras, J. M. P., successful trader at Vincennes, 144; assists Clark, 165
Lernoult, Captain Richard, in command at Detroit, 85, 169
Linctot, Captain Godfrey, to assist Clark, 183
Linn, Benjamin, agent of Clark, 101
Linn, Lieutenant William, Virginia agent at New Orleans, 61; brings supplies from New Orleans, 69, 70; joins Clark's expedition, 134
Logan, Captain Benjamin, Kentucky leader, 100
Logan's Station, early Kentucky settlement, 92
Lord, Captain Hugh, commander at Kaskaskia, 58
Louisiana, transferred from France to Spain, 5n.; population of, 19
Louisville, government established in, 186
Lucerne, Comte de, attitude toward Spanish claims, 259, 262
Lyman, General Phineas, grant of land in West Florida, 42, 43

"Martyrs of Louisiana," 8
Massac, Fort, French post on the Ohio River, 135
McIntosh, General Lachlan, commander at Fort Pitt, 133
"Military Adventurers," 42n., 43
Miralles, Juan de, originates Spanish policy with reference to the Mississippi River, 253, 254
Miró, Stephen, Governor of Louisiana, 321, 322
Mississippi Land Company, purpose of, 34
Mississippi River, navigation of, 19, 20; trade on, 53, 54; free navigation of, 106, 109, 199, 291, 298, 310, 315; place of deposit on, 311
Mobile, early settlement, 40, 41; captured by Galvez, 199, 202-204
Montgomery, Colonel John, officer under Clark, 183, 208
Moore, Samuel, agent of Clark, 101
Morgan, George, trader in the Illinois

INDEX 373

country, 46, 47; founds a colony, 50n., 324n.; Indian agent for Middle Department, 93-95; plan for war in the West, 106

Morris, Robert, partner with Pollock in trade, 56; message from Pollock, 70; favors expedition against Pensacola, 107; Superintendent of Finance, 270, 271; sends agent to Havana, 273; and financial crisis of the United States, 279; writes of Pollock, 290, 291

Morris, the, cruiser fitted out by Pollock, 120, 126, 154, 155; sunk by hurricane, 195

Murray, Daniel, trader at Kaskaskia, 102; gives aid to Americans, 136

Murray, William, trader in Illinois country and speculator in land, 57, 58; messenger to Congress for Pollock, 128

Natchez, 40; settlers from New England, 41, 42; description of the region, 118; captured by Willing, 120

New Orleans, trade center, 4; population, 7n.; plan of, 9; fire protection, 9; buildings, 9, 10; police, 10; house furnishings, 10, 11, 12; slaves in, 11, 12; social usages, 13; education of youth, 14; family relations, 14; missionaries, 14; taverns, 15; taxation, 16; market for Illinois products, 23, 32, 33, 48; Great Britain desires capture of, 52, 53; defense against the British, 66, 74, 129, 130; open to American traders, 74; Pollock resumes trade in, 327; almost destroyed by fire, 327, 328

Norfolk, bombarded and burned, 63, 64

Northwest Territory, claimed by Virginia, 35; Pollock's assistance to Clark in gaining, 300-303

Ohio Land Company, grant of land to, 34n.

O'Reilly, Alejandro, general in Spanish army, 4; takes possession of New Orleans, 6, 8; reorganization of government, 8; military training for youth, 14; land holding under, 17; report on Illinois country, 32; returns to Spain, 53n.

Ouiatanon, trading-post above Vincennes, 21

Panis, Captain Jacinto, agent for Galvez at Mobile, 194

Pensacola, 40; capture of, urged by Pollock, 127; captured by Galvez, 228

Pioneers, push into Ohio country, 37, 38

Piqua, Indian stronghold, 210; attacked by Clark, 210, 211

Pittman, Captain Philip, European settlements on the Mississippi River, 6n., 15, 20

Pittsburgh, conference at, 88, 95; military operations from, 235, 236, 239

Point Pleasant, decisive battle in Dunmore's War, 87

Pollock, Mrs. Margaret O'Brien, 4, 289, 290, 305n., 338, 339n.

Pollock, Oliver, place of birth, 1; relatives, 1; education, 1; comes to America, 1, 2; trader in West Indies, 3; acquires Spanish language, 3; removal to New Orleans and marriage, 4; friend of General O'Reilly, 4n., 7; home in New Orleans, 12, 13; speculates in land on lower Mississippi, 44; buys land for Robert Morris, 45; freedom of trade on the Mississippi accorded, 54-56; financial standing, 56; trade relations with Spanish officials, 56, 57; personality, 57, 76, 77, 78; relation to Illinois leaders, 57, 58; decides to aid colonists, 59, 60; serves as mediator for Captain Gibson at New Orleans, 64; first message to Congress, 65; procures gunpowder from Spaniards, 65, 69; order drawn on, by Captain Linn, 70; sends message to Congress and to Virginia Council, 70; meets Governor Galvez, 76; asks for form of credit from Congress, 76; assured assistance by Galvez, 78, 79, 81, 83; personal contributions for Colonial cause, 81, 83; sends supplies to Pittsburgh, 97; favors expedition against

Pollock, Oliver (Cont.)
West Florida, 108, 154, 188; appointed commercial agent, 113, 114; entrusted with blank commissions for privateers, 115; new loan from Galvez, 115, 126; relations with James Willing, 117, 118; knowledge of international principles, 121; captures Tories, 122; letter to Benjamin Franklin, 128; furnishes stores to Clark, 134; relations with De Leyba, 138; assists Clark, 138, 140-147, 156, 161, 173, 174, 212, 215, 216; congratulates Clark, 146; gets rid of Willing, 147; provides for return of Willing's followers, 147, 148; informs Clark of his financial distress, 148, 154, 155; agent for Virginia at New Orleans, 153; in distress, 155, 174-178, 213; Clark continues to draw bills on, 183; problem of deserters, 186; order drawn on, by Montgomery, 189, 190; loss of the *Morris*, 195; serves as *aide* to Galvez, 196; secures the surrender of Natchez, 197, 198; rejects offer of Spanish title, 198; and free navigation of the Mississippi River, 106, 109, 199, 251, 252, 253, 259, 260, 261, 262, 266, 267; receives aid from friends, 214; aids Montgomery, 215; saves garrison at Fort Jefferson, 217, 226; brought to trial by Spanish creditors, 227; and Treasury Board, 230; debt on account of Virginia, 231; summary of assistance by, 241, 242; service in winning the Northwest, 248; financial distress of, 269, 271, 272; sails for Philadelphia, 272; service to Americans in Havana, 273, 274; letter to Governor Harrison, 274, 275; claims against the United States, 277; appeal to Clark, 277, 278; Robert Morris writes Congress about, 278, 279; returns to Richmond, 279, 280; appeals to Congress, 280; agents of the United States appeal to, 281, 282; claim against Congress, 282, 283; appointed commercial agent at Havana, 283-289; prisoner in Havana, 290, 291, 292, 293; accompanies Gardoqui to Philadelphia and gives information on Cuban affairs, 294, 295; presents his claims to Congress, 297; his family in destitute condition, 298, 304; aspersions cast on his character, 298, 299, 300, 301, 302, 303; returns to Virginia, 304, 305; his children, 305; acquires Silver Spring, 305n.; on Spanish demands, 309, 310, 313, 314, 315, 316; Democratic-Republican, 317; influence on Washington, 317; statement to, by John Brown, 326; returned to New Orleans as trader, 327-330; delivers Brown's message to Governor Miró, 330, 331; relations with Wilkinson, 331, 332, 333; meets all financial obligations, 333, 334, 335; amount of money contributed, 335, 336; payments made to, 336, 337; life at Silver Spring, 338; death of Mrs. Pollock, 338, 339n.; a Roman Catholic, 339n.; candidate for membership in House of Representatives, 340, 341, 342; second marriage, 342; petitions Legislature of Virginia, 343; after death of Mrs. Pollock, goes to live with his daughter in Mississippi, 344; death of, 344

Pollock, Mrs. Winifred Deady, 342, 344
Pontiac, chief of the Ottawa, 24
Prairie du Rocher, 21
Proclamation of 1763, 34; ignored by men of the frontier, 37
Putnam, Colonel Israel, associated with General Phineas Lyman in West Florida, 42, 43
Putnam, Lieutenant Rufus, associated with General Lyman, 42, 43

Quebec Act, influence on Protestant leaders, 58, 59

Revolution, American, gains momentum in South, 63; in the East, 71, 72; in the West, 85-104; in the Southwest, 106-115, 228
Robertson, Colonel James, Western leader, 96
Rocheblave, Philippe de Rastel, commander at Kaskaskia, 86, 102; captured by Clark, 136, 137
Rogers, Colonel David, mission to

INDEX

New Orleans, 153, 154; captured by Indians, 189

St. Ange, Louis, commandant in Illinois, 24
St. Louis, 21; population, 22n.; trade center, 50, 51; plan of British to capture, 207, 208
Ste. Genevieve, 21; trade center, 50
Sevier, Governor John, pioneer leader, 96
Shawnee Indians, Governor Dunmore sends expedition against, 86-88; Clark attacks, 236-238
Shelburne, Earl of, Secretary of State, attitude toward Western expansion, 36, 242, 243n.
Slavery, in New Orleans, 11, 12, 16; in Illinois country, 22
Spain, trade restrictions on Mississippi River, 7; free navigation of the Mississippi River prohibited, 53; advantage in alliance with the United States, 62, 63; hesitates to give aid openly, 68; privileges granted to American traders, 75; aid to the American Cause, 108, 110; prepared to receive captured posts, 112; offer to mediate, 193; declares war, 193; claim to territory in the Northwest, 219, 246; and free navigation of the Mississippi River, 254, 258; makes no concessions, 267; control over Indians of the Southwest, 319; loans to the United States, 337
Stock raising, in lower Louisiana, 18
Stuart, John, British Superintendent of Southern Indians, 39, 77, 78, 96; criticized for loss of Natchez, 125

Taffia, 15
Todd, John, Jr., Kentucky leader, 99, 100; county lieutenant in Illinois, 178-180; delegate to Virginia Assembly, 182; aided by Pollock, 212; killed by Indians, 235
Transylvania Company, activities of, 91
Turner, Frederick Jackson, interpretation of Clark's victories, 242

Ulloa, Don Juan Antonio de, Governor of Louisiana, 5; driven out by insurrection, 5, 6
Unzaga, Don Luis de y Ameraga, Governor of Louisiana, 15; message from General Charles Lee, 62, 64; sells powder to Pollock, 65; goodwill toward Americans, 65, 66; prepares to defend New Orleans, 66; Governor of Cuba, 286; harsh treatment of Pollock, 289, 290
Ursuline Sisters, 9; convent, 9n.

Vandalia Colony, 37
Vergennes, Count, Secretary of Foreign Affairs for France, 67, 68; proposes that Spain become an ally of the United States, 109
Vigo, Colonel Francis, friend of the United States, 138, 139, 160, 161; visits Pollock at Silver Spring, 306n.
Vincennes, 20; captured by Americans, 141; recaptured by the British, 157-159; retaken by Clark, 161-167; government established, 172; troops withdrawn from, 206
Virginia, claim to the Northwest, 35; treasury empty, 232, 269; surrenders claim to the Northwest, 335
Voyageurs, 27

Wabash Land Company, 58
Washington, George, explorer on the Ohio River, 40; message on lack of gunpowder, 71; retreat across New Jersey, 71; deficiency of good officers for army, 71, 72; battle of Princeton, 72; adopts Clark's plan, 222, 223; description of Western conditions, 309; view on attitude of men of the West, 317n., 318
Watauga, Indian attack upon, 96
West Florida, 40; plan to capture, 105; possession by United States urged by Pollock, 202
Western settlers, demands for protection, 308, 312, 315-323
Wilderness Road, 91
Wilkinson, General James, in New Orleans, 320; leader in Kentucky, 320; treatment by Governor Miró,

Wilkinson, General James (Cont.) 321; *memorial* of, 321; Spanish subject, 322; relations with Kentucky traders, 325; and John Brown, 325; and "Spanish Conspiracy," 332

Willing, Captain James, descends the Mississippi River, 116; mission of, 117; partner in trade with Pollock, 117, 118; captures Natchez, 120; demands made by British for return of booty, 121; consequences of raid, 125, 126; aided by Pollock, 145, 146; embarks for Philadelphia, 147; captured by the British, 156

(1)